Slavery and the
Romantic Imagination

Slavery and the Romantic Imagination

DEBBIE LEE

PENN

UNIVERSITY OF PENNSYLVANIA PRESS

Philadelphia

10 9 8 7 6 5 4 3 2 1

Published by
University of Pennsylvania Press
Philadelphia, Pennsylvania 19104-4011

Library of Congress Cataloging-in-Publication Data
Lee, Debbie.
  Slavery and the Romantic imagination / Debbie Lee.
    p. cm.
  Includes bibliographical references (p.) and index.
  ISBN 0-8122-3636-X (cloth : alk. paper)
  1. English literature—19th century—History and criticism.
2. Slavery in literature.   3. Literature and society—Great
Britain—History—19th century.   4. Romanticism—Great
Britain.   5. Africa—In literature.   6. Blacks in literature.
I. Title.
PR468.S55 L44   2002
820.9'355—dc21   2001041542

To my families

Contents

Illustrations

Texts and Abbreviations

Unless otherwise stated, all quotations are taken from the following editions:

William Blake, *The Complete Poetry and Prose of William Blake*, ed. David V. Erdman (Berkeley: University of California Press, 1982).

George Gordon, Lord Byron, *The Complete Poetical Works*, ed. Jerome McGann, 7 vols. (Oxford: Clarendon Press, 1980–86).

Samuel Taylor Coleridge, *The Complete Poetical Works of Samuel Taylor Coleridge*, ed. E. H. Coleridge, 2 vols. (Oxford: Clarendon Press, 1912, 1957).

John Keats, *Keats: The Complete Poems*, ed. John Barnard (Harmondsworth: Penguin, 1973).

Mary Prince, *The History of Mary Prince, a West Indian Slave, Written by Herself*, ed. Moira Ferguson (Ann Arbor: University of Michigan Press, 1993).

Percy Bysse Shelley, *Shelley's Poetry and Prose*, ed. Donald H. Reiman and Sharon B. Powers (New York: W.W. Norton, 1977).

Mary Wollstonecraft Shelley, *Frankenstein, or the Modern Prometheus* (The 1818 Text), ed. James Reiger (New York: Bobbs-Merrill, 1974; Chicago: University of Chicago Press, 1982).

William Wordsworth, *The Poetical Works of William Wordsworth*, ed. E. de Selincourt and Helen Darbishire, 5 vols. (Oxford: Clarendon Press, 1940–49).

William Wordsworth, *The Prelude, 1799, 1805, 1850*, ed. Jonathan Wordsworth, M. H. Abrams, and Stephen Gill (New York: W.W. Norton, 1979).

Other frequently cited texts appear in parentheses by the following abbreviations:

B   Samuel Taylor Coleridge, *Biographia Literaria*, ed. John Shawcross, 2 vols. (Oxford: Clarendon, 1902).

CC   Samuel Taylor Coleridge, *The Collected Works of Samuel Taylor*

	Coleridge, Bollingen Series 75 (Princeton, N.J.: Princeton University Press; London: Routledge, 1969–).
CL	Samuel Taylor Coleridge, *The Collected Letters of Samuel Taylor Coleridge*, ed. Earl Leslie Griggs, 6 vols. (Oxford: Clarendon Press, 1956–71).
CM	Samuel Taylor Coleridge, *Marginalia*, ed. George Whalley, 5 vols. (1980–). *CC* 12.
CN	Samuel Taylor Coleridge, *The Notebooks*, ed. Kathleen Coburn, 5 vols., Bollingen Series 50 (London: Routledge; Princeton, N.J.: Princeton University Press, 1957–).
KL	John Keats, *The Letters of John Keats, 1814–21*, ed. Hyder E. Rollins, 2 vols. (Cambridge, Mass.: Harvard University Press, 1958).
Lects 1795	Samuel Taylor Coleridge, *Lectures 1795, on Politics and Religion*, ed. Lewis Patton and Peter Mann (1971). *CC* 1.
SL	Percy Bysse Shelley, *The Letters of Percy Bysshe Shelley*, ed. Frederick Jones, 2 vols. (Oxford: Clarendon Press, 1964).
SP	Percy Bysse Shelley, *Shelley's Poetry and Prose*, ed. Donald H. Reiman and Sharon B. Powers (New York: W.W. Norton, 1977).
SWF	Samuel Taylor Coleridge, *Shorter Works and Fragments*, ed. H. J. Jackson and J. R. de J. Jackson, 2 vols. (1995). *CC* 11.
TT	Samuel Taylor Coleridge, *Table Talk*, ed. Carl Woodring, 2 vols. (1990). *CC* 14.
Watchman	Samuel Taylor Coleridge, *The Watchman*, ed. Lewis Patton (1970). *CC* 2.
W Prose	William Wordsworth, *The Prose Works of William Wordsworth*, ed. W. J. B. Owen and J. W. Smyser, 3 vols. (Oxford: Clarendon Press, 1974).

As to the poetical Character itself, it is not itself—it has no self.
—John Keats

The only absolute value is the human possibility of giving the other priority over oneself.
—Emmanuel Levinas

Introduction

I

I have always been fascinated by the idea that the Romantic imagination can reveal things hidden to the naked eye. So when I began this study I wondered what the imagination revealed about slavery, which was not hidden in the culture but seemed to be missing from the era's most powerful poetry. Since slavery was the great moral question of the age and Romanticism the great aesthetic development, it seemed logical to set these two movements side by side. But I soon became acutely aware of the violence in doing so. What did women forced into rooms that smelled of rape and men burned alive after frenzied revolts have to do with Romantic writers' long hours of peaceful reflection and protected moments of rural retreat? Even when I thought of the Romantic imagination as a purely political construct, the fact that its politics were often contained in poems about Grecian urns or ruined cottages or magical lands like Xanadu made me wonder just what imagination could say about slavery. To put the Romantic imagination in close proximity to the horrifying details of slavery seemed plain wrong.

Still, the more I read from the period's discourses on slavery in parliamentary papers, travel narratives, medical tracts, abolitionist poetry, and slave narratives, the more I began to see signs of slavery in imaginative works. This was especially true of works that had come to be thought of as direct products of the Romantic imagination because they were in some way *about* the imagination, works such as the *Lyrical Ballads*, *Visions of the Daughters of Albion*, *Lamia*, "The Witch of Atlas," and *Frankenstein*. How, I wondered, would someone characterize these works about imagination as being also works about slavery?

Fortunately, because other scholars were asking similar questions, a shared critical language began to emerge, with some of the most exciting work coming from Srinivas Aravamudan, Alan Bewell, Elizabeth Bohls, Laura Brown, David Dabydeen, Markman Ellis, Moira Ferguson, Tim Fulford and Peter J. Kitson, Nigel Leask, Saree Makdisi, Javed Majeed, Timothy Morton, Felicity Nussbaum, Mary Louise Pratt, and Alan Richardson.[1] These scholars, and others like them, take their critical language from both history and current postcolonial theory, and it adeptly accounts for the various responses eighteenth- and nineteenth-century British writers had to the growing empire. These responses seem to fall into one of the following categories: complicity, resistance, or anxiety.

Felicity Nussbaum's 1995 book *Torrid Zones*, for instance, tries to make "the ideological workings of empire and of Englishwomen's complicity within it more legible." [2] Complicity is also the critical lens for Alison Hickey, in a 1998 essay called "Dark Characters, Native Grounds: Wordsworth's Imagination of Imperialism." No matter what critical viewpoint a reader takes, says Hickey, "some sort of imperialism is implicitly ascribed" to the Wordsworthian imagination because it champions "the incorporation of otherness, the forging of unity from difference." She goes on to say that the imagination's prerogative is "triumph," but triumph, in this case, always means "the appropriation" of another person or place and the "suppression of its potentially threatening aspect." [3] Likewise, Saree Makdisi, in his 1999 *Romantic Imperialism: Universal Empire and the Culture of Modernity*, asserts that, though Romantics criticized imperialism, they were also complicit with it (Blake, however, is the exception). They were all part of "modernization," a sweeping, globalizing movement that collapsed difference and defined subjectivity in relation to an imperialist center.

Complicity's flip side — resistance — is the focus of other books on empire. Elizabeth Bohls argues that women travel writers "initiated a counter-tradition of aesthetic thought" to combat the discourses of power so evident in patriarchy and empire. [4] Srinivas Aravamudan, in a very different kind of study, coins the term "tropicalization" as a postcolonial response to eighteenth-century colonial discourse. Essentially a set of "practices of discursive revision and reversal," [5] tropicalization is resistant as a way of reading empire. But, says Aravamudan, "rather than reifying *a* voice of resistance or dissent, the act of reading makes available the differing mechanisms of agency that traverse texts, contexts, and agents themselves." [6]

The most interesting way to view responses to empire is somewhere between the poles of complicity and resistance, in the fertile ground of anxiety and ambivalence. Though John Barrell's 1991 book *The Infections of Thomas De-Quincey: A Psychopathology of Imperialism* is probably the most potent source of British anxiety in response to colonization, it was Nigel Leask who popularized the idea in his 1992 book *British Romantic Writers and the East: Anxieties of Empire*. Alan Richardson, drawing on Leask, highlights the ambivalence that such anxiety produces. He puts it this way: "If the treatment of empire in Romantic-era poetry is characterized as ambivalent, however, each poem manifests ambivalence in its own manner." [7] Anxiety has been used, more recently, in Alan Bewell's excellent study of *Romanticism and Colonial Disease* (1999). One of the goals of Bewell's book is to explore the "deepening British understanding of the scale and extent of colonial disease and mortality and the growing anxiety their insecurity aroused." [8]

Perhaps the best summary of the range of responses that Romantic writers had to empire is found in the introduction to Tim Fulford and Peter J. Kitson's 1998 collection of essays *Romanticism and Colonialism*. "Although nineteenth-century colonialism is a thing of the past," they write, "imperialism is often said to persist in the sense of the continuing global ambitions of Western capitalism. This raises the vexed question of the relationship between culture and imperialism and the complicity of English literature in the imperialist project. . . . Nevertheless, writing of the Romantic period cannot simply be seen as univocal in support of that domination: the contributors to this volume investigate some of the ways in which it articulates *resistance to*, and/or *anxiety about*, cultural imperialism, even as it also, in other areas, remains *complicit with* it" (my emphasis).[9]

Although these critical terms have produced some excellent scholarship toward our understanding of the eighteenth and nineteenth centuries in Britain, I began to wonder if there was yet another way to view the relationship between literature and empire, one that seriously considers how the creative act differs from the imperial act, how imagination is distinguished from colonization. Might writers have had another response, besides complicity, resistance, and anxiety/ambivalence, to empire and, particularly, to the institution of slavery? Since the legacies of both slavery and the Romantic imagination are still very much with us today, this is a question that deserves careful thought. It was at this time that I spent a summer with poets and fiction writers talking about creative activity. Not surprisingly, among present-day poets, the Romantic concept of the imagination is alive and well; many of them conceive of creative writing in Romantic terms, often quoting Wordsworth, Keats, and Coleridge. But, for them, imagination is not a critical term. It is a process, a name for the act of creating poetry. It emphatically is not the self-centered, politically evasive or combative activity that literary critics sometimes portray it as. What imagination actually produces is a decentered self with extremely weak ego boundaries, and it involves — above all else — a denunciation of self in order to understand with compassion the artistic subject. For those who use it to create, imagination is essentially about empathy. It struck me that this idea is at the heart of the Romantic imagination, from Blake's notion of "self-annihilation" to Keats's claim that the poet has "no self."

This book, then, is an attempt to account for empathy in the Romantics' theory of imagination and in literary works that are about both imagination *and* slavery. This is not to say that the products of the Romantic imagination simply obliterated the power differential between self and other in the name of empathy, but that writers forged the Romantic imagination, in large part, because of their continued attempts to write creatively about the complex and glaringly unequal relationships between Africans and Britons.

II

Interpreting Romanticism in light of slavery has not exactly been a popular subject in the history of literary criticism, and one reason for its absence seems to lie in the problem of how middle-class, mostly American and British scholars make sense of this frightening, gruesome, and ultimately depressing legacy in Romantic studies.[10] Still, there is a small body of literature on the subject. The two earliest book-length studies appeared in 1942: Eva Beatrice Dykes's *The Negro in English Romantic Thought* and Wylie Sypher's *Guinea's Captive Kings*.[11] Both of these works comprehensively cite example after example of slavery in both Romantic and abolitionist poetry, but being products of mid-twentieth century literary criticism, there is no attempt to explain underlying theoretical similarities or differences between the Romantic and abolitionist movements. More than fifty years passed before Joan Baum published *Mind Forg'd Manacles* in 1994.[12] Baum considers the abolitionist movement through major Romantic figures of Blake, Coleridge, Wordsworth, Keats, Shelley, and Byron. But Baum, like earlier critics, offers no theoretical explanation of the interaction between the poetry and politics of the day.

The first step toward political analysis appears with Patrick J. Keane's *Coleridge's Submerged Politics* in 1994.[13] Taking his lead from arguments made famous in Romantic criticism by Jerome J. McGann and Marjorie Levinson, Keane analyzes Coleridge's marginal notes to Daniel Defoe's *Robinson Crusoe* and then locates Coleridge's radical politics, especially on the issue of slavery, in the subtext of "The Ancient Mariner." Keane explicitly rejects Coleridge's claim that the poem is a work of "pure imagination," arguing instead that it "may reenact, consciously or unconsciously, the rapidly shifting political events in England."[14] While Keane does recreate the politics of slavery behind the images in the poem, he never explains precisely how "The Ancient Mariner" reenacts radical politics.

In the same vein as Keane, but in a much more wide-ranging study, *Gothic Images of Race in Nineteenth-Century Britain* (1996), H. L. Malchow traces the image of slavery in popular culture and gothic literature, concluding that the gothic was a kind of language that articulated the anxieties Europe had about the cultures they were exploiting. "Both the gothic novel and racist discourse manipulate deeply buried anxieties," writes Malchow; both take up "fear of contamination, both present the threatened destruction of the simple and pure by the poisonously exotic, by anarchic forces of passion and appetite, carnal lust and blood lust."[15] Malchow's book offers a dynamic treatment of the gothic novel, moving from Mary Shelley's *Frankenstein* to Bram Stoker's *Dracula*. But his focus is popular culture, not the Romantic imagination. The two other recent books on the subject of Romanticism and slavery are Helen Thomas's *Romanticism and Slave Narratives: Transatlantic Testimonies* (2000) and Marcus Wood's *Blind Memory: Visual Representations of Slavery in England and America, 1780–1865* (2000). Thomas perceptively explores the written material of the period, examining the complex intersection between those writing slave narratives, travel texts, Romantic poems, and radical political treatises. Wood, like Thomas, explains the abolitionist movement using historical sources, but with a focus on visual arts. He examines a large variety of such sources, ranging from trite propaganda engravings to J. M. W. Turner's grand landscapes.[16]

For a specific inquiry into the Romantic imagination's relationship to slavery, the most helpful recent book is Adam Lively's *Masks: Blackness, Race, and the Imagination*.[17] In his chapter "Race and the Sentimental Imagination," Lively catalogs numerous depictions of the African, the Moor, and the slave in sentimental novels and poetry. As Lively sees it, sentimental feeling for the slave fell under the wider concern of middle-class interest in any kind of victim, from poor street urchins, to abandoned women, to mistreated prisoners. Yet, ironically, the sentimental movement, according to Lively, was devoted to refining the sensibilities of the white liberal middle class—a trend Lively sees in contemporary Britain and America. This results in a view of the imagination as hopelessly sentimental but not empathetic.

Still, Adam Lively's point is well taken. Against such an ignoble system as slavery and the imperialism that followed African exploration, how are we to address the literature of early- nineteenth-century white middle-class Britons with all we now know about the effects of this history? How can we do anything but submit to a rhetoric of blame or, at the very least, a cautious examination of the possible ruptures in these necessarily complicit British texts? There is, after all, ample evidence in Romantic texts to characterize the writers as being complicit with empire or anxious about its effects on others, and even more to suggest they sought to question the workings of empire, including slavery and the racial prejudices that have lingered long after its demise. Blake is a prime example. In "A Song of Liberty" that concludes *The Marriage of Heaven and Hell* (1790), Blake dramatically declares: "Empire is no more!" Yet this same "Song of Liberty" contains some shockingly racist stereotypes that Blake must have known were crucial to the extension of empire: a call to the Jew to "leave counting gold!" and to the African to alter his facial characteristics: "O African! black African (go. winged thought widen his forehead)."[18]

Though such discrepancies sear nearly every poem, this is not surprising, at least according to Toni Morrison, in her stunning explanation of the African presence in the American literary imagination. In *Playing in the Dark* (1992), Morrison argues that blackness permeates the literary imagination in America, even in works where we least expect to find it. A writer's response to African presence may be "encoded, or explicit," she says, but in any case it "complicate[s] texts, sometimes contradicting them entirely." The African presence "serve[s] the text by further problematizing its matter with resonances and luminations." Linguistic responses, most intriguingly, "provide paradox, ambiguity; they strategize omissions, repetitions, disruptions, polarities, reifications, violence. In other words, they give the text a deeper, richer, more complex life than the sanitized one commonly present to us."[19] The African presence, likewise, shaped the British Romantic imagination. Because slavery was such an intimate part of the imagination, writers produced works so distinct that an entire literary period formed around them.

In the broadest sense, this book asks: what is the relationship between the artist and the most hideous crimes of his or her era? In dealing with the Romantic period, the question has to be: what is the relationship between the nation's greatest artists and the epic violence of slavery, described so astutely by Coleridge in 1808 as "the wildest physical sufferings" combined with "the most atrocious moral depravity" (*SWF*, 1:218). The answer is varied, at best, but one of the things Romantic works chronicle is the death of Romantic illusions in the face of slavery. In fact, many of these writers suggest that the enormous violations of their era can only be met with absurdly small acts of recompense, such as the blessing of water snakes in "The Ancient Mariner." Yet key Romantic works like "The Ancient Mariner," *Visions of the Daughters of Albion*, *Lamia*, "The Witch of Atlas," *Frankenstein*, and *Lyrical Ballads*, which seem impossible to lay aside even after we have finished reading them, also deliver something larger: an inquiry into the nature of empathy.

PART I

History and Imagination

1

British Slavery and African Exploration

The Written Legacy

I

In 1816, the British government began pressuring colonial legislatures in the Caribbean to be more accountable for their African populations.[1] At this time, the colony at Berbice started keeping a "book of minutes" recording the complaints of slaves, which were then published by Parliament and distributed throughout Britain. These records are unique. For in the midst of a turbulent controversy on slavery by virtually all classes of British citizens, the voices of slaves were now to be found within official government discourse. Though the words of slaves were written down by British officials and were often in the third person, the fact that they appear at all says something about the significant shift taking place during this period between African slaves and British masters.

Among these complaints, the case of "Tommy" stands out.[2] On 9 February 1819, Tommy appeared before the fiscal (judge) of the colony to state his case. Tommy, a carpenter by trade, belonged to a man named Fraser of the Gladstone Hall plantation. Fraser used Tommy to repair sugar casks. On the day in question, Tommy had gone to the boiling house to fetch some nails for his day's work, where he met another slave who was "heading up sugars." Tommy and the other slave apparently spoke casually for a few minutes. Before he left, Tommy walked over to one of the casks and "took a lump of sugar for the purpose of sweetening three gallons of water" for his personal use. He put the sugar in his apron, along with some rusty nails. While employed repairing sugar casks, Tommy explained to the fiscal, he was in the habit of keeping old nails that he would later use to repair his hut. But as he was coming out of the boiling house, Tommy met Fraser, his "owner."

For his part, Fraser reported that he had bumped into Tommy and immediately noticed "a big bulge" in his apron. Fraser demanded closer inspection. Tommy opened his apron revealing, in Fraser's words, "a great quantity of sugar and nails mixed together." Fraser accused Tommy of theft, a crime that most plantation owners considered an insidious form of resistance. Fraser then proceeded to have Tommy tied to the ground and flogged one hundred times, sixty-one more than the legal limit.

In his complaint, Tommy did not deny taking the sugar and rusty nails. If anything, he adamantly affirmed his "theft." What he objected to was the flogging. Yet when the fiscal asked Tommy to expose his back and posterior to the court, Tommy's body showed only a few faded marks. The fiscal questioned Tommy on this inconsistency, and he explained that "he had been favoured by the drivers, who threw the whips over him," therefore completely missing his body with the whip. Since the case itself did not come to any conclusion because Tommy openly admitted to taking the sugar and rusty nails, and he similarly acknowledged that he had not been flogged, the logical question is: what is it doing here?

Although the legal center of Tommy's case is the number of lashes he was supposed to have gotten, the moral center rests on the objects of the theft: sugar and rusty nails. In this way, Tommy turned the actions of the British, not of the slaves, into a crime. British guilt rested in the crime of excessive flogging, but also in the crime of withholding from slaves the products of their labor. British plantation owners could only make this kind of criminal confusion because they were "distant" — in the sense that they were indifferent to how they treated others. Tommy draws attention to this distance with a subtle vengeance by bringing his case into the rhetorical arena of human rights. He insists on the right to food (sugar to sweeten his water); to shelter (rusty nails to repair his hut); and to ownership of his own body (a restriction on flogging). He demands a say in defining his own humanity to British lawmakers. Through a simple story of sugar and rusty nails, he asks readers and listeners of this case to feel for the humanity of slaves. Tommy and the other slaves who speak through these records ask not for a cursory acknowledgment of their humanity but for a deep awareness of their experience. That they did so in a form that was recorded in the government's official discourse indicates that the British people in the colonies, or in Britain for that matter, could no longer distance themselves from the violence of slavery as they had done for nearly three hundred years.

But how did this brutally distant attitude occur in the first place? Part of it stemmed from slavery's geography. From the perspective of the average Briton, slavery had always been an institution situated in the faraway colonies. In fact, the most famous case in the history of the institution — that of James Somerset — was an effort to keep slavery physically distant. In 1771, nearly half a century before Tommy's complaint, the slave James Somerset was ordered to appear before Judge Mansfield at the Court of King's Bench in London. Somerset, who had been brought from America to Britain by his "master" Charles Stewart, ran away and was immediately returned to Stewart, who then put him on a slave ship bound for Jamaica to be sold.[3] This was the case in a nutshell, and because it was unprecedented, Judge Mansfield had to decide if Somerset, as a slave of Stewart while they had both been in America, could be forced to return to one of Britain's slaveholding colonies—in this case, Jamaica. Mansfield ruled that Stewart could not force Somerset to return to the colonies.

This case is not what it seems. Mansfield, as historians James Walvin and F. O. Shyllon explain, was intensely interested in upholding the property basis of British slavery, and he was not, by any means, proclaiming that all slaves were free in Britain.[4] What Mansfield actually declared was this slippery justification for not deporting Somerset:

The state of slavery is of such a nature, that it is incapable of being now introduced by courts of justice upon mere reasoning or inferences from any principles, natural or political; it *must* take its rise from *positive* law; the origin of it can in no country or age be traced back to any other source: immemorial usage preserves the memory of positive law long after all traces of the occasion, reason, authority, and time of its introduction are lost; and, in a case so odious as the condition of slaves, must be taken strictly.[5]

Still, the case was interpreted in the popular imagination to mean that slavery was abolished on British soil. It gained a huge following and took on a mythological status after it was settled. Long rambling opinion pieces, filled with an eighteenth-century spirit of debate, crowded out lesser news in the *Morning Chronicle, London Chronicle, Gazetteer,* and *Gentleman's Magazine* in 1772. One man calling himself "A Friend of Mankind" wrote, "Every person in England, and every person in a civilized state, has a claim to the protection of its laws, as he is subject to them. . . . No degree of slavery can subsist in a free state; all mankind are created free agents, and it is only arbitrary force that perverts the gifts of God and nature."[6] Others proclaimed it a judgment in "universal liberty" and even the country's fervent abolitionists, such as Granville Sharp, who was more closely connected with the case than most people, took Mansfield's decision to mean "the exercise of the power of a Master over his Slave must be supported by the Law of the particular Countries; but no foreigner can *in England claim* a right *over a Man*: such a Claim *is not known to the Laws of England.*"[7]

Ten years after the Somerset case, which left the issue of slavery securely situated in the colonies, another case brought it uncomfortably close to home, the infamous case of the slave ship *Zong*. In 1781, the *Zong* sailed on a common trade route, from Liverpool to the west coast of Africa, and then with a cargo of 470 Africans bound for Jamaica. Disease and death tore through the ship,

and in less than three months over sixty Africans and seven crew had died. Although this was one of the usual hazards of slave voyages, the reaction of Luke
Collingwood, captain of the *Zong*, was shockingly unprecedented. When it became clear to Collingwood that loss through "natural causes" was inevitable, he
proposed that the crew throw the remaining sick slaves overboard. He argued
that this would only bring a slightly earlier death to people who would die any-
way, which in turn would leave the dwindling water supplies for those who were
well. It was twisted reasoning, but it seemed to be enough for the crew, who
agreed to push fifty-four Africans into the sea on 29 November, forty-two the
next day, and twenty-six the next. Ten of these, in an act of resistance against the
mass murder, committed suicide by throwing themselves overboard in despair.[8]

As if the manner in which Collingwood treated these people was not shocking enough, the way the case was later handled in British courts indicated how
callous the business of slavery and law had become. Although antislavery advocates were horrified, the case was subsumed under British insurance law, and
the insurance company refused to pay slave owners anything. Apparently, death
from "natural causes" was not covered. In a rebuttal, the slave owners insisted
that the slaves were "goods" that had to be sacrificed in this case, and they demanded compensation. It therefore came down to a chilling distinction between
slaves as property and as people. At one point in the trial, the solicitor representing the slave owners said,

What is all this vast declamation of human beings thrown overboard? The question after
all is, Was it voluntary or an act of necessity? *This is a case of chattels or goods.* It is really
so: it is the case of throwing over goods; for to this purpose, and the purpose of the insurance, *they are goods and property: whether right or wrong, we have nothing to do with it.*
This property—*the human creatures, if you will*—have been thrown overboard: whether
or not for the preservation of the rest, that is the real question.[9]

The *Zong* case was never settled. Initially, it was set for a further trial where,
by coincidence, Judge Mansfield, who had presided over the Somerset case, was
set to hear it. However, if there was a second trial, it was never recorded. But the
event was one of the first highly publicized stories that would brand the brutalities of slavery on the British consciousness. As with the Somerset case, so it was
with the *Zong*. Letters to the daily and weekly newspapers brought the case before the public. And just as the Somerset case had won national praise for British
liberty, the *Zong* affair registered a profound sense of British tyranny. A letter
writer in the *Morning Chronicle* of 18 March 1783 who attended the case wrote,
"*The narrative seemed to make every one present shudder.*"[10] It was this event, according to veteran historian James Walvin, that instigated the full unleashing of
antislavery sentiment in Britain. Not only was it behind the abolitionist move-

ment, it was a startling instance of the kind of integrated team work that would eventually bring slavery to an end. The day after the 18 March article, the Nigerian born Londoner Olaudah Equiano personally called on the white abolitionist Granville Sharp to discuss the incident.[11]

Ironically, the Somerset case, which took place in Britain, implied that slavery would be contained in the faraway colonies, while the *Zong* affair, which took place faraway in the middle passage, brought slavery terrifyingly close to home in the sense that it entered the British consciousness in a personal way. The truth was that slavery, by the 1780s, was bound to ideas of proximity and distance. Before this, Europeans had been able to look with cold remove on the slave trade because of its sheer physical distance from them. The trip from a British slave port such as Liverpool, Bristol, London, or Hull to a destination along the coast of East or West Africa ran anywhere from four thousand to six thousand miles and could take months.[12] The middle passage, from Africa to the West Indies was roughly the same distance, lasting anywhere from forty days at the least, to four months at the most. Sailors heading back to Britain from the West Indies would travel another five thousands miles, and depending on where they stopped with their trade goods, this journey too could last months.

But more important than physical distance was psychological distance. Slave owners, up until the late eighteenth century, seemed to have both in their favor. They frequently argued that because of the geographical remoteness of the colonies from Britain, they were absolved of any crime against Africans. The mass majority of people who were not slave owners felt even more psychologically remote. Even as people were beginning to acknowledge that physical distance made no difference in how intimately involved Britain was in the trade, they had been used to viewing slavery with the same indifference that Tommy faced in his complaint against his master. Therefore, it was psychological remove from the plight of slaves, not just geographical remoteness, that seemed an even more ironclad notion.

Early abolitionists emphasized exactly this point. One of the first, the American Quaker John Woolman, whose essay *Some Considerations on the Keeping of Negroes* appeared in 1746, traveled around America as an itinerant minister speaking against slaveholding. Along with those of the American abolitionist and fellow Quaker Anthony Benezet, Woolman's writings were transported to Britain, serving as the initial inspiration behind Britain's antislavery movement: British abolitionist Thomas Clarkson gives Woolman credit for his own conversion to the antislavery cause. Very soon into Woolman's travels around America, he discovered he was up against one grand objection. His parishes argued that because metropolitan centers were at a safe distance from plantations, they were not responsible for what took place there. So Woolman found himself writing things like, "Great distance makes nothing in our favour. To willingly join with unrighteousness to the injury of men who live some thousands of miles off is the same in substance as joining with it to the injury of our neighbours."[13] Woolman used this concept of intimate distance to challenge the psychological remoteness of most Europeans and Americans. The term he used repeatedly to evoke guilt in his readers was "self-interest." "Can it be possible," he wrote, "for an honest man to think that with a view to *self-interest* we may continue slavery to the off-spring of these unhappy sufferers . . . and not have a share of this guilt" (my emphasis).[14] Psychological proximity, Woolman argued, would clarify just what slavery did:

And did we attend to these scenes in Africa in like manner as if they were transacted in our presence, and sympathize with the Negroes in all their afflictions and miseries as we do with our children or friends, we should be more careful to do nothing in any degree helping forward a trade productive of so many and so great calamities.[15]

Following Woolman, British abolitionists considered it standard practice to challenge the idea of self-interest and to combat the belief that ordinary Britons were simply detached parties in a slave system beyond their control. In 1791, the radical abolitionist William Fox wrote specifically about bridging distance based on racial and geographic boundaries: "Can our pride suggest," he asked, "that the rights of men are limited to any nation, or to any colour? Or, were any one to treat a fellow creature in this country as we do the unhappy Africans in the West-Indies; struck with horror, we should be zealous to deliver the oppressed, and punish the oppressor. Are then the offices of humanity and functions of justice to be circumscribed by geographical boundaries?"[16] Others bridged that distance in more rhetorically simple ways. The slave trader turned evangelist John Newton actually became a "a Captive and a Slave myself" among the "Natives of Africa."[17] Similarly, Thomas Clarkson, in an effort to bring the subject of slavery closer to the British mind, wrote part of his *Essay on the Slavery and Commerce of the Human Species* in the first person, but from the perspective of the African witnessing a scene of horror equal to that of the *Zong*. "To place this in the clearest, and most conspicuous point of view," Clarkson writes, "I shall suppose myself on a particular part of the continent of Africa, and relate a scene. . . . At first, I will turn my eyes to the cloud of dust that is before me. It seems to advance rapidly, and, accompanied with dismal shrieks and yellings, to make the very air, that is above it, tremble as it rolls along. What can possibly be the cause?"[18]

Clarkson was by far the most active abolitionist of the Romantic period and the most inclined to make slavery a personal issue. He traveled over thirty-five thousand miles between 1788 and 1795 alone, establishing local antislavery organizations all over the country and collecting facts and artifacts about the

British slave trade that would help convince anyone, from paupers to Members of Parliament, of the inhumanity of slavery.[19] Not only did Clarkson submit facts and figures, numbers and dimensions, and stories of ill treatment, he brought in actual iron instruments used on slave ships: handcuffs, leg shackles, thumb-screws, speculums for force-feeding slaves who would rather die.

One of the most shocking artifacts of Clarkson's travels is a drawing that shows how Liverpool and Bristol slavers regularly crammed hundreds of African bodies into the bowels of their slave ships (Figure 1). The drawing, in fact, has remained a sort of icon of the visual horror of the slave trade ever since. The peculiar way in which the bodies are imagined in the genre of an architectural drawing and cross section says something about the hideous underside of British seafaring. What is most surprising about the drawing, however, is the amount of detail the bodies have. Little leg irons and arm bands cup the limbs of the African males, while the females lie with their breasts exposed. The distance with which these middle passage slave bodies were normally kept from the British people must have made them startling to viewers at this time. This British ship—the *Brookes*—was originally filled with slaves in Africa and emptied of them in the West Indies, far from Britain's clean shores, and it is the close proximity of this conventionally foreign and distant picture that gives it the intensity of a central image of the antislavery movement.[20]

By driving the Liverpool slaver onto the steps of London's parliamentary buildings, Clarkson and the abolitionists brought slavery home, bridged the distance between London and West Africa, between Liverpool and Barbados. Psychologically, they were saying, as Tommy would say some years later in his Berbice complaint, that it was no longer possible for people in Britain to look with myopic indifference on the human suffering and violence of slavery. "As then the inhumanity of this trade must be universally admitted and lamented," the notice on the slave ship poster reads, "people would do well to consider, that it does not often fall to the lot of individuals, to have an opportunity of per-forming so important a moral and religious duty, as that of endeavouring to put an end to the practice, which may, without exaggeration, be stiled one of the greatest evils at this day existing upon the earth."[21]

II

There is very little argument by historians or literary scholars over the claim made by Clarkson and his coworkers in 1788 that slavery was the greatest evil existing upon the earth at that time. But slavery, they were all aware, was an inherited problem. Servitude, bondage, and forms of dependence and forced

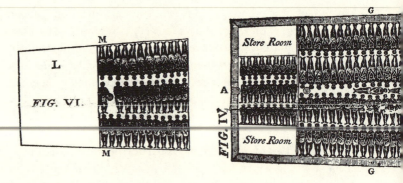

Figure 1. Detail, Thomas Clarkson, 1789. Courtesy of Wilberforce House, Hull City Museums and Art Galleries, UK/Bridgeman Art Library, London.

labor have been aspects of many cultures and time periods. Ancient civilizations in Asia, Africa, Europe, and pre-Colombian America record slavery in its various forms. It has been endorsed by the world's major religious institutions—Judaism, Hinduism, Islam, and Christianity.[22] And long before the transatlantic trade, slavery was practiced in the Mediterranean. During the fourteenth and fifteenth centuries, slave auctions were held all along the coast of North Africa as well as in some of the most fashionable European cities, such as Venice, Seville, Lisbon, and Antwerp.[23] From the fourteenth right through to the eighteenth and nineteenth centuries, India received slaves from Africa, with the trade running from Madagascar and the Red Sea by way of Arab traders. Slaves were also integral to the expansion of the Ottoman Empire.[24] Even in Africa itself, slavery was widespread until the nineteenth century.[25]

But transatlantic slavery was a very different creature. One of the most startling aspects of the early years of the slave trade is how rapidly it expanded from a minor commerce to a full-blown economic enterprise. If one wanted to attach an actual date to the beginnings of the trade it would be 1518, when Charles V of Spain granted the first licenses to Europeans to take African people from their homes and bring them to the Spanish American colonies to be used as slave labor.[26] Within just ten years, by the 1520s, the slave trade was a developed operation managed by the Portuguese, who controlled the basis for slave supply on the west coast of Africa. One hundred years later, during the 1640s, the trade ballooned again when sugar plantations spread from Brazil to the Caribbean. Sugar cultivation could only be profitable if outfitted by cheap labor in the form of slaves. And so during the middle 1640s, the Portuguese, who had controlled

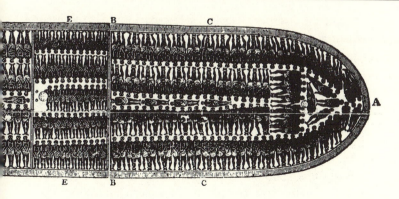

the transatlantic trade for a hundred years, and the Spanish who continued to be involved, were joined by the Dutch, French, Danish, and British. The gruesome baton of massive slave exports passed from the Portuguese, to the Dutch, and eventually to the British, who dominated the trade after 1660.

Britain's very first dealings in the slave trade were amply recorded by Richard Hakluyt in 1582. Hakluyt chronicled the voyage of "Master John Haukins," who "having made divers voyages to the Iles of the Canaries," realized what other European nations had already made disturbingly possible: "that Negros were very good merchandise in Hispaniola, and that store of Negros might easily bee had upon the coast of Guinea." According to Hakluyt, Hawkins immediately "resolved with himselfe to make triall thereof, and communicated that devise with his worshipfull friends of London."[27] Britain's role in the trade continued to expand, as it seized various portions of the Caribbean and exported slaves to its North American colonies, dealing principally in sugar.

In the 1780s, the transatlantic trade reached its peak, with the British leading the way and, ironically enough, it was at this exact moment that the British also began to dominate abolition efforts. One of the landmark events in the abolition movement took place in 1789, when William Wilberforce moved for twelve antislave trade resolutions in the House of Commons. Wilberforce objected to the slave trade on the grounds of British national guilt. This very idea, in fact, formed the moral center of his parliamentary speech: "The motion he meant to offer, was perfectly reconcileable to political expediency, and at the same time to national humanity. It was by no means a party question, nor would it, he hoped, be so considered; . . . He came not forward to accuse the West India Planter; he came not forward to accuse the Liverpool Merchants; he came forward to accuse no one; he came forward to confess himself guilty, for the purpose of shewing to the House, that if guilt any where existed, which ought to be remedied, they were all of them participators in it." [28] The magnitude with which the British exported slaves was now matched, in the popular imagination, only by the guilt each person bore because of it.

Indeed, even though transatlantic slavery was an inherited problem for Romantic audiences, it carried some peculiarly shameful aspects compared to other forms of slavery. Transatlantic slavery was different for several reasons. First of all, its sheer dimension is staggering. By the early nineteenth century, the African slave trade represented the largest migration of people in human history to that point. [29] Millions of people were torn from their homeland and deposited on foreign shores. Just how many millions is a matter of historical debate. The number seems to range from between ten and fifty million. Toni Morrison dedicates her Pulitzer Prize-winning novel Beloved to "Sixty Million and more." [30] Most recent research suggests that around twelve million Africans entered the Atlantic slave trade between 1500 and 1867 with ships of the British Empire alone carrying nearly three and a half million of those slaves from Africa between 1662 and 1807. [31] It is also estimated that 10 to 15 percent of those transported from Africa to the Caribbean and the Americas died on slave ships during the middle passage, which is one of the most horrible and resonating memories of slavery.

Besides its unparalleled magnitude, the other particularly shameful aspect of the trade, one that abolitionists and poets were well aware of, is that plantation slavery turned people into chattels, and this led to the interpretation in Western culture of slavery as the polar opposite of freedom. Transatlantic slavery gave European culture its definition of freedom because in a very real sense, enslaved blacks created freedom for whites in Europe and America. Slavery within Africa, by contrast, did not carry this connotation. While slaves there still suffered in profound ways—for instance, they lost their status and social identity—a slave was not turned into property. [32] Similarly, slavery in the Muslim world included intricate laws and customs regarding how people once enslaved could still make themselves full members of Muslim society. [33]

By the early nineteenth century, the dismantling of the slave trade and the emancipation of slaves was inevitable, but Britons expressed extreme insecurity about its consequences. This feeling is registered most strikingly by George Canning, the leader of the House of Commons, on 16 March 1824, in what is now a famous speech in the history of British slavery. "The question is not," he said, "a question of right, of humanity, of morality merely. It is a question that contemplates a change, great and difficult beyond example; one almost beyond the power of man to accomplish;—a change in the condition and circumstances of an entire class of our fellow creatures; — the recasting, as it were, of a whole generation of mankind." [34]

But what Canning does not admit here is that change was endemic to the period. The American Revolution of 1776 and the French Revolution of 1789 were seen to inaugurate a period of upheaval in which people all over the world could set themselves free from tyranny. The revolutions in Spanish America began around 1810. Simón Bolívar, the liberator of Venezuela, Colombia, and Peru, set up the Congress of Venezuela and the Congress of Colombia in 1819, but he dreamed of a united South America, free from Spanish rule. Closer to home, the Greek war of independence had been sparked as early as 1821 against the Turks of Moldavia and Wallachia. The revolutionary flavor of world politics inevitably spread to the system of slavery — most notably the Haitian revolution of 1791, which lasted many years. On a smaller scale, British slave colonies had continual problems with day-to-day resistance and with major uprisings, such as those of 1816 in Barbados, of 1823 in Demerara, and of 1831–32 in Jamaica. The Jamaica rebellion, in particular, was just what was needed to prompt Parliament to pass the emancipation bill. Samuel Sharpe, a feisty figure who has achieved heroic status, was the leader of the rebellion where 200 slaves were killed and at least 340 more put to death in torturous trials that followed the uprising. Sharpe himself was one of the last to die, on 23 March 1832, a week before Parliament appointed a committee "for the purpose of effecting the Extinction of Slavery." Sharpe reportedly said, just before his execution, "I would rather die upon yonder gallows than live in slavery." [35]

III

But just as Britain was planning a change in the status of slaves, the British were figuring out ways they could exploit Africans in Africa itself. In some bizarre way, they were drawn to Africans or Africa for the entire nineteenth century, whether through slavery or African exploration. At the beginning of the century, as the abolition movement swung into full momentum, Britain was not only the major European sea power, it was the leader (though not far ahead of France) in exploration. At the time, the major contours of Europe, Asia, and North and South America had already been charted, so it was the interiors that presented the most challenging sites for exploration. But those explorers who went in their country's name, and in the name of discovery, also knew that the lands they described would soon become zoned for commercial activity, and beyond that, for colonial exploitation.

Following the three celebrated journeys of Captain James Cook, executed

between 1768 and 1779, Britain initiated thousands more voyages, in an effort to
chart the entire globe. In the South Seas, not only Cook wrote up his travels, but
his shipmates Georg Forster and John Hawkesworth came out with their own
versions. These were followed by other South Seas travelogues, such as George
Keate's 1788 *Account of the Pelew Islands*. In North America, travelers meticu-
lously recorded flora and fauna, as well as Native American Indian customs, as
found in William Bartram's 1791 *Travels through North and South Carolina, Georgia, East and West Florida, The Cherokee Country . . . together with Observations
on the Manners of the Indians*. The more hearty explorers braved the snows and
ice of Canada in search of the elusive Northwest Passage, as recorded in Samuel
Hearne's 1795 *Journey from Prince of Wales's Fort in Hudson's Bay to the Northern
Ocean*. No place was out of reach. The Middle East, India, China and Japan were
scoured under the traveling eyes of men and women alike: James Morier's 1812
Journey through Persia, Armenia and Asia Minor, to Constantinople, and James
Wathen's 1814 *Journal of a Voyage, in 1811 to 1812, to Madras and China*. Even the
places that had been occupied by Britons for hundreds of years were worthy of
travel accounts. There were travels to Scotland, Ireland, and all the countries
in Europe. Caribbean histories and travels also abounded, from William Beckford's early *Descriptive Account of the Island of Jamaica* (1790) to the celebrated
gothic writer Matthew Gregory Lewis, with his *Journal of a West India Proprietor*,
published in 1834, after his death from yellow fever.[36]

As this worldwide exploration and description went on in reasonably systematic fashion, Africa was pursued with more attention than the rest of the
world put together. Africans did not put up a united front against white explorers
the way the Chinese and Japanese did, so this made exploration a more viable
option for the British and the French. As the Industrial Revolution gathered
steam, Africa was also attractive because it offered an expansive market for European trade goods, and the British were determined to corner that market before
the French.[37] So the British set up an official association devoted to learning more
about the continent and how it could be used to Britain's advantage in the face
of the worldwide changes of slavery and French imperialism. The Association
for Promoting the Discovery of the Interior Parts of Africa—or the African Association, as it was called—came into being in 1788 owing to the inspiration of
Sir Joseph Banks.[38]

A round, heavy figure, with darkly defined eyebrows, a dimpled chin, and
sturdy hands, Banks was at the imperial center of Britain for at least fifty years.
Although Banks does not survive in the popular consciousness the way other figures have—like Cook, or Wordsworth, or Napoleon—he was more influential at
the time than any of them, and some of his activities continue to be influential,

even in the twenty-first century. He sailed with Cook, in his circumnavigation of the globe, led the first scientific voyage to Iceland, and in 1778 became president of the Royal Society. A friend of King George III, he also became director of the Royal Botanic Gardens at Kew, making them the world's most impressive repository of international specimens. He was responsible for importing Merino sheep to Australia whose wool to this day is found in sweaters. He planted colonies all over the world and shipped British convicts to Australia. He masterminded the Tahitian breadfruit expedition which ended, of course, with the infamous mutiny on the *Bounty*. He aided Johann Friedrich Blumenbach, the eminent German scientist (also called the father of anthropology) in the development of one of the first scientific efforts to categorize the races of man, which led to our modern racist categories.[39]

Banks developed a grand network of correspondence with scientists and explorers all over the world. Although he shipped men and specimens to the furthest corners of the globe, the most intimate centers of Banks's collection of distant lands were his houses, first at New Burlington Street, then at 32 Soho Square. As if finding the world in a grain of sand, scientists, dignitaries, politicians and explorers discovered here a microcosm of the nature and culture of foreign places. Here Banks assembled a massive library, open to scholars of all kinds, and, more impressively, tens of thousands of specimens, including many of the 30,000 he had collected on the *Endeavour* when he had sailed with Cook. The walls crawled with insects and sprouted plants. One visitor wrote "it would be absurd to attempt a particular description of what I saw there . . . his house is a perfect museum; every room contains an inestimable treasure." In one room, Banks had "warlike instruments, mechanical instruments and utensils of every kind, made use of by the Indians of the South Seas"; in another were "an almost numberless collection of animals, quadrupeds, birds, fish, amphibia, reptiles, insects . . . preserved in spirits." And Banks had his collection available in reproducible form: "the choicest collection of drawings . . . 987 plants drawn and coloured by Parkinson; and 1300 or 1400 more drawn with each of them a flower, a leaf, and a portion of the stalk, coloured by the same hand; besides a number of other drawings of animals, birds, fish, etc. and what is more extraordinary still, all the new genera and species contained in this vast collection are accurately described."[40] In short, scientists and travelers first saw distant lands through Banks's classified information. When they traveled to those lands, when they wrote about them, their perspectives were already shaped by what they had seen at Soho Square. In this way, Banks oversaw almost all voyages of discovery Britain undertook during the Romantic period, but Africa was one of his special favorites.

The African Association was composed of members representing a wide variety of Britain's interests—from scientific to commercial. Interestingly enough, the membership also included the country's two most prominent abolitionists, William Wilberforce and Thomas Clarkson. They hoped, as historian John Gascoigne has demonstrated, that "the Association would be a means of combating the slave-trade." [41] But underlying the association's goals, and those of the abolitionists, was the deeply entrenched belief that British occupation would enlighten Africa. In the process, Britain would enlighten itself about the lands beyond its reach. The original purpose of the association stated, "Certain however it is, that, while we continue ignorant of so large a portion of the globe, that ignorance must be considered as a degree of reproach upon the present age." [42]

The desire to explore and enlighten very soon turned to a lust of conquest. In 1792, Banks said that colonizing Africa "did not in my opinion coincide with the purpose of the association," but just seven years later, in 1799, he recommended "secur[ing] to the British Throne, either by conquest or by Treaty, the whole of the coast of Africa from Auguin to Sierra Leone." [43] He argued that such a colony would make Africans more "happy than they now are under the Tyranny of their arbitrary Princes," and that Britons would support this colonization effort, especially because Africans would then be converted to the "Christian Religion" and the nation could then end slavery "upon the principles of natural justice & Commercial benefit." [44]

This link between African exploration and the demise of British slavery has been carefully critiqued by present-day historians. Most agree, in fact, that abolitionists acted, to a greater or lesser degree, in tandem with the British desire to colonize the world. This particular line of thinking was initiated by Eric Williams, an Oxford historian who went on to become prime minister of postcolonial Trinidad and Tobago, in his 1944 *Capitalism and Slavery*.[45] With originality and striking persuasion, Williams argued that the British slave trade, with all the money and industry it generated, created the conditions for the Industrial Revolution, and this, in turn, funded the large-scale scientific explorations of the nineteenth century. Abolition of the slave trade and emancipation of slaves in the Caribbean, Williams said, was thus a result of economics, not humanitarianism, and it certainly did not have anything to do with transcendental ideals. For historians ever since, Williams's analysis has been the foundation for rethinking the relationship between antislavery opinion and industrial capitalism, humanitarianism and economics. More recently, David Brion Davis has argued that abolitionists were unwittingly acting out of self-interest in pushing for the end of slavery. Since most of them belonged to the rising middle class, it was in their best interest to support abolition, which promised, in turn, to boost capitalism. Davis writes, "British antislavery helped to ensure stability while accommodating society to political and economic change; it merged Utilitarianism

with an ethic of benevolence, reinforcing faith that a progressive policy of lais-
sez faire would reveal men's natural identity of interests."[46] In short, exploration
and subsequent colonization was the flip side of slavery.

In the realm of literature, exploration had different consequences. It
brought Africans—or stories about them—home to Britain, but in different
ways from the stories circulating about slaves. The first to do this with any success was a protégé of Joseph Banks, the Scottish explorer Mungo Park. In July of
1794, Park, an unemployed ship's surgeon, found himself in London's Thatched
House Tavern in a meeting with Banks. Though the two were opposites in many
ways—Banks was rotund, privileged, and, by this time, homebound, whereas
Park was angular, solidly working-class, and moving around the world—they
had in common a curiosity about Africa. So Banks drafted a resolution stating,
"That Mr Mungo Park having offered his Services to the Association as Geographical Missionary to the interior countries of Africa; and appearing to the
Committee to be well qualified for the Undertaking, his offer be accepted."[47]
Even as he signed the commission, Park knew that almost every other European
who had been sent to navigate the Niger River had died in the process. John Ledyard had gone west from Cairo and Daniel Houghton east from Gambia; neither
one returned alive.

Still, Banks vetted, prepared, and sent Mungo Park by way of Gambia, and,
as if to double his chances for successful African exploration, Banks also sent a
young German named Friedrich Hornemann by way of Tripoli the same year.
Both men went in the name of the African Association, and, while Hornemann
died along the way, Mungo Park (whether by ingenuity or, more likely, sheer
luck) returned in 1797, having accomplished most of his mission. Banks had sent
him to explore the Niger Valley with the aim of "rendering the geography of
Africa more familiar to my countrymen, and in opening to their ambition and
industry new sources of wealth, and new channels of commerce."[48] So naturally,
upon Park's return, Banks and the African Association immediately set about
shaping his experiences into a publication designed to open the unknown continent to the eyes of European readers. Banks recruited Bryan Edwards, who
had already written the influential *History, Civil and Commercial, of the British
West Indies* as ghostwriter. Edwards made sure Park's narrative was "interesting
and entertaining," and then he had Banks "cast [his] eye" over each chapter for
final approval.[49] The narrative certainly has dramatic elements, with the requi-
site amount of humor, sex, danger, and violence. At one point, Park himself is
taken captive and is asked to give "ocular demonstration" of his private parts
to a group of Moorish women.[50] At another point he is robbed, stripped naked,
and left for dead.[51]

Such intimate encounters riveted a public that had been saturated with stories of Africans as slaves. In Park's estimation, Africans were sometimes fierce, sometimes friendly, most of the time clever, but never subservient. At one of his particularly vulnerable moments, Park is told by the villagers of Bambarra that he must wait alone the entire night, without food or shelter, and an African woman "returning from the labours in the fields" comes upon him. The woman, says Park, "stopped to observe me, and perceiving that I was weary and dejected, inquired into my situation, which I briefly explained to her; whereupon, with looks of great compassion, she took up my saddle and bridle, and told me to follow her." [52] She and her daughters feed Park, and then sing to him:

The winds roared, and the rains fell. — The poor white man, faint and weary, came and sat under our tree. — He has no mother to bring him milk; no wife to grind his corn. Let us pity the white man; no mother has he, &c. &c.[53]

Park's narrative is filled with modest moments of compassion, and words like "unexpected kindness," "hospitality," and "benefactress" are scattered throughout the pages of his narrative, describing his encounters with Africans. His book thus made readers, who were trained to think of African-European encounter in terms of slaves and masters, imagine Africans in new ways.

For this, and other reasons, the narrative was an instant literary classic, necessitating two more editions after an initial sellout and German, French, and American editions by 1800.[54] Park's observations on Africans were also used by scientists, other explorers, and poets. They were the subject of a play called "Mungo's Address," a song by the duchess of Devonshire called "A Negro Song from Park's Travels" and a poem by Felicia Hemans. James Montgomery quoted Park in his popular abolitionist poem of 1809, *The West Indies*, and Mary Russell Mitford celebrated the narrative itself in "Lines, Suggested by the Uncertain Fate of Mungo Park": "Oh! When secure in Albion's happy land, / He trac'd his dangers with recording hand." [55] After Park, poets portrayed Africa as a place through which the hidden depths of the self could be imagined.

But the imaginative use of Park differed from the political use of him. On 25 May 1799 Banks told the African Association that Park had "opened a Gate into the Interior of Africa into which it is easy for every nation to enter and to extend its Commerce and Discovery from the West to the Eastern side of that immense Continent." If Britain did not "possess" itself of the "Treasures" of Africa discovered by Park, "some Rival Nation" soon would. Chief among those treasures was gold, which Park had seen traded as dust. "Science," Banks stated, "should teach these ignorant savages that Gold which is Dust at the mouth of a river must be . . . in the form of Pebbles when near the place from whence it was originally washed." He also thought Britain should send troops up the Niger to secure the gold reserves: five hundred, supported by artillery, would overcome "the whole Forces which Africa could bring against them."[56] In the end, Britain sent out a more modest expedition. Park led it; he was supported by a troop of soldiers and together they shot their way along until, weakened by disease and ambushed by the Africans, they most likely drowned in the Niger.

Given this fact, it is not surprising that today, among historians and literary critics, Mungo Park and his exploration of Africa are viewed in the same light as African slavery, as a shameful legacy. Mary Louise Pratt, for instance, features Mungo Park as one of the key agents of empire, written about through the myth of "anti-conquest." According to Pratt, "Park's book owes much of its power to [its] combination of humanism, egalitarianism, and critical relativism anchored securely in a sense of European authenticity, power, and legitimacy."[57] Ashton Nichols, in an article dedicated to Mungo Park, also sees Park's journey as intimately tied to the language of domination. He writes: "At a time when British, like European, self-definition had been destabilized in so many ways— political revolutions, social and economic restructuring, class anxiety—Park's Romanticized Africa, and the subsequent romanticization of Park's own life by Europeans, contributes in important ways to the creation of the discourse of the colonizing culture that would soon 'dominate' the globe."[58]

IV

Both African exploration and the antislavery movement coincided with the rise of print culture. While people consumed slave products—tobacco, rum, steel, cotton, indigo, mahogany, coffee, and the addictive white substance, sugar—the vast majority knew about Africans and slaves only through written accounts. From the 1780s onward, the British presses issued millions of pages in the form of parliamentary debates and newspaper columns, sermons and speeches, poems and novels and stage performances, medical tracts and anatomical inquiries, African travelogues and West Indian histories. Legislative debates were often printed in the papers—*Gentleman's Magazine*, for instance, regularly printed the debates, such as the Fifth Session in 1788, which included an open discussion of the revenue produced from the slave trade. It was talked about publicly in the streets—John Bidlake's "The Slave Trade: A Sermon" preached at Storehouse Chapel in December 1788, or Samuel Taylor Coleridge's *Lecture on the Slave Trade* given in Bristol in June 1795. Antislavery discussion and propaganda took many forms—James Montgomery's long poem *The West Indies* (1809), Monk Lewis's play *The Castle Spectre* (1798), Maria Edgeworth's novel *Grateful Negro*

(1804), William Cowper's ballad "The Negro's Complaint" (1788), paintings such as Fuseli's *The Negro Revenged* (1806–7) and Turner's *Slave Ship* (1840), religious tracts such as John Newton's *Thoughts on the African Slave Trade* (1788), narratives such as Olaudah Equiano's *Interesting Narrative* (1789), travelogues like Mungo Park's, and medical treatises like *Letters and Essays on [diseases] of the West Indies* (1787). The debate also impinged upon works of natural history and science like Charles White's *Account of the Regular Gradations in Man* (1799) and James Cowles Prichard's *Researches into the Physical History of Man* (1813), as well as histories such as Bryan Edwards's *History, Civil and Commercial, of the British Colonies in the West Indies* (1793) and Thomas Clarkson's *History of the Rise, Progress and Accomplishment of the Abolition of the African Slave-Trade by the British Parliament* (1808). Each of these genres is more complex than any neat categorization could suggest; they overlap and intertwine to make slavery and African exploration two of the most ubiquitous topics of the era.

Because of changes in print culture and the literary marketplace, many of these writers regarded themselves as having global importance and world-historical influence.[59] As literary historians Jon P. Klancher and William G. Rowland Jr. have shown, a profound shift took place in the early nineteenth-century writer's sense of audience. What made the Romantic period special in this sense, writes Klancher, was that "perhaps for the last time, it was still possible to conceive the writer's relation to an audience in terms of . . . a personal exchange of 'power' between writer and reader." Romantic audiences lived in a "moment of transition," where people's sense of themselves as individual readers was constantly combined with their sense of being part of a larger audience.[60] Klancher says that writers of the British Romantic period shifted between the sense of a personal audience and of a massive audience that they had never met. This could give them either a sense of power or a feeling of despair. Rowland, extending Klancher's idea, argues that Romantic writers' activity "forced them to confront a general feeling of their epoch, sometimes called alienation and sometimes called modern selfhood."[61] "The romantic elevation of the self," writes Rowland, "had its darker counterpart in bourgeois despair, the widespread feeling that individuals can do nothing to change a monolithic social order, composed as it is of a 'mass' of people and the attendant uncontrollable, inexplicable forces."[62] Yet even with this dark alienation closing in on them, Romantic writers clung to the belief that their work had had the force of change. Nowhere is this more strenuously or more eloquently articulated than in Wordsworth's preface to *Lyrical Ballads*:

In spite of the difference of soil and climate, of language and manners, of laws and customs: in spite of things gone silently out of mind, and things violently destroyed; the

Poet binds together by passion and knowledge the vast empire of human society, as it is spread over the whole earth, and over all time. (*W Prose*, 1:141)

The present-day American poet Michael Ryan observes that "by imagining the audience to be permanent and universal instead of immediate and particular, [Wordsworth] awards the poet a larger, lasting, more important role in 'the vast empire of human society,'—far beyond Britain in 1800."[63]

What we also have to remember about the writers of this period and their relationship to social and political issues is that for them writing *was* activism. Their sense of world-historical influence may seem silly in the coolly ironic twenty-first century, but at the time it seemed just the opposite, and it is exactly what fueled both Romantic writing and abolitionist writing. Who else, but someone who thought he or she could make a difference, would publish the large-scale claims found in John Wilson's "On Reading Mr. Clarkson's History of the Abolition of the Slave Trade":

Before him lay a quarter of the world,
A mighty land, wash'd by unnumber'd floods,
Born in her bosom,—floods that to the sea
Roll ocean-like, or in the central wilds
Fade like the dim day melting into night

. . . .
That he by Heaven is chosen to restore
Mercy on earth, a mighty conqueror
Over the sins and miseries of man.
The work is done! The Niger's sullen waves
Have heard the tidings,—and the Orient Sun
Beholds them rolling on to meet his light
In joyful beauty.[64]

Yet despite this grand enthusiasm for global change through poetry, what became increasingly clear was that influential writing had to take up important issues at the same time it had to depart from stale forms and stereotypical images. By the early nineteenth century, so many discourses were saturated with the topic of slavery that writers were hard-pressed to come up with different ways to write about it. In 1809, James Montgomery commented that there was simply no "subject so various and excursive, yet so familiar and exhausted, as the African Slave Trade,—a subject which had become antiquated, by frequent, minute, and disgusting exposure, which afforded no opportunity to awaken, suspend, and delight curiosity, by a subtle and surprising development of plot; and concerning which public feeling had been wearied into insensibility, by the agony of interest which the question excited, during three and twenty years of almost incessant discussion." [65] Coleridge had said exactly the same thing a year earlier, in 1808. In his review of Clarkson's *History of the Rise, Progress and Accomplishment of the Abolition of the Slave-Trade by the British Parliament*, Coleridge explains how slavery's tenacious hold on the nation ensured that other political events never eclipsed it in power and intensity. He writes: "The nation, throughout city, town, and village, was only not unanimous: and though the almost weekly explosion of new events, all of them more or less directly affecting the interests of Great Britain, drew away their attention, or deadened their zeal, for a time, as to this great subject, yet it was only necessary to proclaim the same facts anew— and the same zeal was rekindled, the same sense of duty felt and expressed by all classes" (*SWF*, 1:236). [66]

Given the pervasiveness of the slave issue in the Romantic era, I hope to show in the following chapters how Romantic writing—creative works that concerned themselves with the imagination—took up this issue in more oblique and thus more terrifying ways, as in Coleridge's 1798 poems "The Rime of the Ancient Mariner," with its grimly repetitive "Alone, alone, all, all alone" and its unbearable burden of guilt. Writers like Coleridge took great care to subtly, not brazenly, embroider their poetry with topics that had been treated with ideological righteousness or soggy sentimentalism in most of the literature of the day. Keats felt the same way, as he said in 1818: "We hate poetry that has a palpable design upon us—and if we do not agree, seems to put its hand in its breeches pocket. Poetry should be great & unobtrusive, a thing which enters into one's soul, and does not startle or amaze it with itself but with its subject." [67] Shelley, too, remarked that when poets explicitly try for a moral aim, "the effect of their poetry is diminished in exact proportion to the degree in which they compel us to avert to this purpose." [68] Thus, while Coleridge, Keats, Shelley, and other writers whose works we continue to read, did write about the African and slave presence, they avoided, in Keats's words, putting a "palpable design" on their readers. Since the topic had been made so explicit for so long, such writers considered it most powerful when least obvious, most familiar when most unfamiliar, and truly intimate when seemingly distant.

2

The Distanced Imagination

I

It seems obvious that British Romanticism should be interpreted in the context of the debate on slavery. For one, they share exact dates. British Romanticism, as conventionally defined, begins somewhere in the 1780s (with Blake's publications) and ends somewhere between 1832 (with the passing of the Reform Bill) and 1850 (with Wordsworth's death). The slave question occupied this same period. The first protests against slavery in Britain, initiated by the Quakers, took place in the 1780s, and these led to a massive effort to abolish the slave trade in the 1790s.[1] It was not until 1807 that Parliament outlawed the slave trade, after which followed an even more passionate debate for the emancipation of slaves in the colonies. Although the Emancipation Act was passed in 1833, it did not come into effect until 1834, and then it included a clause regarding apprenticeship that delayed official emancipation until the 1840s.

But beyond sharing dates, slavery and Romanticism are concerned with similar themes. Certainly, one cannot bring the greatest imaginative literature of the period together with the greatest moral question of the age without noticing a common vocabulary of terms like "slave" and "master," "tyranny" and "oppression." Nor are these terms used sporadically in Romantic poetry: they appear with startling regularity. For instance, images of freedom and its British opposite, slavery, are mentioned throughout Blake's poetry, in lines like "the slave grinding at the mill / And the captive in chains," from *The Four Zoas*.[2] Likewise, Mary Wollstonecraft frequently designates women as "slaves" in her *Vindication of the Rights of Woman* (1792). Men, she writes, "will endeavour to enslave woman:—and who can tell, how many generations may be necessary to give vigour to the virtue and talents of the freed posterity of abject slaves?"[3] Both Byron and P. B. Shelley use the idea of slavery in their lyrical dramas. In Byron's *Manfred* (1817), Manfred himself asks the witch, "Obey? And whom? The spirits / Whose presence I command—and be the slave / Of those who served me? Never!" (2.2: 158–60). Throughout *Prometheus Unbound* (1820),

Shelley explores the irony and injustice of slavery. In one striking instance, Asia asks Demogorgon a question about the dialectic of mastery and slavery, "Declare / Who is his master? Is he too a slave?" (2.4: 108–9). Also, Mary Shelley regularly employs the terms "slave" and "tyrant" in exchanges between the monster and Victor Frankenstein in *Frankenstein*.

Although many of these writers may seem to be using the terms "slavery" and "freedom" in abstract and even universal ways, in the sense that everyone is a slave to something and seeking freedom from it, the terms are, in fact, grounded in the historical specificity of the transatlantic trade and plantation slavery, the stories of which surrounded these writers. This study sets out to demonstrate, in detail, just how this is so. In some cases, the historical specificity of slavery is there in clear view, as in Coleridge's "Fears in Solitude" (1798).[4] Coleridge writes,

> Like a cloud that travels on,
> Steamed up from Cairo's swamps of pestilence,
> Even so, my countrymen! have we gone forth
> And borne to distant tribes slavery and pangs,
> And, deadlier far, our vices, whose deep taint
> With slow perdition murders the whole man,
> His body and his soul! (47–53)

Romantic writing operates within the context of slavery, certainly, but what is the relationship between slavery and freedom in the poetry? On one level, Romantic works celebrate a kind of personal freedom that stands in alarming contrast to slavery. This is perhaps expressed most clearly in Coleridge's 1794 "Religious Musings," where he refers to the depths of slavery and then celebrates the expansive and diffusely free British imaginative self:

> The whole one Self! Self that no alien knows!
> Self, far diffused as Fancy's wing can travel!
> Self, spreading still! Oblivious of its own,
> Yet all of all possessing! (154–57)

Indeed, the period might be characterized by this central irony: the British "self, spreading still" and "all of all possessing," springs to life in some Romantic writing at the exact time that the slave self, suicidal and destroyed, haunts other Romantic writing. For instance, John Gorton's 1797 poem "The Negro Suicide" ends with an enslaved African plunging "this pointed steel" into his heart.[5] In 1802, a poem printed by Hannah More called *The Sorrows of Yamba; or, The Negro Woman's Lamentation* speaks of another method of suicide: during the middle passage, many Africans, "sick and sad," died refusing to eat the "Nauseous horse-beans" otherwise forced down their throats.[6] Mary Robinson's "The

Negro Girl" of 1800 ends with yet another form of self-destruction: the slave girl Zelma throws herself "in a wat'ry grave."[7] Perhaps the strangest example of all is in James Montgomery's 1809 poem *The West Indies*, where he records how slaves die "by the slow pangs of solitary care, the earth-devouring anguish of despair." "The Negroes," explains Montgomery in a footnote, "in deep and irrecoverable melancholy, waste themselves away, by secretly swallowing large quantities of earth."[8]

Clearly, many writers who were fascinated with their own vibrant identities were the same ones who were quick to watch slave identities drown in the Atlantic or waste away from a diet of dirt. Yet to say that the literature of the period portrays confident, expanding British selves at the expense of slave selves who submissively disappear is not entirely correct. For there also exists, among some writers, an unstoppable desire to see this expansive British self become *not-self* in the face of the other. In fact, the loss of self recorded with such dramatic intensity by abolitionist poets was integral to the poetic theory of many Romantic writers. In 1819 (to return to the example this book begins with), the same year in which Tommy complained about the analytic distance which was used to dehumanize him, John Keats targeted the concept of aesthetic distance in one of his compelling letters on the imagination. Writing to George and Georgiana Keats on 19 March 1819, Keats mused, "Very few men have ever arrived at a complete *disinterestedness* of Mind: very few have been influenced by a pure desire of the benefit of others. . . . I perceive how far I am from any humble standard of *disinterestedness*" (my emphasis, *KL*, 2:79). In using the term "disinterestedness," Keats means a freedom from self-interest. For Keats, disinterestedness implies a feeling for the suffering of others that is so intimate it can only happen by divesting the self of its own interest.

In his letter, Keats is so taken with the subject that he cannot let it drop. He writes a little later, "Wordsworth says, 'we have all one human heart'—there is an ellectric fire in human nature tending to purify—so that among these human creature[s] there is continu[a]lly some birth of new heroism—The pity is that we must wonder at it: as we should at finding a pearl in rubbish—I have no doubt that thousands of people never heard of have had hearts comp[l]etely disinterested: I can remember but two—Socrates and Jesus" (*KL*, 2:80). As Keats sees it, the imaginative mind produced the self distanced from its own ego. In a letter to Richard Woodhouse of October 1818, Keats had called Wordsworthian imagination the "egotistical sublime," a quality he wanted nothing to do with: "As to the poetic Character itself, (I mean that sort of which, if I am any thing, I am a Member; that sort distinguished from the wordsworthian or egotistical sublime; . . .) it is not itself—it has no self" (*KL*, 1:386–87). But a year later, he seems to have clarified his notion of imaginative distance and could even see in

Wordsworth an aspect of the imagination that felt compelled to divest itself of egotism. Certainly, this idea does occupy a place in the preface to *Lyrical Ballads* (1802). The poet, writes Wordsworth, must "bring his feelings near to those of the persons whose feelings he describes, nay, for short spaces of time, perhaps, to let himself slip into an entire delusion, and even confound and identify his own feelings with theirs" (*W Prose*, 1:138).[9]

The imaginative idea of self-loss was not limited to any single Romantic writer.[10] In 1802, Coleridge wrote, "It is easy to cloathe Imaginary Beings with our own Thoughts and Feelings; but to *think* ourselves in to the Thoughts and Feelings of Beings in circumstances wholly & strangely different from our own . . . who has atchieved it?" (*CL*, 2:810). This same idea gripped Percy Bysshe Shelley in 1821, when he wrote the *Defence of Poetry*, his strangely ethereal poetic treatise, which carefully links the imaginative mind and the distanced heart. "The great secret of morals is Love, or going out of our own nature," says Shelley, with great emotional flourish. This means, in no uncertain terms, "an identification" with a "thought, action, or person not our own. A man, to be greatly good, must imagine intensely and comprehensively; he must put himself in the place of another and of many others; the pains and pleasure of his species must become his own. The great instrument of moral good is the imagination; and poetry administers to the effect by acting on the cause" (*SP*, 487–88). The "creative faculty," he declares, in a statement that is fundamental to his philosophy, is what compels artists to produce poems, novels, and paintings. But like Keats, Shelley views this imaginative faculty, and the products of its labor, as self-distanced in the sense of being divested of ego. The imagination, not taken up with itself, has a special power that enables the self to escape the tediousness of its own interests. It implies sympathy, a "going out of our own natures," but also empathy, the ability to identify with and *feel for* another human being.

One way to think about this distinction between self-interest and disinterestedness, between the expansive self and the loss of self, is through the aesthetic/philosophical categories of intimacy and distance, which were, as Chapter 1 details, also geographic categories. The power of what I am calling the distanced imagination comes from a definition of self as *for the other*. Although literary theorists have not spent much time analyzing the concept of the distanced imagination, its legacy is stubbornly present in modern discussions among poets, critics, historians, and philosophers. The present-day American poet Eleanor Wilner defines distance in two different senses: analytic distance and aesthetic distance. In the case of analytic detachment, writes Wilner, "distance separates and frees a person from *feeling for* what he observes. But what aesthetic distance separates us from is not the emotions but the ego. With poetic imagination, it is precisely this distance from the ego that enables the emotional connectedness we call empathy—and because it is remote from ego-threat, as we enter imaginatively what is actually at a remove from us, we are given both vision and connection."[11] In theory, and in some of their best practical moments, Keats, Shelley, and the other Romantic writers viewed the imagination in this way.[12] But more importantly, it was the African and slave presence in Britain that forced them to articulate the possibilities of the distanced imagination in their creative work.

II

The distanced imagination—a creative faculty at once expansive and self-sacrificing—has its roots in the change in moral consciousness that took place in the eighteenth century.[13] Because this change can be traced both politically (as Chapter 1 argues) *and* theoretically, the two strands must have developed dialectically. In the realm of theory, the Romantics were fundamentally influenced by the astounding number of eighteenth-century texts that celebrated the imagination's expansive capabilities, works such as Joseph Addison's "The Pleasures of Imagination" (1712), Zachary Mayne's *Two Dissertations Concerning Sense and the Imagination* (1728), Archibald Campbell's *Enquiry into the Original of Moral Virtue* (1728), John Gilbert Cooper's *Letters Concerning Taste* (1757), Alexander Gerard's *An Essay on Taste* (1759), and Edmund Burke's *Philosophical Enquiry into the Origin of our Ideas of the Sublime and Beautiful* (1759). These were just a few of the theorists to anticipate Adam Smith's immensely popular *Theory of Moral Sentiments* (1759), a text that explicitly outlined the relationship between imagination and sympathy, a precursor to the Romantic idea of self-sacrifice.[14]

Some of the first important publications on imagination in Britain were Joseph Addison's essays in the *Spectator* titled "The Pleasures of Imagination." These appeared in 1712, a good one hundred years before Keats and Shelley wrote about the imagination. "The Pleasures of Imagination" reads like fairly straightforward eighteenth-century material, dealing with ideas of "taste" and "wit." Addison says the imagination is "*that Faculty of the Soul, which discerns the Beauties of an Author with Pleasure, and the Imperfections with Dislike*" (original emphasis).[15] Yet although he discusses the imagination in conjunction with eighteenth-century taste, his fundamental claim for the imagination is its capacity for enlargement. "It is the Power of the Imagination," Addison says, "when it is once Stocked with particular Ideas, to *enlarge*, compound, and vary them at her own Pleasure" (my emphasis). Magnificent buildings and scenes of nature, he goes on to say, "help to open Man's Thoughts, and to *enlarge* his Imagination" (my emphasis). "Nothing," he emphasizes, "is more pleasant to the Fancy, than to *enlarge* it self " (my emphasis).[16] Certainly the discoveries of the Enlightenment—Newtonian physics, natural history, and geographic exploration—must have influenced Addison's view of the imagination as a faculty of the mind whose purest pleasure came from enlargement. And this claim for enlargement would cling to discussions of imagination in every variation it underwent throughout the eighteenth and nineteenth centuries.

For instance, almost fifty years later, Alexander Gerard, in *An Essay on Taste* (1759), defines the imagination in terms of the expansive mind: "When a large object is presented, the mind expands itself to the extent of that object, and is filled with one grand sensation, which totally possessing it, composes it into a solemn sedateness, and strikes it with deep silent wonder and admiration: it finds such a difficulty in spreading itself to the dimensions of the object, as enlivens and invigorates its frame: . . . it sometimes imagines itself present in every part of the scene which it contemplates; and from the sense of this immensity, feels a noble pride, and entertains a lofty conception of its own capacity."[17] The imagination, in Gerard's view, longs for expansion. "The mind," he says, "acquires a habit of enlarging itself to receive the sentiment of sublimity" and longs to "expand its faculties."[18] Again in 1759, Edmund Burke expresses this idea of imaginative enlargement in its most powerful extreme. What Burke calls "vastness of extent," an aspect of the sublime, finds its ultimate expression in the idea of "infinity."[19]

In contrast to the expansive, powerful imagination of Gerard and Burke, in this same year—1759—Adam Smith published his *Theory of Moral Sentiments*, conceiving of the imagination in terms of self-sacrifice, or what he called "fellow-feeling." "By changing places in fancy with the sufferer," wrote Smith, "we come either to conceive or to be affected by what he feels."[20] The popularity of Smith's arguments can be traced to the heart of distanced imagination. The first part of Smith's essay, "On Sympathy," establishes a new role for the imagination, one that enlarges itself in order to be selfless. "Whatever is the passion which arises from any object in the person principally concerned," he writes, "an analogous emotion springs up, at the thought of his situation, in the breast of every attentive spectator." Here, Smith thinks in terms of proximity and distance and of the coin-cidence one can feel with another. He continues, "In every passion of which the mind of man is susceptible, the emotions of the by-stander always correspond to that, by bringing the case home to himself, he imagines should be the sentiments of the sufferer." The imagination allows one to "bring the case home," implying an intimacy and hospitality in relations between self and other that were, up to this point, unheard of. Clearly, then, the expansiveness of the imagination seen in previous theorists had taken a new turn with Smith, leading to the moral consciousness that would shape the actions and the poetry of the Romantic period.

Since slavery was the most egregious form of suffering, and thus the form of suffering most likely to evoke fellow-feeling, slavery is the first example Smith offers in "On Sympathy." The imagination may be a mental activity, but it implies a bodily experience, an altering of selfhood on the most fundamental level. "Though our brother is upon the rack," writes Smith, "it is by the imagination only that we can form any conception of what are his sensations. Neither can that faculty help us to this any other way, than by representing to us what would be our own, if we were in his case." "By imagination we place ourselves in his situation . . . we enter as it were into his body, and become in some measure the same person with him." [21] Smith makes the enlargement of the imagination not a selfish but a selfless faculty. One expands the ego boundaries of the self in order to feel for the other. Shelley, following Smith, writes much later, "the imagination is enlarged by a sympathy with pains and passions so mighty, that they distend in their conception the capacity of that by which they are conceived" (*SP*, 490).

If imagination defined the self as both expansive *and* sacrificial, these qualities also characterized the political realm. But in politics, expansion was again conceived of as motivated by self-interest. Adam Smith himself provides a striking example: he developed *The Theory of Moral Sentiments* which advocated fellow-feeling and then he turned, less than twenty years later, to champion capitalism, free trade, and the flow of money in *An Inquiry into the Nature and Causes of the Wealth of Nations* (1776). Smith's was the first major work of political economy, examining in detail the consequences of economic free markets, such as division of labor, the function of markets, and the international implications of a laissez-faire economy. Though Smith's two books seem to have opposite emphases — one springing from selfless motives, the other on selfish interests — both, in fact, rivaled one another in popularity for reading audiences. As historian Richard F. Teichgraeber explains, the discrepancy between the assumptions governing these two works has been a problem for Smith scholars ever since the Victorian period, so much so that late nineteenth-century German scholars called it "The Adam Smith Problem." [22]

Curiously enough, a version of the Adam Smith problem is currently the focus for historians of British slavery who have discussed at length the ways in which the two opposed forces of sympathy and capitalism dominated the abolitionist movement. A finely tuned and wonderfully nuanced debate by the veteran historians David Brion Davis and Thomas L. Haskell is notable on several counts. Just as self-sacrifice and self-expansion characterized the nineteenth-century British concept of imagination, these historians agree that humanitarianism and capitalism defined British economics of the same period. In fact, what strikes Haskell as significant is the way in which humanitarian and capitalism attitudes dovetail.[23] "Capitalism fosters self-regarding sentiments, while humanitarianism seems other-regarding," writes Haskell. "What can account for the parallel development in history of two such opposed tendencies?" One answer lies in the fact that despite their antithetical aims, both humanitarianism and capitalism "depend on people who attribute to themselves far-reaching powers of intervention."[24] This power of intervention can also describe the relationship between self-sacrifice and self-expansion in the realm of creativity and imagination. Romantic poets, as Coleridge's poetic exclamation of the spreading self proves, had confidence that their ideas would have national appeal, if not the powers to intervene.

III

One of the best ways to understand the relationships between self-sacrifice and self-expansion of the distanced imagination is, I propose, through the concept of *alterity*. Alterity means "difference," but it also encompasses the idea that because the self is responsible, ethical, and human, it preserves the difference of the other and acknowledges the relativity of subjectivity. Alterity was, from the beginning, a concept of the Romantic imagination. Although the word was used sporadically in the 1600s, the *OED* credits Coleridge for introducing the concept into the language.[25] For Coleridge alterity is a mode of self-consciousness. He claims there can be no consciousness, no being, without alterity. Alterity allows the self to distinguish its own being; it is "namely a distinction of the Scitum from the Sciens" (the thing known from the knowing agent). Although alterity gives the self its consciousness, its distinctness, Coleridge clearly grants the alterity of the "thing known" its own integral status. Alterity's relativity produces "reality": "*outness* is but the feeling of *otherness* (alterity), rendered intuitive . . . because we find this outness and the objects, to which, though they are, in fact, workings in our own being, we transfer it, independent of our will, and apparently common to other minds, we learn to connect therewith the feeling and sense of *reality*" (original emphasis) (*SWF*, 2:929). Further, Coleridge attributes alterity to the Trinity and, therefore, to transcendental being. He opposes "selfness and identity" to "otherness and alterity," whose "synthesis" is the community of the spirit. Identity and alterity, like the Father and the Son, can maintain integral being in the unity of synthesis.

Perhaps Coleridge's clearest definition of the dynamic between alterity and identity is in his marginalia, specifically to the writings of Jakob Bohme. In contemplating the impossible unity of opposites, Coleridge writes:

+A passes into +B to lose itself, and in the next instant retracts itself in order to give an *Alterity* to +B, and this in order to lose itself in another form by loving the self of another as another — (*CM*, 1:680)

Coleridge comes back again and again to the concept of alterity to explore the classic Romantic dilemma of selfhood as simultaneously same and other, alienated and unified, fragmented and whole, connected and distinct. Ultimately he views the self as capable of sacrifice for the other but also as expansive through transcendence.

Today, in philosophy, identity politics, and postmodern theory, in recalling and developing the concept of alterity, we are using Coleridge's terminology and concept of "outness" or "otherness," and are revising a classic Romantic problem of attempts to reconcile seeming opposites. The concept is central to philosophers such as Emmanuel Levinas and Maurice Merleau-Ponty, anthropologists such as Michael Taussig, and literary theorists as diverse as Mikhail Bakhtin and Gayatri Chakravorty Spivak. In 1982, A. J. Greimas and J. Courtes called alterity a "non-definable concept, which is in opposition to another concept of the same sort, identity," two terms which at least can be defined by way of reciprocity.[26] Likewise, Mark C. Taylor's recent study of alterity concedes (using an alternate spelling) that " 'Altarity' is a slippery word whose meaning can be neither stated clearly nor fixed firmly." [27] Though never completely decidable, Taylor says that the linguistic field of "Altarity" can be approached through the network of its associations: "altar, alter, alternate, alternative, alternation, alterity." [28] He provides a thorough genealogy of the concept, starting with Hegel and devoting a chapter each to Heidegger, Merleau-Ponty, Lacan, Bataille, Kristeva, Levinas, Blanchot, Derrida, and Kierkegaard. Thus, despite alterity's nondefinable quality, it is frequently used in Coleridge's original sense, to explain how the self tends toward, desires, seeks, and needs the other in order to distinguish itself and realize its subjectivity.

More importantly, recent discussions have shifted the domain of alterity from transcendental philosophy to social/historical investigation. Galen A. Johnson and Michael B. Smith, for example, in their *Ontology and Alterity in Merleau-Ponty* (1990), designate "alterity" the best word to use in the study of ontology and identity politics. Unlike the term "otherness," " 'alterity' shifts the focus of philosophic concern away from the 'epistemic other' to the concrete 'moral other' of practices — political, cultural, linguistic, artistic, and religious. This is consistent with the movement from the concerns of modern philosophy of knowledge and of the subject to the more decentered philosophies of postmodernism." [29] Although Coleridge does not explicitly reserve alterity for moral otherness, this ethical dimension of alterity is implied in his writings, especially

on slavery. In his *Lecture on the Slave Trade*, Coleridge begins with the grand-
est possibilities for the "Imagination," equating it with "glittering Summits" and
"Alpine endlessness," only to condemn its powerful uses in the execution and
maintenance of colonialism: "horrible has been its misapplication," he writes
(*Lects 1795*, 235–36). The *Lecture* goes on to engage the imagination in alterity
by detailing the sufferings that the slave trade had, up to that time, instigated.
Thus, even though the notion of alterity seems to be transhistorical and trans-
cultural, it does, in fact, lend itself to historical and cultural specifics, like the
relationship between Britons and Africans in the nineteenth century.

Coleridge's investigations into the concept of alterity, its moral possibilities and responsibilities, find their fullest extension in the works of Emmanuel
Levinas (although Levinas was not influenced directly by Coleridge's writings
but developed his philosophy in the phenomenological tradition of Edmund
Husserl and Martin Heidegger). Born in Lithuania, educated in Russia and Ger-
many, and naturalized French in the 1930s, Levinas went on to become one of
the most influential philosophers of the twentieth century, producing a number
of important works, including two major philosophical texts, *Totality and Infinity* and *Otherwise than Being; or, Beyond Essence*.[30] The originality of Levinas's
thought emerges from his synthesis of ethical philosophy and Talmudic commentary, but readers also cannot help sensing the enormous personal energy
that characterizes all his works. This is especially true of the collections of lectures and interviews, such as *Thinking-of-the-Other: Entre Nous* and *Ethics and
Infinity*, the latter a wonderfully readable set of interviews conducted by the philosopher Philippe Nemo.[31]

In fact, the most striking qualities of Levinas's works are their accessibility
and their immediate applicability to politics, aesthetics, and history. Indeed, it
is a little surprising that his work has not been used to examine the relationships between Romanticism and slavery before now. In 1998, a small collection
of essays entitled "Alterity in Discourses of Romanticism" appeared, which suggested applying Levinas's ideas to Romanticism, and in 1999 David P. Haney
wrote an eye-opening essay called "Aesthetics and Ethics in Gadamer, Levinas,
and Romanticism," but neither of these has generated any large-scale studies.[32] It
is safe to assume that Levinas would have welcomed an application of his thought
to questions of slavery and empire, since he was generally enthusiastic when his
philosophy informed political insights and social activism. In 1982, for instance,
Levinas was told that various attempts had been made to apply his philosophy to
Marxism, to which he replied, "I have gotten to know a very sympathetic South
American group that is working out 'liberation philosophy.' . . . I am very happy,
very proud even, when I find reflections of my work in this group. It is a fundamental approval."[33] One of the reasons Levinas's theories are applicable is his

bold rejection of grand philosophical schemes coupled with his use of elegantly simple phrases like "the face-to-face" and "responsibility for the other."[34] But most of all, Levinas's philosophy is attractive because he moves beyond polemics of guilt and blame to a different plane altogether. Levinas's work allows for an ethical connection between self and other in a post-slavery and post-Holocaust world. In this book, I invoke Levinas to provide a philosophical explanation to the previous discussions of the imaginative self as sacrificial and expansive. His work helps explain how some Romantic writers approached the African other of slavery and exploration in their creative work.

Like Coleridge, Levinas describes alterity as the self's responsibility for the other, as the self's imperative to place the other at the center of his or her own being, and as the self's desire to respect and preserve the difference of that other. Alterity in this sense is a relation that does not compromise the selfhood of the other. Because alterity carries an ethical dimension, a reciprocity or responsibility for the other, for Levinas "eros" (as the key dimension of alterity) becomes the only way to recognize the other. Indeed, eros occupies a primary place in relationships. It is, writes Levinas, "a relationship with alterity, with mystery — that is to say, with the future, with what (in a world where there is everything) is never there, with what cannot be there when everything is there — not with a being that is not there, but with the very dimension of alterity."[35] And just as Coleridge attributes alterity to the idea of God and thus to transcendental being, so Levinas describes alterity as the "proximity and the uncanniness of God" who is present in the face-to-face encounter: "Transcendence is what turns its face towards us," he writes. Further, thought awakened to the transcendence of alterity "believes itself to go *beyond* the world or to listen to a voice more intimate than intimacy" (original emphasis).[36] In this way, the imaginative self can be both sacrificial and expansive.

Levinas conceives of consciousness as always involved with the other in a state of proximity, or presence, which he describes as the "face-to-face." This is close to Maurice Merleau-Ponty's description of the intimacy produced by the touch. In Merleau-Ponty, explains Levinas, "one hand touches the other, the other hand touches the first; the hand, consequently, is touched and touches the touching — one hand touches the touching. A reflexive structure: it is as if space were touching itself through the man."[37] The proximity of the face-to-face follows a similar logic. For Levinas, the other *always* presents him or herself as a *face*, and it is the face of the other that "signifies for me an unexceptionable responsibility, preceding every free consent, every pact, every contract. It escapes representations; it is the very collapse of phenomenality. Not because it is too brutal to appear, but because in a sense too weak, non-phenomenal because less than phenomenon. The disclosing of the face is nudity, non-form, abandon of self, aging, dying, more naked than nudity. It is poverty, skin with wrinkles, which are a trace of itself." [38]

Alterity begins with the most important theme of Levinas's work: the relationship between two people. In his ethical philosophy, his Talmudic commentaries, and his political discussions that often hinge on the aftermath of the Holocaust, the well-being of the other person is of utmost concern. In fact, so strong is this idea, that to Levinas, "the only absolute value is the human possibility of giving the other priority over oneself." [39] Levinas develops a philosophy with the politically and socially disenfranchised in mind: the slave, the orphan, the prisoner, the foreigner, the stranger. His philosophy gives us new insights into Romantic writers' use of the imagination to bring the self face-to-face with the alterity of the radical other of that period: the slave self. It approximates Shelleyan "going out of our own natures" and Keatsian "disinterestedness." In fact, Levinas uses the term "dis-inter-estedness" to define the *being-for-the-other* in all human beings. [40]

The essence of being-for-the-other is self-sacrifice, a fundamental condition of human consciousness. Levinas, in fact, defines consciousness as "a preoccupation with the other, even to the point of sacrifice, even to the possibility of dying for him or her; a responsibility for the other. Otherwise than being! It is this shattering of indifference—even if indifference is statistically dominant—this possibility of one-for-the-other." [41] In ways that both recall and go beyond late-eighteenth-century philosophers like Adam Smith, Levinas sees that responsibility, being-for-the-other, must ultimately test itself against suffering: "For me the suffering of compassion, suffering because the other suffers" is one part of the relationship between self and other that is "much more complex and complete at the same time." [42]

But how do we understand this ethical relationship in the writings of British poets? The main problem scholars have in applying Levinas's philosophy to literature is in coming to terms with Levinas's rejection of representation. As David P. Haney points out, Levinas is "suspicious of art" because of its seeming autonomy from the ethical other. Despite this, Levinas does champion critical discussions that relate "the inhuman work of the artist into the human world." [43] Still, if Levinas rejects representation, insisting that the face is *not* a representation and that art has no access to transcendence, how can we face the faceless other, the other of representation? The answer lies in Levinas's notion of "trace." In his essay "The Trace of the Other," he defines "trace" as "the beyond from which a face comes. . . . A face is in the trace of the utterly bygone, utterly past Absent . . . which cannot be discovered in the self by any introspection." [44] Since trace is a substitute for the other, it becomes the way that the absent other appears. Trace thus allows representation to have an ethics. The one bears a responsibility for the represented other, and, in fact, some scholars even believe that trace itself is what constitutes the ethical relationship between self and other.[45]

Along with the idea of trace, another important concept for Levinas, something also directly applicable to art, is his belief that the face of the other is discursive. "Face and discourse are tied," Levinas says. "The face speaks" he continues, and thus "renders possible and begins all discourse."[46] This idea has attracted some of the most influential philosophers of the twentieth century, most notably Jacques Derrida, who delivered a eulogy at Levinas's funeral in 1995, which was published with a speech he gave at a seminar held in Levinas's honor one year later.[47] Here, Derrida reinterprets and extends some of Levinas's ideas, particularly the notion of "hospitality," of meeting the face of the other in discourse. In support, Derrida quotes Levinas's *Otherwise Than Being; or, Beyond Essence*:

> To approach the Other in discourse is to welcome his expression, in which at each instant he overflows the idea a thought would carry away from it. It is therefore to *receive* from the Other beyond the capacity of the I, which means exactly: to have the idea of infinity. But this also means: to be taught. The relation with the Other, or Discourse, is . . . an ethical relation.[48]

In fact, Levinas ends his most important philosophical work, *Otherwise Than Being*, with a summary of the connections he has made between discourse, alterity, proximity, and responsibility: these are the very principles at work in the writings of British Romantics in the face of the other because it is here that the other overwhelms the egoism of the self and causes the self to lose its sovereignty.[49]

To sum up, I am suggesting that Romantic alterity, the philosophical underpinning of the distanced imagination, helped writers form some of the most powerful poetic works of the period. This aspect of the Romantic imagination developed in conjunction with the entire culture's growing awareness of the alterity of Africans and slaves, who were the most discursively visible example of British otherness. Further, I believe that a strand of what has been canonized as Romantic writing explores issues of alterity that are directly linked to slavery.[50] Writers from Wordsworth to Keats, from Blake to Mary Shelley, incorporate the powerful images and ideas of African and slave otherness into their creative works. The literary is the mode through which these writers accomplish proximity, in Levinas's sense of the face-to-face, a discursive responsibility for the other. By using and reshaping information available to them through various discourses, Romantic writers bring Africans and Britons into a relationship of alterity, one that would have been impossible in the original discursive forms — abolitionist poetry, parliamentary papers, or travel literature — that are

either overly sentimental or politically rigid. These forms only reinforce the unequal power relationships between self and other (a typical example would be
the abolitionist medallion, crafted by Josiah Wedgwood, which pictures an African in chains kneeling at the feet of a paternalist white man). On the other hand,
creative works that are modeled on the distanced imagination acknowledge the
unequal power relationship between Africans and Britons, but at the same time
they manage to build an imaginative space for mutual alterity and mutual empathy, in Levinas's sense of the face-to-face.

There are three methodological ways, I suggest, for twenty-first-century
readers to account for the ethics of the faceless other of Romantic representation.
The first, and most important, happens between the artist/poet and his or her
creative subject (for example, Wordsworth's ethical relationship with the black
woman in "The Banished Negroes"; Blake's with the little black boy). In this case,
it is the job of the critic to understand the face as representing an other whose
trace faces the poet him- or herself. The second way to understand Romantic
literature using Levinas's philosophy is simply to read the ethical relationship
between the one and the other within the stories told by poets and writers (for
example, between the ancient mariner and the wedding guest, or between the
monster and Frankenstein), and then to evaluate how these ethical moments
reshape what is being said in other discourses (parliamentary debates, travelogues, abolitionist propaganda). The third way is to accept the possibility of an
ethical relationship between the reader and the trace of the other in representation. To take the example with which this book begins, Tommy's slave complaint
offers a trace, a proxy of the face, which faces the reader, and it is this very trace
that points to an ethics between the one and the other. Similarly, Mary Prince,
whose story concludes this study, establishes, through representation, an ethical
relationship between self and other.

In the chapters that follow, I show how the images drawn from the culture of
slavery, abolition, and African exploration reappear in Romantic literature, with
a difference. With the exception of *The History of Mary Prince*, all the works I examine—Coleridge's "The Rime of the Ancient Mariner," Blake's engravings and
Visions of the Daughters of Albion, Keats's *Lamia*, Percy Bysshe Shelley's "Witch
of Atlas," Mary Shelley's *Frankenstein*, and poems from Wordsworth's *Lyrical
Ballads*—have a critical history of being about the *imagination*, and, while this
is true, they are also about Africans and slaves. I investigate the fever behind
"The Ancient Mariner" but at the discursive forefront of literature on slavery and
African exploration; the monkeys behind Blake's engravings but at the forefront
of race-science debates; the snakes behind Keats's *Lamia* but at the forefront of
discussions on African religion; the African map behind Percy Bysshe Shelley's
"Witch of Atlas" but at the forefront of British exploration; the savage canni-

bal behind Mary Shelley's *Frankenstein* but at the forefront of discussions of slave rebellion and African customs; and the murderous mother behind Words- worth's *Lyrical Ballads* poems and Mary Prince's *History* but at the forefront of debates over slave emancipation. The distanced imagination releases these top- ics from the discourses of power where alterity is impossible and renders them in a language and vision unparalleled in Britain to that time. "For the Eye altering alters all," says Blake in 1800.[51] By drawing on this altering vision — this alterity — Romantic writers created a language that even today offers an alternative to the sterile repetition of history.

PART II

Hazards and Horrors in the Slave Colonies

3
Distant Diseases

Yellow Fever in Coleridge's "The Rime of the Ancient Mariner"

I

Yellow fever of the West Indies, a plague that attacked like an army during the height of British colonial slavery, swept through the body with shocking symptoms. The fever came on suddenly, with fits of hot and cold and violent pain in the head, neck, and back. Not only would the patient's eyes turn watery and yellow, but the whole face would change, appearing "unnatural," denoting "anxiety" and "dejection of mind."[1] Finally, it produced delirium and sometimes madness. During its progress, doctors noted changes "in the great mass of blood itself,"[2] which became putrefied and then oozed from the gums, nose, ears, and anus. The skin turned from flush to yellow or light brown. But it was in the final stages that patients underwent the worst of all symptoms: the black vomit, described variously by medical experts as resembling coffee grounds, black sand, kennel water, soot, or the meconium of a newborn child.

Throughout the late eighteenth and early nineteenth centuries, medical workers and lay people alike considered yellow fever a disease to which Africans were miraculously immune. Dr. Thomas Trotter, a naval doctor famous for implementing mandatory smallpox vaccination in the British armed forces, claimed in 1797 that "African negroes" appeared immune to "contagious fever[s]," while the poet Robert Southey explicitly stated that "yellow fever will not take root in a negro."[3] If yellow fever graciously spared Africans and slaves, it just as ferociously attacked white Europeans who visited Africa and the Caribbean. Yet it was not merely the "new-comers from Europe, in high health" that were "singularly affected with the yellow fever."[4] Many medical experts emphasized British susceptibility. "Britons," noted Dr. William Hillary as early as 1766, were "by the great increased Heat of the Climate, usually not long after their Arrival" in the Caribbean "seized with a Fever."[5] The great Dr. John Hume, a late eighteenth-century expert on tropical medicine, even went so far as to create a catalog of likely British yellow fever candidates: "Strong muscular men are most liable to it, and suffer most."[6]

Yellow fever's insistence on attacking the British body wreaked havoc with the nation's military plans. Since the fever was considered one of Britain's biggest obstacles to successful commerce with Africa and the Caribbean, it often was discussed using terms from military rhetoric. In 1797, for example, Dr. Trotter issued a pamphlet called *Medicina Nautica: An Essay on the Diseases of Seamen*, where he wrote concerning the yellow fever:

The ravages which this fatal Disease have made . . . in our fleets and armies, are beyond all precedent: the insidious mode of attack, the rapid strides by which it advances to an incurable stage, point it out as one of the most formidable opponents of medical skill. It has offered the severest obstacle to military operations, which the history of modern warfare can produce.[7]

This fever turned the British body against itself by turning it into its own foreign enemy. And it did so on an epic scale. Throughout the late eighteenth and early nineteenth centuries, aggressive fever pathogens accounted for 71 percent of all European deaths in the Caribbean, and most of these by far were from yellow fever.[8]

More than yellow fever's military power, it was the geographical movement of this disease that determined its interpretive implications. Because these early medical studies nearly always referred to yellow fever as a Caribbean disease, and since the Caribbean was synonymous with the slave trade and colonial slavery, yellow fever itself became intimately tied to the physical and philosophical effects of slavery. Together, the medical study of yellow fever and the debate on the abolition of the slave trade and of slavery kindled a series of specific concerns—especially among British writers—about what happened when foreign matter, or foreigners, became part of the physical or political body.

No one work from this period is more important for defining these concerns than Coleridge's "The Rime of the Ancient Mariner."[9] "The Ancient Mariner" opened the 1798 *Lyrical Ballads* and so established itself as a first in a new poetics. But when he composed the poem Coleridge himself was thoroughly engaged in the social and political issues of the day, from the latest theories of epidemic disease to the debates on abolition and slavery. Coleridge, along with Robert Southey, was an active abolitionist in Bristol from 1795 to at least 1797–98, the period when he wrote "The Ancient Mariner." The poem, in fact, has frequently been interpreted in light of the slave trade by writers who, in the tradition of John Livingston Lowes, contextualize its major tropes using Coleridge's material concerns with travel literature, colonialism, and the slave trade. J. R. Ebbatson is just one of a number of readers to view the poem as an indictment of British maritime expansion, where "the central act of 'The Ancient Mariner,' the shooting of the albatross, may be a symbolic rehearsal of the crux of colonial expansion, the enslavement of native peoples."[10] Patrick J. Keane has traced many images in "The Ancient Mariner" to their sources in debates on abolition and emancipation.[11]

What has not been exposed in these studies is the extent to which "The Ancient Mariner" takes up issues of slavery and race along with the material conditions of fever, particularly the yellow fever.[12] For example, in the initial stages of the ballad—after the mariner's albatross murder dislodges the ship from the icy fields of the South Pole—fever sets the poem afire. Coleridge takes the reader from climatic realities (the "broad bright Sun," the standing water, and the western wave "all a-flame" [174, 171]) to bodily symptoms ("parched" throats and "cold sweat[s]" [144, 253]) to symbolic fever: the "charmèd water" that "burnt always / A still and awful red" (270–71). But even more dramatic than this is the fever of the British imagination, the "uncertain hour" when "agony returns: / And till my ghastly tale is told, / This heart within me burns" (582–85).

Coleridge was certainly not alone in setting fever to poetry. In 1797, William Roscoe, a Liverpool poet, described the effects of contagion during the slave voyage and in the "polluted islands" of the voyage's destination. But this is nothing compared to Roscoe's final warning. He insists that British consumption will result in both national stagnation and universal pain. Though the "copious stream / Of universal bliss" might seem to flow to every nation, it will "stagnate in its course" and spread "foul and putrid . . . corruption round." British avarice—witnessed so clearly in the case of slavery—was, according to Roscoe, "in nature's breast a dagger" that debilitated all of nature.[13] In Bristol, Hannah More's "Slavery" (1788) portrayed the voice of British liberty in a similar way: "Convulsed . . . and pestilent her breath, / She raves for mercy, while she deals out death."[14] Such writing emphasized how the consciousness of slavery as pestilence partly defined British identity during this time.

But how was it that disease, slavery, and the consciousness of slavery as disease operated in early nineteenth-century British culture, only to be taken up by Coleridge in an extraordinary tale of guilt and redemption? "The Ancient Mariner," like antislavery literature of the period, draws on early nineteenth-century medical and ecological models used to analyze yellow fever—the most deadly and widespread disease for British seamen on slave voyages. In this sense, the diseases of slavery were brought intimately home to the British body, just as the guilt of slavery was brought home to the British psyche. But discussion of fever within the discourse of slavery and discussion of slavery within the discourse of yellow fever also address a wider question: with this new proximity of cultures, could Britain establish a social system free from the diseases of tyranny and guilt?

II

When reading Coleridge's various writings, one has the sense that he could actually imagine a process where British self and foreign other could unite in harmony. He certainly contemplated the philosophic working out of such a process. In his *Marginalia*, for instance, he wrote that "the copula" of "identity" and "alterity" meant the self would "lose itself in another form by loving the self of another as another" (*CM* 1:680). It was in the context of British masters and African slaves, however, where the concepts of "identity" and "alterity" took on a blatant, material reality, and where "losing self in another" by taking on the alterity of that other had complex consequences for both British and African subjectivity. If "The Ancient Mariner" is read through the lens of this potent topic, it must be viewed as a process where the mariner tries to reconcile identity and alterity in a political, as well as a philosophical, way.[15]

In both medical literature and abolitionist poetry, the intersection of slavery and disease nearly always ended in a rethinking of philosophical definitions of identity and alterity. The work of Julia Kristeva provides some help in understanding this aspect of the distanced imagination.[16] Taken together, Kristeva's discussions of the abject in *Powers of Horror* and of foreigners in *Strangers to Ourselves* and *Nations Without Nationalism* offer a compelling theory linking bodily disease and foreign travel through the category of alterity.

Kristeva's writings revolve around a fundamental distinction between "self" and "not-self." Everything that is horrifying, everything that signals our possible inhumanity, everything that reminds us of our mortality, is not-self. As Kristeva has it, the diseased, decaying body (the yellow fever victim's black vomit and bleeding orifices, for example) is the most potent form of the not-self, or what she calls "the abject." And the abject itself, because it is the ultimate expression of the flesh, is an explicit manifestation of sin (at least from the perspective of dominant culture). Blood, urine, excrement, and the human corpse, these are the raw materials of the abject:

corpses *show me* what I permanently thrust aside in order to live. These body fluids, this defilement, this shit are what life withstands, hardly and with difficulty on the part of death. There, I am at the border of my condition as a living being. My body extricates itself, as being alive, from that border. . . . If dung signifies the other side of the border, the place where I am not and which permits me to be, the corpse, the most sickening of wastes, is a border that has encroached upon everything.[17]

We constitute ourselves, according to Kristeva, through abjection by excluding what is not-self. Yet the abject is always part of us, even though it must constantly be ignored, buried, or thrown over the edge of consciousness. The abject is, in this way, the cornerstone of personal subjectivity.

The process by which an individual constitutes personal subjectivity is, for Kristeva, also worked out on a national level. Just as the individual tries to evade death as symbolized in the corpse, so national character shies away from that which is foreign to it:

Hatred of those others who do not share my origins . . . affront me personally, economically, and culturally: I then move back among "my own," I stick to an archaic, primitive "common denominator," the one of my frailest childhood, my closest relatives, hoping they will be more trustworthy than "foreigners."[18]

Foreigners, like Coleridge's mariner, who transgress borders and break taboos, who identify with and touch otherness, are culturally abject. Kristeva maintains a distinctly Coleridgean position by arguing that the unity of the self, though impossible, may be glimpsed by realizing we are all, in some sense, "strangers to ourselves." Her view of the encounter with foreigners is similar to Coleridge's notion of "losing self in another," a process that involves self-alteration and loss of direction:

Confronting the foreigner whom I reject and with whom at the same time I identify, I lose my boundaries, I no longer have a container, the memory of experiences which I had abandoned overwhelm me, I lose my composure. I feel "lost," "indistinct," "hazy."[19]

Throughout her writings, Kristeva describes the marriage of identity and alterity as a boundary-dissolving process, whether those boundaries are individual or national, material or metaphysical.

If nineteenth-century systems of medicine and slavery were about anything, they were about boundaries, or boundary-dissolving processes. In fact, it might be said that these systems of medicine and slavery were designed to reestablish borders that were in the process of dissolving with the increased foreign travel that the slave trade instigated. Dissolving both personal and national borders, after all, is how yellow fever first gained attention. Medical writers who warned that epidemics in the Caribbean could spread throughout Europe conjured up images of the Black Plague of the fourteenth century, which wiped out one-third of the European population.[20] In the meantime, European heads of state put doctors in the service of deflecting national panic. Dr. Gilbert Blane reported in 1819 that Britain, Russia, and Prussia had actually held conferences to dispel the public and medical fear of "importation of this pestilential epidemic [yellow fever], which in the end of last century, and beginning of this, had so afflicted the West Indies, North America, and Spain." [21] In 1797, Dr. Trotter had likewise assured a potentially panicky British audience that there was no danger whatsoever of yellow fever "becoming active on this side of the Atlantic." [22]

The presence of yellow fever could not only disintegrate national borders, it could also redefine political alliances. Dr. Blane recounted an example of French warships that had captured British frigates carrying crews seized with yellow fever. The epidemic spread quickly among the French crews who were then quarantined with British prisoners, despite their status as French enemies. [23] In times of epidemic, it seemed, national identity was as unreliable as the body itself. Unlucky victims were the embodiment of alterity, no matter what their skin color or national status. Not surprisingly, slaves in the Caribbean were even more aware of fever's ability to cross boundaries and render Europeans powerless. In 1799, the traveler Robert Renny recalled being greeted on the shore of Jamaica by a canoe full of slave women sarcastically chanting:

New come buckra,
He get sick,
He tak fever,
He be die,
He be die, &etc. [24]

Yellow fever often killed European individuals who were involved in the slave trade, but what seemed worse to legislators and plantation owners was the imminent death of the slave system itself. With increased pressure from abolitionists like Southey and Coleridge, British culture faced the possibility of a social system that no longer divided itself neatly into masters and slaves. This heightened national anxiety about economic consequences existed most vocally among Caribbean proprietors, many of whom owned failing plantations as it was. Underneath this fiscal fear lay a deeper worry over how the change in the status of African slaves—from foreigners to citizens—would not only infect Europeans, but deplete any differences between the races. Coleridge would later confront this fear in his planned lecture on the "Origins of the Human Race." In this lecture, he opposed the implications being proposed by race theorists, such as Lord Monboddo, that Africans resembled orangutans (*SWF*, 1:1409–10). [25] But this changing view of the slave from inferior to moral equal threatened to dissolve the fragile border of the British self. For there was nothing quite like the abjection of the African slave against which British national character defined itself in the early part of the nineteenth century.

In "The Rime of the Ancient Mariner" Coleridge merges the fear of racial equality with the fear of fever. For example, at the very beginning of the poem, the mariner relates in his story to the unhappy wedding guest how the ship set sail from a British port. But as soon as it moved "below the kirk, below the hill, / Below the lighthouse top" and thus beyond Britain's geographical borders, other borders turned suddenly fragile (23–24). The result of this movement into the waters of foreignness and abjection is a narrative standstill when mariner and crew encounter "Nightmare LIFE-IN-DEATH" upon her "spectre-bark," a vessel which the William Empson (among others) calls "the premonition of a slaver" (194, 202).[26] This encounter turns the crew into a feverish image of the living dead, "for a charnel dungeon fitter," and so has them dancing on the most unbreakable and abject boundary in human experience, that between life and death (435).

By marrying the tropes of fever and slavery, "The Ancient Mariner" also explores slippages between the walled-off categories of self and otherness. In the heat of the poem's fever, the mariner is identified with Englishmen *and* slaves,[27] even though yellow fever underscored what were perceived as natural differences between Britons and Africans in how their bodies weathered forces of nature. The mariner's implied nationality and the wedding guest's response to his "long, and lank, and brown" body links him to British sailors who had been yellow fever victims (226). Because these victims were (according to the Caribbean traveler Robert Renny) "exposed to the burning sun, and a sultry atmosphere by day; chilling dews, and unhealthful vapours by night; obliged to conform themselves to new manners, new employments, new food, and new clothing," their bodies took on a ghostly, unnatural appearance. They became "irritable and weak" and were thus "readily affected" with the fever.[28] During this time, there was also an acute awareness that yellow fever (or "imported contagion") traveled by way of sun-scorched mariners and soldiers from one tropical shore to another.[29] When mariners arrived home, people were naturally afraid of touching these potentially unclean victims of seafaring diseases. It is thus not surprising to find this fear erupting in the opening lines of "The Ancient Mariner." Who can blame the wedding guest for voicing an immediate prohibition against bodily contact, ordering the mariner to "Hold off! unhand me, grey-beard loon!" (11). Like the British seaman whose body changed color in the heat of a yellow fever outbreak, the ancient mariner's shadowy weakness and brown "skinny hand" emerge repeatedly throughout the poem, as if to remind readers that yellow fever took its name from its ability to change the skin color of European victims.

But in the poem's infected environment, the very markers that identify the mariner as a British sailor (the "brown hand") also designate him a slave. He is linked to the bodies of Africans not only through his color, but also through his health. When the mariner assures his listener, "Fear not, fear not, thou Wedding Guest! / This body dropt not down," he acknowledges his own immunity to the fever that struck down all two hundred shipmates, an immunity that aligns him with the alterity of the slave (230–31). For when medical writers, such as Henry Clutterbuck, M.D., observed that infectious fevers were "communicable from one individual to another, either by actual contact, or by the effluvia escaping from the bodies of the sick," they were referring to communication between European and European, not European and African.[30] The wedding guest's fear of touching the Mariner's "skinny hand, so brown," then, also demonstrates a fear of "losing self in another," of being infected and thus profoundly changed by the alterity carried in the blood under dark skin (229).

Boundary-dissolving, a process that "The Ancient Mariner" articulates so powerfully, is the vehicle by which the poem arrives at the distanced imagination. But the proximity of disease and the recognition of how easily national and personal boundaries could break down was also a central issue in the early nineteenth-century medical search for the origin of yellow fever. Medical experts agreed that every disease had its own geographical habitat. For example, Dr. Thomas Beddoes—Coleridge's friend and correspondent—voiced a common opinion when he said "small-pox, yellow fever, and the plague" came from a certain "effluvia" produced in the air of hot regions.[31] Tropical climates—Africa and the Caribbean particularly—were thus carriers of disease, and natives of Britain and America who came in contact with these climates could carry the disease back with them and so become foreigners in their homeland. The search for yellow fever's origin could help reestablish borders between "self" and "other," between "us" and "them," between British and African, which yellow fever itself obliterated.[32]

The search for origins, it seems, was everybody's business. In 1802, a writer named William Deverell published a book proposing to locate yellow fever's origin through a study of Milton, Virgil, and "thence to [the poetry] of Homer, and to the times when the temples of Egypt were founded; and I think it will be seen that the same or a similar disease, arising from the same causes and in the same places, prevailed in each of those ages."[33] Using the *Aeneid*, Deverell established a one-to-one correspondence between Ortygia and Britain, Cyclades and the Caribbean, and "the tabida lues, affecting both animate and inanimate nature" was "most clearly a West Indian or American fever."[34] Coleridge also had an interest in the origin of epidemic disease. He located the origin of smallpox—the seafaring disease most closely associated with yellow fever — and demonstrated its coincidence with commerce, war, and the movement of Africans:

Small pox . . . was first introduced by the Abyssinians into Arabia when they conquered the Province of Hemyen [Yemen]; & they called it the Locust-plague, believing it to have originated in the huge heaps of putrefying Locusts in the Desart. — From Arabia it was carried by Greek merchants to Constantinople — & from thence by the armies of Justinian in his Gothic War to Italy, Switzerland, & France. (*CL*, 2:455)

Coleridge's theory supports the period's belief that, though the instigators of most diseases came from nature, from heaps of putrefying locusts, from "effluvia" of hot climates, or from "decomposing vegetable matter," the growth of disease turned truly epidemic only through cross-cultural interaction.[35]

III

During the early part of the nineteenth century, a radical change took place in the cross-cultural interaction between Britons and Africans. Up until the late eighteenth century, most segments of society accepted, without too many questions, racial hierarchies that placed white Europeans in a superior position to people of color. These hierarchies naturalized the slave system: Africans were considered inferior, and so slavery was justified. But things changed in the 1780s and 1790s. Largely because of the abolitionist movement, but also because of increased slave uprisings, the majority of British people, for the first time in centuries, began to consider Africans as moral others instead of "things." Coleridge articulated a fairly common opinion in an article intended for the *Courier* where he wrote, "A Slave is a *Person* perverted into a *Thing*; Slavery, therefore, is not so properly a deviation from Justice as an absolute subversion of all Morality."[36] As one can imagine, this "subversion of all morality" by the British brought with it an overwhelming sense of guilt. Coleridge and other writers began to see European guilt in the same way doctors saw yellow fever's black vomit: as a primary symptom.

Guilt defined Britain as a sick society. And nowhere is the guilt of slavery and the punishment of disease more apparent than in abolitionist literature. Helen Maria Williams's 1788 *Poem on the Bill Lately Passed* presents a vision of slavery where the "beams direct, that on each head / The fury of contagion shed."[37] The "beams" in this case radiate from the "guilty man" in charge of a slave vessel. While Williams located the origin of contagion in the guilt of British slave traders, Coleridge located the origin of slavery in the guilt of the British consumer. Slavery, he contended in his 1808 review of Thomas Clarkson's *History of the Abolition of the Slave Trade*, was "evil in the form of guilt; evil in its most absolute and most appropriate sense." Guilt, wrote Coleridge, because of its psychological proximity, "will make an impression deeper than could have been left by mere agony of body" (*SWF*, 1:219).[38] Further, guilt was national, and authorized by acts of legislature (*SWF*, 1:219–20). When it came to matters of slavery, Coleridge saw the British nation as a body. "Great Britain is indeed a *living body politic*," he wrote. "London is the true *heart* of empire. No pulse beats there, which is not corresponded to proportionally through the whole circulation" (*SWF*, 1:236).

Those who consumed the products of the trade were just as guilty as slave traders and plantation owners themselves. After all, Coleridge argued, the trade's "final effect" and "first Cause" was "self-evidently the consumption of its Products! and does not the Guilt rest on the Consumers? and is it not an allowed axiom in Morality That Wickedness may be multiplied but cannot be divided and that the Guilt of all attaches to each one who is knowingly an accomplice?" (*Lects 1795*, 247). Wickedness multiplied and spread through the social body, like so many germs, leaving the collective British consumer with an all-consuming guilt.

"The Rime of the Ancient Mariner" struggles with guilt through disease, too. The poem suggests that it is possible to atone for the commerce of slavery, wipe out European guilt, and therefore stop disease from wiping out Europeans. "The Ancient Mariner," according to James McKusick, sails in the shadow of guilt associated with the Western "civilizing" mission. McKusick suggests that the albatross is "an emblematic representation of all the innocent lives destroyed by European conquest," including the guilt associated with the slave trade.[39] But the albatross is just one emblem of guilt. Although the poem does not pinpoint any one source for the mariner's guilt, it seems related as much to the deathly ill state of the crew as to the killing of the bird. Similarly, what arrests the ship "day after day, day after day" (115) is not so much the storm blast or the navigational disaster at the South Pole as it is the outbreak of disease and death. If the ship is on a commercial mission, especially one dealing in slaves, Coleridge implies a moral cause for the epidemic.

Coleridge was well aware of the natural causes of epidemics. But he, like many other writers, turned these natural causes into moral ones. For example, according to many medical experts of the day, stagnant waters combined with the torrid climate of the tropics to produce the yellow fever infection so common to slave vessels. The physician-poet Erasmus Darwin imported this well-known medical tidbit into his exotically charged diatribe *The Botanic Garden*. The poem rails against "Britannia" who invaded the coasts of Africa "with murder, rapine, theft, — and call it Trade!" [40] The poem builds toward a genuine Old Testament plague, put into the modern context of contagion emanating from stagnant waters:

Sylphs! with light shafts you pierce the drowsy FOG,
That lingering slumbers on the sedge-wove bog,
With webbed feet o'er midnight meadows creeps,
Or flings his hairy limbs on stagnant deeps,
You meet CONTAGION issuing from afar,
And dash the baleful conqueror from his car.[41]

Not just contagion, it was believed, but yellow fever in particular, targeted those like the mariner and his crew, floating on an ocean where "the very deep did rot . . . Yea, slimy things did crawl with legs / Upon the slimy sea" (123–26). Slave vessels, stuck without "breath" or "motion" beneath a "hot and copper sky," were especially vulnerable from a medical as well as a moral point of view (116, 111). For instance, yellow fever was portrayed as God's just punishment for the atrocities of the slave trade in James Montgomery's 1809 poem *The West Indies*:

The eternal makes his fierce displeasure known;
At his command the pestilence abhorr'd
Spares the poor slave, and smites the haughty lord.[42]

Similarly, one British traveler to the Caribbean said that "the new world, indeed, appears to be surrounded with the flaming sword of the angel, threatening destruction to all those, who venture within its reach." [43]

In the diseased climate of "The Ancient Mariner," then, it is not just the albatross murder that prompts the crew to hang the bird around the mariner's neck as a symbol of guilt. It is the outbreak itself, the "Spirit that plagued" them with suffocating symptoms: tongues "withered at the root" and "choked with soot," "throats unslaked, with black lips baked," "glazed" eyes reflecting the "bloody Sun" and "death-fires" of the stagnant waters (132, 136, 138, 157, 146, 112, 128). In fact, before he wrote the poem, Coleridge explained how, by way of disease, the slave trade destroyed the British national body by destroying individual bodies. Following Thomas Clarkson, who argued that the slave trade was unfeasible because of the diseases to which crews were exposed, Coleridge said that from "the unwholesomeness of the Climate through which [crews] pass, it has been calculated that every Slave Vessel from the Port of Bristol loses on an average almost a fourth of the whole Crew" (*Lects 1795*, 238). The slave trade, he said, turned British mariners into "rather shadows in their appearance than men," just as in "The Ancient Mariner" disease changes the mariners into a shadowy, "ghastly crew" (*Lects 1795*, 238).

But Coleridge really drives this point home when he locates the source of the disease in the skin of a ghostly white woman. As soon as the crew hangs the dead, white bird around the mariner's neck, the woman-specter, who is "white as leprosy" emerges on a "western wave," and the sailors drop dead (192, 171):

One after one, by the star-dogged Moon,
Too quick for groan or sigh,
Each turned his face with a ghastly pang,
And cursed me with his eye.

Four times fifty living men,
(And I heard nor sigh nor groan)
With a heavy thump, a lifeless lump,
They dropped down one by one. (212–19)

Coleridge thus deviates from the medical community's indictment of the African and Caribbean atmosphere as a carrier of disease for Westerners. In a dramatic reversal, he places foreignness in a white, western woman, who becomes the expression of alterity through disease.

In his notebooks, Coleridge also pictured a white woman as a carrier of disease and moral depravity. In what is now a well-known account of one of his dreams, he told of being "followed up & down by a frightful pale woman who, I thought, wanted to kiss me, & had the property of giving a shameful Disease by breathing on the face" (*CN*, 1:1250).[44] In this case, the diseased white woman is quite clearly the cargo of his fevered mind. But the link between this diseased woman and the pale woman of "The Ancient Mariner" is the link between Western seafaring diseases and sexually transmitted, morally reprehensible diseases such as syphilis.

For Coleridge, at least, there was more to whiteness than met the eye. In "The Ancient Mariner," he folds disease in the envelope of whiteness and thus highlights the extent to which he was conversant with the operations of disease and guilt within antislavery literature. Besides yellow fever, the other disease trope used by abolitionists was leprosy. Thomas Pringle, for instance, in an antislavery sonnet, said sugar "taints with leprosy the white man's soul."[45] Sugar sifted down English channels and dissolved in their teacups, but it remained a disease of white culture.[46] Its cultural twin, leprosy, poisoned instead of sweetened, rotted away white flesh instead of increasing it. Thus, abolitionist writers began to see sugar's deceptive sweetness, like the illusive whiteness of European skin, as something that tainted rather than purified. No wonder that in "The Ancient Mariner," the two apparent hosts of contagion—the leprous white woman and the decaying white bird—destroy the myth of white purity that the British bride symbolizes. The poem, after all, opens in the epithalamic tradition, with the promise of a wedding image of purity, but the mariner's tale nervously disrupts the wedding story. He replaces it with the "Life-in-Deathness" of white disease. The wedding, in fact, is not just contaminated, but completely obliterated from view by the mariner's tale of rot, slime, sickness, and death.

It is not at all surprising that writers like Coleridge and Pringle brought sugar and disease together in literature, given sugar's economic position as the country's foremost slave-produced import. In its refined whiteness, sugar was synonymous with the addiction of the British consumer. And according to Coleridge, guilt sprang not just from consumption of slave products, but from addiction to them. By funneling a variety of such substances into Britain, international trade fed what Coleridge saw as the addictive British personality. "Perhaps from the beginning of the world," he wrote, "the evils arising from the formation of imaginary wants have been in no instance so dreadfully exemplified as in the Slave Trade & West India Commerce! We receive from the West Indias Sugars, Rum, Cotton, log-wood, cocoa, coffee, pimento, ginger, mahogany, and conserves—not one of these are necessary" (*Lects 1795*, 236).[47]

Coleridge was just one of many writers to move the medical to the political level by designating slavery a European disease. Robert Southey's vaccination poem, "A Tale of Paraguay," imagined smallpox as an act of African reprisal. According to the poem's opening lines, Edward Jenner—who had pioneered work on cowpox inoculation to combat smallpox the same year that Coleridge wrote "The Ancient Mariner"—defeated epidemic disease and thus the vengeance of slavery:

Jenner! for ever shall thy honour'd name
Among the children of mankind be blest,
Who by thy skill hast taught us how to tame
One dire disease, . . the lamentable pest
Which Africa sent forth to scourge the West,
As if in vengeance for her sable brood
So many an age remorselessly oppresst.[48]

But if smallpox was a scourge from Africa that could be conquered through British medical technology, yellow fever could not. And so it was most often that abolitionists used the symptoms of yellow fever, as opposed to those of smallpox or other contagious diseases, to demonstrate the interminable vengeance Africa would have on European bodies. In James Stanfield's *The Guinea Voyage* (1789), for instance, yellow fever eats the crew alive. It leaves behind putrid bodies as spoils of war, as condemnation for the "remorseless oppression" of slavery. In military fashion, the "troops of wan disease their march begin":

Now droops the head in faint dejection hung,
Now raging thirst enflames the dry parch'd tongue;
In yellow films the rayless eye is set,
With chilling dews the loaded brow is wet.[49]

The guilt that bleeds through the lines of Stanfield's, Southey's, and, most powerfully, Coleridge's poem is the logical response of the sympathetic imagination, and it is the only response of the distanced imagination. For the culture at large, guilt signaled the beginnings of a dismantling of the slave system that had been in place for so many hundreds of years. Guilt was nothing less than the initial pangs of remorse felt upon recognizing the inhumanity of the British self against the humanity of the African other.

IV

Interestingly enough, recognition of slaves as more than "things" coincided with recognition that slavery created a biological and a psychological rift in the natural environment. From its beginnings in the fifteenth century to its peak in the early nineteenth century, the slave trade represented the largest movement of people in history to that point. It was clear to medical writers of the period that this dramatically disturbed the atmosphere. When Dr. James Clark noted that the activity of the slave trade caused "a deranged state of the atmosphere" and thus "excited this mortal disease in our island,"[50] he was saying that the slave trade disturbed environmental balances, which in turn produced yellow fever.

Moving bodies turned the earth in a dangerous and often fatal direction. Since Africans and slaves appeared to be immune to yellow fever, the only way epidemics spread was among gatherings of freshly arrived Europeans in a tropical locale. As Philip Curtin explains in his book *Death by Migration*, in order to survive, the yellow fever vector *A. aegypti* needed groups of nonimmune subjects "concentrated within the flight range" of the virus. If not, the disease would creep back into the recesses of the tropical jungle, where animals kept it active until a new crop of Europeans arrived.[51] Of course, early-nineteenth-century medical workers did not have germ theories, and they did not even consider the mosquito as a carrier of the virus. But they did understand yellow fever's mode of existence at some level. They knew that the disease stemmed from the European encounter with the tropics. Dr. Thomas Dancer, for one, observed in 1801 how yellow fever "first visits the abodes of wretchedness and squalor, and disappears for a season, or diminishes in virulence to return again and expend its fury over the community at large."[52] American doctors, reporting on the yellow fever epidemic of Philadelphia, recognized that the fever "exists in the West Indies particularly in times of war, when great numbers of strangers are to be found there."[53]

These early medical men clearly believed that the breakdown of the Caribbean ecosystem caused yellow fever to break out. When Dr. Clark insisted in 1799 that yellow fever ran rampant in the Caribbean the more it was "crowded with strangers," he gestured toward the cultural suspicion that yellow fever was the result of environmental trauma. Although Britain had its own socioenvironmental problems (the poverty of the city, the fear of French invasion), nothing of the sort was happening at home. In contrast to the environment of the Quantocks, where Coleridge and Wordsworth first conceived of "The Ancient Mariner," the abolitionist poet William Hutchenson wrote of the Caribbean in 1792:

New cargoes crowd our shores, and on the beach
The squalid multitudes are pouring forth,
From over-loaded ships, which, like the curse
Of vile Pandora's box, bring forth disease,
With misery, and pallid want,
Crippled and maim'd, whose ulcerating sores
Cling to the canker'd chains, that rankle deep.[54]

If the yellow fever outbreaks of the Caribbean frightened Europeans, outbreaks in America created real alarm. The 1793 outbreak in Philadelphia was by far the most referenced and terrifying eighteenth-century yellow fever epidemic precisely because it proved that the disease could be imported like so many slaves and goods. Dr. Trotter blamed the fever on "damaged coffee, that was left to rot on the wharfs, and from which noxious exhalations were spread that first affected the neighbourhood, and afterwards more distant parts of the city."[55] The Americans insisted that this "imported" fever had transgressed the national boundary and thus altered the American environment. Robert Jackson and John Redman, two prominent American doctors, led public opinion in the matter. Yellow fever, said Jackson, had been "imported into Philadelphia from some foreign country" and was "propagated afterwards solely by contagion."[56] Redman traced the infection to "imported clothing or persons who died in the West Indies"; at the very least, the disease stemmed directly from "the neighbourhood of shipping or among persons connected with vessels."[57] So it was that doctors blamed commerce for destroying environmental balances that otherwise kept epidemics at bay. People who carried on the national dirty work of commerce brought fever home. Those, like the mariner, "connected with vessels" were literally on the national border and were somehow held responsible for importing the wrong thing. On the one hand, countries like England and America relied heavily on people associated with the seafaring industry, yet on the other, these individuals were diseased, disturbing, and abject, because of their inevitable contact with foreign cultures.

Many bystanders, however, could not help but use the outbreak of European contracted disease in tropical climates to condemn the slave trade for deforming the environment. Helen Maria Williams asks how slave traders can, in good conscience:

Deform creation with the gloom
Of crimes that blot its cheerful bloom?
Darken a work so perfect made,
And cast the universe in shade? — [58]

Though the moral universe condemned the British slavery system with plagues of yellow fever, the natural universe ultimately paid the price. In James Montgomery's abolitionist poem, yellow fever destroys the British body and thus the entire cosmos:

Foreboding melancholy sinks his mind,
Soon at his heart he feels the monster's fangs,
They tear his vitals with convulsive pangs
. . . .
Now frenzy-horrors rack his whirling brain,
Tremendous pulses throb through every vein;
The firm earth shrinks beneath his torture-bed,
The sky in ruins rushes o'er his head;
He rolls, he rages in consuming fires,
Till nature, spent with agony, expires.[59]

Wordsworth also spoke of slavery in ecological terms. It was, he said, the "most rotten branch of human shame" that ought to "fall together with its parent tree" (*The Prelude*, 10:224–36). From what came to be seen as the center of the Romantic poetic tradition, Wordsworth called the structures of slavery a disease that could outrot the worst atrocities of the French Revolution. Medical experts reinforced this view. "Since the abolition of the slave-trade," wrote Dr. Henderson, "some disorders of African origin, and highly contagious, have almost disappeared." [60]

In "The Ancient Mariner," Coleridge captures sharply the ruination of the universe that the slave trade instigated. His mariner finds disease and thus nightmarish deformation everywhere: it appears not just in the rotting bodies of birds, men, and a white woman, but in heavenly bodies as well, such as the "bloody Sun . . . with broad and burning face" (112; 180). Even the body of the ship is diseased: "The planks look warped! and see those sails, / How thin they are and sere!" (529–30). The Hermit—who is also a figure for decay, as he prays at a "rotted old oak-stump"—likens the ship to the rotting skeletal leaves of the forest, decaying like the planks of the vessel, which Coleridge had already designated as a feature of a slave ship (522). In his *Lecture*, he noted that slaves were "crammed" into the hold of a ship "with so many fellow-victims" that "the heat and stench arising from [their] diseased bodies [would] rot the very planks" (*Lects 1795*, 248–49).

Surrounded as he is by disease and deformation, it is no wonder that when the mariner and his ship pull up to the British bay, only the mariner is alive. By this time, the bay does not seem as pure as it did at the voyage's beginning. Described as "white with silent light," the bay swallows up the mass of contagion that is now practically synonymous with the doubly identified mariner (480). Yet the ship settles in an ambiguous space, neither this side nor that side of Britain's national boundary. It sinks just below the surface of the water. But, like the mariner's tale of guilt, or like the slave population itself, it could emerge at anytime.

Just as the outbreak on the ship coincides with a catastrophic deformation of nature, the rift between the mariner and his environment increases during the journey itself. Coleridge's gloss to the poem indicates how "horror follows" the mariner's meeting of the "spectre-bark." And indeed, the mariner is horrified most of all by the living death of the crew and the quarantined solitude the mariner himself experiences after the crew dies. His hollow repetition, "Alone, alone, all, all alone, / Alone on a wide wide sea!" echoes back through the poem as through a chasm. He is both nowhere and nothing—neither self nor other (232–33). He is disconnected from his environment, from himself, and from other people.

This kind of disconnection is truly a nightmare, and Coleridge uses a fairly standard catalog of gothic images to reinforce slavery's horror. J. R. Ebbatson traces the use of gothic imagery in "The Ancient Mariner"—the spectre-bark, the living-dead crew—to Coleridge's reading of Matthew Gregory Lewis's play *The Castle Spectre*. For Lewis, the gothic symbolized various forms of subjection: each and every character in the play endures the "shame of servitude."[61] The enslaved include the noble Percy, who is imprisoned in a guarded room for just a few hours, and the poor Reginald, who is secretly chained in the castle's subterraneous dungeon for years. Even the evil Osmond, who sets himself up as the master, refers to himself as the "slave of wild desires."[62] One of the reasons Lewis's play was so popular was that it appealed to the early-nineteenth-century British audience's own feelings of subjection.

But if British audiences saw in *The Castle Spectre*'s gothic atmosphere the buried truth of their own slavish condition, Lewis makes it clear that the enslavement of Africans is the real buried secret facing the nation. He does this through two principal characters: a white person and a black one. In contrast to the castle specter, who appears as a "figure" in *"white and flowing garments spotted with blood"* stands Hassan, an African slave.[63] Hassan implies that the castle's inhabitants find themselves in subjection because of the subjection they impose on Africans: "Vengeance!" he cries, "Oh! how it joys me when the white man suffers!—Yet weak are his pangs, compared to those I felt when torn from thy shores, O native Africa!"[64] Slavery is experienced as both a painful reality and a metaphysical condition. "Oh! When I forget my wrongs, may I forget myself!" wails Hassan.[65] The mammoth hypocrisy of all this is, of course, that Lewis later wrote the *Journal of a West Indian Proprietor*, an account of his own slave-labor plantation in Jamaica.[66]

Though Coleridge was influenced by Lewis's long-running play, the aspect of "losing self in another" within a gothic slave story was totally Coleridge's idea. As "Life-in-Death" begins her work on the ancient mariner, he launches the process of trying to reunify his violently ruptured identity. His experiences with emblems of the slave trade—the spectre-bark, Life-in-Death, fever victims, diseased ships—result in a psychological disease that takes him to several levels of self-confrontation. To begin with, his blessing of the slimy water snakes, linked by their "flash of golden fire" to the epidemic waters, is a move to acknowledge what is radically "alter" (281). It is a move to attempt, on a material level, Coleridge's original idea of alterity, of "losing self in another form by loving the self of another as another." It is also a move to release himself from what the wedding guest comes to recognize as the "plague" of Western seafaring missions (80). Who can forget this truly strange moment in the poem when the albatross falls from the mariner's neck:

O happy living things! no tongue
Their beauty might declare:
A spring of love gushed from my heart,
And I blessed them unaware:
. . . .
The self-same moment I could pray;
And from my neck so free
The Albatross fell off, and sank
Like lead into the sea. (282–87, 288–91)

James McKusick has recently suggested that the mariner's ecological enlightenment involves learning to "cross the boundaries that divide him from the natural world, through unmotivated acts of compassion between 'man and bird and beast.' "[67] But it is more than that. This sudden, uncanny recognition of the water snakes is described as a "self-same moment," that is, as a reuniting of oneself and another, of an old and a newly aware self. This moment initiates him in a process of ever-deeper questioning of himself and of the assumptions underlying his culture.

Coleridge's doubly identified mariner tells his guest early on about his feverish mission. Through the simple telling of a tale, he feels he must introduce this two-sided sense of individual self into the British national body. The tale that "burns" within him aligns him with the "storyteller" who, as Michael Taussig explains, has the important cultural job of bringing alterity home. In his book *Mimesis and Alterity*, Taussig says that Coleridge's ancient mariner is the quintessential storyteller. He brings

the far-away to the here-and now as metastructure of the tale. Coleridge provides the classic instance, the Ancient Mariner who has spread his wings in the tradewinds of the world, now returned and beginning his desperate tale, "He stoppeth one of three." And the man apprehended responds: "By thy long grey beard and glittering eye, Now wherefore stopp'st thou me?" It is at this point that the freedom and foreboding bringing the traveler home insists on audience and attains voice, and it is here, in this moment of apprehension, that the listening self is plunged forward into and beyond itself.[68]

So, readers find the mariner again and again trying to convince the wedding guest of his own need to recognize the other as a moral being, trying to plunge the listening self "forward into and beyond itself." Thus, the mariner's dramatic and final claim that "He prayeth best, who loveth best / All things both great and small" is more than a simple moral to a seafaring tale (614–15). It is a lesson about how to relate to what is other than self.

Intimacy as Imitation

Monkeys in Blake's Engravings for Stedman's Narrative

I

On 1 December 1791 the slightly cranky retired captain John Gabriel Stedman recorded in his journal, "I wrote to the engraver Blake, to thank him twice for his excellent work but never received any answer."[1] Blake was in the process of engraving a series of sixteen illustrations to accompany Stedman's *Narrative of a Five Years' Expedition against the Revolted Negroes of Surinam*.[2] As it turned out, within these sixteen engravings are some of the most terrifying images that would ever come before the eyes of the British public. Some of them have permanently lodged themselves in the collective consciousness, showing up in today's academic marketplace with assertive rapidity, as book covers, illustrations, and exhibits in scholarly arguments.[3] "Europe Supported by Africa & America" (Figure 2), which has been reproduced more than almost any other image from the Romantic period, has ensured that slavery remains as intimate as a glance. In the Romantic period these engravings served a more basic function: they illustrated not only Stedman's *Narrative*, which ends with the confession, "I must have hurt both the Eye and the heart of the Feeling reader" (618), but also the terse opening lines of Blake's *Visions of the Daughters of Albion*: "The eye sees more than the heart knows" (plate 1). It is important to know that Blake wrote this poem about slavery at the same time he engraved for Stedman because, for Blake, slavery's proximity came directly through the eye.

But what exactly does the eye see in Stedman's *Narrative*? Part of the answer lies in the two engravings that have a fascinatingly discordant relationship with the other fourteen Blake worked on: "The Mecoo & Kishee Kishee Monkeys" (Figure 3) and "The Quato & Saccawinkee Monkeys" (Figure 4). One could view these two sets of monkeys simply as natural history drawings, along with many other images of birds, fish, and plants in the *Narrative*. But, in fact, Blake engraved only one other natural history drawing for Stedman, a fairly straight-

Figure 2. Blake, "Europe Supported by Africa & America." By permission of the Syndics of Cambridge University Library.

Figure 3. Blake, "The Mecco & Kishee Kishee Monkeys." By permission of the Syndics of Cambridge University Library.

Figure 4. Blake, "The Quato & Saccawinkee Monkeys." By permission of the Syndics of Cambridge University Library.

forward depiction of apples and mammees. The rest of the Blake engravings take a single subject: the sufferings of the African slave population, and in this context the monkey engravings strike one as suggestively ironic.[4] Monkeys in Blake mock and mimic, something Stedman calls repeated attention to with his own clever short-hand, "mock-mimicry." Stedman announces their unnerving ability to copy and thus undermine humans: "Theyr throwing Short Sticks & Excrements, seems to be no more than a Humiliating *Mock-Mimicry* of Human Actions, without any other Use," he writes of the Quato monkeys Blake illustrated (328, my emphasis). In many ways, mock-mimicry not only describes Blake's monkey engravings, it also informs the approach he takes to the other engravings in the *Narrative*, offering an interpretive lens for the entire set. Bringing slavery to the British eye as mock-mimicry meant depicting it as an interpretive quandary, where the eye sees only when the heart tears itself away from what it conventionally knows.

Throughout his poetry, Blake emphasizes that he is more interested in seeing than knowing, and what he wanted Stedman's readers to see was both old and new. Monkey and ape images were seen everywhere in Europe from medieval times onward. The classic study of the human fascination with apes is H. W. Janson's 1952 *Apes and Ape Lore in the Middle Ages and Renaissance*, which was preceded by William Coffman McDermott's authoritative *The Ape in Antiquity*.[5] These two books have spawned similar studies, such as Ramona and Desmond Morris's *Men and Apes* and the collection of essays *Art, the Ape of Nature*.[6] What these studies establish is the pervasive history of monkeys, apes, baboons, and orangutans as creatures of mockery and innate trickiness in European art and literature from the Middle Ages through to Blake's own time. Indeed, among the many animals Blake uses to illustrate his poetic concepts is the monkey, who is featured several times in *The Marriage of Heaven and Hell*, always to demonstrate human folly. In one place Blake writes, "A man carried a monkey about for a shew, & because he was a little wiser than the monkey grew vain, and conceiv'd himself much wiser than seven men" (plate 21). This particular use of the man carrying a monkey may also attest to the fact that these exotic creatures from places like Guiana were increasingly kept as pets and could be seen on the London streets, which may be part of the reason monkeys show up with energetic irony in paintings by Blake's contemporaries: George Stubbs (Figure 5) and William Hogarth.[7] These artists worked alongside Blake, who made his own illustrations of the mischievous monkeys for John Gay's *Fables* (Figure 6).[8] On the more sinister side, apes were also the subject of race debates as scientists compared them to Africans and Europeans. The ape's place in comparative anatomy becomes immediately clear with Pieter Camper's "facial angles," establishing the supposed beauty and thus hierarchical superiority of the European face as op-

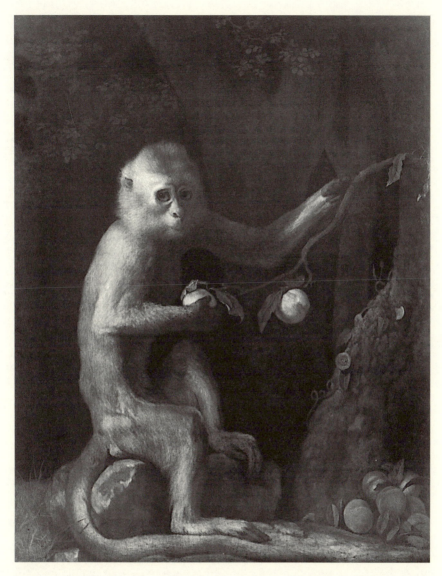

Figure 5. George Stubbs, *Green Monkey*, 1798. Courtesy of the Board of Trustees of the National Museums and Galleries on Merseyside/Walker Art Gallery, Liverpool.

Figure 6. Blake, illustration for John Gay's *Fables*, 1793. By permission of the Syndics of
Cambridge University Library.

posed to the African and the ape (Figure 7).[9] Camper's angles were the basis for
similar studies by Johann Kaspar Lavater, whose works Blake helped engrave.[10]

Monkeys and apes (from here on I use the terms "monkey" and "ape" in
their broadest sense to include the various forms of ape-kind, from monkeys to
orangutans to baboons to gibbons) were thus extremely complicated symbols in
London at the time Blake executed his engravings for Stedman. Indeed, based
on Stedman's account of ape-kind in his *Narrative*, on the art and literary history surrounding Blake's own, and the new accounts of race science published
in London at this time, it is possible to see four complementary threads of ape
lore informing Blake's monkey engravings and thus his numerous depictions of
Africans: the rapist-ape or monkey-lover; the monkey as sinner and devil, or
simia Dei; the ape-artist or *ars simia naturae*; and the classification of the monkey
in eighteenth- and nineteenth-century race science. A fifth thread, what Henry
Louis Gates defined so compellingly in 1988 as "the signifying monkey," is im-

plicit in the engravings.[11] For these reasons, the monkey's strategic significance in Blake's engravings greatly outweighs its otherwise trivial place as a natural history specimen in Stedman's *Narrative*.

II

Apes have long been identified with the wantonness of both masculine and feminine sexuality. The ape was a symbol of sensuality in medieval woodcuts, associated especially with the excesses of female desire, with the term "she-ape" referring to prostitutes in Romance countries. The female ape represented the wiles of women, while the traits of excess and addiction to sensual pleasure "epitomized by the ape were thought to be present in every woman to a greater or lesser extent."[12] However, the more ubiquitous and older tradition is the identification of apes with masculine sexuality. The male ape with a female partner has been so pervasive in Europe over the past four-hundred years that Janson claims it "would be futile to attempt an exhaustive listing of passages concerned."[13] Illustrations of apes and baboons with either maternal breasts or huge penises in early natural histories, for example Ulisse Aldrovandi's 1637 depictions of the powerful cynocephalus in *De quadrupedibus digitatis viviparis*, testify to the ape's reputation for fertility and virility in Europe (Figures 8 and 9).[14]

But this European tradition was also part of the mythology of the Near East. One story—"The King's Daughter and the Ape"—later rehearsed by both Janson and Ramona and Desmond Morris became part of the *Thousand and One Nights*.[15] Richard Burton's 1885 translation of this tale begins by graphically illustrating the ape's ability to outsex the human male:

There was once a Sultan's daughter, whose heart was taken with love of a black slave: he abated her maidenhead and she became passionately addicted to futtering, so that she could not do without it a single hour and complained of her case to one of her body-women, who told her that no thing poketh and stroketh more abundantly than the baboon. Now it so chanced one day, that an ape-leader passed under her lattice, with a great ape; so she unveiled her face and looking upon the ape, signed to him with her eyes, whereupon he broke his bonds and chain and climbed up to the Princess, who hid him in a palace with her, and night and day he abode there, eating and drinking and copulating.

Burton's footnote to this text tellingly unveils how the Eastern myth might have merged with nineteenth-century travel narrative accounts of the woman-ravishing ape. Burton explains, "It is usually the hideous Abyssinian cynocephalus which is tamed by the ape-leader. . . . The beast has a natural penchant

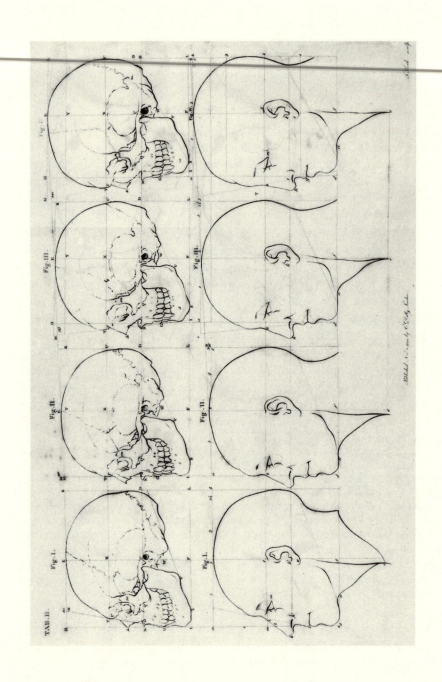

TAB. II.

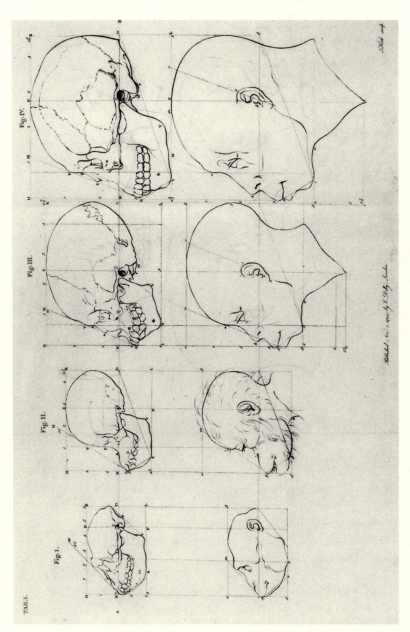

Figure 7. Pieter Camper's "facial angles," from *Works of the Late Professor Camper, on the Connexion between the Science of Anatomy and the Arts of Drawing, Painting, Statuary, &etc.*, 1794. By permission of the Syndics of Cambridge University Library.

Figure 8. From Ulisse Aldrovandi, *De quadrupedibus digitatis viviparis*, 1637. By permission of the Syndics of Cambridge University Library.

for women; I heard of one which attempted to rape a girl in the public street and was prevented only by a sentinel's bayonet." [16]

Blake's monkey engravings for Stedman take up this same mythology, for Stedman calls the female monkeys "lascivious," and takes note of their sexuality: "the females have regularly their Menstra." [17] But he complains more ardently about the sexual promiscuity of the males, who apparently threaten to usurp Stedman's own virility. They "kept following us till we returned to Camp," says Stedman, who then tells his readers, "doctor Bancroft Mentions An ourangoutang in Guiana, that will attack the Males, and ravish the females of the Human Species" (329). The "Doctor Bancroft" Stedman refers to was his contemporary, Edward Bancroft, a politician, naturalist, and chemist. Bancroft had settled in Guiana in 1763 and later published *An Essay on the Natural History of [Dutch] Guiana*.[18] Bancroft was only one among many writers of this period to exaggerate the ape-kind's sexual habits. Lord Monboddo's studies of orangutans, which

Figure 9. From Ulisse Aldrovandi, *De quadrupedibus digitatis viviparis*, 1637. By permission of the Syndics of Cambridge University Library.

Stedman also knew, comment that the males "have a great desire for women."[19] The travelers "Bosman and Gauthier Schoutten," writes Monboddo, attest to the fact that orangutans are "very fond of women, whom they always attack when they meet them in the woods. And Dampier, Forger, and other travellers, affirm that they frequently carry away young girls; and that it is with greatest difficulty that they can be rescued from them."[20] One reason racist writers like Monboddo wanted to believe that apes mated with black women was that, after Buffon's ninety-one-volume *Natural History*, species were defined by their ability to interbreed and sustain progeny.[21]

Closely related to the ape's excessive sexuality was his status as a sinner. From medieval times onward, he appears in woodcuts and sculptures of key biblical scenes: Adam naming the animals, the annunciation, and the crucifixion. But his most telling place is in the Garden of Eden. Early English bestiaries and Bibles show Adam and Eve in the garden, with monkeys hovering overhead on tree limbs, holding apples, or squatting near the snake at the feet of the sinning couple. In Ludwig Krug's depiction of the Fall, for example, a snake appears in the garden above Adam and Eve, but the monkey, who holds an apple, occupies the central position, entwined between their feet as if replacing the snake (Figure 10). This seems to signify that as Adam and Eve sin, they become, like the apple-eating monkey, sexually aware and thus debased. Ironically enough, the ape's association with the Fall of Man is not supported by scriptures at all, yet in iconography from the twelfth to the sixteenth centuries in Europe the ape was generally accepted as a symbol of carnal lust.

An important strand of the ape as fallen man and sexual sinner, one that Blake was definitely conversant with, is the fettered ape. According to Janson, "countless simians . . . enliven the manuscripts" of the thirteenth and fourteenth centuries, and the chained ape "becomes a standard feature of the Late Gothic artist's repertory."[22] The ape tends to represent someone who has become an unconscious prisoner of vice. In Pieter Bruegel the Elder, for example, the fettered ape may "represent the dominance of flesh over reason," and worse, an unconscious resignation to sin and thus to a slavery so entrenched that the victim has no desire to be free (Figure 11).[23] Blake takes this image of the fettered ape to a shocking level in *The Marriage of Heaven and Hell*, which he composed at the same time he was engraving for Stedman. Here, the grisly monkey house represents a state of mind, and an illustration of his proverb, "the man who never alters his opinion is like standing water, and breeds reptiles of the mind" (plate 19). The monkey-house appears in the "Memorable Fancy" of plate 20, where the devilishly ironic narrator shows the angel a vision of simian cannibalism, slavery, and sadistic sexuality. So nightmarish is this scene, it is worth quoting in its entirety:

Figure 10. Ludwig Krug, *The Fall of Man*, 1514. Courtesy of the Bildarchiv Preußischer Kulturbesitz, Berlin.

Figure 11. Pieter Bruegel, "Zwei Affen," 1652. Courtesy of Gemäldegalerie Berlin.

Here, said I! is your lot, in this space, if space it may be calld. Soon we saw the stable and the church, & I took him to the altar, and open'd the Bible, and lo! it was a deep pit, into which I descended driving the Angel before me, soon we saw seven houses of brick, one we enterd: in it were a number of monkeys, baboons, & all of that species, chaind by the middle, grinning and snatching at one another, but witheld by the shortness of their chains: however I saw that they sometimes grew numerous, and then the weak were caught by the strong and with a grinning aspect, first coupled with & then devourd, by plucking off first one limb and then another till the body was left a helpless trunk. this after grinning & kissing it with seeming fondness they devourd too; and here & there I saw one savourily picking the flesh off of his own tail; as the stench terribly annoyd us both we went into the mill, & I in my hand brought the skeleton of a body, which in the mill was Aristotle's Analytics.

Blake imagined the monkeys imitating the most grotesque actions of human beings, but this way of seeing is almost too terrible to acknowledge. It comes as no surprise, then, that this vision arouses the angel's anger: "thy phantasy has imposed upon me and thou oughtest to be ashamed," he says. When the narrator answers, "we impose on one another," the reader understands that Blake is certainly not advocating "imposition." On the contrary, what he champions is "opposition," in the sense of alterity, where the self fully acknowledges the identity of another. He ends this monkey-house plate with the now famous phrase, "Opposition is true Friendship."

Almost all serious Blake scholars acknowledge the repulsiveness of this monkey house. Harold Bloom says "the gruesome lewdness of Blake's vision of the theological monkey-house has not lost its shock value; it still offends orthodoxy. Swift himself could not have done better here, in the repulsive projection of an incestuous warfare of rival doctrines, ground together in the reductive mill of scholastic priestcraft," [24] while David Erdman reads the passage politically, with the monkeys as Tories "clinging to the status quo." "The implication," says Erdman, "seems to be that only those who cannot imagine progressive social change must . . . assume that human relations will be forever those of joyless slavery." [25] Yet, on a deeper level, what seems important in Blake's use of the fettered monkey motif is that it illustrates the exact opposite of another concept he develops in *The Marriage*, the act of alterity. "The most sublime act is to set another before you" (plate 7), he writes in a statement that prefigures, almost word for word, Emmanuel Levinas's definition of intimacy: "The only absolute value is the human possibility of giving the other priority over oneself." [26] The idea is that the human confrontation with another human can be a liberating, imaginative act, that is, an act of "self-annihilation," as Blake refers to it in *Milton*.[27]

In artistic traditions, the ape's slavish sin was simply part and parcel of his role as the *figura diaboli*—that is, he stood for the devil himself. The ape as *figura diaboli* (as well as degenerate man) involved the single worst sin in Christian traditions: the desire to be God.[28] The ape-devil's distinguishing quality was his ambition be acknowledged as creator. Janson tells us that "since the epithet 'ape' had been used to designate spurious pretenders and untrustworthy imitators by both early classical and early Christian writers, the devil, as the unworthy imitator *par excellence*, eventually came to be known as *simia Dei*." [29] Another source of this motif may have been African customs, where the ape was worshiped as a deity who was able to read and write. This ape-god became the ape-devil of Christianity. According to Ramona and Desmond Morris, Martin Luther used the terms "ape" and "devil" synonymously, and the church fathers called the devil an ape, an unholy fake who could do nothing original, but tried to mimic

everything God did.[30] Still, the ape-devil was a compelling figure whose energetic force and uncanny wisdom, his ability to imitate nature, made him a symbol for the artist.

The maxim "art is the ape of nature" is multifaceted, with either diabolical
or noble connotations. In classical antiquity, the imitative qualities of the ape
were so well known that the word "simia" became a synonym for "imitator."[31]
The ape-artist's most popular venue has been painting, where he has embodied
the qualities of trickster who could confuse the distinctions between truth and
lies. One of the most prominent examples of this comes from Alain of Lille,
whose Platonic decree against artists reads: "Oh, the novel miracles of painting!
What cannot have existence is made to exist! Painting, *the ape of truth*, through
play of novel artifice, converts the shadows of things themselves and turns singular lies into truth" (my emphasis).[32] In this early modern view, truth could not
exist in the human imagination, except in God's creation. Yet in the evolution of
the metaphor of the ape-artist, the ape became, in the sixteenth century, an admirable figure. For instance, the ape in Oxford scholar Robert Fludd's *Utriusque
Cosmi Historia* (1617–26) stands for knowledge as he seeks to imitate the infinite
universe. In the eighteenth century, these figures of *ars simia naturae* were used
for satirical purposes, as artists literally painted or sculpted themselves (or each
other) as apes. The German painter and engraver Joachim von Sandrart features
a painting of monkeys at work on canvases, and the Spanish painter and printmaker Francisco Goya, who worked at roughly the same time as Blake, has one
drawing of a monkey rendering a pompous ass into a beautiful horse (Figure 12).

Blake merges the ape-artist and the ape-devil in *The Marriage of Heaven
and Hell*. As artist, Blake becomes the archcreator, and thus the true creator,
with the revelatory powers of the imagination. But Blake's truth is also laced
with simian qualities of trickiness. Indeed, as Harold Bloom has noted in reference to *The Marriage*, its vocabulary is thoroughly ironic. "The specific difficulty in reading *The Marriage of Heaven and Hell*," says Bloom, lies in its "innate
trickery." It is simply difficult to "mark the limits of its irony: where does Blake
speak straight?"[33] Certainly, Blake is not shy about siding with the devil as he
develops his theory of imagination in *The Marriage*. Time and again he takes the
position of the devil, pointing out the limitations of angels who see the world
the wrong way around. Blake writes, at the very beginning of the poem, "The
reason Milton wrote in fetters when he wrote of Angels & God, and at liberty
when of Devils & Hell, is because he was a true Poet and of the Devils party
without knowing it" (plate 6). In addition, it is the "mighty Devil folded in black
clouds" who reads the marvelous "Proverbs of Hell" (plate 6).

While Blake merges the ape-artist and ape-devil in his imaginative treatise,
he also celebrates these tendencies. In doing so, Blake stood alone, because ape

Figure 12. Francisco Goya, *Los Caprichos, Plate 41*, "Ni mas ni menos," 1799. Courtesy of Pomona College, Claremont, California. Gift of Norton Simon.

lore of the classical and early modern periods, where the ape was almost never a noble figure, was at the interpretive center of the ape's connection with Africans in the developing race science of the day. Comparative anatomy was a constant theme in travel texts, and Stedman's *Narrative* is rife with attempts to place monkeys within this bizarre field of inquiry. His own descriptions that accompany Blake's engraving of the Quatos cite "Lord Munboddo" and the "Ourangoutang." "This I know," exclaims Stedman, monkeys "will never Learn to *play upon the* flute as the Ourangoutang Mention'd by *Lord Munboddo*" (329). Monboddo was one in the chain of race scientists whose real beginning was probably Linnaeus's 1758 *Systema naturae* (10th edition). Classification was the trademark of natural historians, and Linnaeus was a first rate categorizer. He called *Homo sapiens* a species, and divided them, as Peter Kitson explains, into varieties: "*ferus* (four-footed, mute and hairy); *americanus* (red, choleric, erect); *europaeus* (white, ruddy, muscular); *asiaticus* (yellow, melancholic, inflexible); *afer* (black, phlegmatic, indulgent); *monstrosus* (several deviant forms)." [34]

Among Linnaeus's predecessors and his successors, twisted debates raged about how to classify ape-kind. While such pseudoscientists thought they were trying to categorize the man of the woods, the Hottentot, the Pygmy, and the orangutan, what they really revealed was the paucity of zoological evidence in the face of a proliferation of racist myths. A prime example of this comes from Edward Tyson's 1699 *Orang-Outang, sive Homo Sylvestris: or, the Anatomy of a Pygmie compared with that of a Monkey, an Ape, and a Man*. When Tyson writes, "since in so many Parts, the Orang-Outang imitates Man," he is not referring to legend or ape lore but to the striking anatomical similarities between apes and man that could be scientifically described.[35] But for all his classification, Tyson himself remains unsure. He writes, "the Ancients were fond of making Brutes to be Men: on the contrary now, most unphilosophically, the Humour is to make Men but meer Brutes and Matter. Whereas in truth Man is part a Brute, part an Angel; and is that Link in the Creation that joyns them both together." [36]

The most startling aspect of Tyson's work, and indeed of those who followed him, is the grisly obsession with dissecting creatures for comparative anatomy. Tyson's full-page engravings of a monkey and dissected Pygmies (Figure 13), whom he describes as "Animals . . they were not a Race of Men, but Apes" led other natural historians into the same activities, notably the Dutch anatomist Pieter Camper, whose discussions of anatomy and art of 1794 boast dissections of many animals, including orangutans and elephants.[37] Through dissection, Camper provided a spooky tutorial for artists in anatomical draftsmanship. His angles also claimed to prove, as Peter Kitson notes, that as the facial angle grew wider, "one progressed from apes through to Africans, Indians, Tartars (or Calmucks) to Europeans and then to the heroic statues of classical

Greece."[38] Camper's work went on to influence British scientists like Charles White, whose *Account of the Regular Gradation in Man* (1799), also uses ape images and facial angles to establish the so-called racial supremacy of the European and thus the inferiority of the African who was closest to the ape.[39]

What did Blake learn from Stedman about the ape's place in race science? Stedman was not racist in the modern sense of the term. Many of the phrases that do appear racist now were in fact added to Stedman's original manuscript by his editor.[40] Still, Stedman was aware of ape-kind's central place in the science debates that promoted racism, but the closest he comes to any kind of a theory is his high praise of "that wonderfull chain of Gradiation, from Man to the most diminutive of the above Species [the monkey]" (144). Mostly, Stedman is a wishy-washy apologist for race science. He elides the evolutionary step between ape, orangutan, and human when he calls the Quato monkeys "that Link in the Chain of *Cercopethicaus* [old world monkeys], Which is Only divided by the *Ourangoutang*, from the Appearance of Man" (328) and then proceeds to liken Guianese monkeys to Indians. He yo-yos between identifying with the monkey and distancing himself from it, between calling Africans "monkeys" and calling them "brothers." Stedman even thinks of himself as a monkey at one point, when he writes that monkeys are "too conspicuous not to inspire me with humility, and think more of these wandering little objects, who if wisely viewed and desected, bear such general resemblance with nay little difference from myself" (144). At the same time, Stedman merges the monkey with the African, saying "does not the face, Shape, and Manner of the african Negroe whom in every respect I look on as my brother I say does this not often put us in Mind of the Wild Man of the Woods or *Orangoutang*? While on the other hand what is *this* still'd more than a large Monkey?" (144). But for all his uneasiness about categories, one striking feature of Stedman's *Narrative* is his continual speculations about the monkeys' significance. In this regard, Blake's engravings support Stedman. It is possible to see a resemblance between human and monkey in Blake's rendition of the Quatos [Figure 4], who uncannily stare out at the reader, as well as in his grim portrait of the manacled monkeys of *The Marriage*. In both cases, Blake's monkeys mock the deadly conventional aspects of human society.

Just as early nineteenth-century race scientists postulated a connection between monkeys and Africans to disenfranchise blacks, in 1988 Henry Louis Gates used this same connection to empower them, when he made famous the "signifying monkey." Gates says that "signifyin(g)" is fundamentally "black," yet there are definite parallels between his trickster figure and the various features of the monkey as it had come to be known in Blake's time. After all, the very people whom Gates uses to locate the early form of signifying—Anglo-African writers such as Ukawsaw Gronniosaw, Ottobah Cugoano, John Jea, and Olaudah

Fig. 1

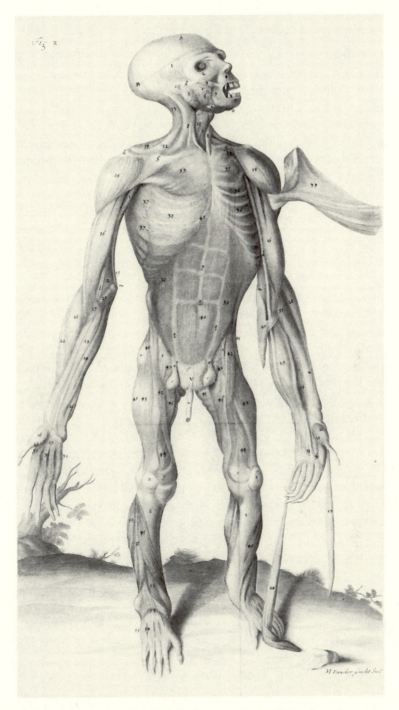

Figure 13. From Edward Tyson, *Orang-Outang, sive Homo Sylvestris: or, the Anatomy of a Pygmie Compared with that of a Monkey, an Ape, and a Man*, 1699. By permission of the Syndics of Cambridge University Library.

Equiano—lived and wrote in the London underclass at the same time as Blake, and like him, their texts are full of inversions, reversals, and trickery.[41] According to Gates, the signifying monkey centers on the Yoruba god Esu, whose role as interpreter "survived the middle passage accompanied by both the Monkey and the tree in which monkeys lived."[42] A small figure of dark skin and a large erect penis, Esu/the monkey underwent a merging and a transformation in the Middle Passage, and then reappeared in late-eighteenth-century Britain and America. In the Anglo-African and African-American writing Gates has studied, the signifying monkey came to represent "individuality, satire, parody, irony, magic, indeterminacy, open-endedness, ambiguity, sexuality, chance, uncertainty, disruption and reconciliation, betrayal and loyalty, closure and disclosure, encasement and rupture."[43] But true to the nature of the monkey, his meaning always eludes categorization. If anything, he is a "classic figure of mediation and of the unity of opposed forces."[44]

To illustrate this, in the course of his book Gates rehearses the stories told about the signifying monkey, and of these stories, one in particular is quite revealing. The story runs as follows: two friends worked in a field side by side, priding themselves that they agreed on everything. Meanwhile, Esu made a "cloth cap," whose "right side was black, the left side was white," and rode his horse between the two men. Afterward, both commented on the stranger. But when they came to describe him, one said he was white, the other, black. While the two were fighting, Esu mediated, revealing his cloth cap.[45]

In this tale, Esu discloses what Blake calls in *Visions* "atmospheres unknown," a place where reality never ceases to transform those elements that seem most fixed (4:18). And the trickster disrupts social order not for sheer pleasure, although this is an important element, but to prove that human interpretation is multiplex. Even if Blake was not explicitly aware of the signifying of black writers Gronniosaw, Cugoano, Jea, and Equiano, he certainly engraves this figure in his rendition of Gay's *Fables*, where "a flippant monkey, spruce and smart, / Hard by, profess'd the dappar art" of mocking human folly.[46]

The multiple meanings of the monkey as Blake knew him also signify within the Stedman engravings. The engravings, that is, enact mock-mimicry, become places where the social order can see itself. The transforming activity of the trickster is invincibly bound up with aesthetic irony of the kind Blake knew well. And irony is the primary vehicle for realizing life's doubleness. This kind of irony, says Henry Louis Gates, is the divine mission of the signifying monkey, who is a revealer of riddles, a double-dealer, and the source of endless retelling of stories.[47] For the trickster Blake, irony's endless possibility for transformation becomes his way to mediate between two worlds, to bring slavery home through a series of engravings, to let the eye see more than the heart knows.

III

Mockery and mimicry are typical subversive behaviors, but they can also be used by authority figures as a way to control people. In 1984, Homi K. Bhabha wrote an influential essay explaining how colonial discourse tried to use mimicry as a regulating device. In "Of Mimicry and Man: The Ambivalence of Colonial Discourse," Bhabha examines colonial writers during Blake's lifetime, looking specifically at how they presented the other as a limited or "partial" being, one who was, in Bhabha's vocabulary "almost the same, *but not quite.*" [48] The "almost" quality of colonial representation is what Bhabha also designates "the *ambivalence* of mimicry." This ambivalence gives rise to some interesting effects. Because mimicry is a doubling, but also a doubling that is not quite the same, mimicry cannot fully represent the other nor the stereotypes it uses to fix its subject. "Mimicry," writes Bhabha, "does not merely destroy narcissistic authority through the repetitious slippage of difference and desire. It is a process of the *fixation* of the colonial as a form of cross-classificatory, discriminatory knowledge in the defiles of an interdictory discourse, and therefore necessarily raises the question of the *authorization* of colonial representations." [49] For Bhabha, the slippages of mimicry both fix subjects and produce forms of authority that negate the civilizing mission of such discourse. Bhabha's quintessential instance of this occurs in Edward Long's glaringly racist *History of Jamaica* of 1774, where he claims, "Ludicrous as the opinion may seem I do not think that an orangutang husband would be any dishounour to a Hottentot female." [50]

The kind of mimicry Homi Bhabha describes bleeds through colonial texts by authors writing at the same time as Blake, like William Beckford's 1790 *Descriptive Account of the Island of Jamaica.* Beckford fixes slave labor and sugar cultivation in a place of emotional remove from the suffering and pain of slaves, with no ironic undercurrent of opposition. Slaves at work, he says,

sometimes throw themselves into picturesque and various attitudes; and as the different clumps of vegetation begin to fall around them, the light is gradually induced, and shines in playful reflections upon their naked bodies and their clothes; and which oppositions of black and white make a very singular, and very far from unpleasing appearance. Their different instruments of husbandry, particularly their gleaming hoes, when uplifted to the sun, and which, particularly when they are digging cane-holes, they frequently raise all together, and as exact time as can be observed, in a well-conducted orchestra, in the bowing of the fiddles, occasion the light to break in momentary flashes around them.[51]

In Bhabha's view, though someone like Beckford tries to describe slaves in the language of the picturesque, African difference inevitably escapes the sharp spear of aesthetic idealism.

Still, Beckford's mimicry of the colonial body, his desire to slot it into British colonial categories of sameness, had its visible effects on other writers. When Amelia Opie, a friend of Mary Wollstonecraft, wrote in her children's poem *The Black Man's Lament; or, How to Make Sugar* (1826) of the sugar cane as a "beauteous plan," she took her cue from Beckford. In a footnote Opie explains, "a field of canes, when standing in the month of November, when it is in arrow or full blossom, (says Beckford, in his descriptive account of the Island of Jamaica,) is one of the most beautiful productions that pen or pencil can possibly describe," and Opie's poem, because it was directed at children, was accompanied by an engraving of similar colonial mimicry.[52] But engravings, even more than print, as Blake must have known, make the ambivalence of mimicry startlingly clear.

While mimicry of the kind used by Beckford and then Opie was certainly an element of colonial representations, Blake's mimicry falls into another category altogether. His engravings produce a "mock-mimicry," the term Stedman bestowed on the monkeys of Guiana. Unlike Bhabha's notion of "mimicry," mock-mimicry turns self-imposed authority inside out. For instance, despite all his confusion over the status of monkeys in race science, Stedman returns repeatedly to their central quality, trickery and disruption, and in this way he pinpoints the central feature of all ape lore from Aristotle to Henry Louis Gates. "Monkeys," says Stedman, "are often Mischievous near the Plantations where they Commit depredations on the Sugar Canes &c yet of which I but one time have been a Witness" (144). Stedman was not the first to bring monkeys, mock-mimicry, and slave plantations before the British reading public. Indeed, only ten years earlier, the poet James Grainger had written in his highly publicized poem *The Sugar Cane* of these destructive, predatory monkeys. On the "upland sugar-groves," the "monkey-nation preys," like harlequin criminals "in silent parties, they descend by night, / And posting watchful sentinels, to warn / When hostile steps approach; with gambols they / Pour o'er the cane-grove."[53]

Blake — like a monkey among the sugarcane — mocks the mimicry he was hired to produce as commercial engraver for Stedman, and ultimately, for Joseph Johnson, and therefore compels readers of Stedman, and viewers of the engravings, into an alterity they might otherwise resist. We are brought close to our subject by a series of double takes. Sometimes Blake does this by visually matching two images, sometimes by creating a tension between Stedman's text and his image, and sometimes by inscribing contradictory visual information within one image.

Two of the first plates that appear in the *Narrative* are especially striking in this regard. "A Coromantyn Free Negro, or Ranger, armed" (Figure 14) illustrates a group of manumitted slaves whom Stedman calls "Stout Strapping able young fellows, picked from the different Plantations" as if they were nothing more than

Figure 14. Blake, "A Coromantyn Free Negro, or Ranger, armed." By permission of the Syndics of Cambridge University Library.

crops ready to be harvested for British consumption (82). This is ironic insofar as this plate is the flip side of "A private Marine of Col. Fourgeoud's Corps"
(Figure 15). Whether these twin plates are supposed to champion difference or
similarity is open to debate, and, in some sense, that is the point. Certainly, by
placing them side by side, the natural tendency is to look at their startling similarities and disturbing differences. Both figures carry guns and wear headgear
decorated with branches. The marine is flanked with the signs of civilization: a
fortress and a ship; while the ranger is supported by natural strength: bushy trees
and palms. Both are crisscrossed with packs, but the Marine, padded with equip-
ment, booted instead of barefoot, appears straitjacketed and weighed-down.
The ranger, on the other hand, travels light, not needing shoulder pads because
of his natural muscles. The differences are thus clear—black skin, nakedness, and
casual readiness contrast with paleness, the constraints of clothing, and military
stiffness. Since it is impossible to tell which Blake engraved first, which one he
may have intended to be philosophically prior, the only way to make sense of
the two is to see them as responding to and then resisting one another. In any
case, the viewer is thrown into an interpretive doubleness. How are we to make
sense of the sameness and the difference?

Such interlocking relationships and unanswerable questions among the engravings, in fact, emphasize the same points Blake made in the poetry he produced at the time. While *The Marriage of Heaven and Hell* is important in any
assessment of Blake's attitude toward the engravings, it is *The Visions of the
Daughters of Albion* that offers the best clues about how Blake defined perception, seeing, and visual trickery. This may seem like an obvious point, but critics
of *Visions*, with the exception of Steven Vine,[54] have not always noticed this. The
poem, proper, begins in bondage, with the line "ENSLAV'D, the Daughters of
Albion weep," while the opening plate introduces the characters: Oothoon, the
enslaved and sexually violated slave, who in her captivity is somehow able to cry
"Love! Love! Love! happy happy Love! free as the mountain wind!" (7:16); Bromion, the cruel slave master who boasts, "Stampt with my signet are the swarthy
children of the sun: / They are obedient, they resist not, they obey the scourge: /
Their daughters worship terrors and obey the violent" (1:21–23); and Theotormon, the downtrodden slave, who "with secret tears; beneath him sound like
waves on a desart shore / The voice of slaves beneath and sun, and children
bought with money" (2:7–8). For this poem, Blake engraved what is now considered one of the most visually demanding of all his illuminated books: Bromion
and Oothoon manacled together, back to back, with Theotormon sitting above
them, his head buckled between his arms and legs (Figure 16). Although part of
the interpretive puzzle involves defining exactly what Theotormon represents (a
white liberal who despairs over ever getting slavery abolished or an abject slave

Figure 15. Blake, "A private Marine of Col. Fourgeoud's Corps." By permission of the Syndics of Cambridge University Library.

Figure 16. Blake, frontispiece, *Visions of the Daughters of Albion*, 1793 (copy D). Courtesy of the Houghton Library, Harvard University.

who is too abused to even rebel), the critical reception of the poem centers on what Blake had in mind by making Oothoon struggle for freedom, and whether or not he allows her to achieve it.[55] David Erdman, in a classic study, actually roots the poem in Stedman's text; it represents Stedman's inability to free his black slave and wife, Joanna, and also allegorizes the impotence of white abolitionists to end the slave trade in Britain's Parliament.[56] On opposite poles are critics like Susan Fox, who upbraids Blake for creating Oothoon as the ultimate female victim, and Nancy Goslee, who celebrates Blake's Oothoon as an active figure of "multivalent liberty opposed to all sorts of slavery." [57]

While Theotormon's exact identity and Oothoon's eventual liberation are up for debate, what Blake does make clear in the poem is the unstable and manifold nature of perception. *How* a person sees has everything to do with *what* he or she sees. The nature of perception first erupts through the character of Oothoon, who laments, "They told me that the night & day were all that I could see; / They told me that I had five senses to inclose me up," but she is not as perceptually destitute as Theotormon, to whom "the night and morn / Are both alike: a night of sighs, a morning of fresh tears" (2:30–31, 37–38). Still, Oothoon never quits questioning the nature of perception, sense, and how a person uses his or her perception relationally. Oothoon and the Daughters of Albion echo one another with questions like:

How can the giver of gifts experience the delights of the merchant?
How the industrious citizen the pains of the husbandman.
How different far the fat fed hireling with hollow drum;
Who buys whole corn fields into wastes, and signs upon the heath:
How different their eye and ear! how different the world to them! (5:12–16)

Clearly Blake is taking up an idea he had toyed with in *The Marriage*, "a fool sees not the same tree that a wise man sees" ("Proverbs of Hell," 8). Yet with this list of roles—gift-giver, merchant, industrious citizen, husbandman, fat fed hireling—he is saying something more. He underscores that people in industrial Britain saw and heard the world in terms of their occupations. A poet and artist, presumably, would see the world differently from a retired captain, a Blake different from a Stedman, and this division in consciousness is at the heart of the trickery that exists between Stedman's text and Blake's engravings. A person's occupation, according to Oothoon, also supplies him or her an ethics in relation to others. In fact, Oothoon speaks a familiar Blakean idea when she says, "With what sense does the parson claim the labour of the farmer?" or what makes one person think another owes him something for nothing? (5:17).

Oothoon's questions, despite their unanswerable quality, remain straightforward compared to Bromion's. In fact, it seems odd that Blake would place in the mouth of the slaveholder questions that hit the infinite depths of perception:

Thou knowest that the ancient trees seen by thine eyes have fruit;
But knowest thou that trees and fruits flourish upon the earth
To gratify senses unknown? trees beasts and birds unknown:
Unknown, not unperceivd, spread in the infinite microscope,
In places yet unvisited by the voyager. and in worlds
Over another kind of seas, and in atmospheres unknown (4:13–18)

Still, whether the voice is that of the slave master, the resistant slave, or the resigned slave, there is a constant shift away from what is known to what is seen, as if to reinforce the opening lines that the "eye sees more than the heart knows," an insistent urging to follow the eye, not the heart. *Visions*, as the plural of single "vision," makes crystal clear that Blake is interested in multiple ways of seeing.

But how much about the nature of perception could Blake have thrown into the Stedman engravings? This question has raised a surprising amount of critical speculation, but I will say at the outset that I read the Stedman plates as being primarily a statement of Blake's artistic purpose. Although the relationship between Stedman's text, his original watercolors, which are not extant, and Blake's final engravings poses a complex issue of representation, there is quite a bit of evidence to suggest that Blake took extraordinary liberties. To begin with, it is by now widely acknowledged that Blake often put his own imaginative spin on his commercial engravings. G.E. Bentley Jr. argues that "engraving is always a work of translation in which the graphic conventions are different from those of the artist with a brush or pencil,"[58] while Robert Essick shows how Blake often "overstep[ped] the usual barriers between designer and engraver," stamping his own vision onto his commercial works. Essick has made a fascinating study of this, demonstrating that in Blake's representation of a native family of New South Wales from a drawing to a full-fledged engraving, he not only "altered the disposition of the figures, but he has transformed poor and naked aborigines into noble savages."[59]

Although the preliminary drawings Blake used for Stedman's *Narrative* have not survived, a look at one Stedman watercolor engraved by J. Barlow indicates that Blake, too, would have had plenty of opportunity to depict the figures in his own way. Barlow's "Manner of Sleeping &c. in the Forest" replaces Stedman's visual prolixity with a carefully placed composition (Figures 17 and 18).[60] Unfortunately, in turning Stedman's loose watercolor into an symbolically explicit engraving, Barlow also trades fluidity for stiffness. This is due, in part, to the constraints of the engraving process itself, but some of it is Barlow's interpretation of the scene. This particular translation proves that Barlow, Blake, and

Figure 17. Stedman, watercolor, 1776. Courtesy of the James Ford Bell Library, University of Minnesota.

Manner of Sleeping &c. in the Forest.

Rural Retreat—The Cottage—

Figure 18. J. Barlow, engravings for Stedman's *Narrative*, 1791. Courtesy of the James Ford Bell Library, University of Minnesota.

other engravers of the *Narrative* did impose their interpretive visions on Stedman's illustrations. Quite obviously, Barlow took the liberty to rearrange figures, change the layout from vertical to horizontal, and add any number of specific minutiae—a sword above Stedman's bunk, foliage, boxes under the hammock—to the picture.[61] In the watercolors Blake had in his possession, one can only assume that he also had the artistic freedom to turn Stedman's dark ink spots into background details and to add expression to the African faces.

Such liberty on the part of the engraver was not unusual, and this was especially true of Blake. In his execution of commercial engravings for Johann Kaspar Lavater's *Aphorisms* (1788), Erasmus Darwin's *Botanic Garden* (1791), and Henry Fuseli's *Lectures on Painting* (1801), he also had, according to Essick, "an unusual amount of responsibility for the completion of the design, not merely its translation to copper, even if we allow for a good deal of consultation between the two friends. The extant preliminaries, two of which remained in Blake's possession for many years, suggest that Fuseli delivered little more than rough sketches."[62] Because Blake's Stedman drawings were engraved for Joseph Johnson, because Johnson seems to have trusted Blake immensely in his trade, and because Blake and Stedman became good friends during the process, it is also possible that Blake had another kind of liberty. He may have handpicked the sixteen engravings he would execute out of the eighty supplied by Stedman.[63] It seems so, when one considers that out of Stedman's eighty, only twenty-three contain human subjects. Of those twenty-three human subjects, Blake engraved thirteen, or nearly two-thirds.[64]

IV

The act of seeing and being seen shaped the Romantic self.[65] When Blake declared "the eye sees more than the heart knows," he was asking viewers to tap into the transformative potential of interpretive doubleness, to bring their subject close up by disentangling themselves from the self-centered heart. One of the ways Blake achieved this, on a most basic level, was to fashion engravings that directly contradicted Stedman's text. Where Stedman sees lack, Blake sees plenty; where Stedman sees living death, Blake sees spirited energy. The engraving "Group of Negros, as imported to be sold for Slaves" (Figure 19) manages to reveal this on a biblical scale.[66] Stedman describes these figures as "a set of living automatons, such a resurrection of Skin and bones, as justly put me in mind of the last trumpet; seeming that moment to be rose from the grave, or deserted from the Surgeons Hall at the old Bailey—and of which no better description can be given than by comparing them to walking Skeletons covered

Figure 19. Blake, "Group of Negros, as imported to be sold for Slaves." By permission of the Syndics of Cambridge University Library.

over with a piece of tanned leather" (166). But Blake's engraving presents a very different picture. The Africans are not skeletons, but healthy and robust, even if they are driven. Blake, in fact, has engravings of skeletons in "A Negro hung alive by the Ribs to a Gallows" (Figure 20) and "The Sculls of Lieut. Leppar & Six of his Men" (Figure 21) to which these imported Negroes bear no resemblance. They certainly are no less emaciated than the sailor with the bamboo rod, who himself is reminiscent of the child-figures from the *Songs of Innocence and Experience*. One of the women in the center back looks pregnant, while the woman next to her is strong enough to carry a chubby child on her back. Stedman adds prophetic weight to the "Group of Negros" engraving by way of Ezekiel 37:2–3: "And the Lord caused me to pass by them round about and behold there were many in the open valley and lo they were very dry—And he said unto me Son of Man can these bones live? And I answered O Lord God thou knowest" (166–67). But Blake's reading of Ezekiel in *The Marriage* overturns this kind of biblical support: "I then asked Ezekiel. why he eat dung, & lay so long on his right & left side? He answerd, the desire of raising other men into a perception of the infinite" (plate 13). As archprophet, Blake insists that these figures not only live in full flesh, but they will, as Stedman's text later testifies, revolt. In fact, Blake's cagey contradiction of this scene owes part of its meaning to the ideology Stedman hitches it to. Stedman uses this scene to actually justify slavery. "The alwise Creator has ordered *war*," he says, "since like throughout all the other links of the Creation—as one fish lives upon another, Man would eat Man, and prey upon his brother without it" (169). By visually refuting Stedman's initial textual claim about "living automatons," Blake solves the problem of having to execute the "Group of Negros" engraving to support divinely sanctioned slavery.

Sometimes Blake creates a disparity between text and image, and sometimes between the smaller parts of the image itself. There are moments, in all of the Blake engravings, when the eye moves from a central figure to the business behind and below it. The conflict between the central image and the surrounding visual clues is especially jolting in the best orchestrated engravings, where the background is a constant source of mockery and disruption. Everything we *see* in "Family of Negro Slaves from Loango" (Figure 22), for instance, goes against what we are supposed to *know* about them. "In the first place," writes Stedman, "I Will introduce a Negro Family in that State of Tranquil Hapiness to Which they are all entitled When they are Well treated by their Owners" (534). Stedman goes on to say "Under Such a Mild Government no Negroes work is more than a Healthy Exercise, which ends with the Setting sun, Viz at 6. O'Clock & When the Rest of the time is his Own, Which he employs in Hunting, And Fishing" (534). If we take Stedman's text literally, we assume that this family is on its own time. But Stedman's text and Blake's images revolt against one another. Stedman tells

Figure 20. Blake, "A Negro hung alive by the Ribs to a Gallows." By permission of the Syndics of Cambridge University Library.

Figure 21. Blake, "The Sculls of Lieut. Leppar and Six of his Men." By permission of the Syndics of Cambridge University Library.

Figure 22. Blake, "Family of Negro Slaves from Loango." By permission of the Syndics of Cambridge University Library.

readers that the slaves are a picture of industry, productivity and fertility, and indeed they immediately call up images of Christ's feeding of the five thousand with loaves and fishes. But the eye sees something more: true to the nature of the trickster, Blake forces readers into an interpretive quandary where boundaries between knowledge and perception break down. In this image, we see far in the background two dark figures, one with a stick. It is difficult to tell whether these slaves are working, or whether one is hitting the other, as in "The Execution of Breaking on the Rack" (Figure 23), a few pages later in the narrative. In fact, the expressions on the faces of the "Family of Negro Slaves" do not differ at all from the expressions on the faces of the execution scene, as if Blake were saying that in these two extremes of slave happiness and slave horror (both of them imposed by white culture), how are we to believe either one? The "Family of Negro Slaves" emphasizes this even further with the body of a fish, hung from the gills, mouth open, caught with a hook, so reminiscent of the single most disturbing engraving in the book, "A Negro hung alive by the Ribs to a Gallows" (Figure 20). Thus, Blake overturns the picture of the "Pleasantly Situated Negro family" with two distinct images that refer to the more horrifying engravings in the series.

Blake had long been interested in the relationship between text and image and, more often than not, he set the two at odds. Most famously, the "fearful symmetry" of his textual "Tyger" is completely dismantled by the cartoonish visual he provided in *Songs of Experience*. The same kind of impulse is behind the Stedman engravings, and in the "Family of Negro Slaves from Loango," he plays an even more startling trick with text and image. Stedman tells readers that the Loango man's body bears Stedman's own initials — "the letters J.G.S. being the enitials of my name, And Supposed to be the Cypher by which each master knows his Property" (534). In the engraving, however, these are initials barely discernible on the upper left corner of the Loango man's breast. If the reader were not explicitly told by Stedman they exist, it would be difficult even to see them. What the eye does see are the "marks on the man's Body," marks that have nothing to do with white ownership. These five-dot patterns brand the man as a member of the *Loango Nation*. Through the body and through the eye, Blake identifies the slave not as a white possession, not as a written symbol of white culture, but as a self-possessed subject with his own nationality.

V

In many of the Stedman engravings, Blake was not simply interested in where the viewing eye was sent. The compositional novelty of many of these images lies

Figure 23. Blake, "The Execution of Breaking on the Rack." By permission of the Syndics of Cambridge University Library.

in the way the subject looks out at the viewer. In this sense, no other artist of this period pictured Africans and slaves quite as Blake did. In his "Surinam Planter in his Morning Dress" (Figure 24) "Europe Supported by Africa and America," and "March thro' a swamp," double vision comes through seeing what the African or slave sees. "A Surinam Planter in his Morning Dress" seems a straightforward depiction of the indifferent mastery to which Stedman attributes the rebellion in the first place. In fact, the planter's parted legs suggest the kind of brutal sexuality motivating him. The eye moves repulsively from the planter to the female slave, naked from the waist up, pouring him a dram, which presumably he is going to drink. The viewer looks where she looks, back at the planter. But why she looks at him, rather than at the drink she pours, is more of a mystery. She is no doubt second guessing his actions, but the way Blake depicts her casual movement forward, her raised foot about to glide her surreptitiously to the rigid planter, suggests she also has the kind of self-possession necessary to carry out any one of the many forms of slave revolt that Stedman enumerates. One of these was the widespread practice among slaves of poisoning, especially household slaves poisoning the drinks of masters.[67] Stedman peppers his text with references to poisoning, but slaves' poisoning of masters' drinks was a central fear in both abolitionist poetry and travel writing from 1790 onward.[68] Though it is impossible to claim the household slave in this engraving is poisoning the planter, Blake clearly describes her in active, not passive, terms. He thus disrupts the mastery of the planter with the self-mastery of the slave.

Self-possession finds its fullest expression in Blake's most famous engraving of the series, "Europe Supported by Africa & America" [Figure 2]. This one has received more critical attention than the rest put together. David Erdman and Anne Mellor have observed that though a cord unites the three sisterly continents, it is Europe being supported. This, according to Steven Vine, is the central irony of the image. Blake grounds this Enlightenment fantasy in the realities of slavery, thus undermining Stedman's accompanying description:[69] "Going now to take my last Leave of *Surinam* after all the Horrors & Cruelties with which I must have hurt both the Eye & the heart of the Feeling reader, I will Close the Scene with an Emblematical picture of *Europe* Supported by *Africa* & *America* Accompanied by an Ardent Wish that in the friendly manner as they are Represented they may henceforth & to all Eternity be the Prop of each other; I might have included *Asia* but this I omitted as having not Connection with the Present Narrative—we All only differ in the Colour but we are Certainly Created by the same hand & After the Same Mould" (618). It has thus been difficult for Blake critics to decide if, in this engraving, he is supporting Stedman's text or resisting it. This is because Blake's Stedman engravings are constantly engaged in avert-

Figure 24. Blake, "A Surinam Planter in his Morning Dress." By permission of the Syndics of Cambridge University Library.

ing the viewing eye from what it conventionally knows. It is tempting, that is, to read these figures symbolically, as big ideas — it is even Blakean to do so. After all, he composed poems called *Europe* and *America* during this time. But it is also Blakean to look from abstractions, in which women represent political bodies, to the small, unnoticed details crawling through his images. Thel learns from a clod of clay, the speaker in *Songs of Experience* from a mere fly. By this same principle, viewers are drawn to what is almost too insignificant in this engraving: the rope that binds and unites the figures.[70]

The hand-colored engraving makes this verdant rope the center piece of the image and thus makes stunningly clear that in the context of Stedman's narrative, the rope is a "nebee," an intriguing growth of the Guianese trees, both powerful and poisonous. Stedman explains, "The *nebees* are a kind of ligneous ropes of all Sizes, both as to length and thickness that grow in the Woods and which climb up alongst the trees in all directions, and are so plentiful and wonderfully dispersed that . . . they make the forest appear like a large fleet at anchor, killing many of the trees by mere Compression, and entwining themselves with each other to the thickness of a Cable of a Ship." They hang down from the branches, "take root and reassend." "Sometimes the thin nebees are so closely interwoven, that they have the appearance of fishing nets . . . these nebees are exceedingly tough, and may be used for mooring large vessels to the Shore — Having only added that some of them are poisonous" (192). If nebees are used as Stedman's ship cables, however, they are also the delicate ropes that support the "The Mecoo & Kishee Kishee Monkeys" (Figure 3), where they drape through the engraving, like strings of pearls, but tough enough to give the monkeys places to jump from. They are therefore liberatory in nature. As a rope to bind the three continents (in "Europe supported by Africa & America"), then, the nebee is a yoke of contradiction at once strong, liberatory, and poisonous, providing natural mobility for untamed monkeys and calculated mooring for civilized ships.

If the nebee is a place for Blakean correspondences and contraries, no place is it more sinister and beneficent than in "March thro' a swamp or Marsh in Terra-firma" (Figure 25). Compared with Blake's other engravings, the sky and trees in this image are more heavily crosshatched, throwing a dark pall over the entire scene. It is as if everything were weighted down, from the dark figure in the back carrying the basket, to the men with their rifles, to the trees, the sky, and the water itself. The small water reeds in the foreground even bend under the weight of the engraving. It is ironic, then, that through the massive density of this plate Blake describes four central white men, in a kind of pattern, wading through a swamp. The only figure who has escaped this linear trap is a black guide, in the foreground, left, leading the way. But so deliberate is his gaze upward, to the branches of the tree, that the viewing eye is hard-pressed to stay

Figure 25. Blake, "March thro' a swamp or Marsh in Terra-firma." By permission of the Syndics of Cambridge University Library.

with the white men in the swamp. For the eye sees what the black guide sees, that the palms towering overhead hold the bodies of black men with guns. Indeed, Stedman himself seems as responsible as Blake is for this visual diversion. The drawing, says Stedman, "Represents *Col: Fourgeoud* Preceded by a negro Slave as a Guide, to give Notice when the watter is too Deep, And followed by some of his Officers and Private Marines, Wading through the Marsh in a heavy shower of Rayn till Above Their Middles, and Carrying their Ammonition & their Accoutrements Above their Heads as they Can, to Prevent them from Dragging through the Swamp While in the Offing may be seen how the Slaves Carry the Burdens, And in What manner sometimes the rebel Negroes fire on the Troops, out of the Palm trees & And which Situation of Marching is Certainly the most Dangerous in Surinam." (402).[71] For Blake, who returned again and again in his illustrations and his poetry to the liberatory spirit of resistance, this engraving must have been especially satisfying. The revolted Africans, like the monkeys, hang high in the trees, disrupting the work of white military men, while the black guide smirks in the foreground, leading the soldiers deeper into the marsh.

VI

As a commercial engraver, Blake toiled under the yoke of subjection. It is well known that he felt a nagging sense of alienation from the British artistic community. In 1803, while in Sussex, he tellingly commented how imitation, that is, engraving other people's designs, was especially limiting for a man of his creative energies: "My unhappiness has arisen from a source which if explord too narrowly might hurt my pecuniary circumstances. As my dependence is on Engraving . . . I find on all hands great objections to my doing anything but the meer drudgery of business & intimations that if I do not confine myself to . . . I shall not live."[72] It is easy to see how he took this personal disenfranchisement to a symbolic level in much of his poetry of this time. He figures it on an epic scale in the trilogy *Europe*, *America*, and *Song of Los*, which can be read as a connected history of subjection and rebellion on both personal and universal scales. Certainly, the illustrations he did for his poetry during this time crystallize this theme: what one is struck with most emphatically in *Visions*, *The Marriage*, and *Songs of Innocence and Experience*, and what makes this all the more important for interpreting the Stedman engravings, is how often his subject is subjection. Theotormon and Oothoon's enslavement is one version of the chained monkeys in *The Marriage*, but even these seem to be part of the human condition. Who can forget Blake's "bound and weary" child, leaping into the "dangerous world," "struggling in" his father's hands, and "striving against" his "swadling bands" ("Infant Sorrow," 7, 2, 5, 6, from *The Songs of Experience*). Similarly, in the Stedman engravings, we are forced to acknowledge each subject's precarious subjectivity: even the Europeans look brutally seized, not artistically posed.

The unnerving quality of the engravings is their balance between subjectivity and subjection, between humanity and violence, and perhaps no engraver in England at the time but Blake could hold these contradictory themes together. This task becomes extremely difficult in the most offensive engravings, "A Negro hung alive by the Ribs to a Gallows" [Figure 20] and "Flagellation of a Female Samboe Slave" [Figure 26]. Here, Blake depicts the central figure's pain in such unbearable terms that the viewer must look away to the incidental detail surrounding the image, but in Blake there are no detached perspectives. What little reprieve there is from the sheer physical pain of the "Negro hung alive by the Ribs" is found in the bones and skulls scattered at his feet, visually underlining what Stedman's text says outright: the book is literally filled with skulls. And like some mad scientist, Blake uses these skulls to emphasize the mutual violence of the slave system. His engraving of "The Sculls of Lieut Leppar & Six of his Men" [Figure 21] shows heads that are obviously those of Europeans. Stedman states that the sergeant who found them "Came to me Declaring that the Sight of the Sculls &c. had made him terribly Sick" (404). Blake uses this engraving as an ironic border for the "Negro hung alive by the Ribs." It is as if the edge of "A Negro hung alive by the Ribs" begins at the border of "The Sculls of Lieut. Leppar," so that, as in the correspondence between the "Negro Ranger" and the white "Marine," the engravings signify upon one another in mutual violence and subjection.

Along with skulls, Stedman's text is full of slaves being tortured and killed for arbitrary reasons, cases where the punishment is extraordinarily disproportionate to the crime, and scenes where Stedman himself claims to feel no guilt or moral responsibility. Nowhere is this more evident than in the "Negro hung alive by the Ribs." A man tells Stedman the story: "Not long ago . . . , I saw a black man hang'd alive by the ribs, between which with a knife was first made an incision, and then clinch'd an Iron hook with a Chain — in this manner he kept living three days hanging with his head and feet downwards and catching with his tongue the drops of water, it being the rainy season" (103). And then the man says, "Shortly after which he was knocked in the head by the More Comiserating Sentry who stood over him — with the butt end of his Musquet." The skull and bones on the ground may imply this slave's grim future, but in fact the viewer does not know if the skull is European or African, or even if it is human because, strangely enough, the bones next to it are more simian than human: the hand, at least, is a monkey's by Stedman's definition of it as having "only 4 Fingers, without a Thumb on its hands, or fore feet" (328).

The fragmented, skeletal hand of a monkey highlights the way Stedman staggers between his extreme violence against monkeys and his intense identification with them. One of the most personally intense scenes in the *Narrative* involves Stedman's encounter not with a rebel Negro, but with a monkey. He sees a monkey mocking him from the other side of a river. At first Stedman and the monkey sense an immediate camaraderie: he "examined me with attention and the greatest Marks of Curiosity, no doubt taking me for a Giant of his own Species." But no sooner is there an identification, than the monkey falls into mimicry and mockery; he "shewed his teeth perhaps by way of laughing— chattered prodigiously—and kept dancing and shaking off the bough on which he rested with incredible strength and velocity" (141). Spooked by this imitative mockery, Stedman performs a dark arbitrary murder, reminiscent of the violence enacted against the "Negro hung alive by the Ribs" and foreshadowing that of the ancient mariner. Stedman shoots the monkey for no other reason than because he can, yet he knows immediately that he has violated an ethical relationship because he acknowledges that he is not simply killing an animal but murdering it:

The Miserable Animal was not dead but mortally Wounded, thus taking his Tail in both my Hands to end his torment, I swong him round and knock'd his head against the Sides of the Canoo with such a force, that I was covered all over with blood and brains; but the Poor thing still continued alive, and looking at me in the most Pitiful manner that can be conceived, I knew no other Means to end this *Murder* than by holding him under Water till he was drown'd, while my heart felt Seek on his account. (141, my emphasis)

If Stedman's heart felt "seek," it was because the monkey's "dying little Eyes still Continued to follow me with seeming reproach till their light gradually forsook them and the wretched Creature expired" (141). This acute guilt foregrounds similar acts of racial violence enacted by white plantation owners. In fact, the monkey accuses Stedman of the same kinds of crimes Stedman performs against the revolted Negroes, but for which Stedman seems to feel no guilt whatsoever. For instance, the engraving by Francesco Bartolozzi for the *Narrative*'s frontispiece shows Stedman—gun in hand—towering over a black man who lies prostrate on the ground, and like the monkey, with a "mortal wound" in his side. The original inscription for the engraving read: *My hands are guilty, but my heart is free.*[73] Like Stedman's encounter with the monkey, this brings to startling clarity the arbitrariness of violence against Africans.

The same is true of the obvious and grisly correspondences between the "Flagellation of a Female Samboe Slave" (Figure 26) and "The skinning of the Aboma Snake, shot by Cap. Stedman" (Figure 27). By visually pairing these two engravings, Blake enacts a sharp indictment of Stedman himself. Of the

Figure 26. Blake, "Flagellation of a Female Samboe Slave." By permission of the Syndics of Cambridge University Library.

Figure 27. Blake, "The skinning of the Aboma Snake, shot by Cap. Stedman." By permission of the Syndics of Cambridge University Library.

female slave, Stedman explains the absolute absurdity of the punishment: "On my having enquired since for the cause of such barbarity, I was too Credibly informed, that her only Crime had consisted in her firmly refusing to submit to the loathsome Embraces of her despicable Executioner, which his Jealousy having Construed to Disobedience, she was thus Skinned alive" (266). The Aboma snake, like the woman, is skinned alive, for no other reason than that he is a snake. Cruelty here is completely arbitrary. And in both, a Stedman-like figure stands below, in bare feet, pointing up at the captured victim.[74]

Blake's Stedman engravings are more visually demanding than the engravings of any other travel narrative of the day. Further, the images had to be some of the most epically disturbing ones Blake himself would ever design, even in the context of his later prophetic work, and there is a kind of courageousness present here, a desire to bring the full horror of slavery to the British eye, to bring the self face-to-face and into responsible proximity with the other. For Blake was intensely interested in the subjectivity, and intersubjectivity, of all creatures. "For everything that lives is holy," he repeated in *The Marriage* and *America*. Such an approach to relationships was obviously not the one taken by the British and Dutch in Guiana, and the engravings tortuously bear this out. Blake must have taken pleasure, then, in making the most ideologically free figure in the *Narrative* — "The celebrated Graman Quacy" (Figure 28) — a vessel of monkey-like mockery. We are told by Stedman that this man is "one of the most Extraordinary Black men in Surinam and Perhaps in the World" (581–82). "By his insinnuating temper and industry this negro not only Obtained his Freedom from a State of Slavery . . . but by his Wonderful artifice & ingenuity has found the means of Acquiring a verry Competant Subsistance — For instance having got the name of a *Loocoman*, or *Sorcerer* among the vulgar Slaves, no Crime of any Consequence is Committed at the Plantations but *Graman* Quacy . . . is Sent for to Discover the Perpetrator, & Which he so verry Seldom misses by their Faith in his Conjurations, & looking them Steadily in the Face." He also sells "*Obias* or *Amulets*" to the "Corps of Rangers & all fighting free negroes." Stedman writes, "He not only has done a Deal of Good to the Colony but fill'd his Pockets with no inconsiderable Profits Also" (582).[75]

"Artful," "extraordinary," "artifice" and "ingenuity." These are the terms used by Stedman, but we can glean from this description, and from Blake's engraving, that this man probably took advantage of both cultures. He was a mediator between them — a kind of signifying monkey, using artifice and ingenuity to straddle the two cultures. And the engraving itself depicts him that way. He has black skin and bright white hair. He is a perverse mockery of George III, and presumably of what that king represents. Behind him stand a plantation and

Figure 28. Blake, "The celebrated Graman Quacy." By permission of the Syndics of Cambridge University Library.

a fortress on the edge of the colony, which his sad cleverness reduces to mere facade.

The "The celebrated Graman Quacy" might actually provide another way to look at Blake's most famous and most perplexing statement on African otherness: "The Little Black Boy." This poem is a knot of contradictions and scholars cannot agree on what Blake meant by it. Did he endorse slavery? Was he complicit with slavery even though he despised it? Did he necessarily reproduce the racist views of his age? Eva Beatrice Dykes, David Erdman, and Wylie Sypher locate the poem in the antislavery tradition;[76] others see it as an ironic poem questioning the dualisms Blake so fiercely detested.[77] More recently, Alan Richardson and Anne Mellor represent the two major points of view regarding the poem's use of racist and colonialist ideologies. Richardson observes that the poem's multiple ironies result from Blake's "subtle critique of the racialist and colonialist aspects of most anti-slavery writing," especially of its desire to Christianize Africans, while Mellor argues that Blake is not critical of the racist views of his day; rather the child speaks and has learned a desire to serve the white boy and be like him.[78] Assimilation is demonstrated through the change in Blake's coloring of the plates: in early copies the little black boy was left "white," while later copies have him colored black. Both Lauren Henry and Michael Echeruo, who read the poem against African writings — Phillis Wheatley, Ukawsaw Gronniosaw, Olaudah Equiano, Ottobah Cugoano — view Blake as complicit with the racist views of his day that forced Britain's black citizens into envisioning only a white, Christian future.[79]

But poets of Blake's own day may have read his poem in yet another way. Coleridge, who was given a copy of the *Songs* to read in 1817, rated "The Little Black Boy" the highest of them all: "Θ:yeaΘ+Θ!" (*CL*, 4: 836–38). Coleridge's enthusiasm may recognize that the poem was one of the first to bring into a relationship of proximity, even alterity, the otherness of Africa and the sameness of Britain. Certainly, if we read it from the perspective of mock-mimicry, the poem's ironies, or internal contradictions, its ability to signify upon itself, ensure that hierarchies shatter and tumble to the ground just as fast as they are constructed. For example, one could read the poem as an apology for hierarchies that reinscribe racism: human and divine, children and parents, African and Christian, black and white. But this reading is undercut. If black skin is a curse to the black boy, why does it seem to be a blessing to the white boy, in the sense of a shade from the burning "love" of the Christian God? If the black boy's skin is black and his soul is white, why are both black and white also referred to as clouds — formations that block vision? The poem, like the engravings, mocks and mimics the ideologies that surround it, making way for an altering vision, where both self and other are preserved. This is also the point of *Visions*, when

Oothoon says "Can that be love, that drinks another as a sponge drinks water?" The answer is obviously no. Neither the slave master—Bromion—nor the sulking slave—Theotormon—act out of love. Both are so absorbed in self that they absorb the other, and thus both lack the perceptual distance that love, or alterity, requires.

PART III

Fascination and Fear in Africa

5

African Embraces

Voodoo and Possession in Keats's Lamia

I

In the final scene of Keats's *Lamia*, the "bald-headed philosopher" Apollonius destroys the wedding ceremony of young Lycius and his bride Lamia by gazing so intensely at her that he reveals she is not the woman she seems to be:

... the sophist's eye,
Like a sharp spear, went through her utterly,
Keen, cruel, perceant, stinging: she, as well
As her weak hand could any meaning tell,
Motioned him to be silent; vainly so,
He looked and looked again a level — *No!*
"A Serpent!" echoed he; no sooner said,
Than with a frightful scream she vanishèd. (2:299–306)

Apollonius's impaling gaze cuts with remarkable precision to the heart of a "knotty problem" Keats had been pondering about the poet's role (2:160). In 1818 he wrote to Richard Woodhouse claiming "What shocks the virtuous philosop[h]er, delights the camelion Poet . . . because he has no Identity—he is continually in for—and filling some other Body" (*KL*, 1:387). By connecting himself as poet to the chameleon—an animal identified by early-nineteenth-century European explorers as a mysterious reptile indigenous to Africa—Keats gives both shape and color to that state of "being in uncertainties, Mysteries, doubts" while "remaining content with half knowledge" (*KL*, 1:193–94).

It comes as no surprise, then, that in the summer of 1819, when Keats started *Lamia*, he chose an unknowable serpent-woman, who lay hidden in the "dusky brake" of an exotic island, to enact this chameleon transformation (1:46). For Keats, Lamia was mysterious in three senses. Not only serpent and woman, she was also African. According to John Lemprière's *Classical Dictionary*, one of the sources Keats used for the poem,[1] "Lamiae" were "certain monsters of Africa, who had the face and breast of a woman, and the rest of their body like that of a serpent. They allured Strangers to come to them, that they might devour them; and though they were not endowed with the faculty of speech, yet their hissings were pleasing and agreeable." Keats embraces Lamia's African mysteries and so reenlivens his poetic imagination. At the same time, he seems aware that the intimacy he imagines is dangerous to both African and European cultures.

Though *Lamia* is clearly set in Greece, the poem's images have overwhelming parallels with those of African and Caribbean travel narratives. This is not surprising, given the relationship between Africa, Britain, and the Caribbean between 1818 and 1820, the time Keats conceived of *Lamia* and published it. This point, midway between the abolition of the slave trade in 1807 and that of slavery in the colonies 1833, generated strikingly contradictory portraits of Africans. To take just one example, Captain G. F. Lyon's *Travels in Northern Africa in the Years 1818, 19, and 20* with his companion, the surgeon/explorer Joseph Ritchie, is typical in presenting Africans as both trustworthy and treacherous.[2] Ritchie, whom Keats had met at a dinner party, and George Lyon, a naval officer, were to go to Africa from Tripoli in 1818. They were sent by the secretary of the admiralty, John Barrow, who hoped to find the Niger and Nile connected, which would make a continuous trade river through Africa for Europeans to use. Though Ritchie died of fever eight months into their journey, Lyon returned home convinced that he had solved the riddle. The Niger, he said, ended in a lake in the Sahara.[3] His geographical contribution was as perplexing as his depiction of Africans, whose characteristics changed from one day to the next. The most striking example of this double-characterizing comes in Lyon's and Ritchie's encounters with an African sultan. When informed of Ritchie's "proposed journey and plans respecting the interior," the African sultan extends "the most flattering promises of protection," pledging to "act towards Mr. Ritchie as a brother, and assist him in all things to the utmost of his power."[4] At the same time, Lyon designates the king a duplicitous man, strongly implying that Ritchie's death is hastened by, if not caused by, the king's illwill.[5]

Just before beginning work on *Lamia*, Keats had expressed interest in those pursuing knowledge of Africa. In January 1819, he wrote his brother George about a travel narrative describing the "discovery of an african Kingdom." Referring to Thomas Edward Bowdich's 1819 *A Mission from Cape Coast Castle to Ashantee*, Keats recounted the uncanny "romance" where familiar British adventurer meets foreign African customs:

They have window frames of gold—100,000 infantry—human sacrifices—The Gentleman who is the adventurer has his wife with him—she I am told is a beautiful little sylphid woman—her husband was to ha[ve] been sacrificed to their Gods and was led through a Chamber filled with different instruments of torture with the privilege to choose what death he would die, without their having a thought of his aversion to such a death they considering it a supreme distinction — However he was let off and became a favorite with the King who at last openly patronized him; thoug[h] at first on account of the Jealousy of his Minister he was wont to hold conversations with his Majesty in the dark middle of the night — All this sounds a little Bluebeardish — but I hope it is true. (*KL*, 2:28)

For Keats, "human sacrifice," a complete giving over of the self, is not only the result of the African-European encounter, but an example of his theory of imaginative disinterest. By saying that the African story is "Bluebeardish," Keats equates this teetering on the brink of sacrificial death in an African village with the poetically productive moment, where, as he put it to Woodhouse, the poet "has no self." Further, for Keats, this African-European exchange generates a tale whose rhythm defies stable identities, approximating a state of negative capability. The story is one of mystery, uncertainty, and doubt, one neither wholly European nor fully African, located somewhere between Bluebeardish fiction and true fact. But, as Keats ironically acknowledges in this passage, for all their mystery, African-European encounters were fraught with the politics of domination. Thus, what one culture lost in identity, the other gained in patronizing power.

Such a dangerous clash between light and dark cultures underlies the structure of *Lamia* from the beginning, giving the reader a sense that this clash is always a threat to the individual. Keats situates the poem at the dawn of a history of conquests, or of increasingly more technological and tyrannical military takeovers, when the English fairies "drove Nymph and Satyr from the prosperous woods," while "King Oberon's bright diadem, / Sceptre, and mantle, clasped with dewy gem, / Frighted away the Dryads and the Fauns" (1:2–5).[6] These conquests also get "whiter" in Keats's retelling as the satyrs — traditionally associated with dark-skinned people — are overtaken by Oberon, whose name comes from the Latin word "albus" meaning "white."[7] The poem's early whiteness foregrounds Lamia's dusky origins. She is both "Proserpine" and "Eurydice," dark distinctions no doubt stemming from the first Lamia's mythological status as Zeus's Libyan mistress (1:63, 248).[8] Further, like Aeneas's Dido, her encounter with white culture destroys her; it turns her "deadly white" (2:276).

Lest we imagine such violent encounters as somehow natural or accidental, Keats figures the poem's protoconquest as an act of self-interested possession by a prodigal god. Hermes, who commissions himself to uncover the secret bed of the lovely nymph, flies from "vale to vale" and "wood to wood," in quest of "amorous theft" to find the "unseen" maid, whose freedom is inextricably linked to her invisibility (1:27, 8, 99). In staging this conquest, Keats draws on travel writers who insisted that, though their activities involved a certain amount of "amorous" probing, the primary road to the control of Africa lay in passionately possessing its secrets. Mungo Park's inaugural address in *Travels in the Interior Districts of Africa* (1799), for instance, burns with a "passionate desire to examine into the productions of a country so little known."[9]

Keats uses this exoticism to interrogate the new proximity of African culture, but first he sets up an exotic scene. The wedding of Lamia and Lycius contains the poem's richest deposit of travel narrative descriptions. Imported images that mimic both Park and Bowdich (who called the verdant lushness of African vegetation "romantic") decorate Lamia's wedding banquet hall.[10] "Mimicking a glade," the hall opens into "Two palms and then two plantains, and so on, / From either side their stems branched one to one / All down the aisled place" (2:125, 127–30). This elaborate counterfeit is just like the canopied African valley described by Bowdich, "profusely covered with pines, aloes, and lilies; and richly varied with palm, banana, plantain, and guava trees."[11] Interestingly, these same exotic descriptions occurred in travel tales of the slave colonies. William Beckford's description of Jamaica comes curiously close to the vegetation of the English countryside:

The first appearance of Jamaica presents one of the most grand and lively scenes that the creating hand of Nature can possibly exhibit: mountains of an immense height seem to crush those that are below them; and these are adorned with a foliage as thick as vivid, and no less vivid than continual. The hills, from their summits to the very borders of the sea, are fringed with trees and shrubs of a beautiful shape and undecaying verdure; and you perceive mills, works, and houses peeping among their branches, or buried amidst their shades. . . . The verdure of England, in the midst of summer, can hardly vie with that of Jamaica for seven, eight, or nine months in the year; and as there are but few apparently deciduous trees and shrubs, that verdure seems to be, upon the mountains, unfading and perennial.[12]

Keats obviously imports these images, but he does more than just transplant tropical vegetation from travel literature. He shows how such beauty is threatened by the "dull catalogue[s]" and scientific systems of the naturalist (2:233). The "charms" of Lamia's wedding hall—whose lushness literally overtakes part two of the poem—dissipate as soon as the scientific Apollonius "force[s] himself" upon the "wealthy lustre" of the banquet room (2:229, 166, 173). Although not all African explorers were alike, Keats aligns Apollonius with the methods of the explorer who would "conquer all mysteries by rule and line, / Empty the haunted air, and gnomèd mine—/ Unweave a rainbow, as it erewhile made / The tender-personed Lamia melt into a shade" (2:235–38). Yet because Keats attempts to capture the charms of Lamia within the "rule and line" of his consciously mysterious poetic, he raises questions about just what kind of inscription can possess African magic without sucking the life out of it. For as the writing of the period demonstrates, through the discourse of either exploratory writing or poetry, Europeans who represented what they did not understand enacted — to different degrees — a process of deadly possession. African snakes, for example, were cataloged by scientific writers like Bowdich, Lyon, and Ritchie as natural manifestations of the African landscape and therefore as fair game for not just observation, but dissection. Indeed, most of the natural history plucked from African shores came home dead. A telling example of this is the chameleon, the very creature Keats used as a metaphor for the poet. Bowdich's discussion of African reptiles captures the chameleon in a sterile, scientific description, understanding the creature as part of the "natural" magic of Africa that could be mined, categorized, and expended.

With *Lamia*, Keats also takes up this chameleon quality, but to a different end. Unlike Bowdich's account of the reptile, Keats's poem is such a "gordian" knot of ambiguity to many readers precisely because he refuses to coldly categorize Lamia (1:47).[13] Instead, he exposes her only to protect her — to some extent, at least — from complete possession. When Hermes first lays his possessive eyes on the serpent, he finds her an excessive, magnificent creature:

Vermilion-spotted, golden, green and blue;
Striped like a zebra, freckled like a pard,
Eyed like a peacock, and all crimson barred;
And full of silver moons, that, as she breathed,
Dissolved, or brighter shone, or interwreathed
Their lustres with the gloomier tapestries (1:48–53)

While this passage in some sense participates in stereotypes that exoticize Africa, it also serves to highlight Lamia's destabilizing transformation when, "left to herself, the serpent now began / To change" (1:146–47). She is literally "undressed" of her colors and masked in white skin, her entrée to the busy metropolis of Corinth (1:161). From this point on, the poem marks her as "fair" but never ceases to hint at the serpent coiled beneath that skin (1:181, 2:110). "The serpent — Ha, the serpent! Certes, she / Was none," writes Keats, declaring her both a serpent and not a serpent (2:80–81). Thus, he identifies her in terms of continual transformation that undermines notions of a possessive, territorial-minded self of travel writers, that self posited so confidently in Bowdich's account of Ashantee.[14]

In contrast to Bowdich, Keats's poetry interacted with Africa in a way that caught the attention of William Hazlitt, who wrote about this very subject to illustrate his idea of imagination. In 1822 Hazlitt reviewed the art collection of William Beckford's Fonthill Abbey for *London Magazine* with sarcastic disappointment because its "frippery and finery" lacked the air of "impenetrable mystery" he had expected to find. He concludes such mystery could better be found among the "wastes and wilds" of Abyssinia, or better, among the dynamic of cultural exchange, like "a volume of Keats's poems [which] was carried out by Mr. Ritchie to be dropped in the Great [Sahara] Desert." [15] Throughout 1818, as it happens, Keats had followed the African travels of Ritchie, whose expeditions Keats likened to those of Mungo Park (*KL*, 1:198). Keats had sent a copy of *Endymion* with the explorer asking him to cast it into the heart of the Sahara, to which Ritchie replied by letter in December 1818: "*Endymion* has arrived thus far on his way to the Desert, and when you are sitting over your Christmas fire will be jogging (in all probability) on a Camel's back 'over those Afran Sands immeasurable' " (*KL*, 2:16).[16] There is something chilling about Ritchie (while traveling with a slave caravan, no less) carrying *Endymion* into Africa while carrying out plans for the British government to explore the continent in order to possess its most powerful resources. But the idea of Ritchie tossing Keats's poetry into Africa as a declaration that he is "the great poetic luminary of the age to come" mirrors Keats's own conception of his poetry as something that could coexist with cultural difference (*KL*, 1:198 n.5). Keats, with his usual irony, wrote to his brother George that copies of *Endymion* commingled with the mysterious worldwide: "One is in the Wilds of america — the other is on a Camel's back in the plains of Egypt" (*KL*, 2:16).[17]

Lamia further demonstrates Keats's awareness that questions of proximity through cultural interaction are inseparable from questions of poetic imagination. By invoking the "rule and line" of the explorer/colonist within the "wide expanse" of his own poetic, Keats implies that the transformations of a certain kind of poetic practice can interact with cultural difference without annihilating it.[18] Rather, self-annihilation must occur. The opening canto in "The Fall of Hyperion" — which he composed while he was writing *Lamia* — records an imaginative interchange between Keats's "fine spell of words" and the "shadows of melodious utterance," "sable charm," and the heavenly dreams of the "savage" (1:1–11). With *Lamia*, Keats casts doubt on ideologies that would impose a sovereign identity onto a space rather than allowing an identity to fill it. To inscribe the "sands of Africa," its "Whirlpools and volcanoes," in the "dull catalogue of common things" — to place the African serpent's chameleon transformations under the static view of the scientific writer or the possessive gaze of colonial authority — is, Keats realizes, to kill it utterly (*KL*, 1:101; *Lamia* 2:233).

Yet, Keats must have been aware that the symbolic meaning of Lamia's serpent nature was a question in which many cultures had a stake. The serpent Lamia (for a Western audience) immediately suggests the smooth-talking reptile and the induction of evil into the world in Christian mythology. By making his serpent a woman, Keats combines Eve and the satanic slitherer. Her "serpent prison" where we find her at the outset of the poem is the reverse of the Satanencasing serpent of *Paradise Lost*. Keats, in fact, wrote in the margins of his own copy of *Paradise Lost*: "Whose head is not dizzy at the [possible] speculations of satan in this serpent prison—no passage of poetry ever can give a greater pain of suffocation."[19] He sympathizes with this satanic colonial outcast because, like Lamia, Milton's serpent-as-transformed-animal seduces his prey and then has his legs, if not his entire body, dissolved by a greater force.

If the serpent formed one basis for Christianity, it also had rich meanings for African and Caribbean society in the early nineteenth century. Even as many travel accounts characterized Africa as a paradise, the serpent played a central role in African voodoo during European exploration. Explorers record the centrality of the serpent in African religion, known as *Vaudoux*, Obeah, or at least as some type of fetish worship. Moreau de Saint-Mery's account in *Description de la partie française de Saint-Domingue* (1797–98) of the mysterious "cult of the serpent" of Saint Domingue, led by the "pythonisse" or "*Vaudoux* mistress," emphasizes the serpent's non-European significance:

Vaudoux signifie un être tout-puissant et surnaturel, dont dépendent tous les événemens qui se passent sur ce globe. . . . Connaissance du passé, science du présent, prescience de l'avenir, tout appartient à cette couleuvre.

[*Vaudoux* signifies an all powerful and supernatural being upon whom depends all the events that take place in the world. . . . Knowledge of the past, the present, and the future, all these belong to this grass snake.][20]

Yet, throughout European literature of the Romantic period, the value Africans grant to the serpent is repeatedly represented as a locus of uncomfortable uncertainty because of its unknowability.[21]

Africans and snakes are brought together ideologically during the Romantic period most often in the debate on the slavery. For example, the widely circulated but anonymously published tract *An Apology for Negro Slavery: or The West India Planters Vindicated from the Charges of Inhumanity* (1786) targets snake worship among other justifications for slavery. Before the Europeans came to Africa, the author alleges, "the people were immersed in the grossest ignorance, idolatry, and barbarism. They worshipped snakes . . . and other wild beasts imagining that the homage they paid them would hinder them from doing them any harm."[22] Given the Christian ideology, which underwrote most discourse on slavery, African snake worship could only imply devotion to something evil. It did not take long for Africans who "worship serpents, and even reptiles and entertain very unbecoming and confused notions of Deity" to become West Indian slaves "without any religion but that called *Obeah*, or belief in a demon."[23]

Snake worship's reputation as an ever present danger to white planters became inextricably related to its unknowability. Bryan Edwards's 1819 edition of *History, Civil and Commercial, of the British West Indies* awkwardly attempts to understand the practice, imposing European knowledge onto it by defining Obeah through etymological meaning. He finds that

A serpent, in the Egyptian language, was called *Ob*, or *Aub*. — *Obion* is still the Egyptian name for a serpent. — Moses, in the name of God, forbids the Israelites ever to inquire of the demon *Ob*, which is translated in our Bible, Charmer, or Wizard, Divinator, [and] Sorcilegus. The woman at Endor is called *Oub* or *Ob*, translated Pythonissa; and *Oubaois* . . . was the name of the Basilisk or Royal Serpent, emblem of the sun, and an ancient oracular Deity of Africa.[24]

Edwards unwittingly sees the serpent as a shared symbol for both Europeans and Africans, but one which takes on a notably different interpretation in each culture. The beguiling serpent in "our Bible" is demonized, whereas the "Royal Serpent" of African cultures radiates life. Though African power originated with the snake, Europeans (including Edwards) remained in the dark about the nature of this power. While some dismissed Obeah as nonsense, others (such as the Jamaican surgeon Benjamin Moseley) claimed that its practitioners could cast spells causing disastrous epidemics on plantations.

However little the British knew about its specific function, they clearly linked Obeah ceremonies to slave rebellions, insurrections, and other threatening acts, especially in the Caribbean. The abolitionist poet James Montgomery warned in his poem *The West Indies* of 1809:

Tremble Britannia! While thine islands tell
The appalling mysteries of Obi's spell;
The wild Maroons, impregnable and free,
Among the mountain-holds of liberty,
Sudden as lightning darted on their foe,
Seen like the flash, remember'd like the blow.[25]

Many islands even established laws, often holding Obeah trials to prevent this frightening practice. Nowhere is this more evident than in the Privy Council inquiries of 1788 in Jamaica. The testimonies here read like a panicked crescendo of the British government's fear of slave rebellion. The questioners begin simply enough, with "Are Negro Slaves or their Children in general baptized?" and then, suddenly, they turn to the topic that dominates the inquiry: "Whether Negroes called Obeah-Men, or under any other Denomination, practising Witchcraft, exist in the Island of Jamaica?" Some of the fear registered here boils down to practical economics: the money Obeah practitioners made by selling their amulets, the number of slaves killed by Obeah-induced poisoning, and the opportunity for slave rebellion through organized Obeah-meetings threatened colonial profits. Worse still, in the opinion of these questioners, was the control Obeah practitioners seemed to hold over the mind. There were the amulets themselves, a sort of emblem of abjection, reportedly consisting of "Rags, Feathers, Bones of Cats, and a thousand other Articles." Then there was the worship of snakes. These were just part of what the government identified as the main problem with Obeah—it produced a "disturbed imagination." Said the representatives from Jamaica, "the Terrours of *Obi*" most certainly "originate from Causes deeply rooted in the Mind," and are thus so powerful that they "will baffle the Skill of the ablest Physician." [26]

Keats's use of the African serpent, or pythoness, would have conjured up scenes of Obeah possession described by John Gabriel Stedman in his 1796 *Narrative of a Five Years' Expedition against the Revolted Negroes of Surinam* (discussed in Chapter 4). Stedman called these the "dance of the mermaid," performed by the "*Sibyls*, who deal in oracles," then dance and whirl

round in the middle of an assembly, with amazing rapidity, until they foam at the mouth, and drop down as convulsed. Whatever the prophetess orders to be done during the paroxysm, is most sacredly performed by the surrounding multitude; which renders these meetings extremely dangerous, as she frequently enjoins them to murder their masters, or desert to the woods.[27]

Stedman's account repeats Moreau's description of the *Vaudoux* mistress, who is mounted by the spirit through the serpent, and who presides over the ceremony:

Tout-à-coup il prend la boîte où est la couleuvre, la place à terre et fait monter sur elle la Reine *Vaudoux*. Des que l'asile sacré est sous ses pieds, nouvelle pythonisse, elle est pénétrée du Dieu, elle s'agite, tout son corps est dans un état convulsif, et l'oracle parle par sa bouche.

[All of a sudden, he takes the box where the grass serpent is, puts it on the ground where it mounts the *Vaudoux* mistress. As soon as the sacred sanctuary is under her feet, she is instantly pythoness, she is filled with her god, she becomes disturbed, her whole body shakes with convulsions, and the oracle speaks through her lips.] [28]

Such anguished ecstasy, in fact, characterizes Lamia's spell-binding transformation:

. . . her elfin blood in madness ran,
Her mouth foamed, and the grass, therewith besprent,
Withered at dew so sweet and virulent;
Her eyes in torture fixed, and anguish drear,
Hot, glazed, and wide, with lid-lashes all sear,

. . . .
The colours all inflamed throughout her train,
~~She writhed about, convulsed with scarlet pain:~~ (1:147–54)

The "gordian" contradictions of the woman mounted by her god through the serpent completely mystified European logic. For example, while the pythoness had power through possession, she was also, according to Moreau, "prone to more violent agitations" and delirium than any other practitioner.[29] These contradictions, inherent in the religious practices of slaves, help explain Lamia's labyrinthine inconsistencies. Her physical incarnations make sense: the "palpitating snake" (1:45) first appears trapped in a "wreathèd tomb" (1:38), yet she is simultaneously incorporated into Hermes's imperial value system, emblemized on his "serpent rod" (1:89). She performs medical miracles by "unperplex[ing] bliss from its neighbour pain" and dressing "misery in fit magnificence" (1:192; 2:116). She lives in both freedom and slavery, enacting the "unconfined Restraint," the "imprisoned liberty" Keats claimed in *Endymion* as the "great key . . . to all the mazy world / Of silvery enchantment" (1:455–61). Significantly, from within her "serpent prison-house," Lamia sends her spirit "where she willed," from the pearly bowers of the sea goddess to the rioting blend of teeming mortals (1:203, 205).

To the European mind, the most puzzling aspect of *Vaudoux* or Obeah possession was its power to liberate *and* enslave its practitioners, what Moreau described as a "a system of both domination and blind submission."[30] The same paradox described so apprehensively by Moreau, Stedman, and others, is at the heart of *Lamia*. Lamia's voodooistic crisis seems to manifest her freedom in several senses. She sloughs off her colorful skin and dark origins, possessing instead "white arms," a "neck regal white," and a "new voice luting soft" (1:287, 243, 167). This whiteness affords her social mobility. As a "lady bright," she wins the love of Lycius who gives her the opportunity to move from slave dwelling, to the house of the master, from "love in a hut" to "love in a palace" (1:171; 2:1, 3).[31] Such freedom, however, only serves to underscore the enslaving function of possession. Like the West Indian slaves she partially recalls, Lamia is entangled in the continual process of giving herself up. The core contradiction of the ritual, one that has a probable explanation in the realities of slavery, is that a person achieves dominance only through complete submission to the possessing spirit.[32] The crux of West Indian voodoo, the suicidal question for slaves, and the ultimate question for Lamia are the same: where does the possibility of giving oneself up stop, once a person is in the possession of a white body?

Possession by whiteness signified evil and, ultimately, death for the West Indians and West Africans alike. Bowdich records that during the Ashantee rituals he witnessed, "they spill a little liquor on the ground as an offering to the fetish; and on rising from their chairs and stools, their attendants instantly lay them on their sides, to prevent the devil (whom they represent as white) from slipping into their master's places."[33] John Adams's *Sketches taken during ten voyages to Africa* (1822) more explicitly notes that "the evil spirit . . . the blacks conceive invariably to be of white color."[34] In Keats's poem, Apollonius, whose "baldness" literally means the "mark of whiteness" and whose "demon eyes" conjure images of the devil, exemplifies Britain's systematic and therefore most destructive side. When he arrives at the feast where Lamia is to become Lycius's possession in a marriage bond, Apollonius's "calm-planted steps," his methodically "patient thought," and his exacting "eye severe" turn poor Lamia into properties that he can then "thaw," "solve and melt" (2:157–63).

In order to escape the threat of such piercing whiteness, slaves cloaked their ceremonies with secrecy. According to Edwards, the Jamaican slaves threw "a veil of mystery" over their rituals, practicing religious ceremonies only during "the midnight hours," to "conceal them from the knowledge and discovery of the White people,"[35] while Moreau observed the sacred oaths of secrecy taken by practitioners in Saint Domingue. Ceremonies were thus conducted during the middle of the night as a kind of protective curtain that made slaves invisible to planters. Throughout *Lamia*, therefore, Keats provides the "half retired" serpent woman with a similar kind of nocturnal concealment (1:312). The entire narrative takes place in the protective covering of night, moving from "evening dim," to "wide-spreaded night," to "eventide," to "midnight" (1:220; 1:354; 2:17; 2:84). When Lamia emerges from darkness on that bright "day" of her wedding, she is married, revealed, and dissolved (2:107).

II

Keats's desire to reinvest the Western story (in both its biblical and Greek versions) of the serpent-as-transformed-animal with a newly charged exoticism constitutes part of the early European fascination with the newly perceived proximity of Africa. Thus, Keats's activity does parallel that of Bowdich, Park, and Ritchie, in their attempts to gather aspects of the African terrain into their classificatory scheme and take possession of what they saw as natural magic. But Keats's text is vexed because, unlike the accounts of travelers, he not only embraced the magic of Africa, but was embraced by it. By choosing a sympathetic poetic figure with African origins who enacts aspects of West Indian religious magic, Keats manages to celebrate the imaginative power of Africa, whose force comes from a reversal of colonial methods, from being the possessed instead of the possessor, from keeping power hidden instead of displaying it, from working in darkness instead of panoptic visibility.

Michel Foucault, analyzing Jeremy Bentham's politics of visibility in late-eighteenth- and early-nineteenth-century English culture, comments on the European preoccupation with eradicating darkness and creating a transparent society:

A fear haunted the latter half of the eighteenth century: the fear of darkened spaces, of the pall of gloom which prevents the full visibility of things, men and truths. It sought to break up the patches of darkness that blocked the light, eliminate the shadowy areas of society, demolish the unlit chambers where arbitrary political acts, monarchical caprice, religious superstitions, tyrannical and priestly plots, epidemics and the illusions of ignorance were fomented. . . . The new political and moral order could not be established until these places were eradicated.[36]

This same British gaze oversaw West Indian slaves while it tried to make visible voodoo rituals and other covert activities where slave rebellions could be planned and executed.

In much the same way, Lamia becomes the object of various sets of "imperial eyes," to use a phrase suggested by Mary Louise Pratt. As Pratt observes, for some African explorers, Mungo Park in particular, gazing was a reciprocal activity.[37] Park recorded not only what he saw, but what saw him. The women he met in Bondou, for example, "rallied me with a good deal of gaiety on different subjects; particularly upon the whiteness of my skin . . . [which] they said, was produced when I was an infant, by dipping me in milk."[38] Keats, too, begins his poem with a type of reciprocal gaze.[39] Lamia strikes a bargain with Hermes through the power of her vision. The oath Hermes swears "by [her] eyes" transpires only when "she breathe[s] upon his eyes" (1:90, 124). This exchange gives Lamia volcanic vision: "Her eyes in torture fixed, and anguish drear, / Hot, glazed, and wide, with lid-lashes all sear, / Flashed phosphor and sharp sparks, without one cooling tear" (1:150–52). It also turns her into the poem's first "seer," or fully conscious character. Like Milton's Eve in her newly born body, Lamia stops "by a clear pool" to see "herself escaped," yet the very moment she becomes conscious of her own freedom, she loses that freedom to the binding forces of the culture she enters (1:182–83).

In Lamia's world, as in Keats's, reciprocity does not last long. Lamia's eyes are "ever watchful, penetrant" (2:34) when she lands at the border of Corinth, but within that border it is Lycius's watchful eyes that turn her into a mirror of colonial desire and Apollonius's penetrant gaze that harpoons her. When Lycius first observes Lamia, he bends to her "open eyes / Where he was mirrored small in paradise" (2:46–47). He falls desperately in love with her, literally consuming her with his eyes: "his eyes had drunk her beauty up, / Leaving no drop in the bewildering cup, / And still the cup was full" (1:251–52). A visual alcoholic, Lycius is instantly addicted, as he declares "Ah Goddess, see / Whether my eyes can ever turn from thee!" (1:257–58). Like the master whose identity comes from the work of the slave who is the source of his or her power, Lycius is "chain[ed]" to Lamia so strongly that he predicts what his fate will be when she ceases to mirror him: "Even as thou vanishest so I shall die," he moans (1:260). Indeed, he feels horror at Lamia's unsightly death precisely because she no longer reflects him. After Apollonius impales Lamia with his own "juggling eyes," the panicked Lycius

. . . gazed into her eyes, and not a jot
Owned they the lovelorn piteous appeal;
More, more he gazed; his human senses reel;
Some hungry spell that loveliness absorbs;
There was no recognition in those orbs.[40] (2:256–60)

But Keats strongly indicts both the addictive gaze of Lycius and the piercing vision of Apollonius. At Lamia's death, Lycius impugns Apollonius's eyes — eyes that hover between "unlawful magic" and "enticing lies" — warning that the gods will "pierce them on the sudden with the thorn / Of painful blindness" (2:286; 281–82). In commanding the common Corinthians to "look upon that greybeard wretch! / Mark how, possessed, his lashless eyelids stretch / Around his demon eyes! Corinthians, see!" Lycius punishes Apollonius by making a spectacle of his eyes, while the poem wraps Lycius up as the final imaginative exhibit (2:287–89).

Moreau warned of the disruptive nature of West Indians in connection with *Vaudoux*, where slaves would explicitly ask for "the ability to manipulate the spirit of their masters." One of the ways this happened was through what he calls "the magnetism" created in white masters who gazed too curiously on this practice of blacks and slaves:

Des Blancs trouvés épiant les mysteères de cette secte, et touchés par l'un de ses membres qui les avait découverts, se sont mis quelquefois à danser, et one consenti à payer la Reine *Vaudoux*, pour mettre fin à ce châtiment.

[Some whites found spying on the mysteries of the sect and touched by one of the members who had discovered them are actually driven to dancing and consenting to pay the *Vaudoux* mistress a fee in order to put an end to this chastisement.] [41]

Just like Keats, who turns Lycius's addictive gaze into a "love trance" from which he cannot escape, Moreau records not only the intense desire of the white community to gaze on the powerful African customs, but also the fear of being mastered by a practice they could not control (2:241).

If Keats's poem condemns a certain kind of seeing eye, it equally celebrates the unseen and explicitly links it to freedom. During her interchange with Hermes, Lamia insists that the nymph, whom Hermes has traveled all this way to see, is "invisible, yet free / To wander as she loves, in liberty" (1:108–9). "She tastes unseen; unseen her nimble feet," explains Lamia, "she plucks the fruit unseen, she bathes unseen" (1:96, 99). And in the context of the island, it is Lamia's power that keeps "her beauty veiled / To keep it unaffronted, unassailed / By the love-glances of unlovely eyes" (1:100–102).[42] Lamia also demonstrates a desire to keep herself "veiled" and "unassailed" in her move to the Corinthian market-place, which was, after all, both an imperial metropolis and the largest slave market in ancient Greece.[43] Given this fact, who can blame Lamia for hiding out, even during her first face-to-face encounter with Lycius, when he literally sees right through her, as she stands "so neighboured to him, and yet so unseen" (1:240)? She dwells unseen in Corinth, and though the voyeuristic crowds try to look on, even "the most curious / Were foiled, who watched to trace them to their house" (1:392–93). This seclusion makes her suspect, yet for a time she maintains her invisibility and thus her power.

It is this focus on secret space destroyed by the consumptive context of the market, where bodies become possessions, that characterizes Lamia's and Lycius's fateful union. As Marjorie Levinson notes, the reciprocity between Lamia and Lycius means that "each lover becomes to the other a property."[44] Hidden away in their chamber and veiled by "midnight silence," they are together too short a time "to breed distrust and hate, that make the soft voice hiss" (2:84; 2:9–10). But if she does not hiss, Lamia at least senses Lycius's mental return to the noisy world, the very conditions that would reframe their experience and cause him to "desert" and "dismiss" her (2:43–44). Lycius destroys this context not simply by proposing marriage to — and by extension ownership of — Lamia, but by reconceiving of her as a "prize" that make his "foes choke" and his "friends shout afar" (2:57, 62). Mutual passion and possession turn into ownership, and the result is dangerous, if not deadly.

Lamia's loss of self, identity, *and* power begins with the unveiling of her secrets by Lycius. In his effort "to reclaim / Her wild and timid nature to his aim," he insists on displaying her before the public in a wedding ceremony, even though Keats as narrator explicitly condemns this kind of visibility: "O senseless Lycius! Madman! wherefore flout / The silent-blessing fate, warm cloistered hours" (2:70–71; 1:147–48). The same was true for the European traveler's relationship to Africa. For it was not merely the one traveler observing the magic of Africa that killed it, but the act of publicizing such a place in representations for all to see. Lamia, like Africa, becomes the object of the gaze for an entire population. At her ceremony, "The herd approached; each guest, with busy brain, / Arriving at the portal, gazed amain" (2:150–51). When Apollonius, as a figure for the center of white culture, destroys Lamia by piercing her with the eye that has learned her secrets, he merely finishes the job that Lycius starts. Thus, while Keats exposes Lamia to the demon eyes of Apollonius, he nonetheless admonishes those like Lycius, inclined to display the vast treasure of African mysteries, to "show to common eyes these secret bowers" (2:149). And though Apollonius reveals Lamia's mystery and leaves Lycius in a dead stare, Keats seems to warn against probing too deeply into the heart of her secrets.

III

Though Keats draws on African symbolism to produce his poetry, this same drive also powerfully records fears resulting from the possession of Africa by European cultures. No other topic registers both the fear of and desire for Africans more than that of interracial love. Such love stories tell themselves at first through a discourse of reciprocity, but this is a dynamic that inevitably disintegrates, leaving the African or Caribbean either dead or enslaved.[45] Keats deliberately pairs Lamia and Lycius in ways that imitate numerous interracial love stories of his period, stories of love, domination, possession and dispossession.[46]

No literate person of the period would have thought about interracial love without thinking of Stedman. His affair with the slave girl Joanna, whom he described in his *Narrative* with succulent details like "Cheeks through which glow'd / in spite of her olive Complexion / a beautiful tinge of vermillion when gazed upon," was relished by readers who had weathered so many gruesome stories of slavery.[47] Stedman's Joanna is not just built on beautiful descriptions. The sadly strange thing about the story is its combination of stereotypical sentiment, biting racism, and genuine tenderness. It is inevitable, though, since the relationship becomes immediately entangled in the shadowy practices of colonial policy and the arbitrary rules of plantation governance. Joanna, Stedman tells us, is the daughter of a "*Gentleman*" and a "black Woman," but is the personal property of a Mr. Demelly, with whom Stedman must negotiate for a right to marry her. Marry her he does, but not before he manages to lace the narrative with statements that contradict one another with increasing intensity. At one point, he objectifies her, lamenting that had she been given the "education of a Lady," she would have been "an ornament to Civilized Society."[48] At another, he places Joanna in the subject position, quoting her supposed words, "but I have a Soul I hope not inferior to the best European."[49] At one point, he says he is her captive, at another he calls her his. Such agitated responses to his own tangled story of interracial love indicate just how highly charged this topic was during the period.

Stedman is all too aware of the interracial love story genre, virtually asking readers to consider his case in narrative terms. He talks of his depiction of Joanna as "producing such a Slave upon the Stage," and then adds "those alone who have read the history of *Incle* and *Yarico* as related by the Spectator with pleasure and *approved* of that Gentlemans Conduct — I here make an Apology." [50] *Inkle and Yarico*, the most popular interracial love story of its kind, evolved in England and France over a one-hundred-year period (from early 1700 to mid-1800).[51] For several months in 1818, the year before Keats wrote *Lamia*, George Colman the Younger's popular drama, *Inkle and Yarico* — published by Longman and introduced by Elizabeth Inchbald — was advertised in the London *Times*.[52] The British reading public knew the story well. Inkle, a shipwrecked British merchant, makes his way to a foreign land.[53] Yarico, an emblem of dark beauty, finds the sea-soaked Inkle, and nurses him back to health, at which point the two proclaim their love for one another. Soon, however, they are rescued by a British vessel headed for Barbados where Inkle, overcome by avarice, sells Yarico into slavery.

Since Colman's version of interracial love and British greed portrays Yarico as an American Indian, Inchbald added a note to the play, confirming that British readers would expect the story to depict Yarico as African. Highly aware of the logistics of sea travel and the constraints of dramatic unity, Inchbald concedes that "it would undoubtedly have been a quick passage, to have crossed a fourth part of the Western globe" between the first and second acts. All the same, she favors a representation that mimics the realities of trade, arguing that "as the hero and heroine of the drama are compelled to go to sea — imagination, with but little more exertion, might have given them a fair wind as well from the coast whence slaves are *really* brought." [54] Any story of cross-cultural union at the time Keats wrote *Lamia* would have been informed by the story of Yarico and Inkle, just as *Inkle and Yarico* in 1818 was informed by encounters between Africa and Britain.

The same year Keats published *Lamia*, J. Rusher published yet another version of Yarico and Inkle in which "the author has altered the names of Yarico and Inkle to Meracato and Barsina." [55] Like *Lamia*, this poem draws heavily on travel narratives designed to sensationalize foreign cultures, while it also explores the concept of mutual love (and its failure). The exoticized Barsina (Yarico) appears in "jetty tresses flowing hung behind, / And wildly wanton'd in each breeze of wind, / Refulgent jewels, plac'd with artless care, / And shining bugles glitter'd on her hair." [56] Meracato (a name taken from the famous sixteenth-century cartographer, Mercator, who invented the Mercator projection for drawing the map of the world), falls instantly in love with this vision of dark beauty. The two spend only a few months in a "sequester'd grove" before entering an English ship where their relationship is recontextualized in such a way that "no more Barsina's beauties now can move."[57] Rusher's *Inkle and Yarico* makes explicit what Keats's *Lamia* also implies: that once brought into the daylight of Western representational systems which uphold distinctions based on color, and value systems where profit triumphs over love, the beauties of Barsina and the charms of Lamia disappear.

When disembodied from her serpent's nature and occupying the body of a woman, Lamia places interracial union in the context of trade with Africa in this transitional period between 1807 and 1833, this time of the "gradual abolition" of slavery. Miscegenation, which had always been a concern for the European ruling class, was viewed with heightened attention during this time because it brought into sharp focus how alterity might seep into the blood and bear witness through the body. It is a difficult task to pinpoint the source of the British fear of miscegenation, but as Joan Dayan points out, most of it revolved around the myth of contamination.[58] Some historians of the West Indies brought back news that black women's blood as well as their breast milk was tainted, while others believed close contact with blacks would infect whites with "ill customs."[59] Worse, contamination highlighted contradictory myths about sexual promiscuity. While writers like Edward Long churned out diatribes about the sexual lasciviousness of black women, others, such as the former slave Olaudah Equiano and the former slave trader John Newton, exposed the sexual violence forced on black women by "white savages."[60]

It was not just the idea of contamination that bothered white planters, merchants, and European culture at large, but the mulatto offspring that resulted from interracial unions. A mulatto represented a precarious blurring of boundaries, for as Bryan Edwards noted, in every island in the West Indies, it was skin color, with some few exceptions, that distinguished freedom from slavery.[61] When color could no longer be distinguished, it would be impossible to tell the possession from the possessor. So was the sentiment of proslavery writer F. G. Smyth, who reminded that "the offspring of white men and Mestize women [are] the last gradation of slavery."[62] Even before West Indian slavery was outlawed by parliamentary legislation, it was possible for slaves to pass from black to white and thus from bondage to freedom in three generations.[63] But in reality, British law was especially slippery in its distinctions between freedom and slavery, black and white. For instance, this distinction can be read in Edward Long's comment that "offsprings of miscegenous unions remain in the same slavish conditions as their mothers,"[64] making it possible, over many years of cross-cultural marriages, for those of Europeans ancestry to be slaves. On the other hand, African women who had long-standing unions with white masters had a better chance of gaining manumission, and hence becoming a "free black," that glaringly uncomfortable British term.

While Keats himself benefited from slavery by virtue of his nationality, he also blatantly condemned the profiteers of slavery and the effects of such exploitative possession. For example, in *Isabella*, another title piece from the collection in which *Lamia* appears, Keats contemptuously characterizes Isabella's brothers, who capitalize from slavish servitude: "for them many a weary hand did swelt / In torchèd mines and noisy factories, / And many once proud-quivered loins did melt / In blood from stinging whip — with hollow eyes" (107–10). Worse still, these brothers commit a most grisly murder for the simple reason that Lorenzo, one of their slaves, "the servant of their trade designs," falls in love with Isabella and earns her love in return (165). Keats associates Lorenzo — even more than Lamia — with Dido, and thus with classical expansionist literature's motif of interracial reciprocity destroyed by the empire-building activities of white travelers.[65] Keats considered *Lamia* an improvement on the sentiment expressed in *Isabella*, and indeed, *Lamia* presents a much more entangled plot of love that attempts to cross or redefine class or racial boundaries. Moreover, *Lamia* deals explicitly with issues of proximity and distance between Africans and Europeans. Despite the dangerous consequences to both Lamia and Lycius, Keats examines what happens when Lamia lands in the middle of so-called civilized culture, bringing her exotic customs with her.

In a letter of September 1819, Keats attempted to define his efforts in *Lamia* as a poetic of possession, one in which the reader is also possessed by the serpentine tale. "I am certain there is that sort of fire in it which must take hold of people in some way," he wrote (*KL*, 2:189). Keats forces readers to embrace the poem's main narrative through Lamia's trance and therefore through her affinity with African religious magic. But readers not only embrace the poem; it embraces them. They come to identify with Lamia and thus establish alterity through an unsettling process that shifts between mortal and goddess, snake and human, African and European, visible and invisible, freedom and bondage, possession and dispossession.

A month after he read *Lamia*, Richard Woodhouse was still so taken by Keats's poetic zombification that he wrote Keats's publishers about it. Specifically, Woodhouse pondered Keats's conception of the imagination as alterity between self and other. How, wondered Woodhouse, could Keats move from subject to object, throw his soul into any object he sees, or imagines, and so "speak out of that object — so that his own self will with the Exception of the Mechanical part be 'annihilated' "? Woodhouse's practical dilemma, one which

Keats, as a poet, took for granted, centered on how the poet as man could be stripped of identity. Woodhouse astutely concludes, "As a man he must have Ident[ity]. But as a poet he need not." [66]

In some sense, Keats's *Lamia* replicates the changing nature of race relations in early-nineteenth-century Britain as slavery and Africa were brought close to home. Keats tries to find a place for African experience in the poem, even as he inscribes Africa within Western classicism, where he identifies the serpent so intimately with Milton's Satan. If Lamia is like Africa, then no matter how much Keats tries to reimagine her symbolic value, evil is writ large across the dark continent. At once fascinating and chilling, Africa is sublimely tamed on the artful page of poetry, as explorers tamed the land and its women. In this sense, Keats reinforces the pattern of the interracial love story, the dark mistress who dissolves in the light of respectability (the wedding in white) and then slithers away into slavery or death. But this is only part of the story. For in *Lamia*, Keats as poet becomes possessed by the other and thus dispossessed of self. The poem thus celebrates, in passages of extraordinary clarity, the alterity of Africa. In a time of changing ideas about race, slavery, and mastery, in a time of increasing cultural exchange between Africans and Europeans, Keats's capability to not reach irritably "after fact & reason" (*KL*, 1:193) was a fitting answer to the painful and sacrificial contradictions of this new proximity.

6

Mapping Interiors

*African Cartography, Nile Poetry, and Percy Bysshe Shelley's
"The Witch of Atlas"*

I

A pivotal episode in Shelley's "The Witch of Atlas" occurs when the "Wizard-
lady" crafts a creature called "Hermaphroditus," which, as its name implies, is
a strange blurring of essential categories—neither man nor woman, yet somehow, both. She sets Hermaphroditus at the prow of her fragile boat for a grand
tour of Africa's interior, navigating the continent's "earthquaking cataracts" and
"panther-peopled forests" (377, 347). She "glide[s] adown old Nilus, where he
threads / Egypt and Aethiopia"; she explores the "Moeris and the Mareotid
lakes"; she uncovers the secrets of "the fabulous Thamondocana," the ancient
name for Timbuktu (498–99, 505, 424).[1] The witch is obviously a well-seasoned
traveler, and, as such, she is drawn to Africa. "The Witch of Atlas" is, in fact,
the only Romantic poem to take up Africa's interior geography with such intensity and in such detail, and given this, it is surprising that it has not been
read strictly in terms of African geography. The poem's narrative elusiveness, its
calculated ambiguities and its deliberate irony have urged most readers to view
this interior as a purely poetic or, at the very most, a psychological one.[2] As it
turns out, the lady-witch and her hermaphrodite also capture with precision two
issues at the heart of African travel during Shelley's own day: what exactly was
the connection between exploration of Africa's interior and exploration of the
human interior by Romantic writers? And how did gender codes coincide with
the mapping of both?

Exploration of Africa was systematic business to men, like Joseph Banks
(whom I discussed in Chapter 1), deciding colonial policy. It was urgent business, too. As the institution of slavery slowly crumbled, British lawmakers were
desperate to find new ways to uphold the slave-based economy. African colonization presented, in their view, a viable alternative. But the geography of

Africa's interior remained almost entirely unknown to Europeans until the mid-nineteenth century. In 1801, Christian Damberger best summed up the allure of the continent: "Of all the parts of the earth, there is none, respecting which we are so deficient in geographic knowledge, as Africa; every fact, therefore, which tends to make us better acquainted with the still numerous unknown districts of this extensive quarter of the world, is highly interesting."[3] Fabled mountains, strange monsters, magical plants, and tales of gold captured the Western imagination, so much so that in 1788 the African Association was formed in London (by Joseph Banks, and several others) to sponsor exploration. It sent a series of travelers to follow James Bruce, who in the 1760s and 1770s had independently explored the Nile and then amazed London with stories of life at the Abyssinian court in his subsequent narrative, *Travels to Discover the Source of the Nile*. In the 1790s, the African Association sent Friedrich Hornemann and Mungo Park to explore the Niger, visit the legendary city of Timbuktu, and write up their accounts.

But they were not alone. Between 1790 and 1820, over fifty travel books appeared in Britain alone bearing titles of Africa's interior. London booksellers would have carried a rich array of titles, including François Le Vaillant's 1790 *Travels into the Interior Parts of Africa*; W. G. Browne's 1799 *Travels in Africa, Egypt and Syria*; Sir John Barrow's 1801 *Account of Travels into the Interior of Southern Africa*; Captain Philip Beaver's 1805 *African Memoranda: Relative to an attempt to establish a British Settlement on the Island of Bulama, on the Western Coast of Africa, in the year 1792*; Henry Salt's 1814 *Voyage to Abyssinia*; John Campbell's 1815 *Travels in South Africa*; R. Tully's 1816 *Narrative of a Ten Years' Residence at Tripoli in Africa*; Johan Ludwig Burckhardt's 1819 *Travels in Nubia*; Thomas Edward Bowdich's 1819 *Mission from Cape Coast Castle to Ashantee*; J.G. Jackson's 1820 *Account of Timbuctoo and Hausa*; Captain George Francis Lyon's 1821 *Travels in Northern Africa*; John Adams's 1822 *Sketches taken during ten voyages to Africa*; William Burchell's 1822 *Travels in the Interior of Southern Africa*; G. B. British's 1822 *Narrative of the Expedition to Dongola and Sennar*; J. Dupuis's 1824 *Journal of a Residence in Ashantee*; and Hugh Clapperton 1829 *Journal of a Second Expedition into the Interior of Africa . . . to which is added the Journal of Richard Lander*.

In these books, readers could count on African travelers to describe unexpected meetings with natives, distressing hardships suffered by the traveler, and a variety of encounters between African women and European men, some explicitly sexual, but most not. Such details made for good stories, but travelers also felt obliged to satisfy a more scientifically minded audience. African travelers thus also included some mention of the slave trade, a variety of natural history descriptions and drawings, as well as tables, catalogs, and most importantly, maps. By 1820, when Shelley composed "The Witch of Atlas," he was well-versed in the travel narrative genre, including accounts dedicated to mapping Africa's interior. He had explored ancient travel sources like Herodotus and contemporary ones such as Mungo Park, where he was especially struck with Park's account of slavery. Park had written, "whatever difference there is between the Negro and European in the conformation of the nose and the colour of the skin, there is none in the genuine sympathies and characteristic feelings of our common nature."[4] This statement became a powerful tool against those, such as Edward Long, who argued that blacks were a separate, inferior species. Shelley, in this respect at least, sided with Park. In 1814, Shelley sent Mary Shelley a letter printed in the *Times*, based on Park's *Travels*, detailing the horrors of slave caravans in the African interior. Shelley writes, "I send you the Times Newspaper. See where I have marked with ink & stifle your horror & indignation until we meet" (*SL*, 1:408–9). In the same letter, Shelley translates the "horror" of Africa's interior into a metaphor for the horror of his own state of mind brought on by financial and personal problems. He does so by referring to both in the same universal terms which he had used to address Africa's interior problems: "my imagination is confounded by the uniform prospect of the perfidity and wickedness and hard heartedness of mankind."

Given Shelley's interest in African geography, it is not surprising he set it to poetry.[5] But in "The Witch of Atlas," the witch is strangely disembodied from herself and from the African interior she inhabits: Shelley describes her as "a lovely lady garmented in light / From her own beauty—deep her eyes, as are / Two openings of unfathomable night" and the Africa she inhabits "like the fleeting image of a shade" (81–83, 139). This physical and geographical disembodiment probably explains why, in most critical assessments of the poem, the witch has come to stand not for a geographic interior, but for the interior workings of the mind, with its random movements, its sheer disorder. It was Shelley's friend, Leigh Hunt, who first identified the poem with the movements of the mind, calling the witch "a personification of the imaginative faculty in its most airy abstractions."[6]

But because the poem so obviously takes up psychological and geographic interiors, it asks to be considered in terms of how a specifically African geography, alive in Shelley's day, came to stand for European interiority. "The Witch" couples the foreign interior of Africa with intimate human interiority, suggesting their fundamental connectedness to European sensibility, the extent to which exploration of one prompted exploration of the other. Yet, given the possessive nature of European exploration of the continent and enslavement of Africans, Africa would seem to be the least likely place for a relationship of alterity and *being-for-the-other*. But for Shelley, the opposite is true. Alterity is possible because Shelley's witch travels, both literally and psychologically, a space where randomness and error replace the supposedly accurate and orderly progressions of Britain's charting of Africa.

II

Explorers and the colonial policy makers sending them forth were not poets. Explorers thus did not undertake their voyages with notions like alterity in mind, but how could they when they were governed by a discourse founded on principles of scientific rigor. The result, as Michel Foucault explains in *The Order of Things*, was that explorers sought to organize not to empathize with the world. Foucault writes, "The sciences always carry within themselves the project, however remote it may be, of an exhaustive ordering of the world."[7] Further, he suggests that in the seventeenth and eighteenth centuries, the "center of knowledge" was "the *table*."[8] Tables organizing natural history specimens, charts calculating minute changes in weather conditions, and maps marking out political borders permitted travelers to display, in increasing detail, an intense knowledge of the geographic world. This knowledge, as Edward Said has observed, helped "the mind intensify its own sense of itself by dramatizing the distance and difference between what is close to it and what is far away."[9] The map was essential here because it provided a miniature and thus accessible form of the faraway. New in this period, explains the historian John Gascoigne, was "the extent to which the natural world [was] refashioned in a scaled-down" form.[10] This enabled those at its center to manipulate it from afar. Travelers seemed to place the remote within Europeans' reach; they could, in the words of science historian Bruno Latour, "travel through all the continents, climates and periods."[11] According to Latour, the kind of information African travelers brought back to Britain was vital in giving Europeans the confidence to believe they knew Africa, even though they were just beginning to explore it. Travelers thus gave Europe power to act from a distance, for they produced a kind of virtual reality, in which the time and space, the history and geography, of remote areas were reconstructed from the metropolis. As Latour puts it, "nothing is unfamiliar, infinite, gigantic or far away in these centres that cumulate traces; quite the opposite, they cumulate so many traces so that everything can become familiar, finite, nearby and handy. It seems strange at first to claim that space and time may be constructed locally, but these are the most common of all constructions. Space is constituted by reversible and time by irreversible displacements."[12]

Scaling down the continent through mapping was one thing. But another, related development in African cartography took place simultaneously. As

Shelley would surely have known, a geographic undressing of the continent was under way. A comparison of pre- and post-Enlightenment maps makes this clear.[13] Britain's first atlas compiler, John Speed—in an effort to deny blankness and lack—displayed Africa in his *Prospect of the Most Famous Parts of the World* (1626) as overflowing with mythological creatures, crowded with villages, and brimming with mountain ranges, lakes, and rivers (Figure 29). Even though Europeans had little idea of what Africa was like, Speed's Africa resembled some of the most populated places in Europe, with this difference: Africa was the only continent where elephants, anteaters, and giant snakes stood in otherwise blank spaces on the map. This peculiar habit of make-believe mapping is exactly how Jonathan Swift, in the eighteenth century, characterized cartography:

So Geographers in *Afric*-Maps,
With Savage-Pictures fill the Gaps,
And o'er unhabitable Downs,
Place Elephants for want of Towns.[14]

This gap-filling was by no means a purely British phenomenon. Speed and others were influenced by the renowned Dutch cartographer Willem Blaeu.

But these representations of Africa's interior, which were mostly fabrication, would not do for an era that claimed to be dedicated to science and objective truth. And so there was only one thing to do: strip the globe of all false geography. A series of maps printed by Robert Sayer from 1754 to 1789 illustrates the slow geographic draining of the continent between the eighteenth and nineteenth centuries. The 1754 map mimics earlier maps in many ways (Figure 30). Although it lacks the mythological creatures of Speed's variety, it is bound by pictures of Africans, showing them to be industrious, social, artistic, all features of so-called European civility. The 1770 map, based on the "great improvements from the Sierus D'Anville & Robert" appears scientific, actually highlighting the lack, emptiness, and blankness with a white space bearing the inscription: "Ethiopia: This country is wholly unknown to the Europeans" (Figure 31). By 1789, all attempts at filling white space with mythology and fabricated geography are gone (Figure 32). This is nowhere more evident than in Major James Rennell's 1800 *The Geographical System of Herodotus compared with Modern Geography* (Figure 33). Rennell promises to display the continent according to the travels of Herodotus, but what he really does is replace Herodotus's mythological features with modern ones. The feared and revered kingdom of Dahomey, for instance, which shows up on Rennell's map, was not even established until the early seventeenth century, some two-thousand years after Herodotus. A fusion of ancient speculation and modern scientific discovery thus guided the charting of Africa's interior as the nineteenth century began.

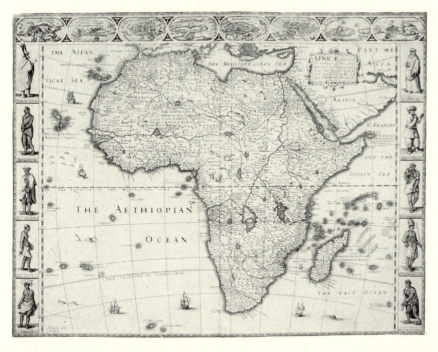

Figure 29. Map of Africa from John Speed's *Prospect of the Most Famous Parts of the World*, 1626. By permission of the British Library.

No one outlined the British fascination with blank, explorable interiors (thus bringing together geographical and psychological interiors) better than Captain James Cook. With Cook, maps became uncanny unfoldings, telescoping thousands of miles within a single field of vision, cataloging strange and foreign places with familiar names like "King George's Strait." Cook not only served as the transitional figure from exploration by sea to exploration by land that led Britain to chart interiors; his opening of the South Pacific also opened the expanding British consciousness.[15] Indeed, a 1784 article in the *Political Magazine* offered Cook as a national example in this regard:

Traveller! contemplate, admire, revere, and emulate this great master in his profession: whose skill and labours have enlarged natural philosophy; have extended natural science; and have disclosed the long concealed and admirable arrangements of the Almighty in the formation of this globe.[16]

Writings like these are typical, giving the noble navigator Cook, and not "the Almighty," the true credit for arranging and forming the globe. Forming the

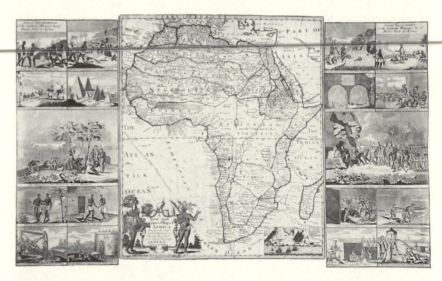

Figure 30. *A New and Correct Map of Africa*, printed by Robert Sayer, 1754. By permission of the British Library.

world, however, went hand in hand with "extending" and "enlarging" British consciousness, which benefited from the globe of outlines, boundaries, perimeters, and "undisclosed" interiors that Cook's "Grand General Chart" offered. Cook specifically asked his cartographer Lieutenant Henry Roberts to construct a "grand out-line of the whole" world, leaving interiors "vacant" and "unfinished" for the exploring European.[17]

But from Jean-Baptiste Bourguignon d'Anville to Cook, it was Africa that remained the most mysterious. Here, in pristine purity, was a continent waiting to be filled up by travelers and poets alike. At the turn of the century, four of the most remarkable African travelers were James Bruce, François Le Vaillant, Mungo Park, and C. F. Damberger. Although the four were notable for different reasons, all had a similar interest in marking Africa as a natural site of male sexual desire. Le Vaillant, who took to the interior as a naturalist in his 1790 *Travels in the Interior of Africa*, called "the interior parts of Africa . . . a Peru — It was a virgin land."[18] Park, in Africa on a commercial fact-finding mission, hoped to "render the geography of Africa more familiar" to British investors, thus establishing a greater "commercial intercourse" with the continent.[19] But whereas Le Vaillant and Park employed long-established sexual conceits to naturalize and thus justify masculine exploration, C. F. Damberger — in his famous and scandalous account of 1801 — claimed that "Vaillant [and] Park . . . added but little to our knowledge, and after all their efforts, the map of Africa remained

Figure 31. *A New Map of Africa*, printed by Robert Sayer, 1770. By permission of the British Library.

still disfigured by a blank space entitled '*Pars wholly unknown to Europeans*.'"[20] By focusing his narrative so intently on what rival explorers were doing, Damberger pointed out how mapping Africa was really a contest between men over a feminized space.

Damberger was not alone in pointing out the ulterior motives of European explorers in Africa. Travelers like Bruce, Le Vaillant, and Park, who were guided by a combination of scientific inquiry, sexual invasion, and pure curiosity, often found themselves at the center of public scrutiny. Condemnation of exploring and mapping finds its most direct expression in didactic poems of the day, which placed male sexual energy at the heart of discovery. On 1 January 1817 the *Morning Post* printed a poem titled "The African Expedition," where the author warns the sons of "Albion" to "check the schemes of prurient enterprise." He charges explorers and cartographers alike with putting geographic designs on "ev'ry trackless wild of Timbuctoo," on the "Niger's doubtful source," and on "the wild mazes of the Congo's course." In "Slavery" (1788), poet Hannah More likewise condemns the "spirit of discovery" as carried on by men like Cortez, Columbus, Cartouche, and Caesar, whom she labels "White Savage[s]" ruled by "uncontrolled" "lust of conquest" and "lust of gold."[21] Ignoble explorers and their cartographers, from More's perspective at least, "pant to tame earth's distant bound."[22] Rapacious, systematic, and murderous, these apparent men of valor sever families and social bonds, making "Discoverers" a "curse to man"

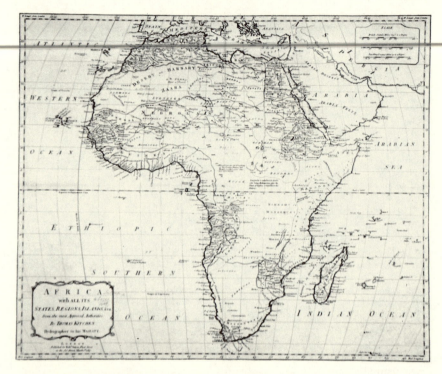

Figure 32. *Africa with all its States, Regions, Islands &c.*, printed by Robert Sayer, 1789. By permission of the British Library.

and thus "Conquest . . . pillage with a nobler name."[23] More was dead serious here, but other writers got the same point across with a less ponderous tone. One early poem, by an anonymous author, entitled "Transmigrations," in 1778, mocks Cook's *Endeavour* voyage where Joseph Banks frolicked with Tahitian women. The poem figures scientific exploration as thinly veiled sexual exploitation:

ATTEND ye swarms of MODERN TOURISTS
Yclept [so-called], or Botanists or Florists:
Ye who ascend the cloud-capt Hills,
Or creep along the tinkling Rills;
Who scientifically tell
The Wonders of each COCKLE-SHELL;
And load the Press with Publications,
With *useless, learned* DISSERTATIONS.
Ye who o'er Southern Oceans wander
With simpling B—ks or sly S—r;

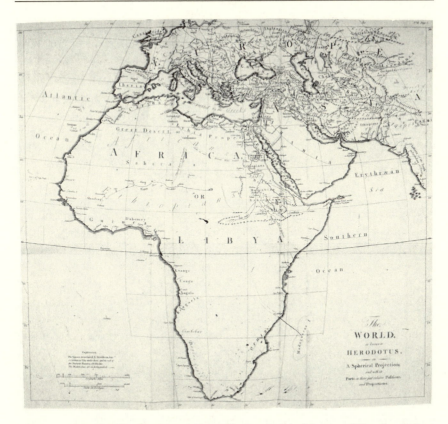

Figure 33. Map of Africa from James Rennell's *Geographical System of Herodotus*, 1800. By permission of the British Library.

Who so familiarly describe
The Frolicks of the wanton Tribe,
And think that simple Fornication
Requires no sort of Palliation

. . . .

Behold, a Queen her Gul o'er-reaches;
First steals, and then she wears his Breeches,
Such luscious Feats, when told with Ease,
Must Widows, Matrons, Maidens please;
Nor can they blush at heaving read
What ye so modestly have said:
Yet though ye strive to dress your Story,
And make (what is your Shame) your Glory,
With us this makes no Variation;
Still is it simple FORNICATION.[24]

But geographic consumption was a two-way street. On the one hand, the public viewed travelers as predatory or ridiculously curious, while on the other hand, travelers charged the public with these same sins. In 1790, the French traveler Vivant Denon wrote in his account of Egypt under Napoleon:

Here the pitiless reader, sitting quietly at his table with his map before him, will say to the poor, hungry, harassed traveller, exposed to all the trouble of war: "I see no account of Aphroditopolis, Crocodilopolis, Ptolemais — what is become of all these towns? What had you to do there, if you could not give an account of them? . . . And have I not relied upon you to give me some information on all these subjects?"[25]

As Denon has it, European readers feasted on the emaciated traveler and the emptiness of the blank map. Still other African travelers complained about how psychologically deprived they became while sending a constant stream of ethnographic and geographic information back to Europe. Park's alienation sticks in the heart of his narrative like a sliver. "I was a *stranger*, I was *unprotected*, and I was a *Christian*," he realizes at the beginning of his course to the Niger (original emphasis).[26] Even after several years in the interior of Africa, and on his way home, Park still describes himself as "a stranger in a strange land."[27] According to Park, while Africa became more familiar to the public through the map, Park himself became stranger.

Despite the antagonistic relationship between explorers and the public, the records of African journeys were the basis for a great deal of cartography, which became the scaled down, and thus symbolic, manifestation of Britain's possession of the continent. It was during the Romantic period that the British became world leaders in African cartography, just as the French and Dutch did before them. The sheer size of Aaron Arrowsmith's *A New Map of Africa* — four large sheets, each measuring 29 by 25 inches — issued in 1802 for the African Association (based on information brought back by Mungo Park), boasts the large-scale confidence Britain had in its ability to master the continent. Nor was mastery limited to official organizations. Thomas Brookes's *New Map of Africa from the Latest Authorite* (1818) takes the form of a popular jigsaw puzzle for use by the British middle class (Figure 34). It is no coincidence that at the end of the eighteenth century, when the British became world leaders in map making and successful, at least in their eyes, in bringing the world within their geopolitical lines, a British engraver and cartographer named John Salisbury invented the jigsaw puzzle using his own maps and charts. Map-puzzles gained popularity as both teaching tools for young students and geographical stimulation for the middle and leisured classes who could organize the world from their drawing rooms. For entertainment, British players competed in table games where they constructed,

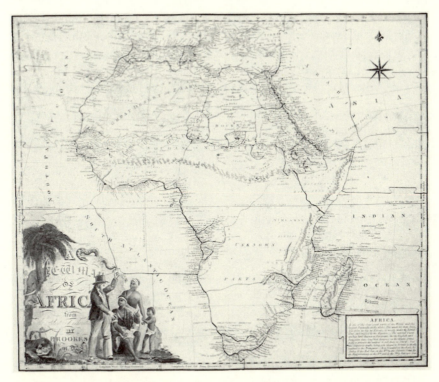

Figure 34. Thomas Brookes, *A New Map of Africa from the Latest Authoritie*, 1818. By permission of the British Library.

from misshapen pieces and fragments, the outline and interior of Africa, so as to demonstrate their command over the continent.[28]

At the same time, what played a more subtle and thus more powerful role in command over Africa was its gendered status in the European mind. Africa, in all its feminine beauty, became a symbol for the male traveler's own mental landscape. In Park's narrative, for example, although he lays eyes on the land's "fertility and abundance" for commercial purposes, during a moment of psychological despair his discovery of Africa's interior helps him rediscover himself:

I saw myself in the midst of a vast wilderness in the depth of the rainy season; naked and alone; surrounded by savage animals, and men still more savage. . . . At this moment, painful as my reflections were, the extraordinary beauty of a small moss, in fructification, irresistibly caught my eye. I mention this to shew from what trifling circumstances the mind will sometimes derive consolation; for though the whole plant was not larger than the top of one of my fingers, I could not contemplate the delicate conformation of its root, leaves, and capsula, without admiration.[29]

The scene's poetic combination of the intimate and the distant, the minutely particular and the expansively general, its portrayal of Park's utter vulnerability in the African landscape, and its mixture of natural science and sexuality, probably accounts for its popularity. In literary renditions of Park, for instance, this scene was a favorite. Mary Howitt fixed upon the incident in her "Ode to Botany":

... when sore distress
O'ertook him in the wilderness;
When courage failed, and dark Despair
Scowled on him in the withering air,
And home-thoughts in his heart sprung up —
The bitterest drops in his bitter cup;
As then — a little flower could reach
His spirit's core, and proudly preach
Of Him whose eye-lids never fall: —
Of Love, which watcheth over all.[30]

As another testament to the scene's appeal, and to one like it in Le Vaillant, Felicia Hemans used Howitt's references to Park as the epigraph of her "Flower of the Desert."[31] Hemans writes, zeroing in on Park and Le Vaillant, "Who does not recollect the exultation of Vaillant over a flower in the torrid wastes of Africa? The affectionate mention of the influence of a flower upon the mind, by Mungo Park, in a time of suffering and despondence, in the heart of the same savage country, is familiar to every one."

Just as often as Africa's flowering, fertile interior reflected itself onto the European mind, African women mirrored the mind of male explorers. Le Vaillant's notorious encounter with a young African woman revolves around his need to transform her into the image of his own mind, which, curiously enough, takes the shape of a flower. "I found her name difficult to pronounce, disagreeable to the ear, and inapplicable to my ideas," he states, "I therefore re-named her Narina, which in the Hottentot language signifies a flower, desiring her to retain this name for my sake" (Figure 35).[32]

III

Given the pervasiveness of mapping in this era, it comes as no surprise that poets employed cartographic metaphors to chart the enlarging human interiority, and that, like the travelers who inspired them, most poets adopted a stance of domination. In Wordsworth's "Ode: Intimations of Immortality from Recollections of Early Childhood," the growing poet sets "at his feet, some little plan

Figure 35. "Narina, a Young Gonaquais," from François Le Vaillant, *Travels into the Interior Parts of Africa*, 1790. By permission of the Syndics of Cambridge University Library.

or chart . . . shaped by himself with newly-learned art" (90, 93). Wordsworth's elliptical portrait draws a striking likeness to Keats, who, "On First Looking into Chapman's Homer," imagines himself charting the heavens and the seas alike, as "some watcher of the skies" or "stout Cortez" staring with "eagle eyes" at the uncharted vastness of the Pacific (9, 11). Keats thus underscores the insepara-bility of geographic and psychological structures within the symbolic order of reading and writing. Like Keats's metaphoric use of exploration, charting, and conquest, Wordsworth's sense in the "Ode" of the "Soul's immensity" urges the middle-aged poet to travel as a "Creature / Moving about in worlds not real-ized" (110, 145–46). This motif of wandering in the unknown world of the soul expands in *The Prelude*, where Wordsworth describes how the "horizon of [his] mind enlarged," how the "sanguine schemes" of his youthful days are expanded by the "intellectual" eye of imagination (13:56, 65, 57). Wordsworth even finds an apt metaphor in the overflowing Nile in a section that begins with the "Imagi-nation!—lifting up itself / Before the eye and progress of my song" and ends with the mind, "Strong in itself, and in the access of joy / Which hides it like the overflowing Nile" (6:525–26, 547–48).

It is just this sort of traveling mind, diffusing itself on fancy's spreading wing (to use Coleridge's terms) that opened up the wonders of "worlds not realized" to the British imagination in travel literature. For example, Park conceives of "fancy" as his travel guide when he claims that "Fancy had already placed me on the banks of the Niger, and presented to my imagination a thousand delightful scenes in my future progress." [33] Coleridge's expanding self is also a prerequi-site for exploratory accounts like the 1816 "Mission to the Congo," which failed (with half the men dying, and half turning back) because of the British self's desire to "possess all in all." A 10 January 1817 report in the *Morning Post* on the mission's failure diagnosed precisely this problem: "An anxious zeal and over eagerness . . . to acquire all the information that could possibly be obtained, seem to have actuated every one, from the lamented commander to the com-mon seaman and private marine, and led them to attempt more than the human constitution could bear." [34]

Like Wordsworth, Felicia Hemans employed the Nile as a metahor, only her lyric takes as its setting the travelogue of James Bruce, whom she describes in conqueror's terms:

The rapture of a conqueror's mood
Rush'd burning through his frame,—
The depths of that green solitude
Its torrents could not tame;
Though stillness lay, with eve's last smile—
Round those far fountains of the Nile. [35]

The poem is an accurate translation of the moment when Bruce mistakenly believes he is standing at the source of the Nile (actually, it was the source of the Blue Nile). The personal and national aggressiveness harbors nothing:

It is easier to guess than to describe the situation of my mind at that moment — standing in the spot which had baffled the genius, industry, and inquiry, of both ancients and moderns, for the course of near three thousand years. Kings had attempted this discovery at the head of armies, and each expedition was distinguished from the last, only by the difference of the numbers which had perished, and agreed alone in the disappointment which had uniformly, and without exception, followed them all. Fame, riches, and honour, had been held out for a series of ages to every individual of those myriads these princes commanded, without having produced one man capable of gratifying the curiosity of his sovereign, or wiping off this stain upon the enterprise and abilities of mankind, or adding this desideratum for the encouragement of geography. Though a mere private Briton, I triumphed here, in my own mind, over kings and their armies.[36]

Bruce's narrative conquest obviously renders impossible the distanced imagination — distance from the ego and a relationship of alterity with the other. It thus distorts the ethical relationship between intimacy and distance. No sooner does Bruce arrive at what he believes to be the Nile's source, than he thinks of it all as "trifling" and remembers "that magnificent scene in my own native country, where the Tweed, Clyde, and Annan, rise in one hill; three rivers, as I now thought, not inferior to the Nile in beauty." [37] The distant and intimate are at odds here. Bruce establishes a power hierarchy between African and British landscapes; he longs for the superiority of home where, as Hemans puts it, "a thousand streams of lovelier flow / Bathed his own mountain land! / Whence, far o'er waste and ocean track, / Their wild, sweet voices called him back." And then, his restless mind is described in metaphors of African topography: "darkly mingling with the thought / Of each familiar scene, / Rose up a fearful vision, fraught / With all that lay between; / The Arab's lance, the desert's gloom, / The whirling sands, the red simoom!" [38]

Yet not only Africa's interior, but the interior of Africans fascinated Europeans. Readers of African travels would expect to find accounts of the customs, habits, and resources of African states, as well as glimpses into the African state of mind. Descriptions of intimate interracial love affairs and friendships were highly popular with readers precisely because such stories highlighted the extent to which Europeans could know themselves by possessing intimate knowledge of another. François Le Vaillant (though he was ardently opposed to the slave trade and slavery) exudes sentiments of equality in regard to the Hottentots of Caffrinia. But equality here carries a peculiar meaning. Le Vaillant stresses the African-European encounter as one where the African can mirror the interiority of the European. In a friendship with a Hottentot named Klaas, for example, Le Vaillant remarks, "Klaas was . . . my equal, my brother, the confidant of my hopes and fears; more than once has he calmed my agitated mind, and re-animated my drooping courage."[39] The African mind thus not only soothes Le Vaillant's troubled mind, but becomes part of his identity as confidant of his "hopes and fears."

Poets—including the young Shelley—who specifically found feminized Africa a handy construct for discovery of the poetic imagination, aligned themselves with the ideologies of men like Bruce, Park, and Le Vaillant.[40] In "Alastor," for instance, Shelley is nourished by an Arab maiden as one of the mysteries that "dark Aethiopia in her desert hills / Conceals" (115–16). Here, as in Park's and Le Vaillant's accounts, it is the poet's interior—not Africa's—that is blank. In fact, the poet "gaze[s] and gaze[s]" on Africa's inmost mysteries "till meaning on his vacant mind / Flashed like strong inspiration" (125–28).[41] As he wanders through this foreign landscape, another maiden appears to him, and this time she does more than feed him. She becomes one with the poet's interiority: "her voice was like the voice of his own soul" (153).

This fusion of African interiority with British psychological landscape emerges most potently in the Nile sonnets of Keats, Shelley, and Hunt. In 1818, the three poets gathered at Leigh Hunt's Hampstead cottage for a poetry writing contest on the subject of the Nile. The "Nile" in these poems may have referred to the Nile River, but it also had a broader frame of reference, for at the time of the sonnet contest, the term "Nile" was given to any large river in northern Africa.[42] In the fifteen minutes the poets had to compose the sonnets, all three liberally used Egyptian and African cartography, thus showing not only the extent to which mythological and contemporary map knowledge was at their fingertips, but also the well-traveled analogy between Africa's interior and the interiority of the British psyche. Keats's sonnet begins with the "old moon-mountains African" then imagines the Nile's flow "'twixt Cairo and Decan," both contemporary dots on the African map ("To the Nile," 1, 8). Hunt employs similar geographic markers, as the Nile "laps[es] along / Twixt villages" then flows in the direction of Egyptian and African topography past "caves, pillars, pyramids" ("The Nile," 12–13, 5).[43] Similar images characterize Shelley's sonnet, where Nile rains "drench" Africa's "secret Aethiopian dells" then stream across the continent from the scorching sands of the Sahara to the "desert's ice-girt pinnacles" in the Atlas Mountains ("To the Nile," 2–3).[44] By instinctively linking the mythology of Egypt to contemporary geographic knowledge of Africa, Keats, Hunt, and Shelley reveal the logical connection between Egypt and Africa and the extent to which British familiarity with Egypt became a way to imagine what was unknown about the African continent as a whole. In the *St. James Chronicle* of 27–29 January 1801, for instance, a writer claimed that Bruce's expedition into the continent by way of Egypt revived "the striking and long continued parallel between Egypt and the extensive settlement at the Cape of Good Hope." Among many points of comparison, the main one was that "with the help of water both Countries are equally fertile."[45]

It was precisely the issue of fertility that prompted Keats, Hunt, and Shelley to make the leap from Africa's geographic interior to their own imaginative interiors. All three poets expand African mysteries to make them stand for the British imagination, especially in their barrenness and fruitfulness, lack and plenty. The flow of Hunt's Nile induces an emptiness and silence, but the bone-dry "void" also highlights the "fruitful" waters that flow in the poet as they flow into Africa (11, 12). Here Hunt emphasizes how neither geographical nor psychological emptiness can be "weighed" until it is measured, in both cartographic and poetic terms (11). The sonnet's carefully measured lines and iambic feet unfold in ways analogous to the cartographer's expansive map, spanning thousands of miles and years on a single sheet of paper. Hunt's Nile rushes past indigenous populations, but urges British mental travelers to "think how we shall take / Our own calm journey on for human sake" (13–14). The poet in his journey for growth aligns himself with the Nile as African traveler, seeking fruitfulness, insight, and calm reflection. For Keats, too, the Nile's journey into Africa is analogous with imaginative fertility. His sonnet asks, "Art thou so fruitful?" and then it answers (6):

'Tis ignorance that makes a barren waste
Of all beyond itself. Thou dost bedew
Green rushes like our rivers, and dost taste
The pleasant sun-rise. Green isles hast thou too,
And to the sea as happily dost haste. (10–14)

Shelley's sonnet is similarly positioned on a fanciful comparison between the physical geography of the Nile and the psychological geography of Western "man." "O Nile," he declares in one breath and "O man" in another, stressing their fundamental interdependence (10, 13). Shelley suggests that "knowledge" is apprehended by the British mind as the floods of the great African river, whose "soul-sustaining airs and blasts of evil / And fruits and poisons spring where'er thou flowest" (11–12).

Yet fertility was about more than imagination. Africa was represented as a fertile mother, giving birth to society, human history and mythology.[46] This made her all the more appealing as an object of poetic conquest. Europeans had to discover Africa's identity in order to discover their own; what she contained in order to find what they contained; what processes governed her to see what processes governed them. The Nile sonnets suggest how, specifically, Africa's

interior was understood as a creative category: in its fruitfulness and barrenness, Africa was linked to the "inward span" of the enlarging poetic imagination
(Keats, "To the Nile," 4). Through their provocative chemistry of geography,
topography, and legend, all three sonnets offer Africa as the source and thus
the interior of contemporary human society. "Egypt and its sands," according
to Hunt, provide an "eternal" vision, so that Africa reflects "the young world"
paved by European civilization (1, 4, 6). This myth of primitivism emerges in
Keats, too, whose nurturing Nile is "Nurse of swart nations since the world
began" (5). Similarly, in "Alastor," Shelley insists on "Dark Aethiopia" as the
land "of the world's youth," hiding in its caverns and hills "the thrilling secrets
of the birth of time" (115, 122, 128). By following the Nile through its African
shifts, Keats takes the imagination to the "moon-mountains," linking Ptolemy's
classical source for the Nile to what was labeled on nineteenth-century maps
as the "spine" or "backbone of the world." As this phrase implied, Africa became like the mythological "Atlas," supporting the world on its back. In his
turn, Shelley takes to the Atlas Mountains, with their indecisive movement between "Frost and Heat," between "blasts and meteors Tempests," and so moved
from an imaginative backbone to a geographic hybrid space (4, 6). In 1818, in
fact, the Atlas Mountains extended across the continent, separating two completely different regions: the Mediterranean basin and the Sahara. And it is these
Atlas Mountains—with their literal and imaginative blend of fire and ice—not
the ones in northern Africa, where Shelley sets a major portion of his "Witch
of Atlas."

IV

Whereas travel accounts and some Romantic poems interiorize Africa by relying
on a particular gendering of it, both Damberger's *Travels* and Shelley's "Witch of
Atlas" hinge on sexual ambiguity and thus undermine the feminization of Africa
by both kinds of explorers. Shelley goes one step further to use the feminine as
the ultimate site for alterity. Because Shelley adopts a deliberately ironic tone in
"The Witch"—one that half-parodies his use of Africa in "Alastor"—the poem
can be read in the tradition of Damberger's equally ironic travel narrative. For
it is the irony of Damberger, not the male aggressiveness of Bruce, Park, and Le
Vaillant, that Shelley plays out in his poem.

Damberger, a German from Leipzig, was believed to be the first to cross the
entire African continent from the Cape of Good Hope to Morocco and to write it
up in his 1801 *Travels Through the Interior of Africa*, so naturally his book was an
instant sensation in Europe, with entire sections of the *St. James's Chronicle* and

other London and Paris papers printing generous extracts.[47] Damberger's narrative promised to surpass previous accounts, which gave "merely a glimpse into the interior of that vast continent, and a thousand miles in a straight line from the coast, has been the extremity of every former excursion, while our present author has explored an extent of ten thousand miles through the very heart of the country."[48] But at a time boasting a new scientific ethos for African travel and cartography, Damberger's account had one serious flaw: it was pure fabrication. He never traveled through Africa at all.

Fake travel narratives abounded in Europe at this time, in part because the difficulties of international travel made it nearly impossible for others to discount travel records, especially in the African interior, since it was the most challenging place to penetrate. A certain segment of the public demanded that both travel narratives and their cartographic contributions demonstrate an ethos of truth over error, science over fiction. In 1800, one reviewer of African travel literature defined the genre's foremost criterion as "Truth of relation."[49] Thus, when a travel narrative was proved inaccurate, the press severely chastised the traveler. Mungo Park's geographic contribution was important to the British public, above all, because of its accuracy. Unlike James Bruce, who had gone before Park into Africa, but whose enthusiasm led him to create a fictitious source for the Nile, Park emerged as a navigator whose geographical "veracity has never been called into question."[50] Still, at the level of dramatic interest, another segment of the British reading public did not much care if an African travel narrative told the truth. In 1807, an abridged volume of "celebrated African travels" appeared featuring Mungo Park's and Damberger's narratives side by side. The compiler, William Mavor — "ever anxious for the satisfaction or our readers" — based his choices not on geographic accuracy but on imaginative hunger for foreign adventure "at a period, marked by the exertions of European travelers, and replete with the most excellent publications on geography of foreign countries."[51] Damberger's narrative would have been a highlight in this volume since, although it was not true, it was truly interesting.

Perhaps it was Damberger's unprecedented ease in crossing the continent (an ease also enjoyed by Shelley's witch) that first prompted readers to doubt the veracity of his narrative. Or maybe it was, simply, that he pushed the bounds of the believable. Not only did he claim to travel the continent by running from a series of amorous African women, he says he spent some time with a tribe of homosexual "Muhotians" and had an encounter with an African man who requested to wear a pair of Damberger's undergarments on his head. Reviewers seriously doubted it. *Gentleman's Magazine* cautioned that "upon first perusal it carries strong marks of romance; but as the reader proceeds he will be disgusted with narratives as indecent as untrue."[52] The *British Critic* indignantly called the

Travels "a most impudent and fraudulent publication," a "farrago of falsehood and nonsense."[53] But, as is often the case, their warnings to the British public served to entice, not to deter readers. His narrative continued to be published and read in Britain, as the abridged version of 1807 proves.

At first glance, it would seem that Damberger fabricated the narrative simply to make money. As a printer in Leipzig, he no doubt had reproduced many travel accounts — sure best-sellers for a European public hungry for geographic knowledge — and the commercial benefits must have tempted him. Yet in a climate of European obsession over Africa's interior, Damberger makes clear that this was more than just a moneymaking venture. That is, the text repeatedly calls attention to itself as hoax, as fabrication, and, like Shelley's "Witch of Atlas," emphasizes its own irony. Shelley's witch crosses standard literary conventions and she crosses Africa, and thus she "tell[s] no story, false or true"; she exists beyond "those cruel Twins . . . Error and Truth" (4, 49, 51). In her African travels, Shelley's witch also crafts out-and-out fabrications, playing "pranks" on "mortal men," "entangling them in her sweet ditties" (665–67).

Damberger's pranks are equally bewitching. For example, he uses Park's and Le Vaillant's travels as the basis for his fraudulent account, yet he repeatedly accuses them of the very literary crime he himself commits. In the midst of his own *pretend* account, he asserts: "I am surprized that M. Vaillant should *pretend* to have been in the country of the Kaminrukis" (my emphasis).[54] And he uses his own *erroneous* geography to declare that "Mungo Park has *erroneously* represented this town as lying beyound Houssa" (my emphasis).[55] Damberger's map is even more ironic: the central part of the continent is marked out by a path titled "Part of Damberger's Route which it is not easy to determine," while another section of his journey reads, "Doubtful part of the Author's Route" (Figure 36). He thus extends the hoax to the cartographic representation itself, calling attention not so much to Africa's blank center as to the European drive to penetrate it.

Damberger makes his most important ideological move by undermining the gender codes of Park and Le Vaillant. At one point, Damberger visits some Muhotians who proudly show him "a horrible spectacle . . . the bodies of five white men, pierced with innumerable wounds, and who had probably been murdered with javelins!"[56] A day later, Damberger personally encounters the chief's son-in-law:

One morning, when I was at a neighbouring thicket cutting some wood . . . the villain made me a proposal of a most shocking nature. I started back with abhorrence, and resisted his infamous attempt: but he began to employ force, threw me on the ground, and beat me so unmercifully, that my whole body was covered with bruises and livid spots. Cries and tears had no effect upon him; at last, however, when he saw that not even the

Figure 36. Map of Africa for C. F. Damberger's *Travels*, 1801. By permission of the Syndics of Cambridge University Library.

most violent treatment could extort my consent to the gratification of his abominable desires, he desisted and let me go.[57]

Damberger, of course, soon finds out that the whole Muhotian tribe wished "to obtain possession of me for the same abominable purpose; and indeed, other attempts were afterwards made to seduce me."[58] Homosexuality in the heart of Africa was unheard of in the travel narrative genre, even when it was a prank.[59] Yet as shocking as it was to early nineteenth-century readers, Damberger uses it to put a unique spin on the gendered economy of African exploration. As a feminized space, Africa could be reduced symbolically to a reflection of European man. And like African women, the continent itself became a commodity, exchanged and arranged by European explorers, cartographers, and commercial supporters back home. By eliding this naturalized version of exploration with violent homosexuality, Damberger demonstrates how conquest was more truly an encounter and a contest between men, even when it seemed to be a sexual interaction.

IV

Shelley takes this notion one step further in "The Witch of Atlas." Whereas Damberger employs homosexuality to uncover the male economy of African exploration, Shelley employs asexuality. Such ambiguity, as I mentioned at the outset, is symbolized most clearly in the hermaphrodite whom Shelley describes as a "sexless thing" (329). The hermaphrodite, although alluring, is disappointingly ineffectual precisely because its difference, and thus its essential alterity, has been stripped away. But, at the same time, the hermaphrodite is effective as a disturbing blur of sexual identity, whose job in the poem is to power the witch's touring boat. It thus critiques the use of gender codes to explore interiors.[60]

The witch's own gender confusion reinforces this conclusion. Not only does she perform her work like a "sexless bee," her genealogy clearly makes her an analogue of feminized Africa, as well as a figure who promotes masculine exploration of that terrain (589). "Her mother was one of the Atlantides" (57), which were, according to Lemprière's *Classical Dictionary*, "a people of Africa, near mount Atlas." Feminized African terrain is the witch's very womb and birth canal; this is where she "took shape and motion" in the "enwombed rocks" and emerged as a "wonder new" (79, 126, 88). Though her mother is linked to African territory, her father — Apollo (a European god) — is territorial. Shelley consistently writes this Greco-Roman god's purpose in imperialistic terms, as the "all-beholding Sun" who makes "wide voyage[s] o'er continents and seas," reigning over "all the regions which he shines upon" (58–59, 216). Given the witch's diverse genealogy, it is no wonder she herself appears to be both an imperial target and an imperializing agent.

Never satisfied with one version of things, Shelley's witch is both lack and plenty. In her identification with feminized Africa, the witch also reverses the blankness of contemporary African map knowledge. Her Africa is not just full, but overflowing with the chartable and the unchartable, the familiar and the strange, the obvious and the obscure. The Nile, for instance, spans "Aethiopia" then falls down through "chasms unfathomable" to a "subterranean portal" (379, 381). Ethnographic information follows a similar logic. The witch communes with the "spotted cameleopard" and the "fearless elephant," as well as "rude kings," "Pigmies," and "shapes . . . neither alive nor dead, / Dog-headed, bosom-eyed, and bird-footed" (89–90, 133–36). With these locales and creatures, Shelley plants his witch in an African atlas much like that of John Speed, filling it with the mythology that early-nineteenth-century cartographers had stripped away.

Even though the witch identifies herself with a version of Africa that pre-dates British exploration of the continent, she also performs her own stripping away of the continent. Just as soon as she emerges from her "dewy" cave, she "tame[s]" the predatory "beasts" that surround her (78, 93). It is not only the African wildlife she tames: "The magic circle of her voice and eyes / All savage natures did imparadise" (103–4). Along with the taming tendency, which paral-lels the activities of male travelers in Africa, the witch predicts an environmental apocalypse. "Fountains," she warns, will be "drained and dried," "solid oaks" will be stripped of "strength, and strew / Their latest leaf upon the mountains wide," the "boundless Ocean" "will be consumed," the "stubborn centre" "scat-tered, like a cloud of summer dust," and all the creatures "will perish one by one—" (226–33). It is this explosive wreckage of the formerly pristine landscape that causes the witch to make a radical shift from one who is the embodiment of African landscape to one who will travel through it, and play within it.

This taking flight makes Shelley's witch not a symbol of the vulnerability to conquest but of vulnerability to an ethical relation between self and other. This kind of vulnerability is described beautifully by Emmanuel Levinas. According to Jacques Derrida, the feminine in Levinas is synonymous with "home" and "interiority." As Derrida explains,

Levinas always opens recollection upon welcoming. He recalls the opening of recollection by the welcome, the welcome of the other, the welcome reserved for the other. . . . Levi-nas describes the intimacy of the home or of the "at home" [*chez-soi*]: these are places of gathered interiority, of recollection, certainly, but a recollection in which the hospitable welcome is accomplished.[61]

Intimacy, then, depends on the concept of the feminine, which is "the condition for recollection, the interiority of the Home, and inhabitation."[62]

Like blank Africa of the early nineteenth century, Levinas's feminine alterity is, according to Derrida "marked by a series of lacks," although this is not a bad thing.[63] On the contrary, the feminine is, as Derrida explains, a place of "vul-nerability," the embodiment of "a being that prohibits violence at the very place it is exposed to it without defense," and this is precisely what "seems to figure the face itself, even though the feminine 'presents a face that goes beyond the face,' where eros 'consists in going beyond the possible.' "[64] Indeed, Levinas de-scribes the feminine as the ultimate alterity. And it is in this sense that Shelley's mysterious witch and his mysterious Africa merge in a moment that parallels Levinas's wonderful description of the feminine as:

A flight before light . . . feminine alterity does not consist in the object's simple exteriority. Neither is made up of an opposition of wills. The Other is not a being we encounter that menaces us or wants to lay hold of us. . . . Alterity makes for all its power. Its mystery constitutes its alterity.[65]

Levinas further argues that under feminine alterity the other is not "initially characterized as freedom, from which alterity would then be deduced; the other bears alterity as essence."[66] "Alterity is accomplished in the feminine," Levinas says.[67] Derrida understands the feminine in Levinas as that which allows "one to transcend, in a single movement, at once the ego and the world of light" (that is, the domination of Western philosophical systems).[68]

"The Witch," as a statement of feminine alterity, reveals Shelley's deviation not only from narratives of conquest and domination, but also from traditional poetic practice of his own era. Mary Shelley's notes to the poem point out how Shelley, in composing "The Witch," deliberately rejected turning his poetry into something he could simply sell for a profit. She desired "that Shelley should increase his popularity, by adopting subjects that would more suit the popular taste than a poem conceived in the abstract and dreamy spirit of 'The Witch of Atlas.'" "I felt sure," she continues, "if his poems were more addressed to the common feelings," they would achieve public attention and his name would be praised instead of viciously attacked for its unorthodoxy. Mary Shelley rightly calls "The Witch" something "wildly fanciful," a poem that disregards "common feelings" in order to "revel in the fantastic ideas" of the imagination.[69] His hybrid treatment of geographical and poetic forms reveal how systems of representations like the English language and the British map allow readers to lay claim to unknown worlds. Shelley seductively challenges the reader to "unveil" his witch, but he makes such an unveiling impossible, since this interiorized world, utterly vulnerable but utterly inviolable, cannot be held down, like so many unknown lands.

This unorthodoxy was born out in the world of commerce. Unlike Bruce, Park, Le Vaillant, and the African Association, neither Damberger nor Shelley was successful in his venture. In 1801, just after the European world discovered the prankish nature of Damberger's *Travels*, the book *Of the Shoemaker Schroter, the Printer Taurinas, and the Traveler Damberger, three travelers who never traveled at all but invented their stories in one manufactory* forced the fake traveler to come clean.[70] As for "The Witch of Atlas," Ollier refused to publish it during Shelley's lifetime, so the witch never made her mark on the poetic territory of the day. But both texts help us understand that in order to read between the lines of the map and the poem, it is necessary to understand the ways travel brought Africa inside the British imagination. Both texts made the foreign distant again, unrecognizable, in order to present it as an intimate space beyond British systematizing.

Shelley places his witch in a wavering world, none of its interiors solvable, none of its outlines resolvable. With all of the witch's geographical instability, "the dim brain whirls dizzy with delight / Picturing her form" (85–86). From beginning to end, she remains as elusive as her "vapor"-like mother, but she also engages in extensive travels like her father, during which she surveys and names places. Shelley can thus have it both ways. Interaction with Africa, like Keats's use of Africa and slavery in *Lamia*, provides imaginative energy for the poetic mind, even though Shelley recognizes its harmful potential in the context of Africa's proximity through travel narratives. Shelley presents Africa as a playful witch so that he can present it as one that resists being taken over. At the same time, this playfulness becomes an enactment of the mapping and naming that was one of the telltale signs of European imperialism. With this double function and attitude, Shelley's witch of Atlas becomes witch of *the* atlas, that European book of maps and charts whose newest and most exciting space—in the British mind—was Africa.

PART IV

Facing Slavery in Britain

7
Proximity's Monsters

Ethnography and Anti-Slavery Law in Mary Shelley's Frankenstein

I

No one work from the Romantic period has haunted Western culture more than Mary Shelley's *Frankenstein*. Yet, from its beginning, the novel was destined to make its mark on the national consciousness.[1] When it first appeared in 1818, it became a major best-seller. Public interest warranted a second printing in 1823, which was also the first year that the novel bore Mary Shelley's signature.[2] That same year, it appeared as the stage play *Presumption, or the Fate of Frankenstein* at the British Opera House.[3] The play hit a deep cultural vein, at least according to a reviewer in the *London Magazine*, who wrote: "The audience crowd to it, hiss it, shudder at it, loathe it, dream of it, and come to it again. The piece has been damned by full houses night after night, but the moment it is withdrawn, the public call it up again — and yearn to tremble once more before it."[4] Packed with myths and metaphors, loaded with cultural knowledge, it was no wonder the public "call[ed] it up," like a phantom, or a Hamlet's ghost. The story of a doctor pursued by his creature riveted audiences because one of the things it did best was blur the lines between the extremes of man and monster, and thus between the country's own cultural extremes of rich and poor, citizen and foreigner, male and female, master and slave.[5]

More recent responses to *Frankenstein*, namely those of the latter twentieth century, have also seen the novel in light of these ideological categories of class, gender, and race.[6] H. L. Malchow, in particular, argues that the monster was based on "evolving contemporaneous representation of ethnic and racial" difference.[7] Malchow admits the lack of hard evidence to establish Mary Shelley's intimate knowledge of abolitionist literature. But it is significant that she began the book in 1816, when the first heated debates over the emancipation of slaves took place in Britain, which were provoked by a major slave revolt in Barbados, one of Britain's most lucrative islands. It was here, on Easter Sunday of 1816, that slaves laid waste to seventy plantations and lit a third of the island on fire. They burned cane fields and houses as the whites fled to the nearby cities of Bridgetown and Oistins. The white plantocracy immediately established martial law, and besides the 100 slaves who were killed in the uprising, 144 more were executed, 170 deported, and hundreds of others sentenced to death or excessive punishments.[8]

Mary Shelley may very well have been aware of this well-publicized conflict when she began the novel, because, although she was living in Switzerland, it was this same year that she met Matthew Gregory Lewis, who stopped to visit the Shelleys and Byron on his way home from his Jamaican plantation.[9] Lewis fascinated them with ghost stories and stories detailing the "mysteries of his trade," which Percy Shelley then transcribed into Mary's journal the day following Lewis's visit.[10] Lewis himself was keeping a journal of his Jamaican voyage, and on his way to see the Shelleys he had written a strange poem called "The Isle of Devils," whose central figure is a rejected African. Described as a "demon," a "fiend," and a "monster," he is the mirror image of Shelley's creature. Indeed, it is hard not to see the resemblance between the African figure in Lewis's poem and Frankenstein's monster. What is especially striking is the sad rejection, the painful ugliness, and the unfulfilled longing that Lewis's creature and Shelley's monster share. When we first hear him, Lewis's creature utters "a moan, / So full, so sad, so strange — not shriek — not groan — / Something scarce earthly." [11] And like Shelley's monster, Lewis's creature evokes genuine sympathy in the reader. He is introduced, from the point of view of the poem's heroine, in these terms:

> —a form,
> Gigantic as the palm, black as the storm,
> All shagged with hair, wild, strange in shape and show,
> Towered on the loftiest cliff, and gazed below . . .
> On *her* he gazed, and floods of sable fires
> Rolled his huge eyes, and spoke his fierce desires . . .

> . . . Sad and slow
> He rose, resumed his club, and turn'd to go.
> Reproachful was his look, but still 'twas kind;
> He climb'd the rock, but oft he gazed behind;
> He reach'd the cave; one look below he threw;
> Plaintive again he moan'd, and with slow steps withdrew.[12]

This is the description we get when we first meet Lewis's creature. When we finally leave Shelley's, we get almost this same picture. As Walton enters the cabin and sees Frankenstein

. . . over him hung a form which I cannot find words to describe; gigantic in stature, yet uncouth and distorted in its proportions . . . his face was concealed by long locks of ragged hair; but one vast hand was extended, in colour and apparent texture like that of a mummy. When he heard the sound of my approach, he ceased to utter exclamations of grief and horror, and sprung towards the window. (216)

Clearly, Shelley and Lewis were thinking in similar terms. But besides Lewis's timely visit, Shelley at least knew enough about the emancipation debate to boycott sugar in protest over slavery. It seems logical to contend, then, that Mary Shelley drew on attitudes toward Africans and slaves in her depiction of the monster.[13]

While Romantic-period audiences were busy reading the 1823 edition of *Frankenstein* and watching the stage version, agitation over slave emancipation reached an all-time high. The year 1823 marks the emancipation movement at its most intense, most complex, and most articulate point. That year, the abolitionist lobby gave themselves an official name, the Anti-Slavery Society, and established a regular publication, the *Anti-Slavery Reporter* (both of which still exist today). And 1823 was also the year of the Demerara uprising, where the colony's well-established British plantocracy was overtaken by some 30,000 rebel slaves.[14] It started on just two plantations, the Success and Le Resouvenir, but it quickly spread across fifty estates, covering most of the land between Demerara's two major coastal cities, Georgetown and Mahaica, with rebel leaders announcing, "the negroes [are] determined to have nothing more or less than their freedom." [15] In retaliation, the planters declared martial law and then killed over one hundred slaves, set fire to their huts, and sentenced the rest to one thousand lashes or lives of hard labor in chain gangs.[16]

The revolt accompanied the famously volatile emancipation debates of 1823–24 held in the British Parliament. The most widely publicized speech during this period was issued by George Canning, the leader of the House of Commons, and here he compared the eager-to-be-emancipated slaves to Frankenstein's monster:

In dealing with the negro, Sir, we must remember that we are dealing with a being possessing the form and strength of a man, but the intellect only of a child. To turn him loose in the manhood of his physical strength, in the maturity of his physical passions, but in the infancy of his uninstructed reason, would be to raise up a creature resembling the splendid fiction of a recent romance; the hero of which constructs a human form, with all the corporeal capabilities of man, and with the thews and sinews of a giant; but being unable to impart to the work of his hands a perception of right and wrong, he finds too late that he has only created a more than mortal power of doing mischief, and himself recoils from the monster which he has made.[17]

Whatever sources in the slave debate Mary Shelley drew on, one thing is clear: the slave debate drew on her. Indeed, what has not been adequately appreciated is the way Shelley's novel literally shaped the content of debates after 1818. Because it actually furnished some of the metaphors for the debates over the status of slaves, *Frankenstein* occupies a singular place in Romantic literature. Canning's speech, it turns out, evokes the first murder scene in the novel, when the abandoned creature grabs little William, who then cries, "monster! ugly wretch! you wish to eat me, and tear me to pieces" (139).[18] The British could expect no less from the violent slave population, Canning predicted. To free slaves would be to "let loose one-half of mankind upon the other."[19] "You will occasion an insurrection of all the blacks. You will cause the murder of all the whites," one proslavery M.P. said, simply.[20] Mary Shelley, however, would not have agreed. For in *Frankenstein* monstrosity and murderish consumption were not just intimately tied; they were qualities that characterize all men. In fact, one of the novel's memorable lines, spoken by Frankenstein's bride Elizabeth, that all men are "monsters thirsting for each other's blood," provides a capsule history of British paranoia over slavery by emphasizing two of its more grizzly metaphors: monstrosity and vampirism/cannibalism (88). These metaphors, when read back through the cultural history *and* through the novel, illustrate the devastating failure of alterity, as monstrosity and vampirism/cannibalism are used to describe first Africans and slaves, and then the British themselves.

II

Both Mary Shelley and British lawmakers used monstrosity and cannibalism metaphorically, but the terms were taken literally in British ethnographic literature.[21] One of the more widely read sources of the day (which Mary Shelley knew) was Bryan Edwards's 1793 *History, Civil and Commercial, of the British West Indies*. Edwards, who had traveled to the Caribbean and back since the age of sixteen, and who went on to become a credible member of Britain's scientific community, presented a picture of the native "Caraibees" (as he called them) that would make any Briton queasy. "Restless, enterprizing and ardent," he described them, "it would seem they considered war as the chief end of their creation, and the rest of the human race as their natural prey; for they devoured without remourse the bodies of such of their enemies . . . as fell into their hands."[22] Cannibalism—taking the rest of the human race as natural prey—rendered the native Caribbeans "the fiercest monsters of the wilderness; since they who shew no mercy are entitled to no pity."[23] With this comment, Edwards foregrounded the nineteenth-century European belief that cannibalism was the root of monstrosity.

Edwards drew most of his information about native Caribs from his reading of historical sources. Just as present-day ethnographers debate over the actual practice of cannibalism, eighteenth-century writers also had cannibal debates. These began with the writings of Christopher Columbus, who claimed he saw in the native Caribs' cottages "the head and limbs of the human body recently separated, and evidently kept for occasional repasts." [24] Others, such as the natural historian Edward Bancroft, in his 1769 *Essay on the Natural History of [Dutch] Guiana*, disagreed that native populations ate human flesh as if it were chicken or beef. Bancroft said that "Carribbees" of Guiana "never eat any of the human species, except their enemies killed in battle." [25] In fact, the casual consumption of chicken and beef, in which the average Briton daily indulged, was actually worse, in Bancroft's view, than the flesh-eating Caribs who at least ate only their enemies. Bancroft asked his readers to "survey, without an involuntary horror, the mangled carcasses of inoffensive animals, exposed in a *London* market, who have been killed to gratify our appetites." [26] And so in one swift move, Bancroft conflated native cannibalism and British consumption, turning a literal practice into a metaphor.

Edwards was definitely influenced by Bancroft's text, and he may also have known the classic text on cannibalism, William Snelgrave's 1734 *A New Account of Some Parts of Guinea and the Slave Trade*. Snelgrave, like previous agents of the Western civilizing mission, had an agenda that involved describing the sacrilegious practices of Africans in order to rationalize Western expansion. It helped that he was describing the kingdom of Dahomey, which, in the eyes of Europeans, was the fiercest of all African tribes. As he tells it, Snelgrave arrives in Dahomey just in time to save a "little Negroe-Child, tied by the Leg to a Stake driven in the Ground, and flies and other vermin crawling on him, and two Priests standing by" ready to sacrifice and cannibalize the child.[27] If this is not enough, Snelgrave details the practice, though willingly admitting he was no "Eye-witness" [28]:

Then he [the Priest] gave the sign of Execution, to a Man that stood behind the Victim with a broad Sword, who immediately struck him on the nape of the Neck, with such force, that the Head was severed at one Blow, from the Body; whereupon the Rabble gave a great Shout. The Head was cast on the Stage, and the Body, after having lain a little while on the Ground, that the Blood might drain from it, was carried away by Slaves, and thrown in a place adjoining to the Camp. The Linguist told us, the Head of the Victim was for the king, the Blood for the *Fetiche*, or God; and the Body for the common People.[29]

Snelgrave thus establishes the Dahomeans as a monstrous band of Africans who eat human flesh. But he does so in order to justify the European consumption of slave labor, saying "That tho' to traffick in human Creatures, may at first sight appear barbarous, inhuman, and unnatural," this is no worse than the cannibalism of the Dahomeans. For so many Africans "would be inhumanly destroyed, was there not an Opportunity of disposing of them to the *Europeans* . . . especially to the *Sugar Islands*, which lying in a Climate near as hot as the Coast of *Guinea*, the *Negroes* are fitter to cultivate the Lands there, than white People."[30] Snelgrave's (and others') descriptions of cannibalistic practices in Africa merged with what were thought to be similar practices in the Caribbean. In this way, Africans forced into West Indian slavery were seen simply to be moving from one cannibal culture to another.

Throughout Western history, cannibal cultures have been interpreted in a variety of ways. As early as the sixteenth century, the French thinker Michel de Montaigne wrote that cannibals simply had a "zealous concern for courage." Later, in the early twentieth century, Freud claimed that among the higher motivations for consuming another person is the belief that "by incorporating parts of a person's body through the act of eating, one at the same time acquires the qualities possessed by him."[31] In the eyes of eighteenth-century Europeans, cannibal cultures were equally fascinating, but they were characterized primarily as immoral. The anthropologist Christy G. Turner has said that, as far as cannibalism is concerned, morality is the operative word: "Eating someone is disruptive, inconsiderate, evil. Cannibalism is bad, and bad people are cannibals."[32] It was this moral ethnography to which abolitionist and Romantic writers responded. In the first few pages of George Colman's 1808 play *The Africans*, for instance, viewers are reminded that though Africans seem to possess some admirable qualities, they are dangerous cannibals who devour their enemies.[33] Colman declares it "an humiliating truth that the nobler virtues are more practised among the barbarian tribes than by civilized society;—that the savage heathen, who wages war to extermination and devours his captives, not unfrequently displays a glorious self denial."[34] In the same breath, however, Colman calls Britons "cannibals" because through slavery they feed on "human mutton."[35] Even in the so-called ethnographic accounts of the Caribbean and Africa, where readers might not expect anthropological terms to be used so freely, there are questions about who are the real monsters, and who are the cannibalistic consumers. Indeed, in Bryan Edwards's *History*, European disgust in response to cannibalism is matched in intensity only by native Caribbean horror in response to slavery. Edwards acknowledges how the European "repugnance" to the custom of eating humans in the same section where he speaks of the Charib's "abhorrence of slavery."[36]

Early abolitionists took earnest delight in pushing these ethnographic terms (cannibalism and monstrosity) off their literal footings, past their metaphoric moorings, and clear through to the other side of meaning, where the terms were then used against the likes of Columbus, Snelgrave, and Edwards. Robert Southey's 1797 "Poems Concerning the Slave Trade," for instance, are vigorously explicit in linking monstrosity with the man-eating British consumers. On Africa's "plain," the British are like "gorged vulture[s]," clogging their "beak[s] with blood."[37] This hideous activity makes them "pale fiend[s]" who "sip the blood-sweeten'd beverage."[38] In Southey's view, this desire for blood is then transferred to the slave himself who drenches his sword's "thirsty blade / In the hard hearts of his inhuman lord."[39] Southey, of course, was not the only abolitionist to use such terms. Because of the Briton's consuming "rage for blood . . . men call'd *Christians* may be monsters too," wrote the poet Mary Birkett.[40] William Roscoe's poems "Mount Pleasant" and "The Wrongs of Africa" also call British commerce "a bloated monster,"[41] and then warn the entire world about the "demon form, / That tramples o'er creation."[42] Abolitionist poetry took the terms of ethnographic literature, turned them into metaphors, and then thrust them back onto British consciousness: British monstrosity and cannibalism caused monstrosity and cannibalism in the slave population. Mary Shelley's novel necessarily reflected the complex history of these ethnographic terms because Frankenstein identifies intensely with his creature at the same time he repeatedly refers to the creature as a "monster," a "demon," and a "fiend."

If the British were monsters, their monstrosity centered on the consumption of sugar. Since a large percentage of British slaves worked in sugar production, sugar itself became the central way to talk about Britain's consumption of slaves.[43] What is astounding is the sheer number of variations this metaphor underwent in the increasingly explosive slavery debate. One of the most powerful uses was by Coleridge, in his *Lecture on the Slave Trade*. Here, the jarring equation of sweetness and slavery must have stirred something in his audience, especially since he broke out in a sweat of exclamation marks whenever he set slavery and sugar in close proximity. For Coleridge, slavery not only negated the Christian mealtime blessing, but also cast a heavy shadow on the very idea of the sacramental body and blood:

Gracious Heaven! at your meals you rise up and pressing your hands to your bosom ye lift up your eyes to God and say O Lord bless the Food which thou hast given us! A part of that Food among most of you is sweetened with the Blood of the Murdered. Bless the Food which thou hast given us! O Blasphemy! Did God give Food mingled with Brothers blood! Will the Father of all men bless the Food of Cannibals — the food which is polluted with the blood of his own innocent Children? (*Lects 1795*, 248)

It is impossible not to notice the fiery tone of this speech, as Coleridge insists that the British are elbow-deep in guilt for their consumption of slave products. The result is nothing less than blasphemy, the unforgivable sin. But as we have seen, although Coleridge was the most passionate, he certainly was not the only one to speak of slavery in these terms. In fact, he called upon well-known sources to defend his choice of cannibalism as a metaphor for slavery. According to Abbé Raynal, whom Coleridge quoted, "nine millions of Slaves had been consumed by the Europeans" (*Lects 1795*, 246).

Of all the slave-produced goods—and Coleridge names quite a few, including "Rum, Cotton, logwood, cocoa, coffee, pimento, ginger, indigo, mahogany, and conserves"—it was sugar that became the cultural nexus, the crossroads of British economics, British slavery, and British high culture (*Lects 1795*, 236). The most striking example of sugar's complex status comes from the works of the Jamaican physician Benjamin Moseley. Moseley had studied medicine in London, Paris, and Leyden, and had settled in Jamaica in 1768, where he was appointed surgeon-general of the island. From this position, he treated plantation owners and slaves (though he had a reputation for actually losing the lives of patients, not saving them) and became an expert in tropical medicine. He seems to have made a fortune from his medical practice in the West Indies. One of the high points of his career was treating Lord Nelson for malaria in 1780. Moseley returned to England where he increasingly became known for his unscientific thinking.[44] Part of this had to do with the vigorous campaign he led against vaccination developed by Edward Jenner in 1802 and publications such as his *Treatise on Sugar*, which was published in 1799, with a second edition in 1800.

Moseley strongly advocated the consumption of sugar for the health of Britons, explaining in his *Treatise on Sugar* that civilized people needed sugar just as much as they needed slaves.[45] "The loss of sugar" to the "diet of Europe" could not be estimated, he claimed, adding that "there is more nourishment in a pound of sugar, than in a load of pulse, or vegetables." Some sugar theorists, or "saccharine enthusiasts," as Moseley called them, attributed the "extinction of the plague" to the introduction of sugar into the European diet. Nor was sugar simply a talisman against disease. It formed the essential civilized British character. The "formation of the body" and the "inclination of the mind" both depended on a steady intake of sugar.[46]

Belief in sugar as the food of the civilized, in "SUGAR CANE" as "the heart of the solar world," led Moseley to warn how sugar's absence from the British diet would result in a very dangerous form of monstrosity.[47] To illustrate this, Moseley's *Treatise on Sugar* carried the remarkable story of a vegetarian tiger and its dramatic plunge from sugared civility to blood savagery. He tells of a

Mr. Parker, in Jamaica, who brought up a "Spanish tyger" on "milk and sugar ... from the time it was newly born, until it was nearly full grown. It slept in his room, and went about the house like a spaniel." One day, Mr. Parker "was taken ill of a fever. I directed him to be bled. Soon after the operation he fell asleep, with the tyger ... on the bed. During his sleeping, the arm bled considerably. The tyger, which as yet had never seen blood, while Mr. Parker was sleeping," chewed "his shirt sleeve, and the bloody part of the sheet into a thousand pieces. He also got at the bleeding orifice of the vein, and licked up the blood running from it." Then, "Forgetting in a moment his domestic education, and the kindness of his master, began to use the arm with some roughness with his teeth, which awakened Mr. Parker. Soon, the tyger and master were in mutual consternation. The tyger gave a spring, and jumped on a high chest of drawers in the room; from that, to the chairs, and tables, and ran about the house in wild and horrible phrenzy. I arrived at the house at the time of this confusion. The tyger escaped into the garden: — where he was shot." [48]

Throughout his works, Moseley seems to be particularly bad at matching up his claims with appropriate examples, and this story is no exception. The vegetarian tyger is not convincing as an example of sugar-tamed savagery because the story strikes readers as poignant and tragic; it is the caged and domesticated tiger, not Mr. Parker's ravaged arm, and certainly not Moseley's mock heroism, that evokes sympathy. However, what is most interesting is that the story appears *only* in the second edition of the *Treatise on Sugar*, where it completely replaces a story of slave revolt through Afro-Caribbean magic. This story is the one about the rebel slave Jack Mansong, which was the basis for a number of dramatic pieces. It became a hit on the British stage, first in pantomime just a year after Moseley's account, and later as a melodrama called *Obi, or Three Finger'd Jack*. In Moseley's first edition of the *Treatise on Sugar*, the Three Finger'd Jack story was originally meant to illustrate the very same principle that the vegetarian tiger illustrates in the second edition: that sugar tames savagery.[49] The slaves of Jamaica, who existed on a diet of vegetables, meat, and vengeance, who made sugar but were prevented from eating it, become Moseley's examples of humans gone awry.

Hailing sugar as the civilized person's commodity, Moseley reversed the antislavery claim of sugar consumption as cannibalism. British cannibalism, in the eyes of saccharine enthusiasts, instead coincided with eating meat. One only had to walk down the streets of London, said Moseley, where "blood flows in almost every gutter. In the very central, and most frequented places in the town, — what a horrid picture do the slaughter houses present!" [50] Substituting sugar for animal food was, according to Moseley, the brainchild of Pythagoras, who hoped "the earth would cease to represent a grazing ground, for slaughter; and its bloody inhabitants a mass of cannibals." [51] Moseley and others like him completely ignored the widely publicized abolitionist link between slave blood, sugar, and British cannibalism to claim sugar as the mainstay of civilized European culture. Such was the importance of the "agriculture of half a million Africans" to the British. [52]

If sugar theorists promoted sugar consumption, antislavery advocates just as stubbornly called for sugar boycotts. For as the poet Mary Birkett said—addressing her "sisters" (women who collectively fought for abolition)—sugar abstinence formed the only possible action for the high-minded humanitarian. The British consumer could aid in the emancipation of slavery "If we the produce of their toils refuse, / If we no more the blood-stain'd lux'ry choose; / If from our lips we push the plant away / For which the liberties of thousands pay." [53] Other poets, like William Cowper, took a satirically damning approach. Cowper's "Pity for Poor Africans" mimics the voice of British consumers, who were decidedly against depriving themselves of sugar and rum:

I pity them greatly, but I must be mum,
For how could we do without sugar and rum?
Especially sugar so needful we see;
What, give up our desserts, our coffee, and tea? [54]

But in Cowper's most famous antislavery poem "The Negro's Complaint," which became a highly popular abolitionist broadsheet, he addressed the pain of Africans, this time from within the voice of slaves:

Why did all-creating Nature
Make the plant, for which we toil?
Sighs must fan it, tears must water,
Sweat of ours must dress the soil.
Think, ye Masters, iron-hearted,
Lolling at your jovial boards;
Think how many backs have smarted
For the sweets your Cane affords. [55]

In this case, Cowper blames "all-creating Nature," or God himself, for making the "plant" so addictive to British consumers. The slave's body fluids and emotions—sweat, tears, and sighs—nurture the sugarcane which, in turn, the unthinking white consumer drinks down. Sugar and cannibalism were major themes in The Anti-Slavery Album, a volume featuring a number of prominent poets such as Cowper and Hannah More. [56] An anonymous poem entitled "The Sugar Cane" describes the plant in this way:

... the eastern plant, ingrafted on the soil,
Was till'd for ages with consuming toil,
While with vain wealth it gorged the master's hoard,
And spread with manna his luxurious board.[57]

The poet imagines labor "consuming" the slave, while Europeans "gorge" themselves on the product of that labor. Several other poems in the *Anti-Slavery Album* are particularly concerned with sugar's intimate link with slave blood. Amelia Opie's "The Black Man's Lament" considers that the sugarcane's "tall gold stems contain / A sweet rich juice," and for this "the Negro toils, and bleeds, and *dies*." [58] And sugar's sweetness opposes the bitter cup of life slaves endure in Timothy Touchstone's *Tea and Sugar, or the Nabob and the Creole*:

This is the sweet ingredient, SUGAR call'd.
Made by the sweat and blood of the enthrall'd,
Bitter their cup, alas! who makes this sweet,
Poor Slaves! whose hearts, in sad affliction beat . . .[59]

As all of these poems demonstrate — and these are just a small sample of the hundreds that exist on the subject — sugar emphasized that slavery turned on the axis of consumption.

The emancipation debates of 1823–24 incorporated the ideas of monstrosity and cannibalism into their language as if these terms just naturally explained the state of slavery. In Parliament, this was especially true: "Now what is the commodity in dispute?" asked one M.P.: "The body of the black man . . . roused from [his] rest by the yells of the man-hunter." [60] Similarly, Thomas Folwell Buxton, who had introduced the first bill for immediate emancipation, said it was "monstrous" for the British to make slaves out of "seven hundred thousand" Africans who were, by definition, now British citizens.[61] But the British were worse than monsters, according to Buxton. They were, at least in the metaphors of the rhetoric, outright cannibals. They feasted on what he referred to as the "bones" and "muscles" of slaves, and the nation, therefore, was "satiated with slavery." [62] William Wilberforce had been much more explicit some years earlier. He had cited the incident of an "overseer" on a Jamaican estate who "threw a slave INTO THE BOILING CANE JUICE" where he died and partially disintegrated.[63] With this horrifying example, Wilberforce implied that oftentimes Europeans literally consumed Africans when they consumed sugar.

But abolition of slavery was objected to in similar terms. Abolition, one M.P. protested, would "occasion an insurrection of all the blacks, [and] cause the murder of all the whites."[64] Another proslavery advocate, the Rev. John Hampden, made the alarming comment that emancipation would "inevitably be the ruin of a numerous class of our fellow subjects; the sacrifice of an important branch of territory; the sunset of British light, and influence in these regions of the western hemisphere, and the protracted reign of darkness, vice, and barbarism."[65] This embarrassingly racist statement comes from Hampden's 1823 pamphlet titled *A Commentary on Mr. Clarkson's pamphlet, entitled "Thoughts on the necessity of improving the conditions of the Slaves in the British colonies, with a view to their ultimate emancipation,"* and it is a good example of issues at the heart of this debate. Hampden was a member of the West Indian planters, the strongest lobby against abolitionists like Thomas Clarkson. Clarkson, in fact, was the planters' particular foe, because he was the most active and personally persuasive abolitionist. Hence, Hampden's attack on Clarkson in this pamphlet. Clarkson's own pamphlet, published in 1823, was probably his most powerful abolitionist work because it is here he introduced the argument that slavery was actually a criminal offense. He also addressed the problem of the increasingly frequent slave insurrections, which the planters had come to fear as a Frankenstein's monster. Planters blamed revolts on antislavery agitation in Britain, claiming that whenever slaves learned of supposed reforms in Parliament, they would then take matters into their own hands. But Clarkson defended the slaves' right to rebel, arguing that colonial legislatures must take the blame for having done nothing toward either improvement of slave conditions or emancipation.

In the initial days of 1823, the Anti-Slavery Society had sought the support of George Canning, who had argued in favor of abolition of the trade years earlier. But on the emancipation issue, Canning had sympathies in both directions. He had two prominent West Indian friends in Parliament, Charles Ellis and John Gladstone. On 22 April 1823, Ellis held a meeting of the London Committee of the West India Merchants and Planters. This group established a variety of changes to the existing institution to avoid sweeping changes that the imperial Parliament, under pressure of the Anti-Slavery Society, might impose. In the end, to the disappointment of the Anti-Slavery Society's members, Canning sided with the planters by comparing the slave population to Mary Shelley's *Frankenstein*, and thus reinforcing that monstrosity and cannibalism were qualities to fear in slaves, not in British lawmakers. But when these terms are read back through the novel in light of the emancipation debate, they show that just as Frankenstein has trouble distinguishing between himself and his creature, so the British had increasing trouble distinguishing between themselves and the worst characteristics they attributed to slaves.

III

Frankenstein deliberately sets up a troubling relationship between consumption and monstrosity: creatures—human or otherwise—must consume, but the more they do, the more insatiable they become, until finally they become monstrous, "thirsting for each other's blood" (88). Such symbolic cannibalism is given power in the novel, first and foremost, through its heavy emphasis on actual food and eating. Eating and hunger, in fact, mark all the creature's inaugural human experiences. In his first moment of consciousness, it is the monster's appetite that raises him up from his laboratory bed: he explains how he "felt tormented by hunger and thirst" which "roused" him "from [his] nearly dormant state" (98). He goes into the world not to become a social being, but to eat. "I often spent the whole day searching in vain for a few acorns to assuage the pangs of hunger," he relates (100).

Appetite provides the motivation for most of the creature's activities. It is because of his appetite that he learns language: his first words are *"fire, milk, bread,* and *wood"* (107). Also, his first encounters with human communities stem from his appetite. "I arrived at the village," he declares concerning his first human encounter, and "how miraculous did this appear! . . . The vegetables in the gardens, the milk and cheese that I saw placed in the windows of some of the cottages, allured my appetite" (101). And, his first moral act arranges itself around appetite. He explains how he "had been accustomed, during the night, to steal" the DeLacey food for his "own consumption" (106), but as pangs of morality and kindness register in his being, he decides that taking the food produced by another is wrong. Appetite also becomes the focus for the creature's climactic personal encounter with the DeLaceys. Old DeLacey greets the creature by saying, "I am afraid I shall find it difficult to procure food for you," to which the creature replies, "I have food; it is warmth and rest only that I need" (129).

If the creature's appetite and desire for companionship bring him to life, appetite and a need for community also control Frankenstein's behavior. His own appetite increases the closer he comes to confronting his monster. After destroying the creature's half-finished mate, Frankenstein sits "on the shore, satisfying" his "appetite, which had become ravenous" (267). On his monster-hunt, Frankenstein views food and natural appetite as a kind of salvation:

overcome by hunger, sunk under by exhaustion, a repast was prepared for me in the desert that restored and inspirited me. The fare was indeed coarse, such as the peasants of the country ate; but I may not doubt that it was set there by the spirits that I had invoked to aid me. Often, when all was dry, the heavens cloudless, and I was parched by thirst, a slight cloud would bedim the sky, shed the few drops that revived me, and vanish. (201)

Not only does spiritual food, like manna from heaven, sustain Frankenstein, but when he is on the brink of death, ingestion revives him. They restore "him to animation by rubbing him with brandy," and forcing him to "swallow a small quantity" (20).

Hunger is, of course, a basic human need. It is therefore the natural, if not strictly physiological, outcome of the creature's and Frankenstein's exhausting trek over the Alps. But since the novel intentionally constructs both the creature's and Frankenstein's higher motives using the discourses of consumption, eating, vampirism, and cannibalism, it calls attention to the ways those same discourses were used in the British social-political world: in antislavery literature, in slave legislation, and in Afro-Caribbean ethnography. The interplay of these discourses makes it apparent that, in African-British relations, it was difficult to tell who were the monsters and who were the cannibals.

This confusion raises an unsettling question: how does one become so addicted to consumption in the first place? The creature identifies himself as "a vagabond and a slave" who turns to cannibalism only after he suffers rejection and a deep sense of wrong at his master's hand (115). He enacts his first revenge on little William who links the creature to the "monstrous" practice of cannibalism. William cries, "monster! ugly wretch! you wish to eat me, and tear me to pieces" (139). William declares the creature a monster and a cannibal; the creature accepts this as a self-fulfilling prophecy. He kills William and digests the thought of successful revenge within his own bloated body. Shelley tells us that as the monster gazes on the limp William, his "heart swell[s] with exultation and hellish triumph" (139). This important scene parallels George Canning's emancipation speech, when he imagined the rejected and abused slaves would exult in "hellish triumph" over the whites once the slave system was dismantled.

Other politicians in the 1823–24 pamphlet war, which followed Canning's speech, were more specific about monstrosity, consumption, and the system of slavery. In *A Letter to the Rev. Mr. Hall . . . in Answer to His Attack on West Indian Proprietors, with Some Observations on the General Question as to the Abolition of West Indian Slavery*, James Barstow summarizes the central issue of the debate, as well as of the novel. In the system of slavery, master and slave become one:

By subjecting one human creature to the absolute control of another, it annihilates the most essential prerogative of a reasonable being, which consists in the power of determining his own actions, in every instance in which they are not injurious to others. . . . Slavery introduces the most horrible confusion, since it degrades human beings from the denomination of persons to that of things; and by merging the interests of the slave in those of the master, he becomes a mere appendage to the existence of another, instead of preserving the dignity which belongs to a reasonable and accountable nature.[66]

In the novel, slave and master merge through the consumptive tendencies of both Frankenstein and his creature. They become incorporated into one another. And it was this aspect of British-African relations that Parliament most feared: mutual devouring and mutual death, when all become "as monsters thirsting after one another's blood." Monstrosity defines the creature's "insatiable thirst for vengeance," a quality that no doubt stirred legislators like Canning, who feared the slave population had a similar "thirst for vengeance," as they saw in the frequent insurrection attempts either on board ship or after slaves were torn from their families in the Caribbean (218). It is a similar tearing away of "family" bonds that motivates the creature to retaliate. After his eviction from the DeLacey household, thoughts of retribution take hold. As he tells Frankenstein, "feelings of kindness and gentleness, which I had entertained but a few moments before, gave place to hellish rage and gnashing of teeth" (138). With this dismemberment of the familial DeLacey bonds, he begins to feed on human misery: "no incident occurred from which my rage and misery could not extract its food," he laments (136).

The more the creature seeks revenge, the more Frankenstein reveals his own vengeful appetite. The creature's "insatiable thirst for revenge" takes on its colossal proportions only when Frankenstein recognizes the creature's insatiability as his own: "revenge," he explains, becomes "the devouring and only passion of my soul" (198). Frankenstein, in fact, spends most of his time merely reflecting the creature, the "murderer, whom [he] turned loose upon society" (198). Even with this sort of dire warning spelled out in the novel, it seems to have been beyond the imaginative range of Canning and other conservative members of Parliament to view themselves as Frankensteinian creators who engineered a type of cannibalistic monstrosity that would fold back on and become one with the creators themselves. Yet this is exactly how Frankenstein assesses his relationship with the creature. He speaks in despair of

the being whom I had cast among mankind, and endowed with the will and power to effect purposes of horror, such as the deed which he had now done, nearly in the light of my own vampire, my own spirit let loose from the grave, and forced to destroy all that was dear to me. (72)

Like the British attitude toward the slave population, Frankenstein looks reflexively at himself by seeing the creature as a monstrous murderer, and so he makes his other the vampire, even as he ("my own spirit") is the consumer of others. Justine and William, he recognizes, are actually his victims. He thus avoids and evades his own vampirism even as he admits it: "I, not in deed, but in effect, was the true murderer" (88).

As many readers of *Frankenstein* have noted, Coleridge's ideas had influenced Mary Shelley in the composition of the novel. "The Ancient Mariner" provided a model not only for Robert Walton on his "voyage of discovery towards the northern pole" (20), but, more strikingly, for Frankenstein himself. The parallel between the mariner's sick soul and Frankenstein's hungry one occurs most pointedly when Frankenstein first brings his monster to life. As he rushes out of the room in horror, in fact, Coleridge's "Rime" is foremost on Frankenstein's mind:

My heart palpitated in sickness of fear; and I hurried on with irregular steps, not daring to look about me: —
   Like one, who on a lonely road,
   Doth walk in fear and dread,
   And, having once turned round, walks on,
   And turns no more his head;
   Because he knows a frightful fiend
   Doth close behind him tread. (54; cf. "The Rime of the Ancient Mariner," 446–51)

To quote this, of all the passages, from Coleridge's poem is to invoke the mariner's fear of a shadowy alter ego, a doppelgänger his own guilt has created. It is, effectively, to call up alterity's failure, a situation where the self is constituted in its relationship to another without ethics, without taking responsibility for that other.

By making Frankenstein and his creature not only doubles, but vampiric doubles, of each other, Mary Shelley again calls forth some of the rhetoric that was so frequently used by advocates both for and against emancipation. Because the figure of the vampire derives much of its symbolism from Christian scriptures, where it stands for the Antichrist, or the incarnation of evil, it was a powerful figure in evangelical arguments against the slave system. Christ at the Last Supper asked his followers to drink his blood and eat his body for eternal life, which is symbolic as a spiritual communion between creator and creature. The vampire perverts this communion, requiring a sinister drinking of literal blood for his or her eternal life.

Just as abolitionists used cannibal metaphors, they also used vampire images to emphasize how slavery perverted Christian values. "But woe to the winds that propitiously breathe," wrote James Montgomery, and "waft" the British slaver "in safety to port":

Where the vultures and vampires of mammon resort
Where Europe exultingly drains
The life-blood from Africa's veins.[67]

Anna Letitia Barbauld found Africa's blood to be the commodity directly consumed in slavery; "still Afric bleeds; / Unchecked, the human traffic still proceeds." Blood, the life of the slave, the "milky innocence of infant veins" was viewed as sucked out by British commercialism.[68] The speaker in "The Dying African," a poem printed in *Gentleman's Magazine* in 1791, says

Here my faint limbs have borne the bloody gash,
Here have I sunk beneath the tyrant's lash:
But still, while rolling on the parched land,
I felt the tortures of his ruthless hand:
Soft sons of luxury, I toil'd for you,
To grace your feast, and swell your empty shew:
The rich ingredients of your costly boards,
Our sweat, our pangs, our misery affords:
Think, think, amid your heaps of needless food,
How much is tainted with your brother's blood.[69]

The bloody, gashed limbs that reach up out of the British breakfast, heaped with the "needless food," recalls Cowper's vivid description of "merchants rich in cargoes of despair," who "buy the muscles and the bones of man."[70]

Surprisingly, abolitionist literature, which is not exactly known for its subtlety, took on the full range of nuances when it came to the metaphors of cannibalism and vampirism. For instance, in vampire lore, the victim of a vampiric repast never dies completely. The victims are simply turned into vampires themselves. It is just this sort of vampire reproduction that takes place in abolitionist literature. In an effective answer to Montgomery, Bryan Edwards grimly pointed out in "Ode on Seeing a Negro Funeral" how British people could easily become the "prey" for "Afric's proud revenge," since British consumption would surely send Africans on a desperate search for the British blood:

Now, Christian, now, in wild dismay,
Of Afric's proud revenge the prey,
Go roam th' affrighted wood;—
Transform'd to tigers, fierce and fell,
Thy race shall prowl with savage yell,
And glut thy rage for blood![71]

There were other such variations on the monstrosities of slavery. James Stanfield's *Guinea Voyage* repeatedly refers to British slavery itself as "the monster," and at the same time the Africans get revenge by calling forth their "native monsters"—tigers, serpents, and crocodiles—that will in an act of vengeance monstrously devour the British consumer.[72] In Colman's play *The Africans*, the character Selico designates slave traders the "monsters of blood" and promises revenge through "some deed" that will "strike them all with terror."[73] In all of these poems, the problem with vampiristic hunger is that it is insatiable. This kind of unquenchable blood thirstiness is what Frankenstein had in mind when he said of his creature, "nor do I know where this thirst for vengeance will end" (218).

Within the discourse of the emancipation and abolition debates, the business of consumption in the commercial districts of Liverpool, Bristol, and London effectively turned men into vampires. William Roscoe's poem, ironically titled "Mount Pleasant" is about the commercial district in early nineteenth-century Liverpool. British businessmen turned vampires are without restraint. They "drink, the beverage of the chrystal flood . . . purchas'd by a brother's blood."[74] The more they revel in the blood of slaves, the more they want. In the companion poem "The Wrongs of Africa," Roscoe imagines the entire British population to be consumed by the "thirst of gain," "crush[ing]" and then "condens[ing]" the bones of living slaves. "Deluded fool," writes Roscoe, "The cup, thy giddy rage has fill'd too high, / Like that of Tantalus shall soon o'erflow, / And leave thee wondering at the sudden void."[75]

Although these poets used the terms "monster," "cannibal," and "vampire" metaphorically, the literal meanings were never far from the surface, since the slave system was based on such brutal bodily violence. Such violence is what anthropologists speculate to be the worst problem with mutual cannibalism. For a society in which two diverse cultures are trying to live, cannibalism operates on the principle of terror, which in turn creates social chaos. Christy G. Turner, in *Man Corn* (1999), contends that cannibalism, in some cultures, is a form of social control; it is order by terrorism. Terrorism, mutilation, murder, "what better way to amplify opponents' fear than to reduce victims to the subhuman level of cooked meat?" says Turner.[76] Indeed, the social system in which Frankenstein and the creature consume each other makes them mutual terrorists. It also makes them subhuman, for they become slaves to one another. The creature repeatedly calls himself a "slave" and thus a "monster, a blot upon the earth" (116). These feelings of rejection are compounded by the monster's appetite. He distinguishes himself from the DeLaceys and from humankind in general because of his ability to "subsist upon a coarser diet" (116). By this point in the novel, it becomes apparent that the homeless, unloved, and exploited creature must inevitably use the language of monstrosity and slavery to define himself. It also becomes obvious that Frankenstein himself experiences a sense of slavery through identification with the monstrous slave he has created. Frankenstein, pursued by the creature, obsessed by such thoughts, wishes for "some accident" to "destroy him" and thus "put an end to my slavery for ever" (150). For, he concludes,

"I was the slave of my creature" (151). Worse still, this kind of mutual slavery is by nature cannibalistic, so that Frankenstein's soul, and by extension that of his creature, is consumed by the devices of a system of slavery. Frankenstein says as much when he confesses to Walton:

For an instant I dared to shake off my chains, and look around me with a free and lofty spirit; but the iron had eaten into my flesh, and I sank again, trembling and hopeless, into my miserable self. (158)

The apparent cannibalism of the creature further foregrounds Frankenstein's own tendencies in his construction of the creature. Different from "cannibal" which refers to eating human flesh, the word "cannibalize" means literally to remove parts from one body or organization for use in the construction or repair of a completely different body or organization. Though the use of this term did not enter the language until the 1900s, the idea was present in the 1800s, since Frankenstein certainly cannibalizes human bodies. He pursues nature's "hiding places," where he "dabbled among the unhallowed damps of the grave" and "tortured the living animals to animate lifeless clay" (49). The more he cannibalizes, the more gruesome his activities become. Behind the dark walls of "charnal houses" and within the grave, he steals the "intricacies of fibres, muscles and veins," bones, blood, and yellow eyeballs (47, 48). His second cannibalizing attempt (the creature's mate), however, leaves him not only sickened, but with a strange inability to distinguish between death and life, between the abject other and the supposedly straightforward self: "The remains of the half-finished creature, whom I had destroyed, lay scattered on the floor, and I almost felt as if I had mangled the living flesh of a human being" (167). The creature threatens Frankenstein with a more haunting, because more symbolic, form of cannibalism, telling his master, "if you refuse" to create a mate, "I will glut the maw of death, until it be satiated with the blood of your remaining friends" (94). The creature even predicts that he, and "thousands of others, shall be swallowed up in the whirlwinds of its rage" (96). The abyss of death itself is imagined as a great, insatiable mouth.

IV

Mary Shelley's novel sets up a dialectic between master and slave through Frankenstein and the creature, but when the novel takes up the issue of colonial consumption, she accuses only Western culture. From the beginning, Frankenstein speaks of his scientific quest in terms of consumption and its metaphoric extensions—cannibalism and vampirism. He describes himself repeatedly "thirst[ing] for knowledge" or "greedily imbib[ing]" the ancient philosophy of Albertus Magnus and Paracelsus (236, 41). Scientific thought and cultural progress provide intellectual nourishment:

In other studies you go as far as others have gone before you, and there is nothing more to know; but in a scientific pursuit there is continual food for discovery and wonder. (46)

Frankenstein's "food for discovery"—the nature of the human body and of the universe—are the two divisions of knowledge that reveal the consumptive character of Western philosophical understanding. This passage has cannibalistic overtones because the universe is devoured as an expressive face and a body to be dissected. Of the universe, Frankenstein observes,

The most learned philosopher . . . had partially unveiled the face of Nature, but her immortal lineaments were still a wonder and a mystery. He might dissect, anatomise, and give names; but . . . a final cause . . . [was] utterly unknown to him. (238)

As his narrative opens, Frankenstein directs his hunger and thirst to "secrets." "The world was to me a secret which I desired to divine" (236), he admits, and in this sense Mary Shelley aligns his motives with those of most travel writers of the day who had dangerous curiosity about the secrets of other cultures. Frankenstein's thirst for the unknown is matched in intensity only by Robert Walton's North Pole probe and Henry Clerval's Oriental conquest. Walton saturates his letters to his sister with what appears to be standard travel narrative discourse, but Mary Shelley intimates that this venture is motivated by a need to consume. Walton explains:

I shall satiate my ardent curiosity with the sight of a part of the world never before visited, and tread a land never before imprinted by the foot of man. (10)

Walton's curiosity for the unknown is something that, at the end of his own quest, Frankenstein recognizes immediately as a matter of consumption. "Have you drank also of the intoxicating draught?" he begs after Walton. "Hear me,—let me reveal my tale, and you will dash the cup from your lips!" (232). Consumption and insatiability are the concepts that fuel the novel, since these are the very notions that cause Frankenstein and Walton to set their stories in motion. More than any other character in the novel, Henry Clerval stands for unrestrained colonial appetite. Clerval's "taste" for Oriental studies, notes Frankenstein, made him like one "transported to Fairy-land," where he "enjoyed [happi]ness seldom tasted by man" (153). Everything was to him "an appetite"[.] [The] trouble with this taste for the exotic flavor of the Orient, as Mary

Shelley distinctly points out, is that it inevitably leads to slavery. The desire to devour discursively also leads to personal and cultural destruction. If this desire were quelled, Frankenstein wisely observes at his own bitter end, then "Greece had not been enslaved; Caesar would have spared his country; America would have been discovered more gradually; and the empires of Mexico and Peru had not been destroyed" (51). Frankenstein echoes the sentiments of abolitionist poets such as Cowper and More, who construed the slave system within the larger dynamic of colonial consumption. In her poem "Slavery," More asks,

Does thirst of empire, does desire of fame,
(For these are specious crimes) our rage inflame?
No: sordid lust of gold their fate controls,
The basest appetite of basest souls;
Gold, better gained by what their ripening sky,
Their fertile fields, their arts, and mines supply.[77]

In the novel, and in the abolitionist literature that preceded it, the emphasis on "appetite" and "thirst" for the spoils of conquest is matched only by the "insatiable" and "unquenchable" desire that drives the cannibal and the vampire.

Inevitably, Frankenstein learns a lesson about the nature of the political universe: devouring other cultures results in the compulsive consumption of one's own. This is the painful knowledge he tries repeatedly to impart to Walton. Frankenstein himself "thirsted for the moment" when he could discern the secrets of the world, but this same thirst "swallowed up every habit of my nature" (85, 50). In the same way, the cannibalized creature he constructs from body parts leaves him with a sense of guilt akin to that of the ancient mariner. He relates to Walton how the "fangs of remorse tore my bosom, and would not forego their hold" (80). The death of Henry Clerval brings to a grim culmination Frankenstein's experience of being eaten alive by the conquering spirit that surrounds him. Clerval's death virtually lodges in his throat, which becomes "parched with horror" (173). For this, Frankenstein can only wish the same retching experience for the creature. "Let the cursed and hellish monster drink deep of agony," he groans (200).

But it is the quest for knowledge that Frankenstein somehow transmits to his creature, who anxiously consumes any bit of knowledge that he gets his hands on. Ironically, in the very spot where he "collected" his "food," the creature finds "a leathern portmanteau, containing . . . some books" (123). Instead of literal food, then, the creature "eagerly" seizes this food for the mind. In this sense, both Frankenstein and his creature represent the "modern Prometheus," Mary Shelley's subtitle for the novel. Frankenstein is the Prometheus who—like Icarus—reaches too high and therefore falls. Because of this, his creature, on the other hand, never gets off the ground. As Promethean figures, both Franken-stein and his monster echo antislavery poetry. Southey, for instance, portrays the slave as a modern Prometheus, chained to a rock, eaten away by the plantation system:

High in the air exposed the slave is hung,
To all the birds of heaven, their living food!
He groans not, though awaked by that fierce sun
New tortures live to drink their parent blood;
He groans not, though gorging vultures tear
The quivering fibre.[78]

Prometheanism is also linked to Africa itself, which James Stanfield imagines as the god of light and rebellion: Africa "heaves his *Promethean* peak to seize the light, / And thro' conducting veins, with chemic pow'r, / Recruits exhausted nature's fiery store."[79] As one abolitionist poet put it, "Blood will have blood."[80]

Mary Shelley's novel, like these poems, focuses on and returns repeatedly to both the creator and the creature as the center of consumption problems, for the cannibalistic overtones in *Frankenstein* are related to enslavement and servi-tude. Further, conquest itself is the ultimate act of cannibalizing, of removing parts and pieces of one culture in order to maintain and to bolster the produc-tion of another. Reading the novel through the lens of the emancipation debates illuminates the excessive hubris with which some Britons regarded the Afro-Caribbean population. They credited themselves with creating a monster akin to Shelley's own. Like Frankenstein, they cannibalized Africans to create some kind of revolutionary, Promethean power that exceeded their own mastery. The following quotation from *Frankenstein* could just as easily have been spoken by George Canning:

In a fit of enthusiastic madness I created a rational creature, and was bound towards him, to assure, as far as was in my power, his happiness and well-being. This was my duty; but there was another still paramount to that. My duties towards the beings of my own fellow-creatures had greater claims on my attention. (214–15)

This statement exudes a sense of paternalism, which is exactly how the British thought of slavery. Instead of actually freeing Africans, Britons argued about how to father them. Abolitionist Richard Nisbet was just one of many to call attention to the "capacity" of slaves to respond to the "PATRIARCHAL PRIN-CIPLE, which would tend to counteract and to lessen the evil of slavery itself."[81]

Indeed, the parallels between Frankenstein and British lawmakers are strik-ing. Within the emancipation debate itself, lawmakers accused each other of committing the same sin Frankenstein blames himself for: having "bred and reared the negro" but having not measured "out to him, with merciful liberality, all that may conduce to his happiness — and that may advance his welfare." [82] Like Frankenstein, these lawmakers protected the "beings of their own species" — plantation owners and British consumers — rather than courageously solving the monstrous problem they had created. So monstrous was the problem, it was appropriate for Canning to invoke Shelley's novel to help his fellow members of Parliament effectively imagine the problem of consumption in African-British relations. The interaction between Shelley's novel and the parliamentary debates demonstrates how issues of slavery were fundamental to a strain of Romantic imaginative writings. More importantly, it underscores the fear of social chaos Britons imagined as the end of the slave system, and the real face-to-face encounter, drew near. Mary Shelley mapped out one possible course of events: the failure of alterity is pronounced quietly but firmly in the last moments of the novel: "Yet I seek not a fellow-feeling in my misery. No sympathy may I ever find," the creature says as he drifts off into the dark and frozen sea (218).

Intimate Distance

African Women and Infant Death in Wordsworth's Poetry and
The History of Mary Prince

I

On the issue of bringing slave experience home to Britain, Wordsworth is per-haps best known for his 1802 tribute "To Toussaint L'Ouverture." Toussaint, the man who staged the first successful slave-led revolution (in Haiti, then called Saint Domingue), landed in a Paris prison in 1802 and died there in 1803. Words-worth's advice to the Haitian leader, to wear "in thy bonds a cheerful brow" because the British were Haiti's friends, would probably have been of little com-fort to the superbly intelligent Toussaint L'Ouverture.[1] Indeed, we do not nor-mally classify Wordsworth as a poet of male slave experience, let alone black *women*'s experience. But this is the problem with normal classifications. In fact, no poet placed African women at the center of British literary culture during the Romantic period with quite the emotional power of Wordsworth. From the "Negro women in white muslin gowns" of *The Prelude*, to the "negro woman . . . gaudy in array" of his stark sonnet "The Banished Negroes," he devoted a sur-prising amount of time in his poetry to black women and the debates surround-ing them.[2]

Wordsworth said in *The Prelude* that the plight of slaves "had ne'er / Fas-tened on [his] affections," and we tend to believe him.[3] Yet, from the begin-ning of his creative activity, the slave issue was unavoidably present. A mere sampling of his reading at the time of his very first published poems reveals his contact with the issue at almost every literary turn. In 1789 and 1790, when the poet regularly read the *Gentleman's Magazine*, numerous reviews on slave-centered books, pamphlets and sermons appeared.[4] During April 1789 alone, the magazine carried reviews of William Dickson's *Letters on Slavery*, H. E. Holder's *A Short Essay on the Subject of Negro Slavery*, M. Schwartz's *Reflections sur l'Esclavage des Negres*, James Ramsay's *Address to the Publick, on the proposed*

Bill for the Abolition of the Slave Trade, and Olaudah Equiano's *Interesting Narrative*. Needless to say, a literate person in 1790s Britain would have come into constant contact with the subject of slavery.

Indeed, by the mid-1790s, when Wordsworth's serious poetic work was taking shape, he was intimately acquainted with a variety of abolitionist sources. He had read John Newton's slave trading salvation story, where Newton witnesses an interracial marriage and from this is prompted to make his own heavenly union with God and nature on the Guinea shore.[5] Wordsworth had also encountered an extremely powerful and highly common strain of abolitionism, whose rhetorical heart was the destruction of the African family. And in May of 1798, he traveled to Bristol to see Monk Lewis's popular play *The Castle Spectre*, whose most disturbing character was a slave named Hassan.[6] Out of Hassan's lips fly nothing but words of retribution against the white man, and in fact, Hassan points to the destruction of his African family as the root of the entire play's theme of vengeance. Hassan confesses these words to a fellow servant:

Yes, thou art sweet, Vengeance! — Oh! how it joys me when the white man suffers! — Yet weak are his pangs, compared to those I felt when torn from thy shores, O native Africa! — from thy bosom, my faithful Samba! — Ah! dost thou still exist, my wife! . . . My boy, too, whom on that morning when the man-hunters seized me, I left sleeping on thy bosom, say, Lives he yet! — Does he ever speak of me? — Does he ask, "Mother, describe to me my father; show me how the warrior looked?"[7]

In many respects, this speech would have been familiar to Wordsworth, since he had already encountered a similar sentiment in Robert Southey's poems against the slave trade, especially "To the Genius of Africa," a work that mourns and moans with the voices of slaves who have lost their homeland, their families, their freedom.[8] Besides this, Wordsworth was strongly influenced by William Cowper, who had written a number of antislavery poems, including the most popular one of the era, "The Negro's Complaint." Wordsworth did read Cowper's 1782 *Poems*, where he would have heard an African tell, in galloping English verse, how slavery severs "The tender ties of father, husband, friend, / All bonds of nature in that moment end."[9]

This idea of broken bonds must have made its mark on Wordsworth, because he took up the theme in his early poetry and applied it to fragmented British families. The most salient example occurs in his 1800 poem "The Brothers." The poem describes how one of these brothers — Leonard — had left his native England for the seafaring life, in the West Indies no less, and though readers are never sure exactly what kind of seafaring he worked in, a rumor circulates through his village that he had sought his fortune "in slavery among the Moors / Upon the Barbary Coast" (317–18). The poem's action centers on

Leonard's return to Britain, where he searches for his buried past. When he learns that his only brother, and his only surviving family member for that matter, has either fallen off or thrown himself off a cliff to his death, readers are led to believe that the sole responsibility for the family's fragmentation lies with Leonard, who initially turned away from his homeland.[10]

Yet, among the larger poetic community, the broken ties of brothers, fathers, and sons were not nearly as graphic, nor as emotionally powerful, as the painful splintering of mothers and their children, especially slave mothers and children. One of the contexts in which Wordsworth's poetry has not been examined is in literature about slave women where, more often than not, mothers and children were depicted through distressing images of infanticide, or suicide, or—just as likely—both. One popular poem, *The Sorrows of Yamba; or, The Negro Woman's Lamentation*, which Wordsworth also knew, was first published in 1795 by the conservative Bristol poet Hannah More in her *Cheap Repository Tracts*.[11] Though the cause of infant death in this poem is left curiously vague, the African woman Yamba expresses relief when she finds that her "poor child was cold and dead." The poem continues in notes of singsong sanguinity so light they are macabre:

Happy, happy there she lies;
Thou shall feel the lash no-more

. . . .
Thee, sweet infant, none shall sell;
Thou hast gain'd a wat'ry grave,
Clean escap'd the tyrant fell,
While thy mother lives a slave.[12]

The poem's morbid fascination with infant death eerily reflects the way slave women and their children were bantered about in pro- and antislavery writings alike. Women who did, or could, kill their children, and women who were happy when their children died, were discussed in documents of all kinds, though plantation reports are the richest source of information. Plantation owners, doctors, and overseers suspected that slave women regularly gave themselves abortions and otherwise committed infanticide. For instance, the British surgeon Henry Beame reported that, among slave women, "the procuration of abortion is very prevalent . . . there being herbs and powders known to slaves, as given by obeah men and women," while the "white medical men know little." [13] On the other side of the debate, opponents of the slave trade, like William Dickson, concluded that though importing Africans was not the key to successful plantations, if slaves did not "keep up their numbers and strengths by births," many plantations would soon go bankrupt.[14] For this reason, plantation managers felt extreme pressure to maintain slave births, but it was something white men seemed to have little control over. The manager of the Newton Estate in Barbados wrote plaintively in 1797, "I am very sorry our negroes have decreased this year—I know not how it has happened." He did, however, offer that "the women have been unsuccessful generally in breeding and childbirth." Still later, he reported that a slave woman named Mary Thomas, after delivering a child, had set out with her mother and sister to murder it.[15]

These dumbfounded comments on slave women's abortion and infanticide very quickly became confused with stories of white plantation owners who themselves committed infanticide. One of the most disturbing cases recorded on the printed page appears in the slave complaints of Berbice on 4 June 1819. It is the story of a slave woman named Rosa, who was "big with child." On the day in question, Rosa was flogged for not working, and the very next day she miscarried. The slave women who assisted her were called on by the courts to relate the incident. In agonizing detail, they describe the dead child, unequivocally blaming the white owners who ordered the flogging. One witness states, "The child's arm was broken; one eye out, bruised and sunk in the head; it was a fine male child, quite formed; in every respect perfect." To the shock of any reader, the white physician and plantation owner testified otherwise, instead accusing Rosa of "eating green pines" to poison the child while he was still in her womb.[16]

Both the cases of Mary Thomas, in 1797, and of Rosa some twenty years later, in 1819, reflect the highly charged issue of slave reproduction. They also illustrate how, in some instances, slave women took control of the slave system by controlling their own reproduction. It was one sure way, as historians such as Barbara Bush and Hilary McD. Beckles have shown, for women to turn the tables and exert mastery over a system that otherwise mastered them. In fact, low fertility and high infant mortality rates had a singular effect on slavery reform.[17] Plantations, like the Codrington Estate in Barbados, that instituted relatively humane policies for slaves—bigger food rations, fewer floggings—saw a marked increased in fertility and infant survival.[18] Historians have suggested that slave women were less likely to induce abortion or engage in infanticide when they were treated like people instead of property. Still, the sickening truth of the matter was that white owners, managers, and overseers were either directly or indirectly responsible for the death of slave children. The grim circumstances surrounding slave infant death were one reason why it became a major trope in antislavery poetry and has continued to haunt literary imaginations ever since. The most powerful modern manifestation of the image is, of course, Toni Morrison's 1987 novel *Beloved*. The New York poet Noel Jones has also written vividly of this image in her 2000 poem called "Permission":

here on plantations red with rape
slave women with *cotton root bark*
~~thwarted the master's plan~~
for a slave baby crop

.   .   .   .   .   .

and if overwhelmed with her choices
there was always suicide
to stop the voices

regardless of what anyone believes
every desperate
woman with child
has been aware of options
and throughout ancient times until
this moment.[19]

But as early as 1788 in Britain, Helen Maria Williams used slave suicide
and infanticide in her *Poem on the Bill Lately Passed*. She depicts an African
woman on board ship during the middle passage who "in desperation wild . . .
madly strain[s] her grasping child." The woman then throws both herself and
her child into the sea, where they sink "in agonizing death." [20] This same image
appears in one of Wordsworth's *Lyrical Ballads* from 1798, "The Mad Mother."
Like Williams's African mother, Wordsworth's mad mother also hints at infanticide through suicide when she instructs her infant son not to "dread the waves
below, / When o'er the sea-rock's edge we go" (43–44).

In his 1800 preface to the *Lyrical Ballads*, Wordsworth singled out "The
Mad Mother" as a first-rate example of his poetic purpose, which was to encour-
age readers to "follow the fluxes and refluxes of the mind when agitated by great
and simple affections of our nature" (*W Prose* 1:126). By turning from the self
and by "tracing the maternal passions," a reader might bear witness to something more profound than him or herself (*W Prose* 1:126). What Wordsworth
did not want was to drag readers through stereotypical experiences, ones that
had been replayed in ideological poetry, where readers would recognize mere
fixed categories of otherness and would thus process his poems without feeling
sympathy with something beyond themselves. So "The Mad Mother," though
clearly foreign (she comes "far from over the main" and speaks of an "Indian
bower," which might mean West Indian, East Indian, or American Indian), is
not recognizable as any one foreigner, or even as a homeless English woman (4,
55). Instead, she enlists the experience, the fears, and the fierce protectiveness of
motherhood in its most universal sense.

Still, upon closer examination, "The Mad Mother" represents this woman
through a catalog of typical antislavery motifs. She appears in the opening lines

as a woman of color planted in the midst of cloud-ridden Britain. "Her coal black hair," the "rusty stain" or her eyebrows, her "brown cheek," the dark "hue" of "breast," and her dialect, surprisingly in an "English tongue," suggest that she is an exile of Britain's foreign expansion, either American Indian or West Indian, one among countless people who found themselves living in poverty in the major slave ports of London, Liverpool, and Bristol (2, 3, 68, 63, 61, 10). In fact, in the Fenwick notes, Wordsworth linked the wretchedness of the mad mother's situation to a story he had heard about an outcast living in Bristol in 1799.[21] This is important when one remembers that, in 1799, a hot-bed for slavery debate was Bristol, the very place where Coleridge had delivered his 1795 *Lecture on the Slave Trade*. It was a fitting setting, for in Bristol, claimed abolitionists, "every brick in the city had been cemented with a slave's blood." [22]

The mad mother's baby boy, who finds his way into every stanza of the poem by the simple fact that she sings her story to him, is repeatedly described in ways that link both child and mother to slave experience. The first incident that the mother alludes to is a sexual assault, which she relives through the language of a recurring, feverish vision. When she remembers how "fiendish faces, one, two, three, / Hung at my breasts, and pulled at me," she gestures toward a fact of slavery no less true for its lurid details and shameful consequences: slave women were frequently raped during the middle passage and on plantations (23–24).[23] This was not, surprisingly enough, a topic abolitionist poets shied away from. To take just one example, the poet James Stanfield, in his 1789 *The Guinea Voyage*, describes a slave woman "with dejected wretchedness enclos'd, / To brutal hand and impious eyes expos'd." The result is that she delivers a mulatto child in a setting nuanced with "foul clouds" of violence and rape.[24]

In Wordsworth's poem, the otherwise inexplicable madness of the mother stems from such a traumatic incident, but the suckling babe releases her from the bondage of ethereal and iron-clad memories alike, and in doing so gestures toward the language of poets who sought to represent slave experience. The baby "cools" her fiery "brain," a common phrase used in abolition poems (32).[25] The phrase appears, for instance, in an anonymous poem *The Wrongs of Alooma*, where the black heroine warns "madness . . . fires my brain." [26] In "Mad Mother," the baby boy also "loosens" the "tight and deadly band" pressing tensely against the mother's chest (36–37). This band, highly suggestive of the slave band or collar—a device frequently used during this time to hold slaves under suspicion of escape—became a synecdoche for slavery among abolitionist writers. James Montgomery, in 1809, writes how manacles bound the slave body and the mind. Slaves thereby wore the "yoke" of British sin around their necks.[27] For other writers, such as Stanfield, the "*fetter'd* band" of slavery recalls with bitter irony the "tender band" of African family ties ripped apart by the trade.[28]

Among Wordsworth's mad motifs that resonate in the antislavery context, the mother's conflicted attitude toward her son is the most compelling. She tells the boy "thy father cares not for my breast, / 'Tis thine, sweet baby, there to rest" (61–62). But then, when she looks back into his eyes, she sees in her child "wicked looks" that "never, never came from me" (86, 88). In fact, this sort of madness most certainly influenced Elizabeth Barrett Browning (who knew her Wordsworth well) in her portrayal of a slave mother, who says to her child:

Why, in that single glance I had
Of my child's face . . . I tell you all,
I saw a look that made me mad!
The *master's* look, that used to fall
On my soul like his lash . . . or worse!
And so, to save it from my curse,
I twisted it round in my shawl.[29]

"The Mad Mother," in short, is close to the telling abolitionist stereotype of the destructive and despairing mother-infant dyad, a stereotype that functioned as the most powerful sentimental campaigning tool in abolitionist literature. The mother wanders randomly, insanely, "o'er the sea rock's edge," through "hollow snows and rivers wide," and then "underneath the spreading tree," while she tells her infant, in less than convincing terms, "Then, lovely baby, do not fear! / I pray thee have no fear of me" (44, 54, 73, 15–16). Whether it be murder, suicide/infanticide, or simply starvation—one way or another—it is clear that this pair is not going to survive. Wordsworth tells us as much. The mad mother's jittery talk of being "dead," her repeated mention of the forces that will work them "harm," evaporate in the sinister conclusion as she leads her babe to the forest, to the "poisons of the shade" where they will "live for aye" (58, 45, 77, 95, 100). Within the logic of the poem, family ties turn into slavish bonds, and the mother is left with little choice: she must destroy one in order to end the other.

Curiously enough, this context is at the very center of another poem from the *Lyrical Ballads*, "The Thorn." Parallels between the two poems also exist through composition date (between March and May of 1798) and through the particular juxtaposition of desperate mothers, deadbeat fathers, and destruction of infants. Wordsworth clearly intended readers to consider the interdependence of both women's situations: The narrator of "The Thorn" gossips how Martha Ray "was with child, and she was mad" (128), and the mad mother finds herself at the center of similar stories circulating about her: "They say that I am mad," she tells her son (11). The "cruel, cruel fire" set in Martha's "brain" the day Stephen Hill abandons her also throbs in the mad mother, who suffers from a "fire" of the "brain" after her own abandonment, which itself resembles a poor man's version of the Rochester and Bertha Mason story ("Thorn" 129, 132; "Mad Mother" 21).[30] Martha Ray's "Oh woe is me! oh misery!" (66) finds an echo in the mad mother who sings "many a sad and doleful thing" (14). Although the mad mother does not go through with suicide or infanticide, Martha Ray of "The Thorn" is a different story. In the poem's chilling conclusion, the narrator — the captain of a trading vessel, as it happens — offers some eerie speculations about the dead baby buried on a lush English hillside:

> . . . some will say
> She hanged her baby on the tree;
> Some say she drowned it in the pond,
> Which is a little step beyond:
>
> . . . .
> "I've heard, the moss is spotted red
> With drops of that poor infant's blood;
> But kill a new-born infant thus,
>
> . . . .
> Some say, if to the pond you go,
> And fix on it a steady view,
> The shadow of a babe you trace,
> A baby and a baby's face,
> And that it looks at you;
> Whene'er you look on it, 'tis plain
> The baby looks at you again. (203–6; 210–12; 214–20)

Ironically enough, while the poem buries the murdered infant, it unearths the context of battered women and infant destruction so intimately tied to the slave woman's experience that Wordsworth and his audiences would have known well.

But if these poems enter the grim areas of maternal madness and infant murder that were most linked with debates on slave women, why are they not explicit about this link? One answer may be in Wordsworth's own connections to slavery in Bristol. When Wordsworth met Coleridge and Southey — both active abolitionists — in Bristol in 1795, he shared their radical views. But he no doubt felt uncomfortable making his own public outcries against the slave trade, for this reason: unlike his new friends and fellow poets, Wordsworth depended directly on the slave trade for his living.[31] Between 1795 and 1797, Wordsworth lived rent free at Racedown Lodge, a house supplied by John Frederick and Azariah Pinney.[32] The Pinney brothers — sons of a rich Bristol merchant and West Indian plantation owner — enjoyed the family fortune built on the backs of slaves whose labor funded the construction of both Racedown and the Pinneys' elegant Georgian home in Bristol, where Wordsworth also stayed for several months. This house, which is, to this day, standing and available for tours, was in Wordsworth's time, as Kenneth R. Johnston states, "a symbol of John Pinney's advancing fortunes" first as a plantation owner, then as a sugar merchant. When Wordsworth stayed in Bristol, Pinney owned "over two hundred slaves, working three different plantations in Nevis: the largest single holding on the smallest of Britain's West Indian" islands. He also ran the Bristol West Indies Trading Company with John Tobin, who was among the most "prominent and intelligent adversaries of the abolition movement." [33] Such was Wordsworth's situation when gathering much of the material for the poems that later appeared in *Lyrical Ballads*. The fragments he wrote during this period, according to Johnston, in fact show the issues that went on to shape Wordsworth's mature poetic work. The subjects of these Racedown pieces were the homeless and rejected, criminals and outlaws, abandoned mothers and their children. All of them, according to Johnston, anticipated "the great solitary set pieces of his mature period: the Discharged Veteran, the Blind Beggar, the Leech Gatherer, and the Solitary Reaper." [34] Though the Pinney brothers encouraged Wordsworth's radicalism in writing about such subjects, his dependence on them meant that he probably did not feel comfortable making open critiques of slavery, or even openly representing ex-slaves among the disenfranchised Britons he wrote about.

Yet this explanation provides only part of the answer. An aesthetic answer is possible, too. As Wordsworth would have known, the antislavery motifs of traumatized, desperate mothers had already, by 1798, become rigid and emotionally cold. By using these images in "The Mad Mother" and in "The Thorn," but by making them opaque enough to hide their explicit political content, Wordsworth avoided formal sterility while expanding the contextual resonances, from the debate on slavery to agricultural poverty to political oppression within Britain. Wordsworth was perfectly clear about the kind of empathy that he wanted "The Mad Mother" to evoke in audiences. He said, when asked much later about the poem, that "while the distance removes her from us, the fact of her speaking our language brings us at once into close sympathy with her." [35] Like Coleridge's "Rime of the Ancient Mariner," Wordsworth's poems became more powerful because they made old tropes mysterious and new, because they turned stereotypes into disturbingly unfixed figures.

II

Poets have all kinds of reasons for choosing their subjects, but one requirement seems to be that the subject must touch them personally. In many of Wordsworth's best poems, this requirement leaps from the page as he identifies intensely with his subject, and in this process readers see a practical working out of his statement in the preface to *Lyrical Ballads*: the poet must "bring his feelings near to those of the persons whose feelings he describes — nay, for short spaces of time, perhaps, to let himself slip into an entire delusion, and even confound and identify his own feelings with theirs" (*W Prose*, 1:138).[36] If a poet is successful in suppressing the ego enough to embrace the otherness of his or her subject, the result is poetry so dynamic that it strikes readers, according to Coleridge, as a luxurious blend "of sameness with difference" even as it subordinates "our admiration of the poet to our sympathy with the poetry" (*B*, 2: 12).

Wordsworth wrote such a poem in 1802, as he sailed from Calais, away from his mistress Annette Vallon and their daughter Caroline, back to Britain. On shipboard, Wordsworth encountered a woman forced into exile by Napoleon's edict banning black people from France. Like Wordsworth, she was traveling to Dover and was not at home in France any longer. Wordsworth, of course, had seen many homeless people in his thirty-two years, but he was emotionally moved by the woman from Calais, as the sonnet he wrote and titled "The Banished Negroes" attests:

We had a fellow-Passenger that came
From Calais with us, gaudy in array,
A negro woman, like a Lady gay,
Yet silent as a woman fearing blame;
Dejected, downcast, meek, and more than tame:
She sate, from notice turning not away,
But on our proffer'd kindness still did lay
A weight of languid speech, or at the same
Was silent, motionless in eyes and face.
She was a Negro Woman driv'n from France
Rejected like all others of that race,
Not one of whom may now find footing there;
What is the meaning of this ordinance?
Dishonour'd Despots, tell us if you dare.

There is in this sonnet a surly sneer back toward France and its dismal failure to achieve liberty, but the poem's true subject is the mysterious character of the "negro woman." In particular, Wordsworth directs his readers to her "face." It is truly a Levinasian moment, a glimpse of alterity through the face-to-face encounter, where the woman is by turns "gay" and "downcast," stone "silent" then weighty with "languid speech." Though "motionless in eyes and face," she nonetheless stirs great emotion in Wordsworth himself. Indeed, Judith W. Page, in her 1994 *Wordsworth and the Cultivation of Women*, provides an insightful reading of this poem, arguing that "Wordsworth does in fact identify with the woman . . . he looks into the woman's eyes and on some level sees part of himself." [37] But though Wordsworth identifies with her, this identification is not comforting. Instead, it becomes a disturbing, haunting presence. She is, he repeats twice in fourteen lines, a "negro woman," so different from himself yet strangely the same. As other, she overwhelms the poet's own egoism, and he loses his own sense of sovereignty. Though this happens only for an instant, the fact that it happens at all is striking. It must have seemed so to Wordsworth himself, because he revised this poem for the next forty-three years, going back, repeatedly, to the black woman's alterity.

In the midst of these revisions, however, Wordsworth had another real-life encounter with black women, and the poem he wrote on this occasion is, frankly, shocking. For whatever flaws of political correctness "The Banished Negroes" has, it is sensitively written with the ambition of telling the truth about the relationship between a white British poet and homeless black woman. The next poem he would write about black women, the queen and princesses of Haiti, was just the opposite. The poem itself sprang from his continuing personal knowledge of the antislavery movement, for it would not have happened if he were not intimate friends with the most active abolitionist in British history, Thomas Clarkson.

Wordsworth and Clarkson met in 1799, right after Wordsworth had settled in Grasmere. Clarkson had actually come to the Lake District before Wordsworth did, in 1794, to recover from the massive travels he had undertaken in his fight against the slave trade, and he would return there to set up antislavery societies throughout the early 1800s. Clarkson's wife, Catherine, soon befriended Dorothy Wordsworth, and after the Clarksons moved away, the two women exchanged letters every few months. The friendship between the two families was close: William and Mary Wordsworth named their younger daughter Catherine after Mrs. Clarkson. And Wordsworth initially showed loyalties to Clarkson and his abolitionist cause. In 1807, when Parliament outlawed the slave-trade, Wordsworth dedicated a sonnet to Clarkson, celebrating his tireless work and emphasizing Clarkson's international influence: "see, the palm / Is won, and by all Nations shall be worn!" (9–10).

Wordsworth was exactly right. And Clarkson would continue to work on an international level. In 1814, Clarkson developed a friendship with the Haitian king Henri Christophe when Haiti was under threat of French invasion. The two corresponded regularly, and Clarkson soon became Haiti's European adviser. Working in conjunction with the Anti-Slavery Society, Clarkson seems to have done all he could for Haiti from 1818 to 1820. He attended the Congress of Aix-la-Chapelle in 1818, for instance, calling on other world powers to put an end to slavery. And then, at Christophe's request, he visited France in 1820 as Haiti's unofficial ambassador, sending a letter back to Christophe saying that though France still harbored great hatred for the island, it would not try to invade it. When Clarkson's letter arrived in Haiti, however, Christophe was dead. In despair over his beleaguered government, he had shot himself with a golden bullet.[38]

A man of action, Clarkson responded to tragedy in ways that other people never dreamed of. In 1822, it would not have occurred to a genteel Briton, even an abolitionist, to bring some of the homeless Haitians back to Britain, but this is exactly what Clarkson did. He invited Christophe's widow and her two daughters to his residence, Playford Hall, where they stayed for nearly a year. What Clarkson did not foresee was the squirmy discomfort his fellow abolitionists, and some of his friends like the Wordsworths, would feel toward the Christophe women. But it certainly struck him, as the months wore on, how there was "a sort of shrink at admitting them into high society." [39] Indeed, upon their arrival, the wishy-washy William Wilberforce wrote Clarkson saying that he "had no time to spare" to help out the Christophes, and even confirmed abolitionists like Zachary MacCaulay were relieved that Madame Christophe was "not likely to come near us." [40] Embodiments of blackness, slavery, and the revolutionary violence of Haiti, the real-life Madame and her daughters left polite abolitionists anxious.

The Wordsworths' reaction was even more puzzling. We know that Dorothy, Sara Hutchinson (his sister-in-law), and Wordsworth himself mused over the situation, because Dorothy wrote to Catherine Clarkson in 1822 with a full report. The letter is so revealingly uneasy, that it is worth quoting here:

If you could see the lively picture I shaped to myself of the Sable Queen sitting with her sable daughters beside you on the sofa in my dear little parlour at Playford you would thank the newspapers for being so communicative respecting your visitors! . . . Sara says, "No! they will sit in the great room" . . . now my Fancy espies them through the window of the court upon the larger Sofa — them and you — and your dear Husband talking French to them with his old loving-kindness.[41]

With this letter, Dorothy enclosed a poem, composed in jest by Wordsworth and Sara. "Oh! how they laughed. I heard them into my Room upstairs," Dorothy wrote to Catherine Clarkson, and she copied out the poem.

And herein lies the problem: When we recall Wordsworth's extremely sensitive and astute acknowledgment of rejected, homeless, and traumatized women — the impossible choices of the mad mother, the red-cloaked misery of Martha Ray, the steely stare of the Negro woman from Calais — it is difficult to know how to interpret the poem he composed about the Christophe women in

1822, where there is little sympathy for the Haitian refugees, little interest in their beliefs, and no acknowledgment of the suffering and violence that had destroyed their lives in the West Indies:

Queen and Negress chaste and fair!
Christophe now is laid to sleep,
Seated in a British Chair
State in humbler manner keep
Shine for Clarkson's pure delight
Negro Princess, Ebon-Bright!

Let not "Wilby's" holy shade
Interpose at Envy's call,
Hayti's shining Queen was made
To illumine Playford Hall
Bless it then with constant light
Negress excellently bright!

Lay thy Diadem apart
Pomp has been a sad deceiver
Through thy champion's faithful heart
Joy be poured, and thou the Giver
Thou that makest a day of night
Sable Princess, Ebon-Bright! [42]

Here, in direct imitation of Ben Jonson's 1600 "Queen and Huntress" (which was addressed to Queen Elizabeth), Wordsworth images the Haitian women as ornaments of exotic otherness, brightening the living room of a country estate. At one moment, he mocks the infighting among Clarkson and Wilberforce with the phrase "Wilby's holy shade," the next he stylizes Clarkson as a faithful champion with a black harem. The women's sole purpose is to exhibit their royal blackness as an ironic beacon to lighten the seriousness of Playford Hall.

The poem was obviously meant to be private since Wordsworth never published it, not even in his 1849–50 collected works. It displays a side of himself that he did not advertise, unlike the more public side he reveals in "The Banished Negroes" and "To Toussaint L'Ouverture," both of which were printed several times during his life. In contrast to these poems, the "Queen and Negress," with its embarrassed half-mocking chivalric tone, its Elizabethan pseudo-idealization of black women as courtly heroines, was a joke as crude and racist then as it is now. It certainly must have come as a shock to Clarkson. Dorothy guessed as much, because when she did not hear from the Clarksons for three full months, she wrote them saying that she feared the "joke" about the "poor fallen royalty" was "displeasing to you." [43]

Wordsworth resolutely turned away from the slavery cause at this point, both implicitly and explicitly. In 1823, when emancipation agitation was at its peak, he advised Clarkson to settle down and write "a History of Africa, as the finishing of his literary labours, and the most appropriate one for him." [44] Clarkson, however, wanted more than an ineffectual academic exercise, and he wanted Wordsworth to do more, too. In 1824, Clarkson asked Wordsworth to distribute antislavery papers in Ambleside, but Wordsworth sternly wrote back, "I could make little use of the Papers your Society sent me" because "nobody at Ambleside appeared in the least interested in the question" of slavery. As a sort of justification, he added, "really, anxiously as I desire to see the condition of the Negroes improved, and slavery abolished, I feel the Question involved in so many difficulties, that I am inclined to leave it to the discretion of Government. The Petitions you are so desirous of obtaining may be of use in giving Ministers courage to act up to their own best wishes; but is it not possible that those very petitions may make the Negroes impatient under their present condition; and excite them to disturbance." [45] Clearly afraid of revolutionary slaves, but with the question of emancipation in the air, Wordsworth turned from political activism to what he could do best: write poetry. But he continued to be haunted by the black woman from Calais.

III

In the meantime, former slaves came to Britain in increasing numbers. Of those, the Antiguan slave Mary Prince left her mark as the first black woman author in Britain. Prince had been a slave all her life, but once in Britain, in 1828, she left her owners and took refuge where she could find it, at the Aldermanbury Anti-Slavery Society, the very society Wordsworth's friend Clarkson had helped to set up. When Prince arrived on the society's doorstep, she was alone and poverty-stricken, her body aching with rheumatism and pain brought on by the harsh labor and physical abuse she had endured in the Caribbean. Although the Anti-Slavery Society did not rescue every former slave who came to their door, they took a special interest in Prince. They gave her a job working for Thomas Pringle, the society's secretary. In return, Mary Prince narrated her riveting story, which the society immediately recognized would move the reading public, and they subsequently published it in 1831 as *The History of Mary Prince, a West Indian Slave, Related by Herself.*

Anyone who reads Prince's thin but powerful *History* will understand that from her point of view, alterity for a former slave woman was unlikely in Britain. But if anyone had the power to achieve it, Prince did. Her narrative's lyrical smoothness and gut-wrenching honesty easily overturned even the most stubborn proslavery claims, like the planters' repeated insistence that slave working conditions were humane, although defeating proslavery arguments does not appear to be the purpose behind the *History*.[46] It is a raw, emotionally driven tale of her life as a slave, and in this capacity it also revised the most heavily symbolic antislavery icon: that of the slave woman. Utterly sentimentalized and in need of pity and salvation, the image of slave woman, and particularly the slave mother, had served poets and abolitionists for over fifty years. But almost never, during this time, was her value as another person, her alterity, recognized. Prince's narrative changed all this.

How does Prince's *History* deal with the British unease of slaves in Britain?[47] How does it recontextualize Wordsworth's depictions of black women and those made by the abolitionists? Arguably, the narrative's most potent content is its conversation with slave reproduction and infant destruction. The most horrifying and therefore most unforgettable scene in the *History* comes early on when Prince, herself still a child, witnesses the senseless death of a fellow slave called Hetty, and the abortion of her child at the hands of the slave master, Captain I____:

Poor Hetty . . . was very kind to me, and I used to call her my Aunt; but she led a most miserable life, and her death was hastened (at least the slaves all believed and said so,) by the dreadful chastisement she received from my master during her pregnancy. It happened as follows. One of the cows had dragged the rope away from the stake to which Hetty had fastened it, and got loose. My master flew into a terrible passion, and ordered the poor creature to be stripped quite naked, notwithstanding her pregnancy, and to be tied up to a tree in the yard. He then flogged her as hard as he could lick, both with the whip and cow-skin, till she was all over streaming with blood. He rested, and then beat her again and again. Her shrieks were terrible. The consequence was that poor Hetty was brought to bed before her time, and was delivered after severe labour of a dead child. (57)

Prince narrates Hetty's death in such graphic detail partly because this is her own introduction to the types of scenarios that await her. The scene marks the death of Prince's childhood innocence by disabusing her of her own sense of freedom. Up to this time, Prince says, "I was too young to understand rightly my condition as a slave," primarily because she belonged to owners who allowed her close contact with her mother and treated her "with as much freedom" as they did their own children (47–48). "But this happy state was not to last long," Prince remembers (49). She goes on to spend the rest of her life (and the rest of her narrative) trying to revive it.

Prince's retelling of the Hetty incident is important, in its literary resonances, because it deliberately opposes the construction of the slave woman eager to put an end to the fruit of her labors or the fruit of her womb. Instead, what Prince notices most about slave mothers is their excessive productivity. Despite the atrocities enacted on Hetty by Captain I____ and his wife, Prince describes Hetty as

the most active woman I ever saw. . . . A few minutes after my arrival she came in from milking the cows, and put the sweet potatoes on for supper. She then fetched home the sheep, and penned them in the fold; drove home the cattle, and staked them about the pond side; fed and rubbed down my master's horse, and gave the hog and fed the cow their suppers; prepared the beds, and undressed the children, and laid them to sleep. (55)

Further, Prince presents her own mother as the productive, and procreative, precursor to Hetty. Altogether, she has twelve children. Yet Prince often talks about her mother in ways that remind readers how slave mothers were degradingly bred like farm animals. Prince's mother, in fact, cannot conceptualize her children nor her own motherly role apart from their place in the West Indian economy. She prepares her "poor slave-brood" to be sold and carries her "little chickens to market" (51). At the market, Prince's mother reminds a young slave mother who "came with her infant in her arms" and "tears in her eyes": " 'your turn will come next' " (51). This connection, between breeding cattle and women, was almost a cliché during the early nineteenth century. Even Thomas Pringle, in his appendix to Prince's work, chides slave holders for "inducing" their slaves to couple and breed like "a pair of lower animals" (94).

Even though Prince must acknowledge the reality, that slave women were forced to become producers of the plantation labor force, she deliberately casts reproduction apart from its commodity function. She maintains that though slave women were aware of their roles as breeding bodies, they had children because *they* wanted families, because close kinship ties were important to *them*. Prince even goes so far as to represent herself as the bridge that reconnects and reunites the women in her family. At one point, for example, she meets her mother after a long absence, and with open arms greets both her mother and the "sweet child with her—a little sister I had never seen, about four years of age, called Rebecca. I took her on shore with me, for I felt I should love her directly" (66).

Prince's emphasis on female family ties as a source of power is supported by other historical documents. The most startling are the Newton papers, some of which include the letters of Sampson Wood, manager of the Newton Estate in Barbados, to the absentee owner living in London. On the estate, Wood repeatedly refers to the "pact of old Doll's family, particularly Dolly, & Jenny & Kitty Thomas the oldest daughter of Mary Ann." He then tells how these women have actually usurped his role as manager. They dictate the amount and kind of work performed by their own children (who make up a majority of the plantation work force), they insist the children learn to read and write, and they control, to some extent, the productiveness of all workers by setting a "bad example" if they choose. Wood both despises and admires the "pact" of women for the influence they wield over the entire plantation.[48]

Prince's description of female family ties has these elements, but since she is writing from the perspective of a slave woman, her view is more complex. She tenderly tells of her mother's attachment to her children, and theirs to her, but this also serves to emphasize their inevitable separation at the auction block. Like Wordsworth in his *Lyrical Ballads*, Prince echoes abolitionist portrayals only to depart from their stereotypical terms. She takes family separation beyond such absurd clichés that are exemplified by this early-nineteenth-century dialect tract:

Massa sell de vife at de auction, and den ve part—go long vay, see no more, den ve veep, and cry, and de heart bleed; me no marry, but me true.—Massa sell de child, and den de other, so vife and children be parted, and den de heart bleed again.[49]

Prince's description is more individual and more disturbing in its figurative terms, for she laces family division with the terms "great grief," "loss," "sorrow," "lamenting," and "mourning" and then goes on to depict the separation as a metaphorical act of infanticide (51–53). She recalls, "Whilst [my mother] was putting on us the new osnaburgs in which we were to be sold, she said in a sorrowful voice, (I shall never forget it) 'See I am *shrouding* my poor children; what a task for a mother!' " (51). By digging up the skeleton of her slave experience, Prince penetrates the "bleeding heart" of the slave mother. Whereas "slavery hardens white people's hearts," it tears the hearts of slave mothers who "could only weep and mourn over their children, they could not save them from cruel masters" (26; 60). Similarly, the feelings of loss well up in Prince so powerfully that she experiences them in a way that mimics abortion. She remembers, "my heart throbbed with grief and terror so violently . . . I could not keep it still, and it continued to leap as though it would burst out of my body" (52). The experience stands in ironic contrast to the feelings of the slave traders and plantation owners who participate most directly in this system: "Did one of the many bystanders, who were looking at us so carelessly, think of the pain that wrung the hearts of the negro woman and her young ones? No, no!" (52).

The pain of the negro woman, however, interested abolitionist poets immensely. They figured her in one of three stereotypical ways: as murderous mother, as activist mother, or as passive, "good" mother. Poetic treatments of murderous mothers, as mentioned in conjunction with Wordsworth's poems, were numerous, but one striking example will suffice here. J. Jamieson's *The Sor-*

rows of Slavery (1798) imagines a slave mother's first words to her new born child:[50]

With transport many a woman would a son
Behold, and all her pangs anon forget;
But I unhappy must the barren bless,
And view my womb's fruit as my greatest curse,
In ripeness dropt into the world's wide field,
But to be crush'd by stern Oppression's tread.
Thrice happy they whose fruit hath in the bud
By some propitious blast been kindly nipt.

Jamieson fuses the slave woman's role as breeding body with the roles of plantation workers in the "world's wide field." He thereby addresses how prenatal obstruction affected the conditions not only of the slave mother's labor, but of slave labor at large.

Poetic portrayals of slave women as revolutionaries were less common than as murderous mothers, though there is plenty of historical support to suggest that slave women were activists, as in the case of the *Amistad*, in which African women helped seize control of a ship in revolt against slavery.[51] Abolitionist poets, however, usually imagined African women as activists by virtue of the fact that they were also mothers. James Montgomery, for instance, pictures black motherhood with a vengeance in his poem *The West Indies* (1809):

A Negro-mother carols to her child:
"Son of my widow's love, my orphan joy!
Avenge thy father's murder my boy!"[52]

A more violent example comes from "The Slave Ship," a broadsheet poem based on the journey of the French ship *Le Rodeur*.[53] When a "terrible malady," a disease of the eyes, renders slaves blind and thus unsalable, the white crew flings them overboard to their deaths. The central scene involves a slave woman intervening for her child:

Help! oh help! thou God of Christians
Save a mother from despair;—
Cruel white man stole my children—
Oh! God of Christians, hear my prayer!
I'm young and strong and hardy;
He's a sick and feeble boy:—
They've killed my child? they've killed my child?
The mother shriek'd,—Now all is o'er;
Down the savage captain struck her,
Lifeless on the vessel's floor.

When abolitionist poets did not write about the slave mother's aggressive or destructive acts, they presented her as helpless, and this became a text that Prince rewrote with particular force. Hetty's energetic and productive example reimagines stereotypes from British poetry, where black women were dismal mothers with children on the verge of death. An extreme example of this is Anna Letitia Barbauld's *Hymns in Prose for Children*, where the "negro woman . . . sittest pining in captivity, and weepest over thy sick child," which points out why the category of good mother was conceived of primarily by white women.[54]

It seems unlikely that these pictures bore much resemblance to actual slave mothers. Yet both poetry and iconography of this period represented slave women as sacrificial mothers who could, as it turned out, speak for the slavish condition of British women.[55] One early nineteenth-century sugar bowl, for example, illustrates a slave woman kneeling as she gently cradles her child under the slogan:

Ye women of England, your influence extend
Ye mothers ye daughters the helpless defend
There strong ties are severed for one crime alone
Possessing a colour less fair than your own.[56]

A similar picture is found on a delicate china plate from the same period carrying the motto (Figure 37):

As borrowed beams illume our way
And shed a bright and cheering ray
So Christian Light dispels the gloom
That shades poor Negro's hapless doom.[57]

What these dinnerware motifs and mottoes point to more emphatically than a perceived parallel between white women and black is the ideological motivation behind slave mother stereotypes. Abolitionist poems relied so heavily on stereotypes that it is impossible to imagine the movement without the standard register of diseased ships, growling captains, clamoring crews, greedy planters, lush tropical isles, shackled slave men, and dejected slave women grabbing after their children. Although these images all had some basis in reality, writers invoked this clichèd catalog for some specific reasons. Like dinnerware and sugar bowls, stereotypes existed through duplication and thrived through mass consumption. The etymology of the word stereotype, in fact, refers to the printing plate used to reproduce many copies of the same material, and therefore emphasizes how abolitionist poets who employed the slave mother stereotype were in the business of sentimental reproduction.

As borrowed beams illume our way
And shed a bright and cheering ray.

I am oppressed undertake for me
Isaiah 38:14

I labour and have no rest
Lam. 5:5

So Christian Light dispels the gloom
That shades poor Negro's hapless doom

Figure 37. Plate with abolitionist motifs and mottoes, white china, printed in brown, early nineteenth century. Courtesy of the Board of Trustees of the National Museums and Galleries on Merseyside/Liverpool Museum.

IV

Prince bridges the distance between the British reading public and the role of slave women not only by bringing slave motherhood to the heart of commercial Britain, but by peopling her narrative with desensationalized characters who resist stereotype and by presenting a genuinely complex picture of the slave system. Prince writes against the stereotype of the good mother who could be protected by white women in her depiction of her last slave mistress, Mrs. Wood. While Mrs. Wood did not flog Prince, she subjected Prince to extreme psychological abuse, verbally berating her, and at one point putting Prince in a cage.

Prince relates how Mrs. Wood would "not lick me herself, but she got her husband to do it for her, whilst she fretted the flesh off my bones" (75).[58] When Prince implicates the behavior of some white British women who treated female slaves as powerless adversaries, not as "sisters" who "possess a colour less fair" than their own, she implies that British women might prove more abusive than British men, and in this sense, she shatters the motifs and mottoes served up on English plates and platters.

More radically, Prince's text inverts the murderous mother stereotype by turning it on white slave owners themselves. Though not a natural parent, Prince nevertheless proves a more productive parent than the white owners she serves. Most of her labors, except her work on Turk's Island, entail nursing her owners' children. In fact, in her role as surrogate parent, Prince binds infants, death, and slavery together in the opening pages of the text. At one of her early jobs, while "nursing a sweet baby, little Master Daniel," she suddenly hears news of her owner's death. Prince's grief is "so great," she runs with the baby in her arms directly to the house, but reaches "it only in time to see the corpse carried out" (49). Prince treats her white charge with love and care, and in this sense she writes against a British fear — real or imagined — of slave women who killed their masters' children, like the "young wench, who had the care of her master's child, [and] disliked the employment so much, that she poisoned the infant, with laudanum."[59]

On Turk's Island, in the employment of Mr. D____, Prince more forcefully acts as protector. She saves his daughter from infanticide in the midst of Mr. D____'s own murderous rage. She tells how Mr. D____ "often got drunk" and proceeded to beat his daughter "till she was not fit to be seen" (67). On one occasion, says Prince:

I heard a great screaming; I ran as fast as I could to the house . . . where I found my master beating Miss D____ dreadfully. I strove with all my strength to get her away from him; for she was all black and blue with bruises. He had beat her with his fist, and almost killed her. The people gave me credit for getting her away. (67)

In grinding detail, the narrative turns the slave mother-figure into the preserver of life and the slave master into the murderous parent of his own white child.

Prince's text gives shape to the abolitionists' hollowed out versions of the slave woman and life to her frozen fixity. But Prince does so on her own terms. To begin with, she lodges herself in the British imagination as a living abortion of the slave system. Right after the Hetty episode, Prince describes how she was thrust into misery at the hands of Captain I____ and God Almighty. She prefaces this scene with a refrain from Christian doctrine, "But the hand of that God whom then I knew not, was stretched over me" (58). The Christian message is here, on one level, to accommodate Thomas Pringle and the Anti-Slavery Society. But God's hand clenches with horror when coupled, as it is in this scene, with the fist of Captain I____ who ties Prince to a ladder, and gives her "a hundred lashes with his own hand" (58). Prince recollects how Captain I____ "When he had licked me for some time he sat down to take breath; then after resting, he beat me again and again, until he was quite wearied, and so hot (for the weather was very sultry), that he sank back in his chair, almost like to faint" (58).

The flogging boldly mixes sadomasochistic sexuality with the nuances of painful childbirth, as the next part of the incident makes terrifyingly clear. To warrant this severe punishment, Prince had picked up Mrs. I____'s "earthen jar," which broke in her hands with "an old deep crack that divided it in the middle" (58). In turn, the flogging Prince receives causes an "old deep crack" in the earth itself, a gaping wound that inadvertently acts as ironic antithesis to the "beauteous heap," or "hill of moss" covering the child murder in Wordsworth's "The Thorn" (36). While Captain I____ rests after flogging Prince, there is a "dreadful earthquake" (59): "The earth was groaning and shaking . . . and the slaves were shrieking," Prince remembers, inextricably linking this earth shattering event to the wrath of Jehovah for the wickedness of Sodom and Gomorrah or Nineveh. Yet here the earth issues forth, not a pillar of salt or a giant fish, but Prince herself, as a testament to the wickedness of Captain I____ and God. Prince thereby portrays herself as the abortive offspring of British slavery, prematurely ripped from her happy childhood by the system and left as its abortive spoil. "During the confusion," she recalls,

I crawled away on my hands and knees, and laid myself down under the steps of the piazza in front of the house. I was in a dreadful state — my body all blood and bruises, and I could not help moaning piteously. . . . I lay there till morning, careless of what might happen, for life was very weak in me, and I wished more than ever to die. But when we are very young, death always seems a great way off, and it would not come that night to me. (59)

Prince's abortive body links her to the other abjected bodies in her narrative, most notably to "a slave called old Daniel" whose flesh was beaten raw with "a rod of rough briar." His open wounds were "full of maggots." In his misery and pain, he became an emblem to the slave gang. "In his wretched case," Prince recalls, "we saw, each of us, our own lot" (64).

Yet Prince engenders the abortive, abject body of slavery in her text only to reenvision its productive value. Though Prince does not have children of her own, she does produce a text and so finds political deliverance through the creative act. It is here that she employs the theme of abortion and infanticide in her narrative as a representational strategy. The literal violence enacted against

Prince and other slaves by their owners continually breaks through the text. It replicates an actual abortion insofar as the content is raw, embryonic, and undeveloped. Quite simply, such brutal violence as was practiced on slaves is beyond development: it literally cannot go anywhere beyond itself. On a structural level, Prince aborts the natural path of the narrative, actually terminating the story's flow in many places, reminding herself, "But I must go on with the thread of my story" (58). Often the narrative's abortive cracks are sites where Prince finds English words and sentiment inadequate. She simply cannot describe some of the abuse she underwent because it is "too, too bad to speak in England" (58). Her loss to "find words to tell you all I then felt and suffered" proves a sharp contrast to the abolitionist poet's repetitive descriptions of the brutalities of slavery (51).

Textual ruptures also signal the *History*'s peculiar status as oral narrative.[60] Although the narrative was designed as a tool for the Anti-Slavery Society and mediated by them, it manages to capture the orality of Prince's retelling. As Moira Ferguson has pointed out, it is impossible to know exactly how much of the narrative Prince authorized, since it was "taken down from Mary's own lips by a lady who happened to be at the time residing" with the Pringles, and Thomas Pringle himself "went over the whole" manuscript and "pruned" it "into its present shape."[61] But this fact also points out the precarious position in which Prince finds herself, a position of abjection, of in-betweenness, at once taking part in and taking note of her culture. Prince herself acknowledges this, pointing out: "Oh the horrors of slavery!—How the thought of it pains my heart! But the truth ought to be told of it; and what my eyes have seen I think it is my duty to relate; for few people in England know what slavery is" (64). Such moments of orality occur after detailed scenes, where Prince as narrator seeks to correct British misconceptions. For instance, to emphasize the terrible conditions on Turk's Island, working for the sexually abusive Mr. D____, Prince diverges from her story to *say*: "Work—work—work—Oh that Turk's Island was a horrible place! The people in England, I am sure, have never found out what is carried on there. Cruel, horrible place!" (64). Her text knifes through the stereotypical and thus nullifying effect of abolitionist poetry with an orality that leaves her text literarily undeveloped, aborted, and all the more powerful for it.

Perhaps most impressively, the text's ruptures signal moments when Prince intervenes for herself. The first and most important of these occurs when Prince runs away from the abusive Captain I____ to her own mother. Her mother, a household slave, does her best to shelter Prince by hiding her in a womblike "hole in the rocks," a space that acts rhetorically as twin opposite to the abortive night she spends under Captain I____'s piazza steps (60). Eventually, she is brought back to Captain I____, but this time it is Prince's words that terminate the story: "I then took courage and said that I could stand the floggings no longer; that I was weary of my life, and therefore I had to run away to my mother" (60). Sometime later, Prince does the same thing. She ends the sexual harassment of Mr. D____, stating that "At last I defended myself, for I thought it was high time to do so. I told him I would no longer live with him" (68).

Most importantly, Prince ends her captivity to Mr. and Mrs. Wood, her last enslavers, through a series of struggles that recall not so much abortion or infanticide, but the intense labor of a successful birth. Prince explains how Mrs. Wood "was always abusing and fretting after" her, always following her around "foot after foot scolding and rating" her (70). Miraculously, for all of the physical abuse Prince has endured, it is at this point of verbal violence that she speaks up and begins to represent herself. She ends the symbiotic mistress-slave relationship through a number of clever maneuvers that begin with her productivity and industry. While her master and mistress are away from home, Prince sets up her own business: "sometimes I bought a hog cheap on board ship, and sold it for double the money on shore" (71). She thus enters the market not as a commodity herself, but as one who exchanges. Then, she strategically places a number of free individuals (according to West Indian law) between herself and the Woods. From making money when her "master and mistress went from home," to marrying a free black, Daniel James, to surrounding herself with abolitionists who listen to and sympathize with her story, Prince induces the Woods to give her up once and for all (71).

But, as if to emphasize the difficult nature of childbirth for slave women, Prince complicates her deliverance from slavery with an eviction scenario that once again symbolically blames white masters for incidents of slave abortion. Kathryn Temple has argued that Prince brought home a threatening view of slavery, and thus the *History* existed as a cultural document to critique the treatment of slaves in the colonies and of black people in Britain itself.[62] Indeed, as Jenny Sharpe points out in a recent essay on Prince, her text does depart from the traditional slave narrative by complicating the notion of escaping to British freedom.[63] When Prince's pain from rheumatism debilitates her, she wryly diagnoses her situation:

I was sorry I had come from Antigua, since mistress would work me so hard, without compassion for my rheumatism. Mr. and Mrs. Wood, when they heard this, rose up in passion against me. They opened the door and bade me get out. But I was a stranger, and did not know one door in the street from another, and was unwilling to go away. (77)

The narrative vacillates between Prince's desire for freedom, the Woods' refusal to let her purchase her freedom, Prince's knowledge that "I was free in England, but I did not know where to go, or how to get my living; and therefore, I did not like to leave the house" (78), and the Woods' continual threats to "send for a constable to thrust" her out (78). Recognizing that freedom in this aborted sense is no freedom at all (because with no money and no employment, she would starve to death), Prince refuses to leave the Woods' until she finds advocacy through the Anti-Slavery Society. At this point, she announces:

This is the fourth time my master and mistress have driven me out, or threatened to drive me — and I will give them no more occasion to bid me go. I was not willing to leave them, for I am a stranger in this country, but now I must go — I can stay no longer to be used. (79)

And with this, Prince delivers herself from slavery in 1828.

When Prince took refuge within the walls of the Anti-Slavery Society, they were busy using the problem of slave reproduction to bolster their rhetoric even as she narrated her story to them. At a May 1830 meeting, for instance, the society — composed of men influential in government policy making — employed the birth metaphor specifically to add a sense of urgency to their message. C. Brownlow, M.P., stated that "the most urgent representation" the Anti-Slavery Society could use to convince Parliament to end slavery was the fact that "under the allegiance of a British Monarch, and within the legislature of a British Parliament, thousands of children continue yearly to be born to no inheritance but that of a hopeless and interminable bondage." [64] Mary Prince's *History* not only reminded these gentlemen that slave mothers, not Parliament, were the real producers of these "thousands of children," but also showed them that a black woman could represent herself in her own terms at the heart of British culture.

On the literary front, Prince made a distant and oppressed figure into a person whose otherness was intimately revealed but not appropriated. Her slave mother is never the simple figure that abolitionist poets thought they knew well enough to manipulate for campaigning purposes. The mother's distance is insisted upon, even as she is made familiar to the reader. In that respect she resembles Martha Ray of "The Thorn" and the mad mother. Yet Prince differs from Wordsworth, for even when he most powerfully realizes women's otherness, he could not, as the example of the Christophe women shows, let them bring it to the cultural center in their own terms. His heroines are challenging in their difference, uncanny in their resemblance to slaves, but they depend on acts of interpretation they cannot make for themselves. Perhaps no other person could make them either, unless that person was Mary Prince, a former slave woman narrating an autobiography in Britain itself.

V

In 1829, a year after Prince came to Britain, Wordsworth wrote another slave poem called "Humanity," where he pondered some of the larger forces that had brought transatlantic slavery into being. He said, for instance, "what a fair world were ours for verse to paint, / If Power could live at ease with self-restraint!" (41–42). Yet the slave in "Humanity" is not an individual like Prince, or even like the woman from Calais, but is reduced to the binary extremes of indignant scorn or pitiable gratitude:

Witness those glances of indignant scorn
From some high-minded Slave, impelled to spurn
The kindness that would make him less forlorn;
Or, if the soul to bondage be subdued,
His look of pitiable gratitude! (64–68)

A few years later, in 1833, a family friend Mrs. W. P. Rawson wrote to Wordsworth asking if she could include "Humanity" in an antislavery anthology she was compiling called *The Bow in the Cloud*. He declined, saying he did not want "to add to the excitement already existing in the public mind." [65]

In 1834, emancipation was made legal. That same year Rawson's *Bow in the Cloud* appeared, without a poem from Wordsworth. Still, what is interesting about the collection is the way the contributors echoed and developed Wordsworth's literary approach to the slave question. His poem "Humanity" contains the lines, " 'Slaves cannot breathe in England' — yet that boast / Is but a mockery! when from coast to coast, / Though *fettered* slave be none, her floors and soil / Groan underneath a weight of slavish toil" (83–86). This very same line opens one of the longest poems in the collection: William Howitt's "West Indian Slavery" starts, " 'Slaves cannot breathe in England, That is true, / But they who forge the chains of Slavery do.' " Howitt then names the following Englishmen as the worst offenders: the senator, the merchant, the gentleman, and father. In short, he indicts Britain's ruling classes and is determined to make oppression abroad be felt at home:

True, — the foul scene that brands us and defiles,
Is held at distance in our Indian isles.
True, — no blood trickles from our bondsman's sores;
No fetter clank, no lash sounds on our shores.
Oh! That they were but near us! [66]

If Howitt's contribution echoes Wordsworth's "Humanity," other verses in *The Bow in the Cloud* might take readers back to Wordsworth's reworking of antislavery motifs of mad and murderous mothers. For example, in "The Negro Mother" we witness a "mother's wild distress" and "frenzied horror" as

... the fiery sunbeams spent
Her frame, not of the scorching ray
She thought, but only how the day,
Hour after hour, might wear away
With her poor abandoned child.[67]

The complementary "Negro-Mother's Cradle-Song" shows a slave singing,

Though a mother's love be mine,
And a daughter's fondness thine,
Yet for thee a parent's breath
Craves the boon of early death.
Worse to live a helpless slave,
Than to fill an early grave;
Better far the silent tomb,
Than the captive's hopeless doom.[68]

Since Wordsworth, in the 1830s, had said things such as that slavery was "in principle monstrous, but it is not the worst thing in human nature," it seemed unlikely that he would return to the slave woman in poetry.[69] But he did. Though he had moved away from his early revisions of antislavery images, though he had turned his back on the activism represented by Clarkson and even produced a poem that unfeelingly mocked the slave's position, and though he had refused to support the antislavery cause poetically, there were at least a few moments when he did express a personal/poetic identification with the alterity of the slave woman. He continued to revise the poem about the woman he had met on the ship from Calais in 1802, returning to it in 1820, 1827, 1836, 1838, 1840, 1843, and 1845, just five years before his death. By 1845, he had changed the title from "The Banished Negroes" to "September 1, 1802," commemorating the exact date of the encounter. In this final version, the woman is as she was in the first, intimate and distant, and perhaps more so, since she retains the fierce otherness that the narrator does not even attempt to classify:

We had a female Passenger who came
From Calais with us, spotless in array, —
A white-robed Negro, like a lady gay,
Yet downcast as a woman fearing blame;
Meek, destitute, as seemed, of hope or aim
She sate, from notice turning not away,
But on all proffered intercourse did lay
A weight of languid speech, or to the same

No sign of answer made by word or face:
Yet still her eyes retained their tropic fire,
That burning independent of the mind,
Joined with the lustre of her rich attire
To mock the Outcast—O ye Heavens, be kind!
And feel, thou Earth, for this afflicted Race![70]

In this 1845 version, Wordsworth highlights the woman's status as rejected French subject by taking this reference from the final lines and placing that information in a headnote, and by making her expulsion a specific example of all forms of tyranny. He writes: "Among the capricious acts of tyranny that disgraced those times, was the chasing of all Negroes from France by decree of the government: we had a Fellow-passenger who was one of the expelled."[71] He reminds readers of the unequal power relations before they even begin the poem, and then he places a gem of alterity at the center in the 1845 text, in the glint of the woman's eye, no less: "her eyes retained their tropic fire, / That burning independent of the mind" (11–12). Nothing in Wordsworth more strongly acknowledges alterity than the single phrase "burning independent of the mind," as if in the forty-three years that had passed between one recounting of this incident and its final incarnation, Wordsworth—despite his struggles with how to conceive of Africans as British citizens—imagined the black woman's fierce resistance to the silence imposed on her.

Afterword

Tracing an iconic Romantic poet — William Wordsworth — through his encounters with slavery and former slaves is a challenge. My purpose in the final chapter of this volume has been to show, by way of conclusion to the book as a whole, that Wordsworth, no more or no less than any creative person of the period, struggled with the poetics of the distanced imagination. On one hand, it is almost impossible to imagine how a writer of this era could have conceived of, let alone represented, the inhuman facts of slavery. But, on the other hand, it was inevitable that such an urgent, alarming, and morally profound history would pay a major role in the Romantics' conception of the imagination. As they created something radically different from themselves and in the process distanced themselves from their own tedious egos, they strove for (as Keats put it) "a complete disinterestedness of Mind," a poetic practice that was absolutely influenced by "a pure desire of the benefit of others" (*KL*, 279).

These flesh and blood "others" in nineteenth-century Britain were slaves — slaves were the very people who gave Britons their definition of freedom. Romantic writers thus necessarily took on the question of slavery as they put their theories of imagination into practice. Hence, there are moments in some of the period's most powerful writing and art — "The Rime of the Ancient Mariner," Blake's engravings and his *Visions of the Daughters of Albion*, Keats's *Lamia*, Percy Bysshe Shelley's "The Witch of Atlas," Mary Shelley's *Frankenstein*, and Wordsworth's poetry — when readers encounter a world immediately familiar and utterly distant, when they are asked to face those whom they will never actually see.

The final chapter has a second purpose as well. Bringing Mary Prince's *History*, the first text authored by a black woman in Britain, up against Wordsworth's portrayal of black women demonstrates how a former slave enacted the distanced imagination. In Prince's text, readers are asked to forget themselves and imagine the alterity of another, and in so doing they are called on to understand the slave experience as never before. In fact, of all the works examined in this volume, none annihilates self-consciousness more swiftly and more shrewdly than *The History of Mary Prince*. The conclusion is clear: as the period wore on and as emancipation drew near, the most powerful representation of the ethical relationship between self and other came not from the imaginations of Romantic poets, artists, and novelists, but from the voice of a former slave woman.

Notes

Introduction

1. Srinivas Aravamudan, *Tropicopolitans: Colonialism and Agency, 1688–1804* (Durham, N.C.: Duke University Press, 1999); Alan Bewell, *Romanticism and Colonial Disease* (Baltimore: Johns Hopkins University Press, 1999); Elizabeth Bohls, *Women Travel Writers and the Language of Aesthetics* (Cambridge: Cambridge University Press, 1995); Laura Brown, *Ends of Empire: Women and Ideology in Early Eighteenth-Century English Literature* (Ithaca, N.Y.: Cornell University Press, 1993); David Dabydeen, ed., *The Black Presence in English Literature* (Manchester: Manchester University Press, 1985); Markman Ellis, *The Politics of Sensibility: Race, Gender, and Commerce in the Sentimental Novel* (Cambridge: Cambridge University Press, 1996); Moira Ferguson, *Subject to Others: British Women Writers and Colonial Slavery, 1760–1834* (New York: Routledge, 1992); Tim Fulford and Peter J. Kitson, eds., *Romanticism and Colonialism: Writing and Empire, 1780–1830* (Cambridge: Cambridge University Press, 1998); Nigel Leask, *British Romantic Writers and the East: Anxieties of Empire* (Cambridge: Cambridge University Press, 1992); Javed Majeed, *Ungoverned Imaginings: James Mill's "History of British India" and Orientalism* (Oxford: Oxford University Press, 1992); Saree Makdisi, *Romantic Imperialism: Universal Empire and the Culture of Modernity* (Cambridge: Cambridge University Press, 1999); Timothy Morton, *The Poetics of Spice* (Cambridge: Cambridge University Press, 2000); Felicity Nussbaum, *Torrid Zones: Maternity, Sexuality, and Empire in Eighteenth-Century English Narratives* (Baltimore: Johns Hopkins University Press, 1995); Mary Louise Pratt, *Imperial Eyes: Travel Writing and Transculturation* (New York and London: Routledge, 1992); Alan Richardson and Sonia Hofkosh, eds., *Romanticism, Race, and Imperial Culture, 1780–1834* (Bloomington: Indiana University Press, 1996).

2. Nussbaum, 210.

3. Alison Hickey, "Dark Characters, Native Grounds: Wordsworth's Imagination of Imperialism," in Richardson and Hofkosh, 283–310 (285).

4. Bohls, 22.

5. Aravamudan, 24.

6. Aravamudan, 14.

7. Alan Richardson, "Epic Ambivalence: Imperial Politics and Romantic Deflection in Williams's *Peru* and Landor's *Gebir*," in Richardson and Hofkosh, 266.

8. Bewell, 12. I have learned especially from Alan Bewell, Tim Fulford, Peter Kitson, and Alan Richardson, and their influence on my work is evident throughout.

9. Fulford and Kitson, 3, 5.

10. Part of the problem for current scholars, according to Malcolm Kelsall, is our critical tendency to read Romantic writers' relationship to imperialism "respectively from

the instantaneous present." "For modern, liberal, cultural historians," he writes, "discussion of empire" and, by extension, of slavery—empire's most shameful branch—"has become involved with the guilt of the post-colonial West," and this "places the liberal in a position of apologetic retreat." Malcolm Kelsall, " 'Once did she hold the gorgeous east in fee . . .': Byron's Venice and Oriental Empire," in Fulford and Kitson, 245. In fact, Stephen C. Behrendt has said something similar about the rereading and remapping of cultural history. Such revisioning requires us to see similarities between the Romantics and our own cultures, but Behrendt warns that we must also be aware of "actual, historical and cultural differences that separate us from our forebears." Stephen C. Behrendt, "Introduction," *Romanticism, Radicalism, and the Press*, ed. Behrendt (Detroit: Wayne State University Press, 1997), 13–29 (13).

11. Eva Beatrice Dykes, *The Negro in English Romantic Thought: or, A Study of Sympathy for the Oppressed* (Washington, D.C.: Associated Publishers, 1942); Wylie Sypher, *Guinea's Captive Kings: British Anti-Slavery Literature of the Eighteenth Century* (reprint New York: Octagon Books, 1969).

12. Joan Baum, *Mind-Forg'd Manacles: Slavery and the English Romantic Poets* (North Haven, Conn.: Archon Books, 1994).

13. Patrick J. Keane, *Coleridge's Submerged Politics: The Ancient Mariner and Robinson Crusoe* (Columbia: University of Missouri Press, 1994).

14. Keane, 195.

15. H. L. Malchow, *Gothic Images of Race in Nineteenth-Century Britain* (Stanford, Calif.: Stanford University Press, 1996), 5.

16. Helen Thomas, *Romanticism and Slave Narratives: Transatlantic Testimonies* (Cambridge: Cambridge University Press, 2000); Marcus Wood, *Blind Memory: Visual Representations of Slavery in England and America, 1780–1865* (New York: Routledge, 2000).

17. Adam Lively, *Masks: Blackness, Race, and the Imagination* (London: Chatto and Windus, 1999).

18. Line 20 and line 12. For a reading of the African in Blake's *Marriage* and "Little Black Boy," see David Bindman, "Blake's Vision of Slavery Revisited," *Huntington Library Quarterly*, ed. Robert N. Essick, 58, 3–4 (1997): 373–82.

19. Toni Morrison, *Playing in the Dark* (New York: Vintage, 1992). All quotations come from page 66.

Chapter 1. British Slavery and African Exploration

1. This was a specific controversy, called the Registry Bill, between government, abolitionists, and plantation owners. In 1812, James Stephen introduced a measure for the general registration of slaves. The proposition would force all planters to make a record of slaves in the colonies, and, in succeeding years, the owners would have to make a record of any changes that had taken place. Since the absence of a name and description in the records was proof of freedom, illicit import of slaves would be prevented. But the main object was to improve the conditions of slaves. The abolitionists thought this would make planters more accountable, but it required an act of Parliament to enforce. In 1815, the abolitionists pressed for the act. On 13 June 1815, William Wilberforce proposed a motion in the House of Commons, but Viscount Castlereagh postponed it. The West Indians

then organized opposition, complaining that this was a way for the imperial government to get power over the colonies, who were better at legislating themselves. Wilberforce thus agreed to let the individual islands pass their own registry bills. By 1820, in each of the islands, registry acts had been passed and a central registry for collecting the colony registers had been established in London by an act of Parliament.

2. *Further Papers Relating to Slaves in the West Indies, Demerara and Berbice*, Ordered by the House of Commons to be printed, 23 June 1825. The complaint of Tommy appears on pages 9–10.

3. F. O. Shyllon, *Black Slaves in Britain* (London: Oxford University Press, 1974), 77. Shyllon says that Somerset was kidnapped on 26 November 1771.

4. James Walvin, *Black Ivory: A History of British Slavery* (London: Fontana Press, 1993), 17–19, and Shyllon, 125–40.

5. David Brion Davis, *The Problem of Slavery in the Age of Revolution, 1770–1823* (Ithaca, N.Y.: Cornell University Press, 1975), 476.

6. *Gazetteer*, 14 February 1772; quoted in Shyllon, 141.

7. *Gazetteer*, 4 June 1774; quoted in Shyllon, 144. From Sharp's personal papers, quoted in Davis, *The Problem of Slavery*, 476.

8. Cited in Walvin, *Black Ivory*, 17. See also Shyllon, 185.

9. Quoted in Walvin, *Black Ivory*, 19. See also Shyllon, 190.

10. Quoted in Shyllon, 188.

11. Shyllon, 189.

12. James Walvin, *Slaves and Slavery: The British Colonial Experience* (Manchester and New York: Manchester University Press, 1992), 99; James A. Rawley, *The Transatlantic Slave Trade: A History* (New York: W.W. Norton, 1981), 283–306.

13. John Woolman, from *Some Considerations on the Keeping of Negroes*, in his *Journal and Major Essays*, ed. Phillips P. Moulton (New York: Oxford University Press, 1971), 233.

14. Woolman, 235.

15. Woolman, 233. Woolman made a journey to Britain in May 1772, the same year as the Somerset trial. He died of smallpox in York on 7 October 1772. For a different discussion of Woolman's place in the antislavery debate, see Thomas L. Haskell, "Capitalism and the Origins of the Humanitarian Sensibility, Part 1 and Part 2," in John Ashworth, David Brion Davis, and Thomas L. Haskell, *The Antislavery Debate: Capitalism and Abolitionism as a Problem in Historical Interpretation*, ed. Thomas Bender (Berkeley: University of California Press, 1992), 107–35, 136–60.

16. William Fox, *An Address to the People of Great Britain on the Utility of Refraining from the Use of West India Sugar and Rum*, 4th ed. (London, 1791), reprinted in *The Abolition Debate*, ed. Peter J. Kitson, vol. 2 of *Slavery, Abolition, and Emancipation: Writings in the British Romantic Period*, ed. Peter J. Kitson and Debbie Lee, 8 vols. (London: Pickering and Chatto, 1999), 2:160.

17. John Newton, *Thoughts on the African Slave Trade* (London, 1788), reprinted in Kitson and Lee, 2:78.

18. Thomas Clarkson, *An Essay on the Slavery and Commerce of the Human Species* (London 1788), reprinted in Kitson and Lee, 2:39–40.

19. Ellen Gibson Wilson, *Thomas Clarkson: A Biography* (Basingstoke: Macmillan, 1989), 29.

20. For an account of the *Brookes*, see Rawley, 283–84.

21. There were many different reproductions of this poster, and the caption quoted here did not appear on all of them. This copy is located in the Wilberforce House Museum, Hull.

22. Bernard Lewis, *Race and Slavery in the Middle East: An Historical Enquiry* (New York and Oxford: Oxford University Press, 1990), 3.

23. Johannes Menne Postma, *The Dutch in the Atlantic Slave Trade, 1660–1815* (Cambridge: Cambridge University Press, 1990), 3.

24. Y. Hakan Erdem, *Slavery in the Ottoman Empire and Its Demise, 1800–1909* (London: Macmillan, 1996).

25. *Slavery in Africa: Historical and Anthropological Perspectives*, ed. Suzanne Miers and Igor Kopytoff (Madison: University of Wisconsin Press, 1977).

26. Postma, 3.

27. Richard Hakluyt, *The Principles of Navigations, Voyages, Traffiques & Discoveries of the British Nation* (1582), 7: 5, quoted in Michael Craton, *Sinews of Empire: A Short History of British Slavery* (New York: Anchor Books, 1974), 1.

28. *The Speech of Mr. Wilberforce . . . on a Motion for the Abolition of the Slave Trade in the House of Commons, May the 12th, 1789* (London, 1789), reprinted in Kitson and Lee, 2:138.

29. Patrick Manning, *Slavery and African Life: Occidental, Oriental, and African Slave Trades* (Cambridge: Cambridge University Press, 1990), 104.

30. Dedication, *Beloved* (New York: Knopf, 1987).

31. Philip Curtin, *The Atlantic Slave Trade: A Census* (Madison: University of Wisconsin Press, 1969), 3–13; Paul E. Lovejoy, "The Volume of the Atlantic Slave Trade: A Synthesis," *Journal of African History* 23 (1982): 496–97.

32. Miers and Kopytoff, 14–18.

33. Erdem, 19.

34. George Canning, *The Speech of the Rt. Hon. George Canning . . . for the Amelioration of the condition of the Slave Population in His Majesty's Dominions in the West Indies* (London, 1824), reprinted in Kitson and Lee, vol. 3, *The Emancipation Debate*, ed. Debbie Lee, 261.

35. Michael Craton, *Testing the Chains: Resistance to Slavery in the British West Indies* (Ithaca, N.Y.: Cornell University Press, 1982), 291–321. Samuel Sharpe is quoted on 321.

36. Captain James Cook, *Voyage to the Pacific Ocean . . . for Making Discoveries in the Northern Hemisphere* (London, 1784); Georg Forster, *A Voyage Round the World* (London, 1777); John Hawkesworth, *An Account of the voyages . . . in the southern hemisphere* (London, 1773); George Keate, *An Account of the Pelew Islands* (London, 1788); William Beckford, *A Descriptive Account of the Island of Jamaica* (London, 1790); Matthew Gregory Lewis, *Journal of a West India Proprietor kept during a residence in the island of Jamaica* (London, 1834); William Bartram, *Travels through North and South Carolina, Georgia, East and West Florida, The Cherokee Country . . . together with Observations on the Manners of the Indians* (London, 1791); Samuel Hearne, *A Journey From Prince of Wales's Fort in Hudson's Bay to the Northern Ocean In The Years 1769, 1770, 1771, and 1772* (London, 1795); Thomas Robert Jolliffe, *Letters from Palestine, descriptive of a Tour through Galilee and Judea* (1819); James Morier, *A Journey through Persia, Armenia and Asia Minor, to Constantinople, in the years 1808 and 1809* (1812) and *A Second Journey . . .* (1818); James Wathen, *Journal of a Voyage, in 1811 to 1812, to Madras and China* (1814); John Crawford, *Journal of an Embassy from the Governor-General of India to the Courts of Siam and Cochin*

China (1828); George Finlayson, *The Mission to Siam, and Hue the capital of Cochin China, in the years 1821 and 1822* (1826)

37. "Africa had also come increasingly under British gaze as a market for the growing volume of goods the Industrial Revolution made possible—particularly as the traditional pattern of trade based on slaves was under challenge with the growth of the anti-slavery movement. French exploration of Africa in the 1780s helped to give greater impetus" to exploring Africa, too. John Gascoigne, *Science in the Service of Empire: Joseph Banks, the British State and the Uses of Science in the Age of Revolution* (Cambridge: Cambridge University Press, 1998), 179.

38. Gascoigne quotes Bryan Edwards as saying that Banks was the "life and soul of the Association," and it was at Banks's house that the first meeting to establish the Association was held (179).

39. Johann Friedrich Blumenbach, *On the Natural Variety of Mankind* (1795), reprinted in Kitson and Lee, vol. 8, *Theories of Race*, ed. Peter J. Kitson, 140–212.

40. Quoted in Patrick O'Brian, *Joseph Banks: A Life* (London: Collins Harvill, 1987), 168–70. This letter refers to the collection when it was located at the house at New Burlington Street.

41. Gascoigne, *Science in the Service of Empire*, 179.

42. Quoted in Gascoigne, 179.

43. Quoted in Gascoigne, 180.

44. Quoted in Gascoigne, 180.

45. Eric Williams, *Capitalism and Slavery* (Chapel Hill: University of North Carolina Press, 1944). In 1933, the Oxford historian Reginald Coupland (who was also William Wilberforce's biographer) published *The British Anti-Slavery Movement* (London: Thornton Butterworth, 1933). He correlated the rise of abolitionism and emancipation with the rise of British humanitarianism, which he claimed was founded on transcendent ideals. Coupland's was the prevailing view among scholars until the publication of Eric Williams's groundbreaking book. See *British Capitalism and Caribbean Slavery: The Legacy of Eric Williams*, ed. Barbara L. Solow and Stanley L. Engerman (Cambridge: Cambridge University Press, 1987).

46. David Brion Davis, "The Problem of Slavery in the Age of Revolution, 1770–1823" (Part 1, "What the Abolitionists Were Up Against"; Part 2, "The Quaker Ethic and the Antislavery International"; Part 3, "The Preservation of English Liberty") in Bender, 17–26, 27–64, 65–103 (102).

47. Peter Brent, *Black Nile: Mungo Park and the Search for the Niger* (London: Gordon and Cremonesi, 1977), 34.

48. Mungo Park, *Travels in the Interior Districts of Africa, performed under the direction and patronage of the African Association, in the years 1795, 1796, 1797* (London, 1799), ed. Kate Ferguson Marsters (Durham, N.C.: Duke University Press, 2000), 68.

49. Manuscript correspondence, 9 October 1798; Banks Collection, Royal Botanic Gardens, Kew: Kew BC, 2:204.

50. Park, 154.

51. In 1799, before the narrative was actually finished, Edwards wrote to Banks describing Park's progress as a writer, "Park . . . improves in his style so much by practice that his journal is equal to anything in the English language." Bryan Edwards to Joseph Banks, 30 January 1797; Kew BC, 2:212.

52. Park, 195.

53. Park, 196. The duchess of Devonshire used this passage to write a poem called "A Negro Song, from Mr. Park's Travels," which was then set to music by G. G. Ferrari and titled "Song from Mr. Park's Travels."

54. Mary Louise Pratt, *Imperial Eyes: Travel Writing and Transculturation* (New York: Routledge, 1992), 74.

55. Mary Russell Mitford, "Lines, Suggested by the Uncertain Fate of Mungo Park, the Celebrated African Traveller," in *Poems* (London, 1811), 49.

56. Quoted in Robin Hallett ed., *Records of the African Association, 1788–1831* (London: Thomas Nelson and Sons, 1964), 168–69.

57. Pratt, 84.

58. Ashton Nichols, "Mumbo Jumbo: Mungo Park and the Rhetoric of Romantic Africa," in Richardson and Hofkosh, 93–113 (97).

59. For the politics of British reading audiences, also see Behrendt.

60. Jon P. Klancher, *The Making of British Reading Audiences, 1790–1832* (Madison: University of Wisconsin Press, 1987), 14, 12.

61. William G. Rowland, Jr., *Literature and the Marketplace: Romantic Writers and Their Audiences in Great Britain and the United States* (Lincoln: University of Nebraska Press, 1996), 5.

62. Rowland, 176.

63. Michael Ryan, "Poetry and the Audience," in *Poets Teaching Poets: Self and the World*, ed. Gregory Orr and Ellen Bryant Voight (Ann Arbor: University of Michigan Press, 1996), 171.

64. John Wilson, "On Reading Mr. Clarkson's History of the Abolition of the Slave Trade," in *The Isle of Palms and Other Poems* (Edinburgh, 1812), lines 31–35, 76–82.

65. James Montgomery in his introduction to *The West Indies, a Poem in Four Parts*, in *Poems on the Abolition of the Slave Trade, by James Montgomery, James Grahame, and E. Benger* (London, 1809), ii. Reprinted in Kitson and Lee, vol. 4, *Verse*, ed. Alan Richardson, 280–332 (285).

66. Coleridge's review was originally published in the *Edinburgh Review* 12 (1808): 355–79 (372).

67. Letter of Keats to John Hamilton Reynolds, 3 February 1818 (*KL*, 1:224).

68. Shelley, *A Defence of Poetry* (*SP*, 488).

Chapter 2. The Distanced Imagination

1. Slave revolts sprang up regularly in the British West Indies, and in Britain itself religious groups posed the first strong objections to slavery. Perfectionist and millennialist sects opposed slavery because it was antithetical to the very principles by which they tried to live: lives devoted to service and selflessness, to which exploitation of other human beings was anathema (Davis, "The Problem of Slavery in the Age of Revolution, 1770–1823," 21). The Quakers, who also called themselves the Society of Friends, and later Christian organizations such as Methodists and Anglican Evangelicals spread the fire of antislavery opinion.

2. William Blake, *The Four Zoas*, 36.9.

3. Mary Wollstonecraft, *A Vindication of the Rights of Woman*, ed. Carol H. Poston, 2nd ed. (New York: W.W. Norton, 1988), 77.

4. Coleridge here uses transatlantic slavery to suggest another frightening form of captivity: Britain's possible subjection to France.

5. John Gorton, *Tubal to Seba: The Negro Suicide: A Poem*, 2nd ed. (London: W. Kemmish, 1797), 40.

6. Hannah More and Eaglesfield Smith, *The Sorrows of Yamba; or, The Negro Woman's Lamentation* (London, 1795), reprinted in Kitson and Lee, 4:224–31 (226). For Alan Richardson's concise account of the complex authorship and printing of this poem, see 4:224.

7. Mary Robinson, "The Negro Girl," from *Lyrical Tales* (London: Longman, 1800), reprinted in Kitson and Lee, 4:267.

8. James Montgomery, *The West Indies*, in Kitson and Lee, 4:311.

9. For a fuller argument about Wordsworth's philosophy of the disinterested self and the creative process, see John G. Rudy, *Wordsworth and the Zen Mind: The Poetry of Self-Emptying* (Albany: State University of New York Press, 1996).

10. In addition to the poets I mention here, William Hazlitt's "Essay on the Principles of Human Action" (1802) was also an important source for this idea.

11. Eleanor Wilner, "The Closeness of Distance, or Narcissus as Seen by the Lake," paper presented at the 25th Annual Centrum Summer Writer's Workshop, 8–20 July 1998, 2. Similarly, Walter J. Slatoff in *The Look of Distance* (Columbus: Ohio State University Press, 1985) observes the way in which aesthetic distance either helps or hinders the moral effects of poetry and novels. One of his most helpful insights comes in a chapter entitled "The Heights and Depths of Distance" where he examines philosophers as diverse as Nietzsche, Arthur Schopenhauer, and Bertrand Russell. Russell is the most articulate exponent of the self's ability to distance itself from itself in its search for freedom within an increasingly confining world. Renouncing selfhood and the neurotic personal wishes that subject people to the "empire of Fate" is a function of the imagination. Its by-product is at least partial freedom from "the resistless forces that control" an individual's outward life (117–18).

12. C. M. Bowra describes it thus: "For the Romantics, imagination is fundamental, because they think that without it poetry is impossible. This belief in the imagination was part of the contemporary belief in the individual self. The poets were conscious of a wonderful capacity to create imaginary worlds, and they could not believe that this was idle or false" (C. M. Bowra, *The Romantic Imagination* [Oxford: Oxford University Press, 1961], 1–2).

15 Over the years, critics have talked about the disinterested imagination using various terms. It is sometimes called the "sympathetic imagination" or the "moral imagination."

14. See James Engell's thoroughgoing book, *The Creative Imagination: Enlightenment to Romanticism* (Cambridge, Mass.: Harvard University Press, 1981). See especially the chapter "The Psyche Reaches Out: Sympathy," 143–60. Other works that take up this topic from various and intersecting perspectives include *The Romantic Imagination: A Casebook*, ed. J. Spencer Hill (London: Macmillan, 1977); T. J. Diffey, "The Roots of Imagination: The Philosophical Context," in *The Romantics*, ed. Stephen Prickett (New York: Holmes and Meier, 1981), 164–201; Eva T. H. Brann, *The World of Imagination* (Savage, Md.: Rowman and Littlefield, 1991); *Platonism and the English Imagination*, ed. Anna Baldwin and Sarah Hutton (Cambridge: Cambridge University Press, 1994), see especially section 4, "The Eighteenth Century," and section 5, "The Nineteenth Century." See

also Nigel Leask, *The Politics of Imagination in Coleridge's Critical Thought* (New York: St. Martin's Press, 1988); John Drew, *India and the Romantic Imagination* (Oxford: Oxford University Press, 1987); Patricia M. Ball, *The Central Self: A Study in Romantic and Victorian Imagination* (London: Athlone Press, 1968); and Jean Hall, *A Mind That Feeds Upon Infinity: The Deep Self in English Romantic Poetry* (London and Toronto: Associated University Press, 1991).

15. Joseph Addison, "The Pleasures of Imagination," in *Selections from the Tatler and the Spectator*, ed. Angus Ross (Harmondsworth: Penguin, 1988), 365.

16. Addison, 385, 390, 399.

17. Alexander Gerard, *An Essay on Taste*, 3rd ed. (1759; London and Edinburgh, 1780), 12.

18. Gerard, 100.

19. Edmund Burke, *A Philosophical Enquiry into the Origin of our Ideas of the Sublime and Beautiful*, 2nd ed. (London, 1759), 127, 129.

20. All quotes from Adam Smith, *The Theory of Moral Sentiments* (1759), ed. D. D. Raphael and A. L. Macfie (Oxford: Clarendon Press, 1976), 10.

21. Adam Smith, 9.

22. Richard F. Teichgraeber III, introduction to Adam Smith, *An Inquiry into the Nature and Causes of the Wealth of Nations* (New York: Random House, 1985). Teichgraeber writes, "In the late nineteenth century, German scholars coined the phrase 'das Adam Smith Problem'. . . . For how could a thinker who had ascribed human conduct to the workings of 'sympathy' later reverse himself in presenting a view of economic affairs which suggested that virtuous conduct was either reducible to enlightened self-interest or simply irrelevant to human purpose" (xii).

23. Haskell agrees that capitalism and the industrial revolution provided the conditions that allowed the abolitionist movement to flourish. But he dismisses the idea that we, in the present day, can ascribe selfish motives—whether that means blatant class interest or more subtle self-deception—to a group of people who took the new moral responsibility to heart and worked to change British attitudes and laws.

24. Thomas L. Haskell, "Convention and Hegemonic Interest in the Debate over Antislavery: A Reply to Davis and Ashworth," in Bender, 200–259 (228).

25. The *OED* cites two sources before Coleridge's writings, one in 1642 and one in 1660 the only two other citations, which give the fullest expression to the term, are from Coleridge's *Table Talk* and *Notes on Shakespeare*.

26. A. J. Greimas and J. Courtés, *Semiotics and Language*, trans. Larry Crist, Daniel Patte, James Lee, Edward McMahon II, Gary Phillips, Michael Rengstorf (Bloomington: Indiana University Press, 1982). 12.

27. Mark C. Taylor, *Altarity* (Chicago: University of Chicago Press, 1987).

28. Taylor, xxviii.

29. Galen A. Johnson and Michael B. Smith, *Ontology and Alterity in Merleau-Ponty* (Evanston, Ill.: Northwestern University Press, 1990), xix.

30. Emmanuel Levinas, *Totality and Infinity: An Essay on Exteriority*, trans. Alphonso Lingis (Pittsburgh: Duquesne University Press, 1969), and *Otherwise Than Being; or, Beyond Essence*, trans. Alphonso Lingis (The Hague: Martinus Nijhoff, 1981).

31. Emmanuel Levinas, *On Thinking-of-the-Other: Entre Nous*, trans. Michael B. Smith and Barbara Harshav (New York: Columbia University Press, 1998) and *Ethics and Infinity: Conversations with Philippe Nemo*, trans. Richard A. Cohen (Pittsburgh: Duquesne University Press, 1985).

32. For a brief discussion of this, see Robert Alexander, Adam Carter, Kevin D. Hutchings, and Neville F. Newman, "Alterity in the Discourses of Romanticism," *European Romantic Review* 9.2 (1998): 149–60. Also, David P. Haney, "Aesthetics and Ethics in Gadamer, Levinas, and Romanticism: Problems of Phronesis and Techne" *PMLA* 114, 1 (1999): 32–45.

33. Levinas, *On Thinking-of-the-Other*, 119.

34. *New York Times*, 27 December 1995, obituary of Emmanuel Levinas.

35. Emmanuel Levinas, *Time and the Other, and Additional Essays*, trans. Richard A. Cohen (Pittsburgh: Duquesne University Press, 1987), 88. See also Johannes Fabian, *Time and the Other: How Anthropology Makes Its Object* (New York: Columbia University Press, 1983).

36. Levinas, *On Thinking-of-the-Other*, 34, 65.

37. Levinas, *On Thinking-of-the-Other*, 111–12.

38. Levinas, *Otherwise Than Being*, 88.

39. Levinas, *On Thinking-of-the-Other*, 109.

40. Levinas, *On Thinking-of-the-Other*, 231.

41. Levinas, *On Thinking-of-the-Other*, xii.

42. Levinas, *On Thinking-of-the-Other*, 107.

43. First quotation from Haney, 43. Second quotation from Levinas, *Otherwise Than Being*, 131, quoted in Haney, 43.

44. Introduction to Levinas, *Time and the Other*, 19.

45. I am indebted to the fruitful discussion at the 2000 MLA after the panel organized by Pamela M. Brown, "Demanding Responsibility: Levinas and Derrida," and to the papers presented by Jennifer Hardy Williams, "Tracing the Author/La trace de l'autre: Derrida avec Levinas," and Robert Eagleston, "Traces, Cinders, Writing: Levinas and Derrida."

46. Levinas, *Ethics and Infinity*, 87.

47. Jacques Derrida, *Adieu to Emmanuel Levinas*, trans. Pascale-Anne Brault and Michael Naas (Stanford, Calif.: Stanford University Press, 1999).

48. Levinas quoted in Derrida, 18.

49. "Signification, the one-for-the-other, the relationship with alterity, has been analyzed in the present work as proximity, proximity as responsibility for the other, and responsibility for the other as substitution," Levinas, *Otherwise Than Being*, 184.

50. The topic has already been partially explored by critics such as Orrin N. C. Wang, Eugene L. Stelzig, and Jeanne Moskal. Wang, "The Other Reasons: Female Alterity and Enlightenment Discourse in Mary Wollstonecraft's *A Vindication of the Rights of Woman*," *Yale Journal of Criticism* 5 (1991): 129–49; Stelzig, "Coleridge in *The Prelude*: Wordsworth's Fiction of Alterity," *Wordsworth Circle* 18 (1987): 23–27; Moskal, *Blake, Ethics, and Forgiveness* (Tuscaloosa: University of Alabama Press, 1994), in a chapter called "Alterity and the Spectre of Urthona," 104–35.

51. "The Mental Traveller," 62.

Chapter 3. Distant Diseases

I would like to thank Alan Bewell, Tim Fulford, Jerry Hogle, Jim McKusick, and Raimonda Modiano for the various contributions they made to this chapter. Alan Bewell's exciting book *Romanticism and Colonial Disease*, which explains in detail how disease, literature, and colonialization merged during the nineteenth century, was unfortunately not available when I wrote this chapter.

1. Charles Powell, *A Treatise on the Nature, Causes, & Cures, of the Endemic, or Yellow Fever of Tropical Climates, as it occurs in the West Indies* (London, 1814), 24; and James Clark, *A Treatise on the Yellow Fever as it Appeared in the Island of Dominica, in the years 1793–4–5–6* (London, 1797), 8.

2. Powell, 23.

3. Thomas Trotter, *Medicina Nautica: An Essay on the Diseases of Seamen* (London, 1797), 184. See Robert Southey, *Selections from the Letters of Robert Southey*, ed. J. W. Warter, 4 vols. (London, 1856), 1:317. The full text of Southey's remark is "I have a sort of theory about such diseases [e.g., smallpox], which I do not understand myself,—but somebody or other will one of these days. They are so far analogous to vegetables, as that they take root, grow, ripen, and decay. Those which are eruptive blossom and seed; for the pustules of the smallpox is, to all intents and purposes, the flower of the disease, or the fructification by which it is perpetuated. Now these diseases, like vegetables, choose their own soil; as some plants like clay, others sand, other chalk, so the yellow fever will not take root in a negro, nor the yaws in a white man."

4. Clark, 63.

5. William Hillary, *Observations on the Changes of the Air and the Concomitant Epidemical Disease, in the Island of Barbadoes*, 2nd ed. (London, 1766), iii.

6. John Hume, "Letter VII: An Account of the True Bilious, or Yellow Fever; and of the Remitting and Intermitting Fevers of the West Indies," *Letters and Essays on the Small Pox and Inoculation, the Measles, the Dry Belly-Ache, and Yellow, and Remitting and Intermitting Fevers of the West Indies* (London, 1788), 237.

7. Trotter, 322.

8. Philip Curtin, *Death by Migration: Europe's Encounter with the Tropical World in the Nineteenth Century* (Cambridge: Cambridge University Press, 1989), 18. For other contemporary books on the subject, see François Delaporte, *Disease and Civilization: The Cholera in Paris, 1832*, trans. Arthur Goldhammer (Cambridge, Mass.: MIT Press, 1986), and François Delaporte, *The History of Yellow Fever: An Essay on the Birth of Tropical Medicine*, trans. Arthur Goldhammer (Cambridge, Mass.: MIT Press, 1991).

9. Peter J. Kitson, "Coleridge, the French Revolution and 'The Ancient Mariner': Collective Guilt and Individual Salvation," *Yearbook of English Studies* 19 (1989): 197–207.

10. J. R. Ebbatson, "Coleridge's Mariner and the Rights of Man," *Studies in Romanticism* 11 (1972): 198. A number of writers have interpreted the poem by looking at it alongside Coleridge's writings on the slave trade and slavery. John Livingston Lowes (*The Road to Xanadu* [London: Constable, 1927]) establishes Coleridge's use of travel reports and ship logs in many of the tropes and descriptions of "The Ancient Mariner." Ebbatson's classic article establishes a logical link between the poem, voyages of discovery, colonialism, slavery, and abolitionist poetry, the most important of which is Robert Southey's 1799 "The Sailor Who Had Served in the Slave Trade." The issues are powerfully discussed in Peter J. Kitson, "Coleridge, the French Revolution and 'The Ancient Mariner': A Reassessment," *Coleridge Bulletin* 7 (1996): 30–48.

11. Keane uses an approach similar to Ebbatson, arguing the assumption that slavery is the hidden politics under the surface of "The Ancient Mariner." Keane's study is especially useful in his rigorous bibliographic unearthing of Coleridge's references to the slave trade and related topics. Coleridge's involvement in the slave trade and its application

to "The Ancient Mariner" is also discussed by Baum; Dykes; James McKusick, " 'That Silent Sea': Lee Boo, and the Exploration of the South Pacific," *Wordsworth Circle* 24, 2 (1993): 102–6; William Empson, " 'The Ancient Mariner': An Answer to Warren," *Kenyon Review* 15 (1993): 155–77. Also Anthea Morrison, "Samuel Taylor Coleridge's Greek Prize Ode on the Slave Trade," in *An Infinite Complexity: Essays in Romanticism*, ed. J. R. Watson (Edinburgh: Edinburgh University Press, 1993); and Charles DePaolo, "Of Tribes and Hordes: Coleridge and the Emancipation of Slaves," *Theoria: A Journal of Studies in the Arts, Humanities and Social Sciences* 60 (1983): 27–43.

12. Critics who see the mariner's experience shaped by Coleridge's concerns with political and historical issues include Jerome J. McGann, "The Meaning of *The Ancient Mariner*," *Critical Inquiry* 8 (1981): 63–86; Daniel P. Watkins, "History as Demon in Coleridge's *The Rime of the Ancient Mariner*," *PLL* 24 (1988): 23–33; and Joseph C. Sitterson, Jr., " 'Unmeaning Miracles' in 'The Rime of the Ancient Mariner,' " *South Atlantic Review* 46 (1981): 16–26. Among critics who also offer psychological explanations for the poem's mysteries are Raimonda Modiano, "Words and 'Languageless' Meanings: Limits of Expression in 'The Rime of the Ancient Mariner,' " *Modern Language Quarterly* 38 (1977): 40–61; Paul Magnuson, *Coleridge's Nightmare Poetry* (Charlottesville: University Press of Virginia, 1974); and Joseph C. Sitterson Jr., " 'The Rime of the Ancient Mariner' and Freudian Dream Theory," *PLL* 18 (1982): 17–35. Readers who, like Lowes, find contextual sources for the poem include Martin Bidney, "Beneficent Birds and Crossbow Crimes: The Nightmare-Confessions of Coleridge and Ludwig Tieck," *PLL* 25, 1 (1989): 44–58; James B. Twitchell, " 'The Rime of the Ancient Mariner' as Vampire Poem," *College Literature* 4, 2 (1977): 21–39; Bernard Smith, "Coleridge's 'Ancient Mariner' and Cook's Second Voyage," *Journal of the Warburg and Courtauld Institutes* 29 (1956): 117–54; Donald P. Kaczvinsky, "Coleridge's Polar Spirit: A Source," *English Language Notes* 24, 3 (1987): 25–28; Arnd Bohm, "Georg Forster's *A Voyage Round the World* as a Source for *The Rime of the Ancient Mariner*: A Reconsideration," *ELH* 50, 2 (1983): 363–77.

13. See William Roscoe, "The Wrongs of Africa" (London: R. Faulder, part 1, 1787; part 2, 1788), reprinted in *William Roscoe of Liverpool*, ed. George Chandler (London: B.T. Batsford, 1953), part 1, 343–59; part 2, 360–78 (355, 378).

14. See Hannah More, "Slavery" (1788), reprinted in *Women Romantic Poets, 1785–1832: An Anthology*, ed. Jennifer Breen (London: Everyman, 1992), 11, lines 37–38.

15. Although it is difficult to tell exactly what Coleridge means by "alterity," in one place, at least, he defines it as "the healthful positiveness of compleat polarity, instanced in that chasm between the Subjective and the Objective" (*CN*, 4:5281 f.33). Tim Fulford has pointed out to me that "The Ancient Mariner" often portrays the physical body as a "slave" to some other force than its own soul. The zombielike state of the crew, for instance, parallels a state of slavery, where the body is controlled by some force external to it.

16. Although I do not explore Kristeva's theory of the alterity that stems from the maternal, this is an important component of her philosophy. Coleridge's "The Ancient Mariner" has been insightfully interpreted using Kristeva's ideas on the maternal and the symbolic by Diane Long Hoeveler ("Glossing the Feminine in *The Rime of the Ancient Mariner*," *European Romantic Review* 2, 2 [1992]: 145–62) and Anne Williams ("An I for an Eye: 'Spectral Persecution' in *The Rime of the Ancient Mariner*," *PMLA* 108, 5 [1993]: 1114–27). Hoeveler sees the mariner "trapped forever in the realm of the linguistic, in patriarchal language, in contrast to the recognition of the power of the 'good' maternal

that he has ostensibly experienced" (158–59). The mariner longs for unity (experienced through the maternal), which he cannot have as a result of being a speaking subject, telling his tale again and again. Williams employs Kristeva to examine how "The Ancient Mariner" "provides a genealogy of Coleridgean Imagination . . . it traces the means by which meaning is constructed out of separation, need, fear, guilt, and the need to repair the primal break" (1117).

17. Julia Kristeva, *The Powers of Horror: An Essay on Abjection*, trans. Leon S. Roudiez (New York: Columbia University Press, 1982), 3.

18. Julia Kristeva, *Nations Without Nationalism*, trans. Leon S. Roudiez (New York: Columbia University Press, 1993), 2–3.

19. Julia Kristeva, *Strangers to Ourselves*, trans. Leon S. Roudiez (New York: Columbia University Press, 1991), 187.

20. For a fascinating account of the cultural meanings of the Black Death, see Philip Ziegler, *The Black Death* (New York: Harper, 1969).

21. Gilbert Blane, *Elements of Medical Logick . . . including a statement of evidence respecting the contagious nature of yellow fever* (London, 1819), 158.

22. Trotter, 333.

23. Blane, 205.

24. Robert Renny, *A History of Jamaica with observations on the climate, scenery, trade, productions, negroes, slave trade, diseases of Europeans* (London, 1807), 241.

25. James McKusick (*Coleridge's Philosophy of Language* [New Haven, Conn.: Yale University Press, 1986]) makes a connection between Coleridge and Lord Monboddo, who first believed the orangutans had the physiological ability to articulate language but could not because of intellectual inferiority. Monboddo implicitly established a link between African man and ape.

26. Empson, 167. Empson states, "The Mariner, at this first magical event in the poem, has a premonition of a Slaver, with its planks rotted off by the insanitary exudations of the dying slaves—that was going to be the final result of his heroic colonial exploration, and well might his heart beat loud."

27. Raimonda Modiano has pointed out to me that Ebbatson inadvertently sees the mariner as doubly identified, also. Ebbatson adds a footnote identifying the mariner as a slave just when he states that the mariner, in killing the albatross and guiltily hanging it around his neck, represents European culture's involvement with slavery. Ebbatson says, "The act of hanging the albatross round the Mariner's neck, though probably derived from religious allegory, might also be an image of the slave laden with ball and chain; and what has usually been dismissed as an absurdly large crew of 200 becomes less remarkable when one recalls that a slave ship would carry double the crew of a normal vessel" (201, n. 76).

28. Renny, 192–93.

29. John Redman, *Proceedings of the college of Physicians of Philadelphia relative to the prevention of the introduction and spreading of contagious diseases* (Philadelphia, 1789), 30.

30. Henry Clutterbuck, *Observations on the Prevention and Treatment of the Epidemic Fever* (London, 1819), 39.

31. Thomas Beddoes, *A Lecture Introductory to a Course of Popular Instruction on the Constitution and Management of the Human Body* (Bristol, 1797), 48.

32. The search for origins was thus central to understanding the fever's most ter-

rifying feature: uncontrollability. For the British, who had been used to controlling the way cultures interacted, yellow fever's uncontrollability was particularly unsettling because it highlighted just how susceptible British physical and political bodies were to the invisible and invidious forces of foreign climates. In 1772, Dr. Charles Blicke (*An Essay on the Bilious of Yellow Fever of Jamaica* [London, 1772]) insisted that the first step toward containing yellow fever was "to know its origin" (11).

33. William Deverell, *Andalusia; or, Notes tending to shew that the yellow fever of the West Indies . . . was a Disease Well Known to the Ancients* (London, 1803), 2.

34. Deverell, 71–72.

35. Beddoes, 48–49; and John Wilson, *Memoirs of the West Indian Fever* (London, 1827), 139. Coleridge's interest in the origin of disease and the notion of "alterity" can be traced to German Romantic philosophy and the medicine of Schelling, Schiller, and Freidrich Schlegel, as Hermione De Almeida (*Romantic Medicine and John Keats* [New York: Oxford University Press, 1991], 139) has pointed out. Coleridge applied his interest in the philosophical "other" to certain contemporary debates on disease and to the debate on slavery, both of which sought out classifications and origins.

36. Quoted in Keane, 70.

37. Helen Maria Williams, *Poem on the Bill Lately Passed for Regulating the Slave Trade* (London, 1788). Reprinted in Kitson and Lee, 4:84–98 (88).

38. Coleridge actually wrote that this "evil in the form of guilt" was "evil in its most absolute and most appropriate sense, that sense to which an impression deeper than could have been left by mere agony of body, or even anguish of mind, in proportion as vice is more hateful than pain, eternity more awful than time" (*SWF*, 1:219).

39. McKusick, 106.

40. Erasmus Darwin, *The Botanic Garden: A Poem in Two Parts*, part 1, *The Economy of Vegetation*; part 2, *The Loves of the Plants* (London, 1791), 1:96, line 424.

41. Darwin, 1:168–69, lines 79–84.

42. Montgomery, *The West Indies*, in *Poems on the Abolition of the Slave Trade, by James Montgomery, James Grahame, and E. Benger*, 33 (part 3 lines 300–302). In a footnote to this passage, Montgomery writes, "For minute and afflicting details of the origin and progress of the yellow fever in an individual subject, see Dr. Pinkard's *Notes on the West Indies* . . . in which the writer, from experience, describes its horrors and sufferings." Reprinted in Kitson and Lee, 4: 317.

43. Renny, 192–93.

44. Molly Lefebure (*Samuel Taylor Coleridge: A Bondage of Opium* [New York: Stein and Day, 1974], 371–73) explains this passage in the context of Coleridge's guilt-ridden opium dreams.

45. Thomas Pringle, "Sonnet on Slavery," in *The Anti-Slavery Album: Selections in verse from Cowper, Hannah More, Montgomery, Pringle* (London, 1828), 3.

46. As Timothy Morton shows in "Blood Sugar," in Fulford and Kitson, 87–106.

47. Coleridge, of course, would go on to see his dependence on opium as one of these imported addictions that acted not just as relief to the pain of disease, but as disease itself, as Roy Porter and Dorothy Porter point out (*In Sickness and in Health: The British Experience, 1650–1850* [New York: Basil Blackwell, 1989], 218–19). See also *The Popularization of Medicine, 1650–1850*, ed. Roy Porter (London: Routledge, 1992).

48. Robert Southey, "A Tale of Paraguay," in *The Poetical Works of Robert Southey Collected by Himself*, 10 vols. (London, 1838), vol. 7, stanza 1:1–7.

49. James Stanfield, *The Guinea Voyage* (London, 1789), 20, 21.

50. Clark, 63.

51. Curtin, *Death by Migration*, 69.

52. Thomas Dancer, *The Medical Assistant; or Jamaica Practice of Physic designed chiefly for the use of families and plantations* (Kingston, 1801), 70–71.

53. Redman, 29.

54. William Hutchenson, *The Princess of Zanfara* (London, 1792), 11.

55. Trotter, 323.

56. Robert Jackson, *An Outline of the History and Cure of Fever . . . vulgarly the yellow fever of the West Indies* (Edinburgh and London, 1798), 219.

57. Redman, 28.

58. Williams, 88.

59. Montgomery, *The West Indies*, in Kitson and Lee, 4:317–18.

60. Stewart Henderson, *A Letter to the Officers of the Army . . . on the means of preserving health and preventing that fatal disease the Yellow Fever* (London, 1795), 43.

61. Matthew Gregory Lewis, *The Castle Spectre* (1797), in *Seven Gothic Dramas*, ed. Jeffrey N. Cox (Athens: Ohio University Press, 1992), 149–221 (186). Coleridge referred to the play in a 1798 letter to Wordsworth.

62. Lewis, *The Castle Spectre*, 175.

63. Lewis, 163, 206

64. Lewis, 199.

65. Lewis, 199.

66. D. L. Macdonald, "The Isle of Devils: The Jamaican Journal of M. G. Lewis," in Fulford and Kitson, 189–205.

67. James McKusick, "Coleridge and the Economy of Nature," *Studies in Romanticism* 35 (1996): 375–92 (387).

68. Michael Taussig, *Mimesis and Alterity* (New York: Routledge, 1993), 41.

Chapter 4. Intimacy as Imitation

1. Geoffrey Keynes, "William Blake and John Gabriel Stedman," *Times Literary Supplement*, 20 May 1965, 400.

2. John Gabriel Stedman, *Narrative of a Five Years' Expedition against the Revolted Negroes of Surinam*, ed. Richard Price and Sally Price (Baltimore: Johns Hopkins University Press, 1988). All subsequent quotations in this chapter from Stedman will be from this edition, cited in parentheses in the text.

3. See the jacket picture for Barbara Bush, *Slave Women in Caribbean Society 1650–1832* (Bloomington: Indiana University Press, 1990), and Timothy Morton, *The Poetics of Spice*, the illustrations in Hugh Honour, *The Image of the Black in Western Art*, 5 vols. (Cambridge, Mass: Harvard University Press, 1989), and in Marcus Wood, *Blind Memory*, and the academic argument in Anne K. Mellor, "Sex, Violence and Slavery: Blake and Wollstonecraft," *Huntington Library Quarterly* 58, 3–4 (1997): 345–70, and Aravamudan, 7, 47.

4. Of the sixteen engravings, all but three depict human subjects. Besides the two monkey engravings, the other is the straightforward natural history illustration of fruit.

5. H. W. Janson, *Apes and Ape Lore in the Middle Ages and the Renaissance* (London:

Warburg Institute, 1952); William Coffman McDermott, *The Ape in Antiquity* (Baltimore: Johns Hopkins University Press, 1938).

6. Ramona Morris and Desmond Morris, *Men and Apes: A Study of the Ape and Monkey in World Mythology* (New York: McGraw-Hill, 1966); *Art, the Ape of Nature: Studies in Honor of H. W. Janson*, ed. Moshe Barasch, Lucy Freeman Sandler, and Patricia Egan (New York: H.N. Abrams, 1981).

7. Robert N. Essick tells us, "In 1788, John and Josiah Boydell hired Blake to engrave William Hogarth's painting of a scene in John Gay's *The Beggar's Opera*. This commission, from England's greatest printseller for Blake's largest copy plate, is the high-water mark of his career in reproductive graphics" (*William Blake's Commercial Book Illustrations: A Catalogue and Study of the Plates Engraved by Blake After Designs by Other Artists* [Oxford: Clarendon Press, 1991], 7).

8. "Fable XXII, the Goat without a Beard," in John Gay, *Fables*, 2 vols. (London, 1793), where three flippant monkeys debase a self-absorbed goat.

9. *The Works of the Late Professor Camper, on the Connexion between the Science of Anatomy and the Arts of Drawing, Painting, Statuary, &etc.* (London, 1794).

10. Johann Kaspar Lavater, *Aphorisms on Man* (London, 1788) and *Essays on Physiognomy* (1781) (Blake engraved one plate for *Aphorisms* and four for *Physiognomy*); Charles White, *Account of the Regular Gradation in Man* (London, 1799). For discussions of apes and race science, see Londa Schiebinger, *Nature's Body: Gender in the Making of Modern Science* (Boston: Beacon Press, 1993), 40–183, and Ashley Montagu's introduction to the 1966 reprint (London: Dawson) of Edward Tyson, *Orang-Outang, sive Homo Sylvestris: or, the Anatomy of a Pygmie Compared with that of a Monkey, an Ape, and a Man. To Which is added a Philological Essay Concerning the Pygmies, the Cynocephali, the Satyrs and Sphinges of the Ancients* (London, 1699). For a discussion of what Blake might have known about facial angles and race science, see Bindman.

11. Henry Louis Gates, *The Signifying Monkey: A Theory of Afro-American Literary Criticism* (New York: Oxford University Press, 1988).

12. Janson, 262.

13. Janson, 266.

14. Ulisse Aldrovandi, *De quadrupedibus digitatis viviparis* (Bonon, 1637). Cited in Janson, 334.

15. Although this story was translated by Richard Burton in the middle of the nineteenth century, Janson thinks it was indeed part of an older Near Eastern tradition; he cites Peter Damian's *De bono religiosi status et variorum animantium tropologia* as evidence (Janson, 268).

16. Richard F. Burton, *A Plain and Literal Translation of the Arabian Nights' Entertainments, Now Entitled the Book of the Thousand Nights and a Night*, 16 vols. (Benares: Kamashustra Society, private printing, 1885), 8:297.

17. This was a hotly debated topic. Scientists deciding whether the ape was a primitive human or not used menstruation as evidence. See Londa Schiebinger, *Nature's Body: Gender in the Making of Modern Science* (Boston: Beacon Press, 1993), 89–91, 124–25.

18. Edward Bancroft, *An Essay on the Natural History of Guiana with an account of the Religion, Manners, and Customs of several Tribes of its Indian Inhabitants* (London, 1769).

19. James Burnett, Lord Monboddo, *Of the Origin and Progress of Language*, 2nd ed., 6 vols (Edinburgh and London, 1774), 1:276

20. Burnett, 1:274.

21. This point was brought to my attention by Peter J. Kitson.

22. Janson, 148–49.

23. Janson, 155.

24. Bloom, "Introduction," in *William Blake's The Marriage of Heaven and Hell: Modern Critical Interpretations*, ed. Harold Bloom (New York: Chelsea House, 1987), 1–24 (20).

25. David V. Erdman, "Blake's Vision of Slavery," *Critical Essays on William Blake*, ed. Hazard Adams (Boston: G.K. Hall, 1991), 41.

26. Levinas, *On Thinking-of-the-Other*, 109.

27. Blake uses *Milton* to explain how self-centered identity must be annihilated before true intersubjectivity can occur:

. . . Individual Identities never change nor cease:
You cannot go to Eternal Death in that which can never Die.
Satan & Adam are States Created into Twenty-Seven Churches
And thou O Milton art a State about to be Created
Called Eternal Annihilation that none but the Living shall
Dare to enter: & they shall enter triumphant over Death
And Hell & the Grave! States that are not, but ah! Seem to be.
Judge then of thy Own Self: thy Eternal Lineaments explore
What is Eternal & what is Changeable? & what Annihilable!
(*Milton*, plate 32: 23–31)

28. Janson, 109.

29. Janson, 19.

30. Morris and Morris, 37–38.

31. Janson, 287, McDermott, 144–45. McDermott cites five Latin examples: Seneca, Pliny, Capitolinus, Horace, and Apollinaris Sidonius.

32. Janson, 289.

33. Bloom, "Dialectic of the *Marriage of Heaven and Hell*," in Bloom, 49–56 (49–50).

34. Kitson and Lee, Peter J. Kitson, introduction to vol. 8, *Theories of Race*, x.

35. Tyson, 2

36. Tyson, 55.

37. Tyson, 2. *The Works of the Late Professor Camper.*

38. Kitson and Lee, 8:xi.

39. Neither Camper nor the most influential race scientist, J. F. Blumenbach, endorsed White's racist conclusion that blacks formed a separate species from whites.

40. See Richard Price and Sally Price's introduction, lxi.

41. Gates, 127–69.

42. Gates,16.

43. Gates, 6.

44. Gates, 6.

45. Gates, 32–35.

46. *Fables by the late Mr. Gay in one volume complete* (London, 1767), 54. Blake's engraving appears in a 1793 edition. See Essick, *William Blake's Commercial Book Illustrations.*

47. Gates, 6–7.

48. Homi K. Bhabha, "Of Mimicry and Man: The Ambivalence of Colonial Discourse," *October* 28 (Spring 1984), 125–33 (127)

49. Bhabha, "Of Mimicry and Man," 131.

50. Edward Long, *The History of Jamaica*, 2 vols (London, 1774), 2: 364; quoted in Bhabha, "Of Mimicry and Man," 132.

51. William Beckford, *A Descriptive Account of the Island of Jamaica*, 2 vols. (London,1790), 1: 255.

52. Amelia Opie, *The Black Man's Lament; or How to Make Sugar* (London, 1826), 3, line 5.

53. James Grainger, *The Sugar-Cane: A Poem in Four Books* (London, 1764), 55.

54. Steven Vine, "'THAT MILD BEAM,' Enlightenment and Enslavement in William Blake's *Visions of the Daughters of Albion*," in *The Discourse of Slavery: Aphra Behn to Toni Morrison*, ed. Carl Plasa and Betty J. Ring (London and New York: Routledge, 1994), 40–63. Reading two images of Blake's Stedman engravings, "Family of Negro Slaves from Loango" (Figure 22) and "Europe supported by Africa & America" [Figure 2], Vine sees Blake's engravings as ironic commentary on implicit racism in Stedman's text.

55. For the various interpretations of Theotormon's racial identity, see Nancy More Goslee "Slavery and Sexual Character: Questioning the Master Trope in Blake's *Visions of the Daughters of Albion*," *ELH* 57 (1990): 101–28: "Theotormon's 'jealous waters' are black and as he sits at the cave's threshold, 'beneath him sound like waves on a desart shore / The voice of slaves beneath the sun, and children bought with money' (2:4, 7–8). Thus we might assume that he is black and doubly powerless" (108). David V. Erdman says Theotormon "is also unable to interfere or to rescue" Oothoon. "Stedman's anxieties shed light on the moral paralysis of Theotormon" (*Blake: Prophet Against Empire* [Princeton University Press, 1977; reprint New York: Dover 1991], 226–42 [234]).

56. Erdman, "Blake's Vision of Slavery." Also see Erdman, *Blake: Prophet Against Empire*.

57. Susan Fox, "The Female as Metaphor in William Blake's Poetry," *Critical Inquiry* 3 (1977): 507–17; Goslee, 102. Also see James A. Heffernan, "Blake's Oothoon: The Dilemmas of Marginality," *Studies in Romanticism* 30 (1991): 3–18; Nelson Hilton, "An Original Story," in *Unnam'd Forms: Blake and Textuality*, ed. Nelson Hilton and Thomas A. Vogler (Berkeley: University of California Press, 1986), 69–104; Fred Hoerner, "Prolific Reflections: Blake's Contortion of Surveillance in *Visions of the Daughters of Albion*," *Studies in Romanticism* 35 (1996), 119–51; Harriet Kramer Linkin, "Revisioning Blake's Oothoon," *Blake: An Illustrated Quarterly* 23 (1990): 184–94; Jane E. Peterson, "The *Visions of the Daughters of Albion*: A Problem in Perception," *Philological Quarterly* 52 (1973): 252–64; Bindman, 374–82.

58. G. E. Bentley, Jr., "The Great Illustrated-Book Publishers of the 1790s and William Blake," in *Editing Illustrated Books*, ed. William Blissett (New York: Garland, 1980), 57–96 (63). Also see G. E. Bentley Jr., *Blake Records* (Oxford: Clarendon Press, 1969).

59. Robert N. Essick, *William Blake Printmaker* (Princeton, N.J.: Princeton University Press, 1980), 53. Essick analyzes "A Family of New South Wales," which Blake made after the watercolor by Governor King for John Hunter's *A Historical Journal of the Transactions at Port Jackson and Norfolk Island*, 1793.

60. Essick says that Blake "has changed the format from vertical to horizontal and made many alterations in the placement and configuration of motifs. It is reasonable to assume that the other engravers were permitted similar liberties" (Essick, *William Blake's Commercial Book Illustrations*, 71).

61. Richard Price and Sally Price bring this watercolor and the engraving together in their introduction to Stedman's *Narrative*, pointing out many of the same features I have repeated here. I would like to thank them for their help in locating and ordering Stedman's watercolor.

62. Essick, *William Blake's Commercial Book Illustrations*, 7.

63. Thanks to Morton Paley and Joe Viscomi for discussing this particular point with me.

64. Stedman liked Blake's work more than that of the other engravers. See Price and Price, xlvi.

65. Hilda Kean, *Animal Rights: Political and Social Change in Britain Since 1800* (London: Reakton Books, 1998): "The very act of seeing became crucial in the formation of the modern person. Who you were was determined by where you were and what you saw—as well as how you interpreted it" (27).

66. Aravamudan reads this plate very differently in the introduction to *Tropicopolitans*, 7.

67. For instance, Stedman tells of a rebel slave about to be hanged who "without motion he first ask'd a dram and then bid them pull away without a Groan—but what gave us the greatest entertainment, continued he, were the fellows Jokes, by desiring the Executioner to drink before him—in case there should chance to be poison in the Glass" (103).

68. The 1788 Privy Council papers record "cases of poison" by astute slaves: "the Skill of some Negroes in the Art of Poisoning has been noticed ever since the Colonists became much acquainted with them. Sloane and Barham, who practised Physic in Jamaica in the last Century, have mentioned particular Instances of it. The Secret and insidious Manner in which this Crime is generally perpetrated, makes the legal Proof of it extremely difficult. Suspicions therefore have been frequent, but Detections rare." In *House of Commons Sessional Papers of the Eighteenth Century*, vol. 69, ed. Sheila Lambert (Wilmington, Del.: Scholarly Resources, 1975), 215–21.

69. Mellor, "Sex, Violence, and Slavery," 357; Erdman, *Blake: Prophet Against Empire*, 231; Vine, 57.

70. This seems to be a truly Blakean engraving because it uses specific figures for big ideas. Blake would later write entire prophetic books called *Europe* and *America* right after these engravings were finished, and the *Song of Los* takes up Africa and Asia.

71. After marching through the marsh, Stedman says, "But here was a Spectacle Almost Sufficient to Damp the Spirits of the most intrepid Soldier, Viz, the ground being Strew'd with the Sculls, bones, and Ribs, Still Covered with Part of the flesh, and Besmeared with the Blood, of those unhappy men kill'd with Capt. Meyland" (401). Stedman moves right from an image of Europeans being murdered by revolted slaves, to the idea of a slave leading through this dangerous marsh.

72. Erdman, *The Complete Poetry and Prose of William Blake*, 724. Letter to Mr. Butts, 10 January 1803.

73. This was apparently replaced in the final published version with a caption that could easily sum up Stedman's attitude toward monkeys and slaves:

From different Parents, different Climes we came,
At different Periods: Fate still rules the same
Unhappy Youth while bleeding on the ground;
'Twas YOURS to fall—but MINE to feel the wound.
(Honour, vol. 4, part 1, 87–89, and 319 n.217.)

74. While Blake certainly mocks Stedman's position in these images, he probably did not make it his personal mission to visually censure Stedman. After all, Blake and Stedman were friends, and Stedman's contradictory position on slavery was more likely a position shared by the majority of people Blake knew, including at times Blake himself.

75. Curiously, he is credited with discovering a root. "Besides these & many other Artful Contrivances he had the Good Fortune to find out the Valuable Root known Under the name of *Qwacy Bitter* of Which this man Was Absolutely the first Discoverer in 1730, & Notwithstanding its being less in Reput in England than formerly is Highly Esteem'd in many other Parts of the World for its Efficacy in strength'ning the stomach, Restoring the Appetite &c." (582).

76. Dykes, 19; Erdman, *Prophet Against Empire*, 226–42; Sypher, 157.

77. Bloom, "Dialectic of the *Marriage of Heaven and Hell*," 49–56; Robert F. Gleckner, "Blake's Little Black Boy and the Bible," *Colby Library Quarterly* 18, 4 (1982): 205–13; Howard H. Hinkel, "From Pivotal Idea to Poetic Ideal: Blake's Theory of Contraries and 'The Little Black Boy,'" *Papers on Language and Literature* 11, 1 (1975): 39–45.

78. Kitson and Lee, 4:158. See also Richardson's "Colonialism, Race and Lyric Irony in Blake's 'The Little Black Boy,'" *Papers on Language and Literature* 26 (1990): 233–48; and Mellor, "Sex, Violence, and Slavery"; Helen Thomas, 120.

79. Lauren Henry, "Sunshine and Shady Groves: What Blake's 'Little Black Boy' Learned from African Writers," in Fulford and Kitson, 67–86, Michael J. C. Echeruo, "Theologizing 'Underneath the Tree': An African Topos in Ukawsaw Gronniosaw, William Blake, and William Cole," *Research in African Literatures* 23 (1992): 51–58.

Chapter 5. African Embraces

1. Robert Burton's account of Lycius, Lamia, and Apollonius in *Anatomy of Melancholy* (III.2.i.I), which Keats extracted in an endnote to the poem, is its most obvious source. For a discussion of Burton's influence, see Jane Chambers, "'For Love's Sake': Lamia and Burton's Melancholy," *Studies in English Literature* 22 (1982): 583–600. For another possible mythic source of the poem, see George C. Gross, "Lamia and the Cupid-Psyche Myth," *Keats-Shelley Journal* 39 (1990): 151–65.

2. George Francis Lyon, *A Narrative of Travels in Northern Africa in the Years 1818, 19, and 20 . . . by Captain G. F. Lyon, R.N., companion of the late Mr. Ritchie* (London, 1821).

3. See Robin Hallett, *The Penetration of Africa: European Enterprise and Exploration Principally in Northern and Western Africa up to 1830* (London: Routledge and Kegan Paul, 1965), and Anna Buckley, "Uncharted Waters (River Niger's Course)," *Geographical Magazine* 66 (December 1994): 28.

4. Lyon, 4.

5. Lyon, 193.

6. John Barnard points out that "the idea that classical nymphs, satyrs, and

gods were displaced by the fairies of English folk-lore is common in Elizabethan and seventeenth-century literature." *The Complete Poems of John Keats*, ed. John Barnard (Harmondsworth: Penguin, 1973), 691 n.

7. See Frantz Fanon, *Black Skin, White Masks*, trans. Charles Lam Markmann (New York: Grove, Weidenfeld, 1967), 161.

8. At the time Keats was writing, "Libya" — on many maps of Africa — designated the space occupied by the Sahara Desert.

9. Park, 67.

10. See Thomas Edward Bowdich, *A Mission from Cape Coast Castle to Ashantee* (London, 1819), 15.

11. Bowdich, 15.

12. Beckford, 1:7–9. Like Bowdich, Beckford refers to the landscape as "romantic" (1:27).

13. For those critics who see the poem as a demonstration of ambiguity arising from various contradictions between philosophy and poetry, rationalism and imagination, good and evil, immortality and mutability, see Timothy Pace, " 'Who Killed Gwendolen Harleth?' Daniel Deronda and Keats's *Lamia*," *Journal of English and Germanic Philology* 87 (1988): 35–48; M. R. Ridley, *Keats' Craftsmanship: A Study in Poetic Development* (Lincoln: University of Nebraska Press, 1933); Joseph C. Sitterson Jr., "Narrator and Reader in *Lamia*," *Studies in Philology* 79 (1982): 297–310; John Daniel Skirp, III, "Intellect, Imagination and the Poet: An Interpretation of *Lamia*," *Journal of Evolutionary Psychology* 7 (1986): 143–47; Jack Stillinger, *The Hoodwinking of Madeline and Other Essays on Keats's Poems* (Urbana: University of Illinois Press, 1971); Earl R. Wasserman, *The Finer Tone: Keats' Major Poems* (Baltimore: Johns Hopkins University Press, 1953, 1967). Terence Hoagwood ("Keats and Social Context: Lamia," *Studies in English Literature* 29 [1989]: 675–95) argues that critics who see the text in these kinds of dichotomies evade the social/political problems the text addresses. Readings that incorporate gender criticism often cite Keats's having a "gordian complication of feelings" for women (*KL*, 1:342); Margaret Hallissy, "Poisonous Creature: Holmes's Elsie Venner," *Studies in the Novel* 17 (1985): 406–19; Martha Nochinson, "Lamia as Muse," in *The Poetic Fantastic*, ed. Patrick D. Murphy (New York: Greenwood Press, 1989); Karla Alwes, *Imagination Transformed: The Evaluation of the Female Character in Keats's Poetry* (Carbondale: Southern Illinois University Press, 1993). Susan Wolfson provides an excellent analysis of Keats's "gordian complication of feelings" with reference to his entire oeuvre in "Keats and the Manhood of the Poet," *European Romantic Review* 6 (1995): 1–37. The word "gordian" in its mythic context, also connotes the power of imperialism. As legend would have it, the intricate Gordian knot, originally tied by King Gordius of Phrygia, was cut by Alexander the Great upon the promise that whoever could undo it would be the next ruler of Asia.

14. Critics seem attuned to the poem's unsettling quality. John Barnard, for example, finds the poem "unsettled and unsettling" (120).

15. *The Complete Works of William Hazlitt*, ed. P. P. Howe, 21 vols. (London, 1930–34), 18:174.

16. The letter is still in Haydon's Journal. Andrew Motion, *Keats* (London: Faber and Faber, 1997), 219–20; Stephen Coote, *John Keats: A Life* (London: Hodder and Stoughton, 1995),117–18.

17. Letter written in 1818, printed by David Garnett, *New Statesman* (10 June 1933), 763 (*KL* 1:198).

18. "On First Looking into Chapman's Homer," 5.

19. This insight was pointed out to me by Alan Bewell. See Beth Lau, *Keats's Paradise Lost* (Gainesville: University Press of Florida, 1998), 153.

20. M. L. E. Moreau de Saint-Mery, *Description de la partie française de Saint-Domingue*, 2 vols. (Paris, 1797–98), 1:64. For a postcolonial treatment of Moreau, see Jean Price-Mars, *So Spoke the Uncle*, trans. Magdaline W. Shannon (Washington, D.C: Three Continents Press, 1983). Translation by Debbie Lee and Robert Tetreault.

21. For the most compelling work on the history and function of West Indian voodoo or vodoun, see Joan Dayan, *Haiti, History, and the Gods* (Berkeley: University of California Press, 1995) and "Vodoun, or the Voice of the Gods," *Raritan* 10 (1991): 32–57. I am grateful to Joan Dayan, who first suggested this line of inquiry to me and to Alan Richardson, whose groundbreaking article "Romantic Voodoo: Obeah and British Culture, 1797–1807" provided the starting point for my work here (*Studies in Romanticism* 32 [1993]: 3–28).

22. *An Apology for Negro Slavery: or, The West India Planters Vindicated from the Charges of Inhumanity* (London, 1786), 10.

23. Renny, 165; *The State of Society in Jamaica: In a Reply to an article in the Edinburgh Review No. LXXV* (London, 1825), 12.

24. Bryan Edwards, *The History, Civil and Commercial, of the British West Indies*, 5 vols. (London, 1819; reprint, New York: AMS Press, 1966), 2:107.

25. See Montgomery, *The West Indies*, in Kitson and Lee, 4:316.

26. The Jamaica Privy Council of 1788 interviewed Mr. Fuller (agent for Jamaica), Mr. Long and Mr. Chisholme, who together replied to the Privy Council's queries, enclosing papers on Obeah from Mr. Rheder and from Fuller himself. See answers nos 16–26 in the Report of the Lords of the Committee of Council appointed for the condition of all matters relating to trade and foreign plantations . . . dated 11th February, 1788, concerning the present state of the trade to Africa, and particularly the trade in slaves: Part 3, "Treatment of Slaves in the West Indies." In Lambert, 69:215–21.

27. John Stedman, *Narrative of a five years' expedition against the Revolted Negroes of Surinam, in Guiana, on the wild coast of South America; from the Year 1772, to 1777: elucidating the history of that Country, and describing its productions . . . with an account of the Indians of Guiana, & Negroes of Guinea*, 2nd ed., corrected, 2 vols. (London, 1806–13), 2:272–73.

28. Moreau, 1:66, trans. by Debbie Lee and Robert Tetreault.

29. Moreau, 1:67, trans. by Debbie Lee and Robert Tetreault.

30. Moreau, 1:65, trans. by Debbie Lee and Robert Tetreault.

31. The dwellings of Africans and slaves on plantations were called "huts" in all travel and abolitionist literature of this period.

32. Erika Bourguignon, *Possession* (San Francisco: Chandler and Sharp, 1976), 48.

33. Bowdich, 269–70.

34. John Adams, *Sketches taken during ten voyages to Africa* (London, 1822), 65.

35. Edwards, 2:109.

36. Michel Foucault, *Power/Knowledge*, trans. Colin Gordon, Leo Marhsall, John Mepham, and Kate Soper, ed. Colin Gordon (New York: Pantheon Books, 1980), 153.

37. Pratt, 69–85.

38. Park, 103.

39. Pratt argues that "reciprocity . . . organizes Park's human-centered, interactive

narrative," but this dynamic is simply an idealization of Park's "expansionist commercial aspirations" whereby Park not only looks at and speculates on Africans, but also "repeatedly portrays himself as subjected to the scrutiny of the Africans" (80–81).

40. Marjorie Levinson's Marxist reading draws a parallel between Lamia's blank eyes and Moneta's eyes which are "like two gold coins" (*Keats' Life of Allegory: The Origins of a Style* [New York: Blackwell, 1988], 268). But even equating Lamia with the gold coin of Keats's day would have linked her to Africa and the slave trade. The "guinea," in which all goods were advertised, literally means "negro land" and takes its name from the fact that it was originally issued in Guinea gold. A good portion of the British slave trade took place on the Guinea Coast.

41. Moreau, 1:68, trans. by Debbie Lee and Robert Tetreault.

42. As Gordon K. Lewis explains, the area around the Mediterranean is often compared to the Caribbean, primarily because both civilizations grew up as seaborne empires surrounded by awesome masses of water. Lewis goes into detail about how similarities in geography and climate have influenced the politics of both (*Main Currents in Caribbean Thought* [Baltimore: Johns Hopkins University Press, 1983]). These were observed even during the Romantic era by at least one interested writer. Olaudah Equiano comments in his slave/travel narrative: "I was surprised to see how the Greeks are, in some measure, kept under by the Turks, as the negroes are in the West Indies by the white people" (*The Interesting Narrative of the Life of Olaudah Equiano, or Gustavus Vassa the African, Written by himself*, ed. Paul Edwards, 2 vols. [London, 1782, reprint, facsimile ed., Coral Gables, Fla.: Mnemosyne, 1989], 1:90). Also see Martin Bernal's work on Africa and Classical civilization. Bernal speculates that Greek culture and mythology, especially as it originated on Crete, was influenced in major ways by Egyptian, Levantian, and North African religion and society (*Black Athena: The Afroasiatic Roots of Classical Civilization*, vol. 1, *The Fabrication of Ancient Greece, 1785–1985* [New Brunswick, N.J.: Free Association Books, 1987]).

43. Corinth was the center of worship for the patron goddess Aphrodite, for which the Corinthians built a magnificent temple housing thousands of slaves and prostitutes for the use of strangers. For historical accounts of slavery in ancient Greece and Rome, see Thomas Wiedemann, *Greek and Roman Slavery* (London: Routledge, 1992).

44. Levinson, 227. Coleman O. Parsons notes that Lycius's "indulging" in public invites his rivals to seize what is being enjoyed ("Primitive Sense in *Lamia*," *Folklore* 88 [1977]: 203–10). Bruce Clarke ("Fabulous Monsters of Conscience: Anthropomorphosis in Keats's *Lamia*," *Studies in Romanticism* 23, 4 [1988]: 555–79) also sees that much of the interaction of the poem is based on ownership and property, so that "Hermes and Lamia together compose an allegory for the participatory exchange of goods in free commerce, the counterpart of theft and dispossession" (569).

45. Pratt, 97.

46. Power and dominance: these are qualities other readers have used to characterize Lamia's and Lycius's relationship, though not in the context of interracial love. Morris Dickstein (*Keats and His Poetry: A Study in Development* [Chicago: University of Chicago Press, 1971]) sees elements of "love, possession, and sadistic desire for domination intermingle" in the union of Lycius and Lamia (239). Clarke contends that "Lamia herself is an incoming, then outcast agent, who will be accused of dispossessing another, who will then be dispossessed herself" (555).

47. John Gabriel Stedman, *Narrative of a Five Years Expedition against the Revolted Negroes of Surinam*, ed. Richard Price and Sally Price (Baltimore: Johns Hopkins University Press, 1988), 88. See Helen Thomas, 125–33.

48. Stedman, ed. Price and Price, 88–90.

49. Stedman, ed. Price and Price, 100.

50. Stedman, ed. Price and Price, 98.

51. Lawrence Marsden Prince, *The Inkle and Yarico Album* (Berkeley: University of California Press, 1937). Another account is found in Peter Hulme, *Colonial Encounters: Europe and the Native Caribbean, 1492–1797* (London: Methuen, 1986). Hulme bases much of his critique on Richard Steele's 1711 version, but he states that "after about 1810 the flood suddenly dried, and Inkle and Yarico were quickly and almost completely forgotten" (227). This is incorrect, for the play was still advertised in the London *Times* as late as 1818, and a version of the poem appeared in 1820.

52. George Colman, *Inkle and Yarico . . . As performed at the Theatres Royal, Covent Garden and Haymarket . . . Printed . . . from the prompt book. With remarks by Mrs. Inchbald* (London, 1806).

53. Depending on the version, it is Africa, America, or India.

54. Inchbald's note in Colman, *Inkle and Yarico*, 4.

55. J. Rusher, *The Secret History and Misfortunes of Fatyma; and the History of Olympia written by themselves, to which is added Inkle and Yarico in verse* (Banbury, 1820).

56. Rusher, 30, lines 37–40.

57. Rusher, 31–32, lines 74, 142.

58. See Joan Dayan, "Gothic Naipaul," *Transition* 59 (1993): 158–70. Dayan points out the extreme classificatory systems of black blood during the early nineteenth century, stating that, "as a metaphysical attribute, blood provides a rational system for classification and distribution of a mythical essence: blood, i.e., race" (167). Also see Joan Dayan, " 'A Receptacle for That Race of Men': Blood, Boundaries, and Mutations of Theory," *American Literature* 67 (1995): 801–13; "Codes of Law and Bodies of Color," *New Literary History* 26 (1995): 283–308.

59. Bush, 15.

60. Bush, 18; Equiano, 1:75; John Newton, *Authentic Narrative of some Remarkable and Interesting Particulars in the Life of John Newton* (London, 1764).

61. Edwards, 2:1–31.

62. F. G. Smyth, *An Apology for West Indians, and Reflections on the Policy of Great Britain's Interference in the internal concerns of the West India Colonies* (London, 1824), 39.

63. Edwards, 2:20; Also see Richard S. Dunn, *Sugar and Slaves: The Rise of the Planter Class in the English West Indies, 1624–1713* (Chapel Hill: University of North Carolina Press, 1972), 255.

64. Quoted in Bush, 32.

65. See Pratt, 96.

66. Letter from Richard Woodhouse to John Taylor, 27 October 1818 (*KL*, 1:389–90). Woodhouse also wrote notes to himself along these same lines. See *The Keats Circle*, ed. Hyder Edward Rollins (Cambridge, Mass.: Harvard University Press, 1965), 2:57–60.

Chapter 6. Mapping Interiors

1. In an interesting note on the poem, Brian Nellist comments that "Thamondocana," which is "something of a crux in the poem," has always been interpreted as Timbuktu by critics of Shelley's poem, as in Donald Reiman's and Sharon Powers's Norton edition, 360 n. 3. However, Nellist doubts that the two names correspond and finds no historical evidence to support this common interpretation. See "Shelley's Narratives and 'The Witch of Atlas,' " in *Essays on Shelley*, ed. Miriam Allott (Totowa, N.J.: Barnes & Noble, 1982), 160–90 (190 n. 33).

2. Most readers interpret "The Witch of Atlas" in the spirit of Harold Bloom, who claims the witch represents imagination (*Shelley's Mythmaking* [1959, reprint Ithaca, N.Y.: Cornell University Press, 1969], 165–204). William Crisman states that "figures" in the poem are "realistic characters whose minds undergo convincing psychological developments and whose activities produce correspondingly individual plots and settings" ("Psychological Realism and Narrative Manner in Shelley's 'Alastor' and 'The Witch of Atlas,' " *Keats-Shelley Journal* 35 [1986]: 126–48 [128]). The most important reading in this regard is that of Jerrold Hogle, whose work I am greatly indebted to. Hogle argues that "The Witch of Atlas" enacts a particular process of mind, or imagination, where both the witch "and her poem are the very pathway of desire releasing the psyche from repressive narcissism, attempting to make the fading coals of previous desires into figures of their own capacity for infinite reproduction" ("Metaphor and Metamorphosis in Shelley's 'The Witch of Atlas,' " *Studies in Romanticism* 19 [1980]: 327–53 [353]).

3. Christian Frederick Damberger, *Travels Through the Interior of Africa from the Cape of Good Hope to Morocco* (London, 1801), 537.

4. Park, 120. François Le Vaillant, *Travels into the Interior Parts of Africa*, 2 vols. (London, 1790).

5. Frederic Colwell, "Shelley's 'The Witch of Atlas' and the Mythic Geography of the Nile," *British Literary History* 45 (1978): 69–92. Ronald A. Duerksen also contends that African geography is essential to the poem in his "Wordsworth and the Austral Retreat in Shelley's 'Witch of Atlas,' " *Keats-Shelley Journal* 34 (1985): 18–20. Nellist acknowledges that "The poem is geography as much as legend" (180).

6. Leigh Hunt, quoted in Theodore Redpath, *The Young Romantics and Critical Opinion, 1807–1824: Poetry of Byron, Shelley, and Keats as Seen by Their Contemporary Critics* (New York: St. Martin's Press, 1973), 409; and Hogle, "Metaphor and Metamorphosis in Shelley's 'The Witch of Atlas,'" 329.

7. Michel Foucault, *The Order of Things: An Archeology of the Human Sciences* (New York: Pantheon, 1970), 74. These insights were pointed out to me by John Willinsky and are part of his book in *Learning to Divide the World: Education at Empire's End* (Minneapolis: University of Minnesota Press, 1998), 26–27.

8. Foucault, *The Order of Things*, 75.

9. Edward Said, *Orientalism* (1978; New York: Vintage, 1979), 55.

10. John Gascoigne, "The Ordering of Nature and the Ordering of Empire: A Commentary." *Visions of Empire: Voyages, Botany and Representations of Nature*, ed. David Philip Miller and Peter Hans Reill (Cambridge: Cambridge University Press, 1996), 107–13 (108).

11. Bruno Latour, *Science in Action: How to Follow Scientists and Engineers Through Society* (Cambridge, Mass.: Harvard University Press, 1987), 225.

12. Latour, 230.

13. For more information on the history of cartography and mapping, see Frank Lestringant, *Mapping the Renaissance World: The Geographical Imagination in the Age of Discovery*, trans. David Fausett (Berkeley: University of California Press, 1994); Lloyd A. Brown, *The Story of Maps* (1949; reprint New York: Dover, 1977); Michael Kwamena-Poh, John Tosh, Richard Waller, and Michael Tidy, *African History in Maps* (Essex: Longman, 1982); Ronald Vere Tooley, *Maps of Africa* (London: Map Collectors' Circle, 1968). For a guide to cartography's interaction with the humanities, see Mark Monmonier, *Mapping It Out: Expository Cartography for the Humanities and Social Sciences* (Chicago: University of Chicago Press, 1993).

14. Jonathan Swift, "On Poetry: A Rhapsody," in *The Poems of Jonathan Swift*, ed. Harold Williams, 3 vols., 2nd ed. (Oxford: Clarendon Press, 1958), 2:639–59 (645–46). Quoted also in Bewell, 196.

15. Bernard Smith, "Coleridge's 'Ancient Mariner' and Cook's Second Voyage," 117–54.

16. "To the Memory of Captain James Cook"; and "Lieutenant Roberts's Account of the Grand General Chart, Prepared by Order of Government, to illustrate the Voyages of the Celebrated Capt. Cook," *Political Magazine* (December 1784): 403–5.

17. *Political Magazine*, 404.

18. Le Vaillant, 1: xxiii.

19. Park, 75, 68.

20. Damberger, translator's preface, iii.

21. Hannah More, "Slavery," in Breen, 17, lines 249–50.

22. More, "Slavery," in Breen, 17, line 257.

23. More, "Slavery," in Breen, 18, lines 280, 266.

24. Cited by Willinsky, unpublished manuscript. From Bernard Smith, *European Vision and the South Pacific*, 2nd ed. (New Haven, Conn.: Yale University Press, 1985), 47.

25. Quoted in the *Edinburgh Review* 1 (1803): 331. From Vivant Denon, *Travels in Upper and Lower Egypt*, trans. Arthur Aikin, 3 vols. (London, 1803), 2:22–23.

26. Park, 149.

27. Park, 227.

28. Linda Hannas, *The English Jigsaw Puzzle: 1760–1890* (London: Wayland, 1972).

29. Park, 126–27.

30. Mary Howitt, "Ode to Botany," in Mary Howitt and William Howitt, *The Desolation of Eyam: The Emigrant, a Tale of the American Woods, and Other Poems* (London, 1827), 256–63, lines 126–35.

31. Felician Dorothea Hemans, "The Flower of the Desert," in *Miscellaneous Poems*, vol. 6 of *The Works of Mrs. Hemans, with a memoir of her life*, 7 vols. (London and Edinburgh, 1839), 279–80 (279).

32. Le Vaillant, 1: 428–29.

33. Park, 145.

34. For a detailed account of this expedition, see Fergus Fleming, *Barrow's Boys* (London: Granta, 1998), 13–28.

35. Hemans, *Miscellaneous Poems*, "The Traveller at the Source of the Nile," 154–56, lines 13–18.

36. James Bruce, *Travels to Discover the Source of the Nile, in the Years 1768, 1769,*

1770, 1771, 1772, & 1773. (1770) 3rd ed. (Edinburgh: Constable and Manners and Miller; London: Longman Hurst Rees, Orme, and Brown, 1813), 269.

37. Bruce, 309.

38. Hemans, "The Traveller at the Source of the Nile," 154–56, lines 27–30, 37–42.

39. Le Vaillant, 1: 252.

40. Gender played a role in geographic mapping in the same way it played a role in poetic mapping. External nature and landscape were often figured as feminine by male Romantic poets, as Marlon Ross and Anne Mellor have demonstrated by calling on key passages in *The Prelude* where Wordsworth conceptualizes the landscape as feminine and then sees the terrain of Mount Snowdon as "the perfect image" of his "mighty mind" (*The Prelude* [1805], 13:69). The poet's interiority seeks to possess, dominate, and ultimately find a mirror in the feminized landscape. See Marlon B. Ross, *The Contours of Masculine Desire: Romanticism and the Rise of Women's Poetry* (New York: Oxford University Press, 1989); Anne K. Mellor, *Romanticism and Gender* (New York: Routledge, 1993).

41. See Saree Makdisi, "Versions of the East: Byron, Shelley, and the Orient," in Richardson and Hofkosh, 203–36. Makdisi writes, "My own reading of *Alastor* proposes that the quest and the terrain on which it unfolds are not coincidental to each other and must be read together" (232).

42. Fleming, 98.

43. *The Poetical Works of Leigh Hunt*, ed. H. S. Milford (Oxford: Oxford University Press, 1923), 248.

44. *Shelley: Poetical Works*, ed. Thomas Hutchinson, corrected by G. M. Matthews (Oxford and New York, Oxford University Press, 1970), 552.

45. *St. James's Chronicle, or British Evening Post*, 27–29 January 1801.

46. On Africa as the origin of European civilization, see Bernal, vol. 1, *The Fabrication of Ancient Greece.*

47. *St. James's Chronicle, or British Evening Post*, 7–10 March 1801.

48. Damberger, translator's preface, iii.

49. Richard Wharton, *Observations on the Authenticity of Bruce's Travels in Abyssinia, in reply to some passages in Brown's travels through Egypt, Africa and Syria; to which is added, a comparative view of life and happiness in Europe in Cafraria* (Newcastle upon Tyne, 1800), 4.

50. *British Critic* 17 (January–June, 1801): 123.

51. William Mavor, *Travels in Africa by Mr. Mungo Park, Surgeon; From the Cape of Good Hope to Morocco by Damberger; and in the Interior Districts of Africa by Ledyard and Lucas* (London, 1807), 1, 137.

52. *Gentleman's Magazine*, vol. 71, part 1 (1801): 249–50.

53. *British Critic* 17 (January–June, 1801): 349.

54. Damberger, 115.

55. Damberger, 452.

56. Damberger, 156.

57. Damberger, 157.

58. Damberger, 158.

59. According to Fleming, the one exception to this may be Clapperton's casual sex with the natives of northern Africa in 1822 (187).

60. For an excellent discussion of the hermaphrodite, see Diane Long Hoeveler, "Shelley and Androgyny: Teaching 'The Witch of Atlas,'" in *Approaches to Teaching*

Shelley's Poetry, ed. Spencer Hall (New York: Modern Language Association, 1990), 93–95.

61. Derrida, 36.

62. Levinas, quoted in Derrida, 36.

63. Derrida, 36.

64. Derrida, 39–40.

65. Levinas, *Time and the Other*, 87.

66. Levinas, *Time and the Other*, 87–88.

67. Levinas, *Time and the Other*, 88.

68. Derrida, 40.

69. Mary Shelley's note to "The Witch of Atlas" in *The Poetical Works of Shelley*, ed. Newell F. Ford (Boston: Houghton Mifflin, 1975), 272.

70. *Of the Shoemaker Schroter, the Printer Taurinas, and the Traveler Damberger, three travelers who never traveled at all but invented their stories in one manufactory* (London, 1801).

Chapter 7. Proximity's Monsters

1. The *Frankenstein* myth was often used by caricaturists to comment on current affairs. See "Frankenstein Creating Peers," *McLean's Monthly Sheet of Characters* (1 March 1832); "The Political Frankenstein," *Figaro in London* (28 April 1832); James Parry, "Reform Bill's First Step Amongst His Political Frankensteins" (1833); George Cruikshank, "Tugging at a High Eye Tooth," published 1 November 1821 by George Humphrey. Details are to be found in Donald F. Glut, *The Frankenstein Catalog, Being a Comprehensive List of Novels, Translations, Adaptations, Stories, Critical Works . . . Featuring Frankenstein's Monster and/or Descended from Mary Shelley's Novel* (Jefferson: N.C. and London: McFarland, 1984).

2. *Frankenstein, or the Modern Prometheus*, 2 vols. (London, 1823).

3. For a discussion of the theater piece, see Steven Earl Forry, *Hideous Progenies: Dramatizations of Frankenstein from Mary Shelley to the Present* (Philadelphia: University of Pennsylvania Press, 1990).

4. *London Magazine* 8 (1823): 322.

5. *Frankenstein* appeared to be the perfect metaphor for racial/colonial otherness in the nineteenth century. John Tenniel, "The Brummagem Frankenstein," *Punch*, 8 September 1866; John Tenniel, "The Russian Frankenstein and His Monster," *Punch*, 15 July 1854; "The Irish Frankenstein," *Punch*, 5 1843; Matt Morgan, "The Irish Frankenstein," *Tomahawk*, 18 December 1869; John Tenniel, "The Irish Frankenstein," *Punch*, 20 May 1882. For collections in which these cartoons appear, see Glut and Forry.

6. For an interpretation based on class and oppression, see Anca Vlasopolos, "*Frankenstein*'s Hidden Skeleton: The Psycho-Politics of Oppression," *Science Fiction Studies* 10 (1983): 125–36. For a Marxist reading, see Warren Montag, "The Workshop of Filthy Creation: A Marxist Reading of *Frankenstein*," in *Frankenstein: Complete Authoritative Text with Biographical and Historical Contexts, Critical History, and Essays from Five Contemporary Critical Perspectives*, ed. Johanna M. Smith, Case Studies in Contemporary Criticism (Boston: St Martin's Press, 1992), 300–311. For a postcolonial reading of the novel, see Gayatri Chakravorty Spivak, "Three Women's Texts and a Critique of Imperi-

alism," *Critical Inquiry* 12 (1985): 243–61. For *Frankenstein* and Orientalism, see Joseph W. Lew, "The Deceptive Other: Mary Shelley's Critique of Orientalism in *Frankenstein*," *Studies in Romanticism* 30 (1991): 255–83. Jerrold Hogle reads the monster as a sign of the "abject," in Kristeva's sense, as that which is neither inside nor outside ("*Frankenstein* as Neo-Gothic: From the Ghost of the Counterfeit to the Monster of Abjection," in *Romanticism, History and the Possibilities of Genre*, ed. Tilottama Rajan and Julia Wright (Cambridge: Cambridge University Press, 1998), 176–210. For readings that stress the influence of Percy Bysshe Shelley, William Godwin, and Mary Wollstonecraft on the production of the text, see Joyce Zonana, "'They Will Prove the Truth of My Tale': Safie's Letters as the Feminist Core of Mary Shelley's *Frankenstein*," *Journal of Narrative Technique* 21 (1991): 170–84; Marc A. Rubenstein, "'My Accursed Origin': The Search for the Mother in *Frankenstein*," *Studies in Romanticism* 15 (1976): 165–94; Ellen Moers, *Literary Women* (Garden City: N.Y.: Doubleday, 1976); and William Veeder, *Mary Shelley and Frankenstein: The Fate of Androgyny* (Chicago: University of Chicago Press, 1986). Among feminist readings of the novel, see Moers; Anne K. Mellor, *Mary Shelley: Her Life, Her Fiction, Her Monsters* (New York: Methuen, 1988); and Sandra M. Gilbert and Susan Gubar, *The Madwoman in the Attic: The Woman Writer and the Nineteenth-Century Literary Imagination* (New Haven, Conn.: Yale University Press, 1979), especially their chapter "Horror's Twin, Mary Shelley's Monstrous Eve," 213–47. Other readings, which deal with the politics of gender, include Barbara Johnson, "My Monster/My Self," *Diacritics* 12 (1982): 2–10; Fred V. Randel, "*Frankenstein*, Feminism and the Intertextuality of Mountains," *Studies in Romanticism* 23 (1984): 515–33; and Marcia Tillotson, "'A Forced Solitude': Mary Shelley and the Creation of Frankenstein's Monster," in *The Female Gothic*, ed. Juliann E. Fleenor (London: Eden Press, 1983), 167–75. Among the other influential treatments of the novel's political themes are Peter Dale Scott, "Vital Artifice: Mary, Percy, and the Psychopolitical Integrity of *Frankenstein*," in *The Endurance of Frankenstein*, ed. George Levine and U. C. Knoepflmacher (Berkeley: University of California Press, 1979), 172–202; see also, in the same volume, Lee Sterrenburg, "Mary Shelley's Monster: Politics and Psyche in *Frankenstein*," 143–71, and Kate Ellis, "Monsters in the Garden: Mary Shelley and the Bourgeois Family," 123–42. Other treatments of the novel's politics include Judith Weissman, "A Reading of *Frankenstein* as the Complaint of a Political Wife," *Colby Library Quarterly* 12 (1976): 171–78, and Mellor, *Mary Shelley: Her Life, Her Fiction, Her Monsters*.

7. H. L. Malchow, *Gothic Images of Race in Nineteenth-Century Britain* (Stanford, Calif.: Stanford University Press, 1996), 92.

8. Michael Craton, *Empire, Enslavement, and Freedom in the Caribbean* (Oxford: James Currey, 1997), 284; and Craton, *Testing the Chains: Resistance to Slavery in the British West Indies* (Ithaca, N.Y.: Cornell University Press, 1982), 262–64.

9. Lewis, though characteristically paternalistic, was disturbed by the treatment of slaves in Jamaica, and he thus had Shelley, Byron, and Polidori witness and sign "a codicil" to his will ensuring that the heirs to his estate would visit it every third year and that the slaves on his plantation would not be split up through sale. *The Journals of Mary Shelley: 1814–1844*, ed. Paula R. Feldman and Diana Scott-Kilvert (Oxford: Clarendon Press; New York: Oxford University Press, 1987), 129 n.

10. *Journals of Mary Shelley: 1814–1844*, 126.

11. Matthew Gregory Lewis, "The Isle of Devils," in *Journal of a West Indian Proprietor*, 261–89 (272).

12. Matthew Gregory Lewis, "The Isle of Devils," in *Journal of a West Indian Proprietor*, 272–73.

13. Malchow believes that Shelley's Gothic portrayal of the monster "drew on contemporary attitudes towards non-whites, in particular on fears and hopes of the abolition of slavery in the West Indies" ("Frankenstein's Monster and Images of Race in Nineteenth-Century Britain," *Past and Present* 139 [1993]: 90–130 [90]).

14. The account of the Demerara uprising is explained in nearly every history of British slavery in the Caribbean. The details of my account are taken primarily from Craton, *Empire, Enslavement, and Freedom in the Caribbean*, the statistics coming from page 289.

15. Craton, *Testing the Chains*, 285.

16. During the uprising, some whites escaped to these cities for protection, but others were placed in the stocks. The slaves, that is, did not enact the rebellion violently, but symbolically: they turned the whites into the criminals by placing them in the very stocks that the planters regularly used to hold the slaves themselves. The whites, however, within hours saw the uprising as blatant evidence of the kind of actions that would take place if slaves were allowed even the slightest bit of freedom (Craton, *Empire, Enslavement, and Freedom in Caribbean*, 298). Also see Craton, *Testing the Chains*, 287–88.

17. Parliamentary Papers, House of Commons, 16 March 1824, 1103.

18. See Malchow's chapter "Cannibalism and Popular Culture" in his *Gothic Images of Race in Nineteenth-Century Britain*, 41–123.

19. Canning, quoting Dr. Paley, Parliamentary Papers, House of Commons, 15 May 1823, 280.

20. Parliamentary Papers, House of Commons, 15 May 1823, 261.

21. In a fascinating and detailed recent study, Peter Kitson explains that "cannibalism" in the nineteenth century had a wide field of significations. Of these, he says, "Cannibalism, one might say, is the most notorious process of colonial "othering," both as an alleged practice and as a critical construct. It is clear that cannibalism was used as process by which imperial Europe distinguished itself from the subjects of its colonial expansion while concomitantly demonstrating a moral justification for that expansion" ("'The Eucharist of Hell'; or, Eating People is Right: Romantic Representations of Cannibalism," *Romanticism on the Net*, 17 February 2000 <http://users.ox.uk/~scato385/17cannibalism.html>).

22. Edwards, 1: 39.

23. Edwards, 1: 41.

24. Edwards, 1: 40.

25. Bancroft, 260.

26. Bancroft, 262.

27. William Snelgrave, *A New Account of Some Parts of Guinea and the Slave Trade* (London, 1734), introduction 9 recto.

28. Snelgrave, 52.

29. Snelgrave, 44.

30. Snelgrave, 160–61.

31. Michel de Montaigne, "On the Cannibals," in *The Essays of Michel de Montaigne*, trans. and ed. M. A. Screech (London: Penguin, 1987, 1991), 228–41 (236). Sigmund Freud, *Totem and Taboo* (1913) in *The Standard Edition of the Complete Works of Sigmund Freud*,

trans. and gen. ed. James Strachey, 23 vols. (London: Hogarth Press, 1953, 1971), 13:1–100 (82).

32. Christy G. Turner, *Man Corn: Cannibalism and Violence in the Prehistoric American Southwest* (Salt Lake City: University of Utah Press, 1999), 1.

33. The play opened in London's Haymarket Theater on 29 July 1808. See headnote to George Colman in Kitson and Lee, vol. 5, *Drama*, ed. Jeffrey Cox, 221–22.

34. George Colman, *The Africans: or, War, Love, and Duty. A Play in Three Acts* (London, 1808; reprint, Cumberland's British Theatre, no. 347, c. 1826), 1.

35. Colman, 1.

36. Edwards, 1: 39, 42.

37. Robert Southey, "Poems Concerning the Slave Trade" (sonnets 1–6 and "To the Genius of Africa"), in *Poems, by Robert Southey* (Bristol: Joseph Cottle; London: G. G. & J. Robinson, 1797), reprinted in Kitson and Lee, 4:243 (sonnet 1, lines 1–2).

38. Southey, sonnet 1 line 12; sonnet 3 line 10, reprinted in Kitson and Lee, 4:243, 244.

39. Southey, sonnet 5 lines 2–3, reprinted in Kitson and Lee, 4:245.

40. M. Birkett, *A Poem on the African Slave Trade, Addressed to Her Own Sex* (Dublin, 1792), part 2 line 14.

41. William Roscoe, "Mount Pleasant. A Descriptive Poem" (Warrington: W. Eyre, 1777), reprinted in *William Roscoe of Liverpool*, ed. George Chandler (London: B.T. Batsford, 1953), 330–42 (334).

42. William Roscoe, "The Wrongs of Africa," 371.

43. For a reading of sugar and consumption, see Timothy Morton, "Blood Sugar," in Fulford and Kitson, 87–106. Also see Morton's *Poetics of Spice*.

44. His most famous work is actually the 1787 *Treatise on Tropical Diseases and on the Climate of the West Indies*, which was translated into German and went into five editions.

45. Benjamin Moseley, *A Treatise on Sugar with Miscellaneous Medical Observations* (London, 1799).

46. Moseley, *A Treatise on Sugar, A Treatise on Sugar with Miscellaneous Medical Observations*, 2nd ed. (London, 1800), 165, 161.

47. Moseley, *Treatise on Sugar*, 2nd ed., 172.

48. Moseley, *Treatise on Sugar*, 2nd ed., 167.

49. Moseley, *Treatise on Sugar*, 1st ed. (London, 1799).

50. Moseley, *Treatise on Sugar*, 2nd ed., 159–60.

51. Moseley, *Treatise on Sugar*, 2nd ed., 161.

52. Moseley, *Treatise on Sugar*, 2nd ed., 164.

53. Birkett, 13–14, lines 21–24.

54. William Cowper, *The Negro's Complaint, a Poem, to which is added Pity for Poor Africans* (London, 1826), 17–22 (17). Also see *The Poems of William Cowper*, ed. John D. Baird and Charles Ryskamp, 3 vols. (Oxford: Clarendon Press, 1980–95), 3:26–27, lines 5–8.

55. Cowper, *The Negro's Complaint*, 2–15 (6–7). Also see Baird and Ryskamp, 3:13–14, lines 17–24.

56. *The Anti-Slavery Album: Selections in Verse from Cowper, Hannah More, Montgomery, Pringle* (London, 1828).

57. *The Anti-Slavery Album*, 9, lines 15–18.

58. Opie, *The Black Man's Lament*, 4, lines 1–4.

59. Timothy Touchstone, Gent. [pseud.], *Tea and Sugar, or the Nabob and the Creole* (London, 1792), 2:63–66.

60. Parliamentary Papers, House of Commons, 15 May 1823, 271–74.

61. Parliamentary Papers, House of Commons, 16 March 1824, 1131.

62. Parliamentary Papers, House of Commons, 15 May 1823, 272, 270.

63. William Wilberforce, "Remarks on the Method of Procuring Slaves with a Short Account of Their Treatment of It in the West Indies," Box 9, Wilberforce House Museum. Box 9 also cites the case of "an overseer on the estate where Mr. J. Rurry of Genada threw a slave INTO THE BOILING CANE JUICE who died four days later."

64. Parliamentary Papers, House of Commons, 15 May 1823, 261.

65. Rev. John Hampden, *A Commentary on Mr. Clarkson's pamphlet entitled "Thoughts on the Necessity of Improving the Conditions of the Slaves in the British Colonies, with a View to Their Ultimate Emancipation"* (London: J. Ridgway, 1824), reprinted in Kitson and Lee, 3:184.

66. The words of Hall, quoted by Barstow in James Barstow, *A Letter to the Rev. Mr. Hall . . . in Answer to His Attack on West Indian Proprietors, with Some Observations on the General Question as to the Abolition of West Indian Slavery* (London, 1824), 2.

67. "The Ocean. Written at Scarborough, in the Summer Of 1805," 66–70, in *The Poetical Works of James Montgomery*, collected by himself, 4 vols. (London, 1841), 1:115.

68. Anna Letitia Barbauld, "Epistle to William Wilberforce, Esq., on the Rejection of the Bill for Abolishing the Slave Trade," 15–16, 52, from *Poems* (London, 1792).

69. *Gentleman's Magazine* 61, part 2 (1791): 1047, lines 31–40.

70. William Cowper, "Charity," in Baird and Ryskamp, 1: 337–53 (138, 140).

71. Edwards, "Ode on Seeing a Negro Funeral," in *The History . . . of the British West Indies*, 2: 104–5.

72. Stanfield, 19, 14.

73. Colman, *The Africans*, 29.

74. Roscoe, "Mount Pleasant," 333.

75. Roscoe, "The Wrongs of Africa," 357.

76. Interview with Turner, *New Yorker*, 30 November 1998, 87.

77. Hannah More, "Slavery" in Breen, 14, lines 153–58.

78. Southey, Sonnet 6 line 1–6, reprinted in Kitson and Lee, 4:246.

79. Stanfield, 9.

80. Touchstone, line 82. The first use of this line was in Shakespeare's *Macbeth*, 3.4.121.

81. Richard Nisbet, *The Capacity of Negroes* (1789; reprint, New York: Negro University Press, 1970), 75.

82. Parliamentary Papers, House of Lords, 16 March 1824, 1131.

Chapter 8. Intimate Distance

1. "To Toussaint L'Ouverture," line 7. C. L. R. James, *The Black Jacobins: Toussaint L'Ouverture and the San Domingo Revolution* (1963; 2nd ed., rev., New York: Vintage, 1989).

2. *The Prelude*, 1805, 7:243. "The Banished Negroes," 1798, 3.

3. *The Prelude*, 1805, 10:218–19.

4. Duncan Wu, *Wordsworth's Reading, 1770–1799* (Cambridge: Cambridge University Press, 1995). Wu suggests that Wordsworth read *Gentleman's Magazine* off and on in 1789 and 1790 (62).

5. Newton, *Authentic Narrative of some Remarkable and Interesting Particulars in the Life of John Newton* (London, 1754), 172, 173–74. Wu notes that Dorothy Wordsworth records into D.C. MS 16 a portion of Newton's *Narrative* (the last part of letter 5), and that Mary Jacobus has put forward the care for Newton's influence on *The Borderers*. Wu notes there is "an apparent reminiscence of Newton's *Narrative* in MS B. of *The Ruined Cottage*, dating from February 1798 (PW v384), suggesting that W took his copy to Alfoxden from Racedown, where it influenced *The Borderers*" (107). Wu also notes that the passage copied by Dorothy is the source of the *Thirteen-Book Prelude*, 6:s160–74.

6. According to Wu, Wordsworth attended *The Castle Spectre* "at the Theatre Royal, when it preceded *The Rival Soldiers* on a double bill. He arrived in Bristol 18 May, and returned to Alfoxden on 22 May, to meet Hazlitt for the first time. Years later, Hazlitt recalled that Wordsworth "had been to see the *Castle Spectre* by Monk Lewis, while at Bristol, and described it very well. He said 'it fitted the taste of the audience like a glove'" (87).

7. Matthew Gregory Lewis, *The Castle Spectre*, 199. It is impossible to know if Wordsworth heard this exact speech since, as Cox points out, it had been marked by the censor for deletion.

8. Written 1794, published 1797. Robert Southey, "Poems Concerning the Slave Trade," in Kitson and Lee, 4:247–48.

9. William Cowper, "Charity," in *Poems in Two Volumes*, 2nd ed. (London, 1782), 1: 182, lines 141–42.

10. In the final line Wordsworth tells us that Leonard leaves the village to become a "seaman, a grey-headed Mariner" (435). Leonard thus becomes a brother to Coleridge's ancient mariner, while his real brother's traumatic death, with all its causes and consequences, lies buried in an unmarked grave in the country churchyard. Bewell gives a fascinating reading of "The Brothers" in terms of calenture. He also observes, "The poem is thus an extraordinary study in the ambiguity and instability of colonial identities. By its end Leonard relinquishes his claim to a 'native' identity. . . . The dialogue takes place in a graveyard—a suitable setting, for one learns not only that James has been dead for twelve years, but also that Leonard is dead to this community" (56).

11. From 1795 to 1797, More edited and was the primary writer for the *Cheap Repository*, a regular pamphlet publication addressed to the middle and lower classes, aimed at social action.

12. More and Smith, *The Sorrows of Yamba*, in Kitson and Lee, 4:226–27.

13. Cited in Michael Craton, James Walvin, and David Wright, *Slavery, Abolition, and Emancipation: Black Slaves and the British Empire, a Thematic Documentary* (London: Longman, 1976), 141. A similar comment came from the abolitionist James Ramsay who wrote to William Wilberforce about the slave population on the Molineaux plantation of St. Christopher, which had "decreased insensibly" due to "a peculiarity in this plantation of their losing their new born infants generally within a month." Infanticide was a possible explanation, but Ramsay also linked slave reproduction to poor plantation practices. He said the "not very frequent fecundity of the young women brought from Africa" reminded him of vines, that when "transplanted in an improper period of

growth . . . seldom take root." In "Observations Made by the Reverend James Ramsay of Teston in a Residence in the Island of St. Christopher of 19 Years Ending 1781 Concerning the Treatment of Slaves" (Wilberforce Papers, box 9, Wilberforce House Museum, Hull).

14. William Dickson, *Mitigation of Slavery* (1814; reprint Miami: Mnemosyne, 1969), 214.

15. Newton Papers, Senate House Library, University of London, 523/316 and 523/288 (Seawells). Also see Hilary McD. Beckles, *Natural Rebels: A Social History of Enslaved Black Women in Barbados* (New Brunswick, N.J.: Rutgers University Press, 1989), 159.

16. *Further Papers Relating to Slaves in the West Indies, Demerara and Berbice*, ordered by the House of Commons to be printed, 23 June 1825. The complaint of Rosa appears on pages 25–27.

17. Quantitative analyses of slave populations and the contributing causes of infertility and infant mortality to patterns of decrease continue to interest historians. The work of Barry W. Higman ("Household Structure and Fertility on Jamaican Slave Plantations: A Nineteenth-Century Example," *Population Studies* 27, 3 [1973]: 527–50; *Slave Population and Economy in Jamaica 1807–1834* [Cambridge: Cambridge University Press, 1976]; "The Slave Populations of the British Caribbean: Some Nineteenth-Century Variations," in *Eighteenth-Century Florida and the Caribbean*, ed. Samuel Proctor [Gainesville: University Press of Florida, 1976], 60–70) and Michael Craton ("Hobbesian or Panglossian? Two Extremes of Slave Conditions in the British Caribbean 1781–1834," *William and Mary Quarterly* 35 [1978]: 324–56) is important here. For studies that deal more directly with the possibility of slave women's intervention in population and reproduction, see the work of Barbara Bush ("Defiance or Submission? The Role of the Slave Woman in Slave Resistance in the British Caribbean," *Immigrants and Minorities* 1, 1 [1982]: 16–38; and *Slave Women in Caribbean Society*, Hilary McD. Beckles, and Michael P. Johnson, "Smothered Slave Infants: Were Slave Mothers at Fault?" *Journal of Southern History* 67 [1981]: 510–15).

18. Of particular interest here is the work of Harry Bennett Jr. (*Bondsman and Bishops: Slavery and Apprenticeship on the Codrington Plantations of Barbados, 1710–1838* [Berkeley: University of California Press, 1958]; "The Problem of Slave Labor Supply at the Codrington Plantations," *Journal of Negro History* 36, 4 [1951]: 406–41).

19. Noel Jones, "permission," *without flinching* (New York: Noel Jones, 2000), 6.

20. Helen Maria Williams, *A Poem on the Bill Lately Passed*, in Kitson and Lee, 4:85–86.

21. In notes dictated by Wordsworth to Isabella Fenwick in 1843, related in De Selincourt and Darbishire, 2:486: "Alfoxden, 1798. The subject was reported to me by a Lady of Bristol who had seen the poor creature."

22. This is quoted in an excellent article on antislavery rhetoric in Bristol by Alan Richardson, "Darkness Visible: Race and Representation in Bristol Abolitionist Poetry, 1770–1810," *Wordsworth Circle* 27, 2 (1996): 67–72 (67).

23. Jennifer Lyle Morgan, "Women in Slavery and the Transatlantic Slave Trade," in *Transatlantic Slavery: Against Human Dignity*, ed. Anthony Tibbles (London: HMSO, 1994), 67.

24. Stanfield, 32.

25. Note on the poem in De Selincourt and Darbishire, 2:486, suggests that Wordsworth also drew on Percy's *Reliques*.

26. *The Wrongs of Alooma, or the African's Revenge: A narrative poem, founded on historical fact* (Liverpool: H. Hodgson, 1788), 8.

27. James Montgomery, *The West Indies*, in Kitson and Lee, 4:327.

28. Stanfield, 19, 5.

29. Elizabeth Barrett Browning, "Runaway Slave at Pilgrim's Point," in *The Complete Works of Mrs. Browning*, ed. Harriet Waters Preston (Boston: Houghton, Mifflin, 1900; facs. ed., 1991), 192–95 (193).

30. This insight was suggested to me by Bruce Graver.

31. Nicholas Roe, *Wordsworth and Coleridge: The Radical Years* (Oxford: Clarendon Press, 1988), 23. Wu states, "in his letter to Wordsworth of 25 March 1796, Azariah Pinney remarks: 'If you should like to have Coleridge's Watchman I will endeavour to have it packed' (Pinney Papers, Family Letter Book 13). Wordsworth would have wished to acquire *The Watchman* and, I presume, accepted Pinney's offer" (30). Issue 4 of the *Watchman* held Coleridge's impassioned *Lecture on the Slave Trade*.

32. Stephen Gill also suggests that Wordsworth was supplied with some money from the Pinney brothers, and which John Pinney Sr. later vehemently objected to (*William Wordsworth: A Life* [Oxford: Oxford University Press, 1990], 116).

33. Kenneth R. Johnston, *The Hidden Wordsworth: Poet, Lover, Rebel, Spy* (New York: W.W. Norton, 1998), 468–69. Johnston provides an illuminating chapter on Wordsworth's Racedown years, "Of Cabbages and Radicals: Racedown Lodge, 1785–97," 468–93.

34. Johnston, 479.

35. Letter to John Kenyon, 24 September 1836, *The Letters of William and Dorothy Wordsworth*, 2nd ed., vol. 6, *The Later Years*, part 3, 1835–1839, rev., arr., Alan G. Hill (Oxford: Clarendon Press, 1967–1993), 292–93. Wordsworth writes "*It was in the English Tongue*—you say 'is not this, in an English poem, superfluous?' Surely here is an oversight on your part; whether the poem were in English, French, or Greek is a matter wholly indifferent as to the expression I have used. She came from afar. The Emigrant Mother came from France, as is told in that other Poem, but I do not think it necessary to say, in this latter case, that her griefs found utterance in French—only that I have put them into verse. But in the instance to which you object it was expedient to specify, that—though she came from far, English was her native tongue—which shows her either to be of these Islands, or a North American. On the latter supposition, while the distance removes her from us, the fact of her speaking our language brings us at once into close sympathy with her."

36. In *The Prose Works of William Wordsworth*, ed. W. J. B. Owen and J. W. Smyser, vol. 1, (Oxford: Clarendon Press, 1974), Owen and Smyser trace this passage to Quintilian, whom they quote: "To paint passion . . . requires the author to have the power of entering deeply into the characters which he draws; of become for a moment the very person whom he exhibits, and of assuming all his feelings . . . there is no possibility of speaking properly the language of any passion, without feeling it" (177).

37. Judith W. Page, *Wordsworth and the Cultivation of Women* (Berkeley: University of California Press, 1994), 76. Page also writes, referring to Marie-Guillemine Benoist's painting *Portrait of a Negress*, "whereas the viewer of Benoist's painting feels an intimacy with the subject, the reader of Wordsworth's sonnet remains at a distance" (75).

38. Long after the fact, Clarkson added a note to this last letter, which reads: "This letter was sent to Christophe; but, alas! He was not living at the time it arrived, . . . so that my labours for . . . the people of Hayti were all in vain, as related to this treaty." Quoted

in *Henry Christophe and Thomas Clarkson, A Correspondence*, ed. Earl Leslie Griggs and Clifford H. Prator (New York: Greenwood Press, 1968), 207.

39. Griggs and Prator, 200–207, 78–79.

40. Quoted in Griggs and Prator, 78–79.

41. Letter of 24 October 1821, *The Letters of William and Dorothy Wordsworth* vol. 4, *The Later Years*, part 1, 1821–1830, 87–88. The poem appears on page 90.

42. A slightly different version of the poem is printed in Ellen Gibson Wilson, 153:

> Queen and Negress chaste and fair!
> Christophe now is laid asleep,
> Seated in a British chair
> State in humbler manner keep
> Shine for Clarkson's pure delight
> Negro Princess, Ebon bright!
>
> Let not "Wilby's" holy shade
> Interpose at Envy's call,
> Hayti's shining Queen was made
> To illumine Playford Hall
> Bless it then with constant light
> Negress excellently bright!
>
> Lay thy Diadem apart
> Pomp has been a sad deceiver
> Through thy Champion's faithful heart
> Joy be poured, and thou the Giver
> Thou that mak'st a day of night
> Sable Princess, ebon bright!

There is also a printing of the poem in William Wordsworth, *Last Poems, 1821–1850*, ed. Jared Curtis, Apryl Lea Denny-Ferris, and Jillian Heydt-Stevenson (Ithaca, N.Y.: Cornell University Press, 1999), 24–25, 418–19.

43. Letter of 16 January 1822, *The Letters of William and Dorothy Wordsworth* vol. 4, 103.

44. Dorothy Wordsworth's letter to Catherine Clarkson, 11 or 12 November 1823, *The Letters of William and Dorothy Wordsworth*, vol. 4, 230.

45. Letter from William and Dorothy Wordsworth to Thomas and Catherine Clarkson, 26 March 1824, *The Letters of William and Dorothy Wordsworth*, vol. 8, *A Supplement of New Letters*, ed. Alan G. Hill (Oxford: Clarendon Press, 1993), 186.

46. This was pointed out by Sukhdev Sandhu in Kitson and Lee, vol. 1, *Black Writers*, ed. Sukhdev Sandhu and David Dabydeen, 343–44.

47. For an astute reading of Prince's text, see Jenny Sharpe, " 'Something Akin to Freedom': The Case of Mary Prince," *Differences* 8, 1 (1996): 31–55.

48. Newton Papers, 523/288, pages 11 & 13.

49. "The Negro Slave's Complaint to the Friends of Humanity" (author and exact date unknown), Wilberforce Papers, box 9, Wilberforce House Museum, Hull.

50. J. Jamieson, *The Sorrows of Slavery* (London, 1789), 25–26.

51. James Walvin and Stephen Small, "African Resistance to Enslavement," in *Transatlantic Slavery: Against Human Dignity*, ed. Anthony Tibbles (London: HMSO, 1994), p. 42.

52. Montgomery, *The West Indies*, in Kitson and Lee, 4:330.

53. "The Slave Ship," broadsheet (London: E. M. Hodges, n.d.).

54. Anna Letitia Barbauld, *Hymns in Prose for Children*, 6th ed. (London, 1794), 66.

55. This argument is made in Moira Ferguson, *Subject to Others*.

56. Located in the Wilberforce House Museum, Hull.

57. Located in the Liverpool Museum, Merseyside.

58. The struggle between white mistresses and black slaves was not, of course, uncommon in colonial slavery. Moira Ferguson suggests that "Two factors unvoiced in the narrative might have exacerbated the series of altercations between Mary Prince and Mrs. Wood. First, the fact that all of Mrs. Wood's privileges as a white slave-owning wife were embodied in the work designated for Mary Prince. Delegating work and responsibilities and enjoying leisure were among the few forms of power and control that Mrs. Wood possessed. . . . Second, Mrs. Wood surely harboured sexual jealously towards Mary Prince. Mr. Wood would have customarily viewed Mary Prince (and other female slaves) as his sexual property" (introduction, *The History of Mary Prince*, 13).

59. William Dickson, *Letters on Slavery* (1789; reprint, Westport, Conn.: Negro University Press, 1970), 20.

60. Surrounding the narrative itself is a complex textual apparatus in the form of testimonies, legal papers, and protests, which prove that the *History* was a distressing firsthand testimony in its own time about how British slavery affected women.

61. Pringle's preface to Prince's *History*, 45.

62. Kathryn Temple, "Libeling the Nation: Mary Prince and the Emergence of a 'British' African Aesthetic," paper delivered at 1995 MLA Convention.

63. Sharpe asserts, "A simple and linear plotting of the slave's quest for emancipation is inadequate for explaining such negotiations. . . . If we are to read *The History of Mary Prince* in the interest of the slave rather than the ex-slave, then we must acknowledge the limitations of a model of subjectivity based on notions of autonomy and/or free will" (53).

64. Minutes of the Anti-Slavery Society, Aldermanbury, 18 May 1830, MSS Br Em, 520E 2/3, Anti-Slavery Society Papers, Rhodes House, Oxford.

65. Letter to Mary Ann Rawson [? May 1833] in *The Letters of William and Dorothy Wordsworth*, vol. 5, *The Later Years*, part 2, 1831–1840, 614–15. For a fuller explanation of Wordsworth's view on slavery at this time, in his own words, see in the same volume the letter to Benjamin Dockray, 23 April 1833, 605–7.

66. William Howitt, "West Indian Slavery," in *The Bow in the Cloud; or, The Negro's Memorial*, collected by M. A. Rawson (London, 1834), 40–41.

67. Mary Howitt, "The Negro Mother," in *The Bow in the Cloud*, 46–47.

68. Bernard Barton, "A Negro Mother's Cradle-Song," in *The Bow in the Cloud*, 33.

69. Letter to Benjamin Dockray, 23 April 1833.

70. Also see William Wordsworth, *Poems in Two Volumes, and Other Poems, 1700–1807*, ed. Jared Curtis (Ithaca, N.Y.: Cornell University Press, 1983), 161–62.

71. Wordsworth, writes Page, is referring to the "French statute of 2 July 1802 regarding the status of 'aucun noir, mulatre, ou autres gens de couleur, de l'un et de l'autre sexe' (any black, mulatto, or other persons of color, of either sex). The ordinance effec-

tively forbade all people of color from entering the continental territories of France, and stated that any people of color currently residing there who did not have government approval would be expelled. A note refers specifically to sending these people to San Domingo, where Napoleon had reinstituted slavery in the summer of 1802, reversing the Convention's abolition of slavery in 1794. As if making explicit the racial fears behind the decree, there is also a clause forbidding intermarriage between whites and people of color. The ordinance, however, does not call for the expulsion of all people of color from France, as Wordsworth suggests, although it certainly makes it difficult for them to remain. It is not clear whether Wordsworth misunderstood the ordinance or whether he deliberately exaggerated or dramatized its effect. For Wordsworth, these racist decrees, along with press reports of the event in San Domingo, particularly regarding Napoleon's betrayal of Toussaint L'Ouverture, were further expressions of despotic rule. Also, considering the faith he had once placed in France, these assaults on human dignity would have been particularly appalling to Wordsworth and would perhaps have served as a reminder of the gulf between 1792 and 1802" (69). Also see Jared Curtis, "Wordsworth and 'The Banished Negroes,'" *Wordsworth Circle* 28, 3 (1987): 144–45.

Selected Bibliography

This selected bibliography contains seven kinds of sources: primary sources on the British slave trade, slavery, and abolition; primary sources on British foreign travel, medicine, and science; current scholarship on the history of the slave trade, slavery, abolition, and foreign travel; current scholarship on medicine, religion, cartography, iconography, and ethnography; current scholarship on British Romanticism and specific Romantic poems; current scholarship in postcolonial studies; work in the philosophy of ethics, alterity, and theories of imagination. The bibliography contains all the references cited in the notes to chapters (except for minor citations), as well as sources that have been formative to my reading and thinking for this book.

MANUSCRIPT SOURCES

Anti-Slavery Society Papers, Rhodes House, Oxford.
DTC, Dawson Turner Copies, Joseph Banks's Correspondence. Botany Library, Natural History Museum, London.
Kew BC, Banks MS Correspondence, Royal Botanic Gardens, Kew.
Newton Papers, Senate House Library, University of London.
Public Record Office, London.
Wilberforce Papers, Wilberforce Museum, Hull.
William Roscoe Papers, Public Record Office, Liverpool.

GOVERNMENT DOCUMENTS

Further Papers Relating to Slaves in the West Indies, Demerara and Berbice. Ordered by the House of Commons to be printed, 23 June 1825.
House of Commons Sessional Papers of the Eighteenth Century. Vol. 69. Ed. Sheila Lambert. Wilmington, Del.: Scholarly Resources, 1975.
Parliamentary Papers, House of Commons, 1780–1840.
Parliamentary Papers, House of Lords, 1780–1840.
Privy Council Papers, 1788.
Records of the African Association, 1788–1831. Ed. Robin Hallett. London: Thomas Nelson and Sons, 1964.

PRIMARY SOURCES

Adams, John. *Sketches taken during ten voyages to Africa, including Remarks on the Country Extending from the Cape Palmas to the River Congo.* London, 1822.

Addison, Joseph. "The Pleasures of Imagination." In *Selections from the Tatler and the Spectator,* ed. Angus Ross. Harmondsworth: Penguin, 1988. 364–405.

"The African's Complaint on-board a slave ship." *Gentleman's Magazine* 63 (August 1793): 749.

Alderson, John. *An Essay on the Nature and Origin of the Contagion of Fevers.* Hull, 1788.

An Apology for Negro Slavery: or, The West India Planters Vindicated from the Charges of Inhumanity. London, 1786.

The Anti-Slavery Album: Selections in Verse from Cowper, Hannah More, Montgomery, Pringle. London, 1828.

Bancroft, Edward. *An Essay on the Natural History of [Dutch] Guiana with an account of the Religion, Manners, and Customs of several Tribes of its Indian Inhabitants.* London, 1769.

Barbauld, Anna Letitia. "Epistle To William Wilberforce, Esq. on the Rejection of the Bill for Abolishing the Slave Trade, London." In *Poems.* London, 1791.

———. *Hymns in Prose for Children.* 6th ed. London, 1794.

Barrow, Sir John. *An Account of Travels into the Interior of Southern Africa.* 1801. Reprint New York: Johnson Reprint, 1968.

Bartram, William. *Travels through North and South Carolina, Georgia, East and West Florida, The Cherokee Country . . . together with Observations on the Manners of the Indians.* Philadelphia, 1791. Reprint as *William Bartram: Travels and Other Writings.* Selected by Thomas P. Slaughter. New York: Library of America, 1996.

Barstow, James. *A Letter to the Rev. Mr. Hall . . . in Answer to His Attack on West Indian Proprietors, with Some Observations on the General Question as to the Abolition of West Indian Slavery.* London, 1824.

Barton, Bernard. "A Negro Mother's Cradle-Song." In *The Bow in the Cloud; or, The Negro's Memorial,* collected by M. A. Rawson. London, 1834. 33.

Beaver, Philip. *African Memoranda: Relative to an attempt to establish a British Settlement on the Island of Bulama, on the Western Coast of Africa, in the year 1792.* London, 1805. Reprint Westport, Conn., Negro Universities Press, 1970.

Beckford, William. *A Descriptive Account of the Island of Jamaica: with Remarks upon the cultivation of the Sugar-Cane, throughout the different Seasons of the Year, and chiefly considered in a Picturesque point of view; also observations and reflections upon what would probably be the consequence of an abolition of the slave trade, and of the emancipation of the slaves.* 2 vols. London, 1790.

Beddoes, Thomas. *A Lecture Introductory to a Course of Popular Instruction on the Constitution and Management of the Human Body.* Bristol, 1797.

Birkett, M. *A Poem on the African Slave Trade, Addressed to Her Own Sex by M. Birket.* Dublin, 1792.

———. "The Slave." In *Tributes of Affection with the Slave; and Other Poems.* By a lady and her brother. London, 1797.

Blane, Gilbert. *Elements of Medical Logick . . . including a statement of evidence respecting the contagious nature of yellow fever.* London, 1819.

Blicke, Charles. *An Essay on the Bilious or Yellow Fever of Jamaica.* London, 1772.

Blumenbach, Johann Friedrich. *On the Natural Variety of Mankind.* In *The Anthropo-logical Treatises of Johann Friedrich Blumenbach.* London, 1865. Reprint in *Slavery, Abolition, and Emancipation: Writings in the British Romantic Period*, ed. Peter J. Kitson and Debbie Lee. 8 vols. London: Pickering & Chatto, 1999. Vol. 8, *Theories of Race*, ed. Peter J. Kitson. 143–212.

Bowdich, Thomas Edward. *A Mission from Cape Coast Castle to Ashantee.* London, 1819.

Bowles, William Leslie. "The African." In *Sonnets with Other Poems.* 3rd ed. Bath, 1794.

Browne, William George. *Travels in Africa, Egypt, and Syria, from the year 1792 to 1798.* London, 1799.

Bruce, James. *Travels to Discover the Source of the Nile, in the Years 1768, 1769, 1770, 1771, 1772, & 1773.* 1790. 3rd ed. Edinburgh: Constable and Manners and Miller; London: Longman, Hurst, Rees, Orme, and Brown, 1813.

Burke, Edmund. *A Philosophical Enquiry into the Origin of our Ideas of the Sublime and Beautiful.* 2nd ed. 1759.

————. *Sketch of a Negro Code.* 1792. In *Works.* London, 1818, vol. 9. Reprint in *Slavery, Abolition, and Emancipation: Writings in the British Romantic Period*, ed. Peter J. Kitson and Debbie Lee. 8 vols. London: Pickering & Chatto, 1999. Vol. 2, *The Abolition Debate*, ed. Peter J. Kitson. 167–208.

Burnett, James, Lord Monboddo. *Of the Origin and Progress of Language.* 2nd ed. 6 vols. Edinburgh and London, 1774.

Burton, Richard. F. *A Plain and Literal Translation of the Arabian Nights' Entertainments, Now Entitled the Book of the Thousand Nights and a Night.* 16 vols. Benares: Kama-shustra Society, private printing, 1885.

Camper, Pieter. *The Works of the Late Professor Camper, on the Connexion between the Science of Anatomy and the Arts of Drawing, Painting, Statuary, &etc.* London, 1794.

Canning, George. *The Speech of the Rt. Hon. George Canning . . . for the Amelioration of the condition of the Slave Population in His Majesty's Dominions in the West Indies.* London, 1824. Reprint in *Slavery, Abolition, and Emancipation: Writings in the British Romantic Period*, ed. Peter J. Kitson and Debbie Lee. 8 vols. London: Pickering & Chatto, 1999. Vol. 3, *The Emancipation Debate*, ed. Debbie Lee. 217–262.

Christophe, Henry and Thomas Clarkson. *Henry Christophe and Thomas Clarkson: A Correspondence.* Ed. Earl Leslie Griggs and Clifford H. Prator. New York: Green-wood Press, 1968.

Clapperton, Hugh. *Journal of a Second Expedition into the Interior of Africa . . . to which is added the Journal of Richard Lander.* London, 1829.

Clark, James. *A Treatise on the Yellow Fever as it Appeared in the Island of Dominica, in the years 1793–4–5–6.* London, 1797.

Clarkson, Thomas. *An Essay on the Impolicy of the African Slave Trade.* London, 1788.

————. *An Essay on the Slavery and Commerce of the Human Species.* London, 1788. Reprint in *Slavery, Abolition, and Emancipation: Writings in the British Romantic Period*, ed. Peter J. Kitson and Debbie Lee. 8 vols. London: Pickering & Chatto, 1999. Vol. 2, *The Abolition Debate*, ed. Peter J. Kitson. 37–74.

————. *The History of the Rise, Progress, and Accomplishment of the Abolition of the Slave-Trade by the British Parliament.* London, 1808. Reprint Frank Class and Co., 1968.

Clutterbuck, Henry. *Observations on the Prevention and Treatment of the Epidemic Fever.* London, 1819.

Colman, George. *Inkle and Yarico . . . As performed at the Theatres Royal, Covent Garden and Haymarket . . . Printed . . . from the Prompt book. With remarks by Mrs. Inchbald.* London 1806.

———. *The Africans: or, War, Love, and Duty, a Play in Three Acts.* London, 1808. Reprint in *Cumberland's British Theatre* No. 347. London, c. 1826.

Coleridge, Samuel Taylor. Review of *The History of the Abolition of the Slave Trade.* By Thomas Clarkson. *Edinburgh Review* 12 (1808): 355–79.

Cook, James. *Voyage to the Pacific Ocean . . . for Making Discoveries in the Northern Hemisphere.* London, 1784.

Cowper, William. "Charity." *Poems in Two Volumes.* 2nd ed. London, 1782.

———. *The Poems of William Cowper.* Ed. John D. Baird and Charles Ryskamp. 3 vols. Oxford: Clarendon Press, 1980–95.

Crawford, John. *Journal of an Embassy from the Governor-General of India to the Courts of Siam and Cochin China.* 1828. Reprint Oxford: Oxford University Press, 1967.

The Crisis of the Sugar Colonies; or, An Enquiry into the Probably Effects of the French Expedition to the West Indies; and their Connection with the Colonial Interests of the British Empire, to which are subjoined Sketches of a Plan for Settling the Vacant Lands of Trinidad. London, 1802. Reprint New York: Negro Universities Press, 1969.

Damberger, Christian Frederick. *Travels Through the Interior of Africa from the Cape of Good Hope to Morocco.* London, 1801.

Dancer, Thomas. *The Medical Assistant; or, Jamaica Practice of Physic designed chiefly for the use of families and plantations.* Kingston, 1801.

Darwin, Erasmus. *The Botanic Garden: A Poem in Two Parts.* London, 1791.

———. *The Temple of Nature: or, The Origin of Society.* London, 1803.

Day, Thomas and John Bicknell. *The Dying Negro, a Poetical Epistle.* London, 1773.

Denon, Vivant. *Travels in Upper and Lower Egypt.* Trans. Arthur Aiken. 3 vols. London, 1803.

Deverell, William. *Andalusia; or, Notes tending to shew that the yellow fever of the West Indies . . . was a Disease Well Known to the Ancients.* London, 1803.

Dickson, William. *Letters on Slavery.* 1789. Reprint Westport, Conn.: Negro Universities Press, 1970.

———. *Mitigation of Slavery.* 1814. Reprint Miami: Mnemosyne, 1969.

Dupuis, J. *Journal of a Residence in Ashantee.* London, 1824.

Edwards, Bryan. *The History, Civil and Commercial, of the British West Indies.* 3 vols. London, 1819. Reprint New York: AMS Press, 1966.

Equiano, Olaudah. *The Interesting Narrative of the Life of Olaudah Equiano, or Gustavus Vassa the African, written by himself.* 1789. Ed. Paul Edwards. Reprint facsimile ed., 2 vols. Coral Gables, Fla: Mnemosyne, 1989.

Examen de l'Esclavage en général, et particulièrement de l'Esclavage des Nègres dans les Colonies Françaises de l'Amérique. Par V. D. C. Ancien Avocat et Colon de St. Domingue. 2 vols. Paris, 1802, 1803. Review article in *Edinburgh Review* (July 1805): 326–50.

Falconbridge, Alexander. *An Account of the Slave Trade on the Coast of Africa.* London, 1788.

Forster, Georg. *A Voyage Round the World in his Britannic Majesty's Sloop Resolution Commanded by Captain J. Cook, during the Years 1772, 3, 4, and 5.* 2 vols. London, 1777.

Fox, William. *An Address to the People of Great Britain on the Utility of Refraining from the Use of West India Sugar and Rum.* 4th ed. London, 1791. Reprint in *Slavery, Abolition, and Emancipation: Writings in the British Romantic Period*, ed. Peter J. Kitson and Debbie Lee. 8 vols. London: Pickering & Chatto, 1999. Vol. 2, *The Abolition Debate*, ed. Peter J. Kitson. 153–166.

Gay, John. *Fables.* 2 vols. London, 1793.

Gerard, Alexander. *An Essay on Taste.* 1759. 3rd ed. London and Edinburgh, 1780.

Gorton, John. *Tubal to Seba: The Negro Suicide: A Poem.* 2nd ed. London, 1797.

Grainger, James. *The Sugar-Cane: A Poem in Four Books.* London, 1764.

Hampden, John. *A Commentary on Mr. Clarkson's pamphlet entitled "Thoughts on the necessity of improving the conditions of the Slaves in the British colonies, with a view to their ultimate emancipation".* London, 1824. Reprint in *Slavery, Abolition, and Emancipation: Writings in the British Romantic Period*, ed. Peter J. Kitson and Debbie Lee. 8 vols. London: Pickering & Chatto, 1999. Vol. 4, *The Emancipation Debate*, ed. Debbie Lee. 145–216.

Hawkesworth, John. *An Account of the voyages undertaken by the order of His Present Majesty for making discoveries in the southern hemisphere, and successively performed by Commodore Byron, Captain Wallis, Captain Carteret and Captain Cook, in the* Dolphin, *the* Swallow, *and the* Endeavour. London, 1773.

Hazlitt, William. *The Complete Works of William Hazlitt.* Ed. P. P. Howe. 21 vols. London, 1930–34.

Hemans, Felicia Dorothea. *The Works of Mrs Hemans, with a memoir of her life.* 7 vols. Edinburgh and London, 1839. Vol. 6, *Miscellaneous Poems.*

Henderson, Stewart. *A Letter to the Officers of the Army . . . on the means of preserving health and preventing that fatal disease the Yellow Fever.* London, 1795.

Hillary, William. *Observations on the Changes of the Air and the Concomitant Epidemical Disease, in the Island of Barbadoes.* 2nd ed. London, 1766.

Howard, Lieutenant. *The Haitian Journal of Lieutenant Howard, York Hussars, 1796–1798.* Ed. Roger Norman Buckley. Knoxville: University of Tennessee Press, 1985.

Howitt, Mary. "The Negro Mother." In *The Bow in the Cloud; or, The Negro's Memorial*, collected by M. A. Rawson. London, 1834. 46–47.

Howitt, Mary, and Howitt, William. *The Desolation of Eyam: The Emigrant, a Tale of the American Woods, and Other Poems.* London, 1827.

Howitt, William. "West Indian Slavery." In *The Bow in the Cloud; or, The Negro's Memorial*, collected by M. A. Rawson. London, 1834. 40–41.

Hume, John. "Letter VII: An Account of the True Bilious, or Yellow Fever; and of the Remitting and Intermitting Fevers of the West Indies." In *Letters and Essays on the Small Pox and Inoculation, the Measles, the Dry Belly-Ache, and Yellow, and Remitting and Intermitting Fevers of the West Indies.* London, 1788.

Hunt, Leigh. *The Poetical Words of Leigh Hunt.* Ed. H. S. Milford. Oxford: Oxford University Press, 1923.

Hutchenson, William. *The Princess of Zanfara.* London, 1792.

Jackson, Robert. *An Outline of the History and Cure of Fever . . . vulgarly the yellow fever of the West Indies.* Edinburgh and London, 1798.

Keate, George. *An Account of the Pelew Islands, Situated in the Western Part of the Pacific Ocean. Composed from the Journals and Communications of Captain Henry Wilson and Some of His Officers who, in August 1783, were there shipwrecked in The Antelope, a Packet Belonging to the Honourable East India Company.* London, 1788.

Knipe, Eliza. "Atomboka and Omaza; an African Story." In *Six Narrative Poems*. London, 1787: 51–60.

Lemprière, John. *Lempriere's Classical Dictionary of proper names mentioned in ancient authors writ large*. 1788. 3rd ed. London: Routledge, 1984.

Letters and Essays on the Small-Pox . . . The Yellow and Remitting and Intermitting Fevers of the West Indies. To which are added Thoughts on the Hydrocephalus Internus . . . . London, 1778.

Le Vaillant, François. *Travels into the Interior Parts of Africa*. 2 vols. London, 1790.

Lewis, Matthew Gregory. *The Castle Spectre*. 1797. Reprinted in *Seven Gothic Dramas*, ed. Jeffrey N. Cox. Athens: Ohio University Press, 1992. 149–221.

———. *Journal of a West India Proprietor, kept during a residence in the island of Jamaica*. London, 1834.

Long, Edward. *The History of Jamaica*. 2 vols. London, 1774.

Lyon, George Francis. *A Narrative of Travels in Northern Africa in the Years 1818, 19, and 20 . . . by Captain G. F. Lyon, R.N., companion of the late Mr. Ritchie*. London, 1821.

Mavor, William. *Travels in Africa by Mr. Mungo Park, Surgeon; From the Cape of Good Hope to Morocco by Damberger; and in the Interior Districts of Africa by Ledyard and Lucas*. London, 1807.

Mitford, Mary Russell. "Lines, Suggested by the Uncertain Fate of Mungo Park, the Celebrated African Traveller." In *Poems*. London, 1811.

———. "Ode to Botany." In *Poems*. London, 1811.

M. L. E. Moreau de Saint-Mery. *Description de la partie française de Saint-Domingue*. 2 vols. Paris, 1797–98.

Montgomery, James. "The Ocean. Written at Scarborough, in the Summer of 1805." In *The Poetical Works of James Montgomery*, collected by himself. 4 vols. London, 1841.

———. *The West Indies, a Poem in Four Parts*. 1809. In *Poems on the Abolition of the Slave Trade, by James Montgomery, James Grahame, and E. Benger*. London, 1809. Reprint in *Slavery, Abolition, and Emancipation: Writings in the British Romantic Period*, ed. Peter J. Kitson and Debbie Lee. 8 vols. London: Pickering & Chatto, 1999. Vol 4, *Verse*, ed. Alan Richardson. 279–332.

More, Hannah. "Slavery." 1788. Reprint in *Women Romantic Poets, 1785–1832: An Anthology*. Ed. Jennifer Breen. London: Everyman, 1992.

More, Hannah and Eaglesfield Smith. *The Sorrows of Yamba; or, The Negro Woman's Lamentation*. London, 1795. Reprint in *Slavery, Abolition, and Emancipation: Writings in the British Romantic Period*, ed. Peter J. Kitson and Debbie Lee. 8 vols. London: Pickering & Chatto, 1999. Vol 4, *Verse*, ed. Alan Richardson: 224–31.

Moseley, Benjamin. *A Treatise on Sugar with Miscellaneous Medical Observations*. 1st ed. London, 1799. 2nd ed. London, 1800.

———. *A Treatise on Tropical Diseases; on Military operations; and on the Climate of the West Indies*. 1787. London, 1803.

Mulligan, Hugh. "The Lovers: An African Eclogue." *Gentleman's Magazine* 54 (March 1784): 199–200.

Newton, John. *Authentic Narrative of some Remarkable and Interesting Particulars in the Life of John Newton*. London, 1764.

———. *Thoughts on the African Slave Trade*. London, 1788. Reprint in *Slavery, Abolition, and Emancipation: Writings in the British Romantic Period*, ed. Peter J. Kitson and

Debbie Lee. 8 vols. London: Pickering & Chatto, 1999. Vol. 2, *The Abolition Debate*, ed. Peter J. Kitson. 75–118.

Nisbet, Richard. *The Capacity of Negroes.* 1789. Reprint New York: Negro Universities Press, 1970.

No Rum! No Sugar! or, The Voice of Blood. London, 1792.

Of the Shoemaker Schroter, the Printer Taurinas, and the Traveler Damberger, three travelrs who never traveled at all but invented their stories in one manufactory. London, 1801.

Opie, Amelia. *The Black Man's Lament; or How to Make Sugar.* London, 1826.

———. *The Negro Boy's Tale, a poem addressed to children.* London, 1824.

Park, Mungo. *Travels in the Interior Districts of Africa, performed under the direction and patronage of the African Association, in the years 1795, 1796, 1797.* London, 1799. Ed. Kate Ferguson Marsters. Durham, N.C.: Duke University Press, 2000.

Powell, Charles. *A Treatise on the Nature, Causes, & Cures, of the Endemic, or Yellow Fever of Tropical Climates, as it occurs in the West Indies.* London, 1814.

Pringle, Thomas. *African Sketches.* London, 1834.

Rainsford, Marcus. *An Historical Account of the Black Empire in Hayti.* London, 1805.

Redman, John. *Proceedings of the College of Physicians of Philadelphia relative to the prevention of the introduction and spreading of contagious diseases.* Philadelphia, 1789.

Rennell, James. *The Geographical System of Herodotus, Examined and Explained, by a comparison with those of other ancient authors, and with modern geography (The Whole Explained by Eleven Maps).* London, 1800.

Renny, Robert. *A History of Jamaica with observations on the climate, scenery, trade, productions, negroes, slave trade, diseases of Europeans . . . .* London, 1807.

Robinson, Mary. "The Negro Girl." In *Lyrical Tales.* London: Longman, 1800. Reprint in *Slavery, Abolition, and Emancipation: Writings in the British Romantic Period,* ed. Peter J. Kitson and Debbie Lee. 8 vols. London: Pickering & Chatto, 1999. Vol 4, *Verse,* ed. Alan Richardson. 259–267.

Roscoe, William. "Mount Pleasant, a Descriptive Poem." Warrington: W. Eyre, 1777. Reprint in *William Roscoe of Liverpool,* ed. George Chandler, intro., Sir Alfred Shennan, preface Vere E. Cotton. London: B.T. Batsford, 1953. 330–42.

———. "Ode to May, written in 1807, on the abolition of the African slave trade." *Poems.* London, 1834. 96–101.

———. "The Wrongs of Africa." London: R. Faulder, part 1, 1787; part 2, 1788. Reprint in *William Roscoe of Liverpool,* ed. George Chandler, intro., Sir Alfred Shennan, preface Vere E. Cotton. London: B.T. Batsford, 1953. Part 1, 343–59; Part 2, 360–78.

Rusher, J. *The Secret History and Misfortunes of Fatyma; and the History of Olympia, written by themselves, to which is added Inkle and Yarico in verse.* Banbury, 1820.

Rushton, Edward. *West Indian Eclogues.* London, 1787.

Salt, Henry. *A Voyage to Abyssinia.* London, 1814

Sancho, Ignatius. *Letters of the late Ignatius Sancho.* 5th ed. 1803. Ed. Paul Edwards. London: Dawson of Pall Mall, 1968.

Sayer, Frank. "The Dying African." *Gentleman's Magazine* 61 (November 1791): 1046–47.

Shelley, Mary. *The Journals of Mary Shelley: 1814–1844.* Ed. Paula R. Feldman and Diana Scott-Kilvert. Oxford: Clarendon Press; New York: Oxford University Press, 1987.

———. *Mary Shelley's Journal.* Ed. Frederick L. Jones. Norman: University of Oklahoma Press, 1947.

"The Slave Chase." [song] Composed by Henry Russell for his new entertainment "Negro Life." Words by Angus B. Reach, Esq. n.d.

"The Slave Ship." Broadsheet. London: E.M. Hodges, n.d.

Smith, Adam. *An Inquiry into the Nature and Causes of the Wealth of Nations.* Ed. and intro. Richard F. Teichgraeber, III. New York: Random House, 1985.

———. *The Theory of Moral Sentiments.* 1759. Ed. D. D. Raphael and A. L. Macfie. Oxford: Clarendon Press, 1976.

Smyth, F. G. *An Apology for West Indians, and Reflections on the Policy of Great Britain's Interference in the internal concerns of the West India Colonies.* London, 1824.

Snelgrave, William. *A New Account of Some Parts of Guinea and the Slave Trade.* London, 1734.

Southey, Robert. *Selections from the Letters of Robert Southey.* Ed. J. W. Warter. 4 vols. London, 1856.

———. "A Tale of Paraguay." In *The Poetical Works of Robert Southey Collected by Himself.* 10 vols. London, 1838.

Stanfield, James. *The Guinea Voyage, a Poem in Three Books.* London, 1789.

The State of Society in Jamaica: In a Reply to an Article in Edinburgh Review No. LXXV. London, 1825.

Stedman, John Gabriel. *Narrative of a Five Years' Expedition Against the Revolted Negroes of Surinam.* Ed. Richard Price and Sally Price. Baltimore: Johns Hopkins University Press, 1988.

———. *Narrative of a five years' expedition against the Revolted Negroes of Surinam, in Guiana, on the wild coast of South America; from the Year 1772, to 1777: elucidating the history of that Country, and describing its productions . . . with an account of the Indians of Guiana, & Negroes of Guinea.* 2nd ed., corrected. 2 vols. London, 1806–13.

Thelwell, John [John Beaufort, L.L.D.]. *The Daughter of Adoption: A Tale of Modern Times.* 4 vols. London, 1801.

Touchstone, Timothy, Gent. [pseud.]. *Tea and Sugar, or the Nabob and the Creole, a Poem in Two Cantos.* London, 1792.

Trotter, Thomas. *Medicina Nautica: An Essay on the Diseases of Seamen.* London, 1797.

Tyson, Edward. *Orang-Outang, sive Homo Sylvestris: or, the Anatomy of a Pygmie Compared with that of a Monkey, an Ape, and a Man. To Which is added a Philological Enquiry Concerning the Pygmies, the Cynocephali, the Satyrs, and Sphinges of the Ancients.* London,1699.

Wharton, Richard. *Observations on the Authenticity of Bruce's Travels in Abyssinia, in rply to some passages in Brown's travels through Egypt, Africa and Syria; to which is added, a comparative view of life and happiness in Europe in Cafraria.* Newcastle upon Tyne, 1800.

White, Charles. *Account of the Regular Gradation in Man.* London, 1799.

Wilberforce, William. *The Speech of Mr. Wilberforce . . . on a Motion for the Abolition of the Slave Trade in the House of Commons, May the 12th, 1789.* London, 1789. Reprint in *Slavery, Abolition, and Emancipation: Writings in the British Romantic Period*, ed. Peter J. Kitson and Debbie Lee. 8 vols. London: Pickering & Chatto, 1999. Vol. 2, *The Abolition Debate*, ed. Peter J. Kitson. 135–152.

Williams, Helen Maria. *Poem on the Bill Lately Passed for Regulating the Slave Trade.* London, 1788. Reprint in *Slavery, Abolition, and Emancipation: Writings in the British*

Romantic Period, ed. Peter J. Kitson and Debbie Lee. 8 vols. London: Pickering & Chatto, 1999. Vol. 4, *Verse*, ed. Alan Richardson. 84–98.

Wilson, John. *Memoirs of the West Indian Fever*. London, 1827.

———. "On Reading Mr. Clarkson's History of the Abolition of the Slave Trade." In *The Isle of Palms and Other Poems*. Edinburgh, 1812.

Wollstonecraft, Mary. *A Vindication of the Rights of Woman*. 1792. Ed. Carol H. Poston. 2nd ed. New York: W.W. Norton, 1988.

Woolman, John. *Journal and Major Essays*. Ed. Phillips P. Moulton. New York: Oxford University Press, 1971.

The Wrongs of Alooma, or the African's Revenge: A narrative poem, founded on historical fact. Liverpool, H. Hodgson, 1788.

Yearsley, Ann. *A Poem on the Inhumanity of the Slave-Trade*. London, 1788.

Secondary Sources

Alexander, Robert, Adam Carter, Kevin D. Hutchings, and Neville F. Newman. "Alterity in the Discourses of Romanticism." *European Romantic Review* 9, 2 (1998): 149–60.

Alwes, Karla. *Imagination Transformed: The Evaluation of the Female Character in Keats's Poetry*. Carbondale: Southern Illinois University Press, 1993.

Anderson, Benedict. *Imagined Communities: Reflections on the Origin and Spread of Nationalism*. London: Verso Editions/NLB, 1983.

Aravamudan, Srinivas. *Tropicopolitans: Colonialism and Agency, 1688–1804*. Durham, N.C.: Duke University Press, 1999.

Ashton, Rosemary. *The Life of Samuel Taylor Coleridge*. Oxford and Cambridge, Mass.: Blackwell, 1996.

Baldwin, Anna and Sarah Hurron, eds. *Platonism and the English Imagination*. Cambridge: Cambridge University Press, 1994.

Ball, Patricia M. *The Central Self: A Study in Romantic and Victorian Imagination*. London: Athlone Press, 1968.

Banton, Michael. *Racial Theories*. New York: Cambridge University Press, 1987.

Barasch, Moshe, Lucy Freeman Sandler, and Patricia Egan, eds. *Art, the Ape of Nature: Studies in Honor of H. W. Janson*. New York: H. N. Abrams; Englewood Cliffs, N.J.: Prentice-Hall, 1981.

Barnard, John, ed. *Keats: The Complete Poems*. Harmondsworth: Penguin, 1973.

Baum, Joan. *Mind-Forg'd Manacles: Slavery and the English Romantic Poets*. North Haven, Conn.: Archon Books, 1994.

Beckles, Hilary McD. *Natural Rebels: A Social History of Enslaved Black Women in Barbados*. New Brunswick, N.J.: Rutgers University Press, 1989.

Behrendt, Stephen C., ed. *Romanticism, Radicalism and the Press*. Detroit: Wayne State University Press, 1997.

Bennett, Henry Jr. *Bondsman and Bishops: Slavery and Apprenticeship on the Codrington Plantations of Barbados 1710–1838*. Berkeley: University of California Press, 1958.

———. "The Problem of Slave Labor Supply at the Codrington Plantations." *Journal of Negro History* 36.4 (1951): 406–41.

Bentley, G. E. Jr. *Blake Records*. Oxford: Clarendon Press, 1969.

———. "The Great Illustrated-Book Publishers of the 1790s and William Blake." In *Editing Illustrated Books*, ed. William Blissett. New York: Garland, 1980. 57–96.

Bernal, Martin. *Black Athena: The Afroasiatic Roots of Classical Civilization*. Vol. 1, *The Fabrication of Ancient Greece, 1785–1985*. New Brunswick, N.J.: Free Association Books, 1987.

Bewell, Alan. *Romanticism and Colonial Disease*. Baltimore: Johns Hopkins University Press, 1999.

Bhabha, Homi K. "Of Mimicry and Man: The Ambivalence of Colonial Discourse." *October* 28 (Spring 1984): 125–33.

———. "The Other Question: Difference, Discrimination and the Discourse of Colonialism." In *Literature, Politics, and Theory: Papers from the Essex Conference, 1976–84*, ed. Francis Barker et al. London: Methuen, 1983. 148–72.

ed. *Nation and Narration*. New York: Routledge, 1990.

Bidney, Martin. "Beneficent Birds and Crossbow Crimes: The Nightmare-Confessions of Coleridge and Ludwig Tieck." *PLL* 25, 1 (1989). 44–58.

Bindman, David. "Blake's Vision of Slavery Revisited." *Huntington Library Quarterly* 58, 3–4 (1997): 373–82.

Blaut, J. M. *The National Question and Colonialism*. London: Zed Books, 1987.

Bloom, Harold. "Introduction." In *William Blake's The Marriage of Heaven and Hell: Modern Critical Interpretations*, ed. Harold Bloom. New York: Chelsea House, 1987. 1–24.

———. "Dialectic of the *Marriage of Heaven and Hell*." In *William Blake's "The Marriage of Heaven and Hell": Modern Critical Interpretations*, ed. Harold Bloom. New York: Chelsea House, 1987. 49–56.

———. *Shelley's Mythmaking*. 1959. Reprint Ithaca, N.Y.: Cornell University Press, 1969.

Bohls, Elizabeth. *Women Travel Writers and the Language of Aesthetics*. Cambridge: Cambridge University Press, 1995.

Bohm, Arnd. "Georg Forster's *A Voyage Round the World* as a Source for *The Rime of the Ancient Mariner*: A Reconsideration." *ELH* 50, 2 (1983): 363–77.

Boime, Albert. *The Art of Exclusion: Representing Blacks in the Nineteenth Century*. Washington, D.C.: Smithsonian Institution Press, 1990.

Bourguignon, Erika. *Possession*. San Francisco: Chandler and Sharp, 1976.

Bowra, C. M. *The Romantic Imagination*. Oxford: Oxford University Press, 1961.

Brent, Peter. *Black Nile: Mungo Park and the Search for the Niger*. London: Gordon and Cremonesi, 1977.

Brown, Laura. *Ends of Empire: Women and Ideology in Early Eighteenth-Century English Literature*. Ithaca, N.Y.: Cornell University Press, 1993.

Brann, Eva T. H. *The World of Imagination*. Savage, Md.: Rowman and Littlefield, 1991.

Brown, Lloyd A. *The Story of Maps*. 1949. Reprint New York: Dover, 1977.

Bush, Barbara. "Defiance or Submission? The Role of the Slave Woman in Slave Resistance in the British Caribbean." *Immigrants and Minorities* 1, 1 (1982): 16–38.

———. *Slave Women in Caribbean Society, 1650–1832*. Bloomington: Indiana University Press, 1990.

Carter, H. B. *Sir Joseph Banks: 1743–1820*. London: British Museum, 1988.

Chambers, Jane. " 'For Love's Sake': *Lamia* and Burton's *Melancholy*." *Studies in English Literature* 22, 4 (1982): 583–600.

Clarke, Bruce. "Fabulous Monsters of Conscience: Anthropomorphosis in Keats's *Lamia.*" *Studies in Romanticism* 24, 4 (1984): 555–79.

Colwell, Frederic. "Shelley's 'The Witch of Atlas' and the Mythic Geography of the Nile." *British Literary History* 45 (1978): 69–72.

Costanzo, Angelo. *Surprising Narrative: Olaudah Equiano and the Beginnings of Black Autobiography.* Urbana: University of Illinois Press, 1986.

Coupland, Reginald. *The British Anti-Slavery Movement.* London: Thornton Butterworth, 1933.

Craton, Michael. *Empire, Enslavement, and Freedom in the Caribbean.* Oxford: James Currey, 1997.

———. "Hobbesian or Panglossian? Two Extremes of Slave Conditions in the British Caribbean 1781–1834." *William and Mary Quarterly* 35 (1978): 324–56.

———. *Sinews of Empire: A Short History of British Slavery.* New York: Anchor Books, 1974.

———. *Testing the Chains: Resistance to Slavery in the British West Indies.* Ithaca, N.Y.: Cornell University Press, 1982.

Craton, Michael, James Walvin and David Wright. *Slavery, Abolition and Emancipation: Black Slaves and the British Empire, a Thematic Documentary.* London: Longman, 1976.

Crisman, William. "Psychological Realism and Narrative Manner in Shelley's 'Alastor' and 'The Witch of Atlas.' " *Keats-Shelley Journal* 35 (1986): 126–48.

Cummins, Alissandra. "Caribbean Slave Society." In *Transatlantic Slavery: Against Human Dignity,* ed. Anthony Tibbles. London: HMSO, 1994. 51–59.

Curran, Stuart. *Shelley's Annus Mirabilis: The Maturing of an Epic Vision.* San Marino, Calif.: Huntington Library, 1975.

Curtin, Philip. *The Atlantic Slave Trade: A Census.* Madison: University of Wisconsin Press, 1969.

———. *Death by Migration: Europe's Encounter with the Tropical World in the Nineteenth Century.* Cambridge: Cambridge University Press, 1989.

———. *The Image of Africa: British Ideas and Action, 1780–1850.* 1964. Reprint, 2 vols in one. Madison: University of Wisconsin Press, 1973.

Curtis, Jared. "Wordsworth and 'The Banished Negroes.' " *Wordsworth Circle* 28, 3 (1987): 144–45.

Dabydeen, David. *Hogarth's Blacks: Images of Blacks in Eighteenth Century English Art.* Manchester: Manchester University Press, 1987.

Davis, David Brion. *The Problem of Slavery in the Age of Revolution, 1770–1823.* Ithaca, N.Y.: Cornell University Press, 1975.

———. "The Problem of Slavery in the Age of Revolution, 1770–1823" (Part 1, "What the Abolitionists Were Up Against"; Part 2, "The Quaker Ethic and the Antislavery International"; Part 3, "The Preservation of English Liberty"). In John Ashworth, David Brion Davis, and Thomas L. Haskell, *The Antislavery Debate: Capitalism and Abolitionism as a Problem in Historical Interpretation,* ed. Thomas Bender. Berkeley: University of California Press, 1992. 17–26; 27–64; 65–103.

Dayan, Joan. "Codes of Law and Bodies of Color." *New Literary History* 26 (1995): 283–308.

———. "Gothic Naipaul." *Transition* 59 (1993): 158–70.

———. *Haiti, History, and the Gods.* Berkeley: University of California Press, 1995.

————. "'A Receptacle for that Race of Men': Blood, Boundaries, and Mutations of Theory." *American Literature* 67 (1995): 801–13.

————. "Vodoun, or the Voice of the Gods." *Raritan* 10 (1991): 32–57.

De Almeida, Hermione. *Romantic Medicine and John Keats*. New York and Oxford: Oxford University Press, 1991.

Delaporte, François. *Disease and Civilization: The Cholera in Paris, 1832*. Trans. Arthur Goldhammer. Cambridge, Mass.: MIT Press, 1986.

————. *The History of Yellow Fever: An Essay on the Birth of Tropical Medicine*. Trans. Arthur Goldhammer. Cambridge, Mass.: MIT Press, 1991.

DePaolo, Charles. "Of Tribes and Hordes: Coleridge and the Emancipation of Slaves." *Theoria: A Journal of Studies in the Arts, Humanities and Social Sciences* (Pietermaritzburg Natal, South Africa) 60 (1983): 27–43.

Derrida, Jacques. *Adieu to Emmanuel Levinas*. Trans. Pascale-Anne Brault and Michael Naas. Stanford, Calif.: Stanford University Press, 1999.

Dickstein, Morris. *Keats and His Poetry: A Study in Development*. Chicago: University of Chicago Press, 1971.

Diffey, T. J. "The Roots of Imagination: the Philosophical Context." In *The Romantics*, ed. Stephen Prickett. New York: Holmes and Meier, 1981. 164–201.

Drew, John. *India and the Romantic Imagination*. Oxford: Oxford University Press, 1987.

Duerksen, Ronald A. "Wordsworth and the Austral Retreat in Shelley's 'Witch of Atlas.'" *Keats-Shelley Journal* 34 (1985): 18–20.

Dunn, Richard S. *Sugar and Slaves: The Rise of the Planter Class in the English West Indies, 1624–1713*. Chapel Hill: University of North Carolina Press, 1972.

Dykes, Eva Beatrice. *The Negro in English Romantic Thought: A Study in Sympathy for the Oppressed*. Washington, D.C.: Associated Publishers, 1942.

Ebbatson, J. R. "Coleridge's Mariner and the Rights of Man." *Studies in Romanticism* 11, 1 (1972): 171–206.

Edwards, Paul. *Unreconciled Strivings and Ironic Strategies: Three Afro-British Authors of the Georgian Era: Ignatius Sancho, Olaudah Equiano, Robert Wedderburn*. Occasional Papers 34. Edinburgh University: Center for African Studies, 1992.

Echeruo, Michael J. C. "Theologizing 'Underneath the Tree': An African Topos in Ukawsaw Gronniosaw, William Blake, and William Cole." *Research in African Literatures* 23 (1992): 51–58.

Engell, James. *The Creative Imagination: Enlightenment to Romanticism*. Cambridge, Mass.: Harvard University Press, 1981.

Erdem, Y. Hakan. *Slavery in the Ottoman Empire and Its Demise, 1800–1909*. London: Macmillan, 1996.

Erdman, David V. "Blake's Vision of Slavery." In *Critical Essays on William Blake*, ed. Hazard Adams. Boston: G.K. Hall, 1991.

————. *Blake: Prophet Against Empire*. 1977. Reprint New York: Dover, 1991.

Ellis, Kate. "Monsters in the Garden: Mary Shelley and the Bourgeois Family." In *The Endurance of Frankenstein*, ed. George Levine and U. C. Knoepflmacher. Berkeley: University of California Press, 1979. 123–141.

Ellis, Markman. *The Politics of Sensuality: Race, Gender, and Commerce in the Sentimental Novel*. Cambridge: Cambridge University Press, 1996.

Empson, William. "'The Ancient Mariner': An Answer to Warren." *Kenyon Review* 15 (1993): 155–77.

Essick, Robert N. *William Blake's Commercial Book Illustrations: A Catalogue and Study of the Plates Engraved by Blake After Designs by Other Artists.* Oxford: Clarendon Press, 1991.

———. *William Blake, Printmaker.* Princeton, N.J.: Princeton University Press, 1980.

Fabian, Johannes. *Time and the Other: How Anthropology Makes Its Object.* New York: Columbia University Press, 1983.

Fanon, Frantz. *Black Skin, White Masks.* 1952. Trans. Charles Lam Markmann. New York: Grove, 1967.

Ferguson, Moira. *Subject to Others: British Women Writers and Colonial Slavery, 1760–1834.* New York: Routledge, 1992.

Forry, Steven Earl. *Hideous Progenies: Dramatizations of Frankenstein from Mary Shelley to the Present.* Philadelphia: University of Pennsylvania Press, 1990.

Foucault, Michel. *The Order of Things: An Archeology of the Human Sciences.* New York: Pantheon, 1970.

———. *Power/Knowledge.* Trans. Colin Gordon, Leo Marshall, John Mepham, and Kate Soper, ed. Colin Gordon. New York: Pantheon Books, 1980.

Fox, Susan. "The Female as Metaphor in William Blake's Poetry." *Critical Inquiry* 3 (1977): 507–17.

Fulford, Tim and Peter J. Kitson, eds. *Romanticism and Colonialism: Writing and Empire, 1780–1830.* Cambridge: Cambridge University Press, 1998.

Gascoigne, John. "The Ordering of Nature and the Ordering of Empire: A Commentary." In *Visions of Empire: Voyages, Botany, and Representations of Nature*, ed. David Philip Miller and Peter Hans Reill. Cambridge: Cambridge University Press, 1996. 107–13.

———. *Science in the Service of Empire: Joseph Banks, the British State and the Uses of Science in the Age of Revolution.* Cambridge: Cambridge University Press, 1998.

Gates, Henry Louis. *The Signifying Monkey: A Theory of Afro-American Literary Criticism.* New York and Oxford: Oxford University Press, 1988.

Geggus, David. "British Opinion and the Emergence of Haiti, 1791–1805." In *Slavery and British Society 1776–1846*, ed. James Walvin. Baton Rouge: Louisiana State University Press, 1982. 123–49.

Gilbert, Sandra M. and Susan Gubar. *The Madwoman in the Attic: The Woman Writer and the Nineteenth-Century Literary Imagination.* New Haven, Conn.: Yale University Press, 1979.

Gill, Stephen. *William Wordsworth: A Life.* Oxford: Oxford University Press, 1990.

Gleckner, Robert F. "Blake's Little Black Boy and the Bible." *Colby Library Quarterly* 18, 4 (1982): 205–13.

Glissant, Edouard. *Caribbean Discourse.* Trans J. Michael Dash. Charlottesville: University of Virginia, 1992.

Glut, Donald F. *The Frankenstein Catalog, Being a Comprehensive List of Novels, Translations, Adaptations, Stories, Critical Works . . . Featuring Frankenstein's Monster and/or Descended from Mary Shelley's Novel.* Jefferson, N.C.: McFarland, 1984.

Goslee, Nancy Moore. "Slavery and Sexual Character: Questioning the Master Trope in Blake's *Visions of the Daughters of Albion.*" *ELH* 57 (1990): 101–28.

Greimas, A. J. and J. Courtés. *Semiotics and Language.* Trans. Larry Crist, Daniel Patte, James Lee, Edward McMahon II, Gary Phillips, Michael Rengstorf. Bloomington: Indiana University Press, 1982.

Gross, George. "Lamia and the Cupid-Psyche Myth." *Keats-Shelley Journal* 39 (1990): 151–65.

Hall, Jean. *A Mind that Feeds Upon Infinity: The Deep Self in English Romantic Poetry.* London: Associated University Press, 1991.

Hallett, Robin. *The Penetration of Africa: European Enterprise and Exploration Principally in Northern and Western Africa up to 1830.* London: Routledge and Kegan Paul, 1965.

Hallissy, Margaret. "Poisonous Creature: Holmes's Elsie Venner." *Studies in the Novel* 17 (1985): 406–19.

Haney, David P. "Aesthetics and Ethics in Gadamer, Levinas, and Romanticism: Problems of Phronesis and Techne." *PMLA* 114, 1 (1999): 32–45.

Hannas, Linda. *The English Jigsaw Puzzle: 1760–1890.* London: Wayland, 1972.

Haskell, Thomas L. "Capitalism and the Origins of the Humanitarian Sensibility, Part 1 and Part 2." In John Ashworth, David Brion Davis, and Thomas L. Haskell, *The Antislavery Debate: Capitalism and Abolitionism as a Problem in Historical Interpretation*, ed. Thomas Bender. Berkeley: University of California Press, 1992. 107–35, 136–60.

———. "Convention and Hegemonic Interest in the Debate over Antislavery: A Reply to Davis and Ashworth." In John Ashworth, David Brion Davis, and Thomas L. Haskell, *The Antislavery Debate: Capitalism and Abolitionism as a Problem in Historical Interpretation*, ed. Thomas Bender. Berkeley: University of California Press, 1992. 200–59.

Heffernan, James A. "Blake's Oothoon: The Dilemmas of Marginality." *Studies in Romanticism* 30 (1991): 3–18.

Henry, Lauren. "Sunshine and Shady Groves: What Blake's 'Little Black Boy' Learned From African Writers." In *Romanticism and Colonialism: Writing and Empire 1780–1830*, ed. Tim Fulford and Peter J. Kitson. Cambridge: Cambridge University Press, 1998. 67–86.

Higman, Barry W. "Household Structure and Fertility on Jamaican Slave Plantations: A Nineteenth-Century Example." *Population Studies* 27, 3 (1973): 527–50.

———. *Slave Population and Economy in Jamaica, 1807–1834.* Cambridge: Cambridge University Press, 1976.

———. "The Slave Populations of the British Caribbean: Some Nineteenth-Century Variations." In *Eighteenth-Century Florida and the Caribbean*, ed. Samuel Proctor. Gainesville: University of Florida Press, 1976. 60–70.

Hill, Spencer J., ed. *The Romantic Imagination: A Casebook.* London: Macmillan, 1977.

Hilton, Nelson. "An Original Story." In *Unnam'd Forms: Blake and Textuality*, ed. Nelson Hilton and Thomas A. Vogler. Berkeley: University of California Press, 1986. 69–104.

Hinkel, Howard H. "From Pivotal Idea to Poetic Ideal: Blake's Theory of Contraries and 'The Little Black Boy.'" *Papers on Language and Literature* 11, 1 (1975): 39–45.

Hoagwood, Terence. "Keats and Social Context: Lamia." *Studies in English Literature* 29 (1989): 675–95.

Hoerner, Fred. "Prolific Reflections: Blake's Contortion of Surveillance in *Visions of the Daughters of Albion*." *Studies in Romanticism* 35 (1996): 119–51.

Hoevelor, Diane Long. "Glossing the Feminine in *The Rime of the Ancient Mariner*." *European Romantic Review* 2, 2 (1992): 145–162.

————. *Romantic Androgyny: The Women Within*. University Park: Pennsylvania State University Press, 1990.

————. "Shelley and Androgyny: Teaching 'The Witch of Atlas.'" *Approaches to Teaching Shelley's Poetry*, ed. Spencer Hall. New York: Modern Language Association, 1990. 93–95.

Hogle, Jerrold E. "*Frankenstein* as Neo-Gothic: From the Ghost of the Counterfeit to the Monster of Abjection." In *Romanticism, History, and the Possibilities of Genre*, ed. Tilottama Rajan and Julie Wright. Cambridge: Cambridge University Press, 1998. 176–210.

————. "Metaphor and Metamorphosis in Shelley's 'The Witch of Atlas.'" *Studies in Romanticism* 19 (1980): 327–53.

————. *Shelley's Process: Radical Transference and the Development of His Major Works*. Princeton, N.J.: Princeton University Press, 1988.

Holmes, Richard. *Shelley: The Pursuit*. London: Weidenfeld and Nicolson, 1974.

Honour, Hugh. *The Image of the Black in Western Art*. 5 vols. Cambridge, Mass.: Harvard University Press, 1989.

Hulme, Peter. *Colonial Encounters: Europe and the Native Caribbean, 1492–1797*. London: Methuen, 1986.

James, C. L. R. *The Black Jacobins*. New York: Vintage, 1963, 1989.

Janson, H. W. *Apes and Ape Lore in the Middle Ages and the Renaissance*. London: Warburg Institute, 1952.

Johnson, Barbara. "My Monster/My Self." *Diacritics* 12 (1982): 2–10.

Johnson, Galen A. and Michael B. Smith. *Ontology and Alterity in Merleau-Ponty*. Evanston, Ill.: Northwestern University Press, 1990.

Johnson, Mary Lynn. "Coleridge's Prose and a Blake Plate in Stedman's *Narrative*: Unfastening the 'Hooks and Eyes' of Memory." *Wordsworth Circle* 13, 1 (1982): 36–38.

Johnson, Michael P. "Smothered Slave Infants: Were Slave Mothers at Fault?" *Journal of Southern History* 67 (1981): 510–15.

Johnston, Kenneth R. *The Hidden Wordsworth: Poet, Lover, Rebel, Spy*. New York: W.W. Norton, 1998.

Jones, Noel. *without flinching*. New York: Noel Jones, 2000.

Kaczvinsky, Donald P. "Coleridge's Polar Spirit: A Source." *English Language Notes* 24, 3 (1987): 25–28.

Keane, Patrick J. *Coleridge's Submerged Politics: The Ancient Mariner and Robinson Crusoe*. Columbia: University of Missouri Press, 1994.

Kelsall, Malcolm. " 'Once did she hold the gorgeous east in fee . . .': Byron's Venice and Oriental Empire." In *Romanticism and Colonialism: Writing and Empire, 1780–1830*, ed. Tim Fulford and Peter J. Kitson. Cambridge: Cambridge University Press, 1998. 243–60.

Keynes, Geoffrey. "William Blake and John Gabriel Stedman." *Times Literary Supplement*, 20 May 1965, 400.

King-Hele, Desmond. *Erasmus Darwin and the Romantic Poets*. London: Macmillan, 1986.

Kitson, Peter J. " 'The Eucharist of Hell'; or, Eating People Is Right: Romantic Representations of Cannibalism." *Romanticism on the Net* 17 (February 2000). <http://users.ox.uk/~scato385/17cannibalism.html>

Kitson, Peter J. and Debbie Lee, eds. *Slavery, Abolition, and Emancipation: Writings in the British Romantic Period*. 8 vols. London: Pickering and Chatto, 1999.

Klancher, Jon P. *The Making of British Reading Audiences, 1790–1832*. Madison: University of Wisconsin Press, 1987.

Kristeva, Julia. *Nations Without Nationalism*. Trans. Leon S. Roudiez. New York: Columbia University Press, 1993.

———. *The Powers of Horror: An Essay on Abjection*. Trans. Leon S. Roudiez. New York: Columbia University Press, 1982.

———. *Strangers to Ourselves*. Trans. Leon S. Roudiez. New York: Columbia University Press, 1991.

Kwamena-Poh, Michael, John Tosh, Richard Waller, and Michael Tidy. *African History in Maps*. Essex: Longman, 1982.

Larkin, Peter. "Lyrical Ballads: Wordsworth's Book of Questions." *Wordsworth Circle* 20, 2 (1989): 106–12.

Latour, Bruno. *Science in Action: How to Follow Scientists and Engineers Through Society*. Cambridge, Mass.: Harvard University Press, 1987.

Lau, Beth. *Keats's Paradise Lost*. Gainesville: University of Florida Press, 1998.

Leask, Nigel. *British Romantic Writers and the East: Anxieties of Empire*. Cambridge: Cambridge University Press, 1992.

———. *The Politics of Imagination in Coleridge's Critical Thought*. New York: St. Martin's Press, 1988.

Lefebure, Molly. *Samuel Taylor Coleridge: A Bondage of Opium*. New York: Stein and Day, 1974.

Lestringant, Frank. *Cannibals: The Discovery and Representation of the Cannibal from Columbus to Jules Verne*. Trans. Rosemary Morris. Berkeley: University of California Press, 1997.

———. *Mapping the Renaissance World: The Geographical Imagination in the Age of Discovery*. Trans. David Fausett. Berkeley: University of California Press, 1994.

Levinas, Emmanuel. *Ethics and Infinity: Conversations with Philippe Nemo*. Trans. Richard A. Cohen. Pittsburgh: Duquesne University Press, 1985.

———. *On Thinking-of-the-Other: Entre Nous*. Trans. Michael B. Smith and Barbara Harshav. New York: Columbia University Press, 1998.

———. *Otherwise Than Being; or, Beyond Essence*. Trans. Alphonso Lingis. The Hague: Martinus Nijhoff, 1981.

———. *Time and the Other, and Additional Essays*. Trans. Richard A. Cohen. Pittsburgh: Duquesne University Press, 1987.

———. *Totality and Infinity: An Essay on Exteriority*. Trans. Alphonso Lingis. Pittsburgh: Duquesne University Press, 1969.

Levinson, Marjorie. *Keats' Life of Allegory: The Origins of a Style*. New York: Blackwell, 1988.

Lew, Joseph. "The Deceptive Other: Mary Shelley's Critique of Orientalism in *Frankenstein*." *Studies in Romanticism* 30 (1991): 255–83.

Lewis, Bernard. *Race and Slavery in the Middle East: An Historical Enquiry*. New York and Oxford: Oxford University Press, 1990.

Lewis, Gordon K. *Main Currents in Caribbean Thought*. Baltimore: Johns Hopkins University Press, 1983.

Linkin, Harriet Kramer. "Revisioning Blake's Oothoon." *Blake: An Illustrated Quarterly* 23 (1990): 184–94.

Lively, Adam. *Masks: Blackness, Race, and the Imagination*. London: Chatto and Windus, 1999.

Lovejoy, Paul E. "The Volume of the Atlantic Slave Trade: A Synthesis." *Journal of African History* 23 (1982): 496–97.

Lowes, Jonathan Livingston. *The Road to Xanadu*. Boston: Houghton Mifflin, 1964.

Magnuson, Paul. *Coleridge's Nightmare Poetry*. Charlottesville: University Press of Virginia, 1974.

Majeed, Javed. *Ungoverned Imaginings: James Mill's "History of British India" and Orientalism*. Oxford: Oxford University Press, 1992.

Makdisi, Saree. *Romantic Imperialism: Universal Empire and the Culture of Modernity*. Cambridge: Cambridge University Press, 1999.

Malchow, H. L. "Frankenstein's Monster and Images of Race in Nineteenth-Century Britain." *Past and Present* 139 (1993): 90–130.

———. *Gothic Images of Race in Nineteenth-Century Britain*. Stanford, Calif.: Stanford University Press, 1996.

Manning, Patrick. *Slavery and African Life: Occidental, Oriental, and African Slave Trades*. Cambridge: Cambridge University Press, 1990.

Mannoni, Octave. *Prospero and Caliban: The Psychology of Colonization*. 1964. Ann Arbor: University of Michigan Press, 1990.

Matheson, Ann. "The Influence of Cowper's *The Task* on Coleridge's Conversation Poems." *New Approaches to Coleridge: Biographical and Critical Essays*, ed. Donald Sultana. London, Vision Press; Totowa N.J.: Barnes and Noble, 1981. 137–50.

McDermott, William Coffman. *The Ape in Antiquity*. Baltimore: Johns Hopkins University Press, 1938.

McGann, Jerome G. "The Meaning of *The Ancient Mariner*." *Critical Inquiry* 8 (1981): 63–86.

McKusick, James. "Coleridge and the Economy of Nature." *Studies in Romanticism* 35 (1996): 375–92.

———. *Coleridge's Philosophy of Language*. New Haven, Conn.: Yale University Press, 1986.

———. " 'That Silent Sea': Lee Boo, and the Exploration of the South Pacific." *Wordsworth Circle* 24, 2 (1993): 102–6.

Mellor, Anne K. *Mary Shelley: Her Life, Her Fiction, Her Monsters*. New York: Methuen, 1988.

———. *Romanticism and Gender*. New York: Routledge, 1993.

———. "Sex, Violence, and Slavery: Blake and Wollstonecraft." *Huntington Library Quarterly* 58, 3–4 (1997): 345–70.

———. "Why Women Didn't Like Romanticism: The Views of Jane Austen and Mary Shelley." In *Romantics and Us: Essays on Literature and Culture*, ed. Gene W. Ruoff. New Brunswick, N.J.: Rutgers University Press, 1990.

———, ed. *Romanticism and Feminism*. Bloomington: Indiana University Press, 1988.

Mendilow, Jonathan. *Romantic Tradition in British Political Thought*. London: Croom Helm, 1986.

Midgley, Clare. *Women Against Slavery: The British Campaigns, 1780–1870*. London: Routledge, 1992.

Miers, Suzanne and Igor Kopytoff, eds. *Slavery in Africa: Historical and Anthropological Perspectives*. Madison: University of Wisconsin Press, 1977.

Miller, David Philip. "Joseph Banks, Empire, and 'Centers of Calculation' in Late Hanoverian Britain." In *Visions of Empire: Voyages, Botany and Representations of Nature*, ed. David Philip Miller and Peter Hans Reill. Cambridge: Cambridge University Press, 1996. 21–37.

Modiano, Raimonda. "Words and 'Languageless' Meanings: Limits of Expression in *The Rime of the Ancient Mariner*." *Modern Language Quarterly* 38 (1977): 40–61.

Moers, Ellen. "Female Gothic." In *The Endurance of Frankenstein*, ed. George Levine and U. C. Knoepflmacher. Berkeley: University of California Press, 1979. 77–87.

Monmonier, Mark. *Mapping It Out: Expository Cartography for the Humanities and Social Sciences*. Chicago: University of Chicago Press, 1993.

Montag, Warren. "The Workshop of Filthy Creation: A Marxist Reading of *Frankenstein*." In *Mary Shelley, Frankenstein: Case Studies in Contemporary Criticism*, ed. Johanna Smith. Boston: St. Martin's Press, 1992. 300–311.

Morgan, Jennifer Lyle. "Women in Slavery and the Transatlantic Slave Trade." In *Transatlantic Slavery: Against Human Dignity*, ed. Anthony Tibbles. London: HMSO, 1994. 60–69.

Morris, Ramona and Desmond Morris. *Men and Apes: A Study of the Ape and Monkey in World Mythology*. New York: McGraw-Hill, 1966.

Morrison, Toni. *Beloved*. New York: Knopf, 1987.

———. *Playing in the Dark*. New York: Vintage, 1992.

Morton, Timothy. "Blood Sugar." In *Romanticism and Colonialism: Writing and Empire, 1780–1830*, ed. Tim Fulford and Peter J. Kitson. Cambridge: Cambridge University Press, 1998. 87–106.

———. *The Poetics of Spice*. Cambridge: Cambridge University Press, 2000.

Morrison, Anthea. "Samuel Taylor Coleridge's Greek Pride Ode on the Slave Trade." In *An Infinite Complexity: Essays in Romanticism*, ed. J. R. Watson. Edinburgh: Edinburgh University Press, 1993. 145–60.

Moskal, Jeanne. *Blake, Ethics, and Forgiveness*. Tuscaloosa: University of Alabama Press, 1994.

Motion, Andrew. *Keats*. London: Faber and Faber, 1997.

Nellist, Brian. "Shelley's Narratives and 'The Witch of Atlas.'" In *Essays on Shelley*, ed. Miriam Allott. Totowa, N.J.: Barnes and Noble, 1982. 160–90.

Nichols, Ashton. "Mumbo Jumbo: Mungo Park and the Rhetoric of Romantic Africa." In *Romanticism, Race, and Imperial Culture, 1780–1834*, ed. Alan Richardson and Sonia Hofkosh. Bloomington: Indiana University Press, 1996. 93–113.

Nochinson, Martha. "Lamia as Muse." In *The Poetic Fantastic*, ed. Patrick D. Murphy. New York: Greenwood Press, 1989.

Nussbaum, Felicity. *Torrid Zones: Maternity, Sexuality, and Empire in Eighteenth-Century English Narratives*. Baltimore: Johns Hopkins University Press, 1995.

O'Brian, Patrick. *Joseph Banks: A Life*. London: Collins Harvill, 1987.

Pace, Timothy. "Who Killed Gwendolen Harleth? Daniel Deronda and Keats' *Lamia*." *Journal of English and Germanic Philology* 87, 1 (1988): 35–48.

Page, Judith. *Wordsworth and the Cultivation of Women*. Berkeley: University of California Press, 1994.

Parsons, Coleman O. "Primitive Sense in *Lamia*." *Folklore* 88 (1977): 203–10.

Peterson, James E. "The *Visions of the Daughters of Albion*: A Problem in Perception."
 Philological Quarterly 52 (1973): 252–64.
Porter, Roy, ed. *The Popularization of Medicine, 1650–1850*. London: Routledge, 1992.
Porter, Roy and Dorothy Porter. *In Sickness and in Health: The British Experience, 1650–1850*. New York: Blackwell, 1989.
Postma, Johannes Menne. *The Dutch in the Atlantic Slave Trade, 1660–1815*. Cambridge: Cambridge University Press, 1990.
Pratt, Mary Louise. *Imperial Eyes: Travel Writing and Transculturation*. New York: Routledge, 1992.
Price-Mars, Jean. *So Spoke the Uncle*. Trans. Magdaline W. Shannon. Washington, D.C.: Three Continents Press, 1983.
Prince, Lawrence Marsden. *The Inkle and Yarico Album*. Berkeley: University of California Press, 1937.
Raben, Joseph. "Shelley as Dionysian." In *Shelley Revalued: Essays from the Gregynog Conference*, ed. Kelvin Everest. Leicester: Leicester University Press, 1983. 21–36.
Randel, Fred V. "*Frankenstein*, Feminism, and the Intertextuality of Mountains." *Studies in Romanticism* 23 (1984): 515–32.
Rawley, James A. *The Transatlantic Slave Trade: A History*. New York: W.W. Norton, 1981.
Redpath, Theodore. *The Young Romantics and Critical Opinion 1807–1824*. New York: St. Martin's Press, 1973.
Reed, Arden. "The Mariner Rimed." In *Romanticism and Language*, ed. Arden Reed. Ithaca, N.Y.: Cornell University Press, 1984. 168–201.
Reynolds, Edward. "Human Cargoes: Enslavement and the Middle Passage." In *Transatlantic Slavery: Against Human Dignity*, ed. Anthony Tibbles. London: HMSO, 1994. 29–34.
Richardson, Alan. "Colonialism, Race and Lyric Irony in Blake's 'The Little Black Boy.'" *Papers on Language and Literature* 26 (1990): 233–48.
———. "Darkness Visible: Race and Representation in Bristol Abolitionist Poetry, 1770–1810." *Wordsworth Circle* 27, 2 (1996): 67–72.
———. "Epic Ambivalence: Imperial Politics and Romantic Deflection in Williams's *Peru* and Lnador's *Gebir*," In *Romanticism, Race, and Imperial Culture, 1780–1834*, ed. Alan Richardson and Sonia Hofkosh. Bloomington: Indiana University Press, 1996. 265–82.
———. "From Emile to Frankenstein: The Education of Monsters." *European Romantic Review* 1, 2 (1991): 147–62.
———. "Romantic Voodoo: Obeah and British Culture, 1797–1807." *Studies in Romanticism* 32 (1993): 3–28.
Richardson, Alan, and Sonia Hofkosh, eds. *Romanticism, Race, and Imperial Culture, 1780–1834*. Bloomington: Indiana University Press, 1996.
Ridley, M. R. *Keats' Craftsmanship: A Study in Poetic Development*. Lincoln: University of Nebraska Press, 1933.
Roe, Nicholas. *Wordsworth and Coleridge: The Radical Years*. Oxford, Clarendon Press, 1988.
Rollins, Hyder Edward, ed. *The Keats Circle*. Cambridge, Mass.: Harvard University Press, 1965.
Ross, Marlon B. *The Contours of Masculine Desire: Romanticism and the Rise of Women's Poetry*. New York: Oxford University Press, 1989.

Rowland, William G., Jr. *Literature and the Marketplace: Romantic Writers and Their Audiences in Great Britain and the United States.* Lincoln: University of Nebraska Press, 1996.

Rudy, John G. *Wordsworth and the Zen Mind: The Poetry of Self-Emptying.* Albany: State University of New York Press, 1996.

Ryan, Michael. "Poetry and the Audience." In *Poets Teaching Poets: Self and the World*, ed. Gregory Orr and Ellen Bryant Voight. Ann Arbor: University of Michigan Press, 1996. 159–84.

Rzepka, Charles. "Slavery, Sodomy, and De Quincey's 'Savannah-La-Mar': Surplus Labor Value in Urban Gothic." *Wordsworth Circle* 27, 1 (1998): 33–37.

Said, Edward. *Orientalism.* 1978. New York: Vintage, 1979.

———. "Representing the Colonized: Anthropology's Interlocutors." *Critical Inquiry* 15 (1989): 205–225.

Schiebinger, Londa. *Nature's Body: Gender in the Making of Modern Science.* Boston: Beacon Press, 1993.

Scott, Peter Dale. "Vital Artifice: Mary, Percy, and the Psychopolitical Integrity of *Frankenstein*." In *The Endurance of Frankenstein*, ed. George Levine and U. C. Knoepflmacher. Berkeley: University of California Press, 1979: 173–202.

Shyllon, F. O. *Black Slaves in Britain.* London: Oxford University Press, 1974.

Sitterson, Joseph C, Jr. "Narrator and Reader in *Lamia*." *Studies in Philology* 79, 3 (1982): 297–310.

———. " 'Platonic Shades' in Keats's *Lamia*." *Journal of English and Germanic Philology* 83, 2 (1984): 200–13.

———. " 'The Rime of the Ancient Mariner' and Freudian Dream Theory." *PLL* 18 (1982): 17–35.

———. " 'Unmeaning Miracles' in 'The Rime of the Ancient Mariner.' " *South Atlantic Review* 46 (1981): 16–26.

Skirp, John Daniel, III. "Intellect, Imagination, and the Poet: An Interpretation of *Lamia*." *Journal of Evolutionary Psychology* 7, 1–2 (1986): 143–47.

Slatoff, Walter. *The Look of Distance.* Columbus: Ohio State University Press, 1985.

Smith, Bernard. "Coleridge's 'Ancient Mariner' and Cook's Second Voyage." *Journal of the Warburg and Courtauld Institutes* 29 (1956): 117–54.

———. *European Vision and the South Pacific.* 2nd ed. New Haven, Conn.: Yale University Press, 1985.

Snead, James. "European Pedigrees/African Contagions: Nationality, Narrative, and Communality in Tutuola, Achebe, and Reed." In *Nation and Narration*, ed. Homi K. Bhabha. New York: Routledge, 1990. 231–49.

Solow, Barbara L., and Stanley L. Engerman, eds. *British Capitalism and Caribbean Slavery: The Legacy of Eric Williams.* Cambridge: Cambridge University Press, 1987.

Spivak, Gayatri Chakravorty. "Three Women's Texts and a Critique of Imperialism." *Critical Inquiry* 12 (1985): 243–61.

Stelzig, Eugene L. "Coleridge in *The Prelude*: Wordsworth's Fiction of Alterity." *Wordsworth Circle* 18 (1987): 23–27.

Sterrenburg, Lee. "Mary Shelley's Monster: Politics and Psyche in *Frankenstein*." In *The Endurance of Frankenstein*, ed. George Levine and U. C. Knoepflmacher. Berkeley: University of California Press, 1979. 143–71.

Stillinger, Jack. *The Hoodwinking of Madeline and Other Essays on Keats's Major Poems.* Urbana: University of Illinois Press, 1971.

———. "The Plots of Romantic Poetry." *College Literature* 15, 3 (1988): 209–23.

Sullivan, Zohreh T. "Race, Gender, and Imperial Ideology in the Nineteenth Century." *Nineteenth Century Contexts* 13, 1 (1989): 19–32.

Sunstein, Emily W. *Mary Shelley: Romance and Reality.* Boston: Little, Brown and Co., 1989.

Sypher, Wylie. *Guinea's Captive Kings: British Anti-Slavery Literature of the Eighteenth Century.* New York: Octagon Books, 1969.

Taussig, Michael. *Mimesis and Alterity.* New York: Routledge, 1993.

Taylor, Mark C. *Altarity.* Chicago: University of Chicago Press, 1987.

Thomas, Helen. *Romanticism and Slave Narratives: Transatlantic Testimonies.* Cambridge: Cambridge University Press, 2000.

Thomas, Mark. "Wither Fled Lamia?: A Search for Signification." *Journal of Names* 37, 1 (1989): 73–78.

Tillotson, Marcia. " 'A Forced Solitude': Mary Shelley and the Creation of Frankenstein's Monster." In *The Female Gothic*, ed. Juliann E. Fleenor. London: Eden Press, 1983. 167–75.

Tooley, Ronald Vere. *Maps and Map-Makers.* London: Batsford, 1952.

———. *Maps of Africa.* London: Map Collectors' Circle, 1968.

Turley, David. *The Culture of English Antislavery, 1780–1860.* London: Routledge, 1991.

Turner, Christy G. *Man Corn: Cannibalism and Violence in the Prehistoric American Southwest.* Salt Lake City: University of Utah Press, 1999.

Twitchell, James B. " 'The Rime of the Ancient Mariner' as Vampire Poem." *College Literature* 4, 2 (1977): 21–39.

Veeder, William. *Mary Shelley and Frankenstein: The Fate of Androgyny.* Chicago: University of Chicago Press, 1986.

Vine, Steven. " 'THAT MILD BEAM': Enlightenment and Enslavement in William Blake's *Visions of the Daughters of Albion*." In *The Discourse of Slavery: Aphra Behn to Toni Morrison*, ed. Carl Plasa and Betty J. Ring. London: Routledge, 1994. 40–63.

Vlasopolos, Anca. "*Frankenstein*'s Hidden Skeleton: The Psycho-Politics of Oppression." *Science Fiction Studies* 10, 2 (1983): 125–36.

Walvin, James. *Black Ivory: A History of British Slavery.* London: Fontana Press, 1993.

———. "The Propaganda of Anti-Slavery." In *Slavery and British Society 1776–1846*, ed. James Walvin. Baton Rouge: Louisiana State University Press, 1982. 49–68.

———. *Slaves and Slavery: The British Colonial Experience.* Manchester and New York: Manchester University Press, 1992.

Walvin, James and Stephen Small. "African Resistance to Enslavement." In *Transatlantic Slavery: Against Human Dignity*, ed. Anthony Tibbles. London: HMSO, 1994. 42–50.

Wang, Orrin N. C. "The Other Reasons: Female Alterity and Enlightenment Discourse in Mary Wollstonecraft's *A Vindication of the Rights of Woman*." *Yale Journal of Criticism* 5 (1991): 129–49.

Watkins, Daniel P. "History as Demon in Coleridge's *The Rime of the Ancient Mariner*." *PLL* 24, 1 (1988): 23–33.

Weissman, Judith. "A Reading of *Frankenstein* as the Complaint of a Political Wife." *Colby Library Quarterly* 12 (1976): 171–80.

Wiedemann, Thomas. *Greek and Roman Slavery*. London: Routledge, 1992.

Williams, Anne. "An I for an Eye: 'Spectral Persecution' in *The Rime of the Ancient Mariner*." *PMLA* 108, 5 (1993): 1114–27.

Williams, Eric. *Capitalism and Slavery*. Chapel Hill: University of North Carolina Press, 1944.

Willinsky, John. *Learning to Divide the World: Education at Empire's End*. Minneapolis: University of Minnesota Press, 1998.

Wilner, Eleanor. "The Closeness of Distance, or Narcissus as Seen by the Lake." Paper presented at the 25th Annual Centrum Summer Writer's Workshop, 8–20 July 1998.

Wilson, Ellen Gibson. *Thomas Clarkson: A Biography*. Basingstoke: Macmillan, 1989.

Winter, Kari J. *Subjects of Slavery, Agents of Change: Women and Power in Gothic Novels and Slave Narratives, 1790–1865*. Athens: University of Georgia Press, 1992.

Wolfson, Susan. "Keats and the Manhood of the Poet." *European Romantic Review* 6 (1995): 1–37.

———. "The Language of Interpretation in Romantic Poetry: 'A Strong Working of the Mind.'" In *Romanticism and Language*, ed. Arden Reed. Ithaca, N.Y.: Cornell University Press, 1984. 43–61.

Wood, Andelys. "Shelley's Ironic Vision: *The Witch of Atlas*." *Keats-Shelley Journal* 29 (1980): 67–82.

Wood, Marcus. *Blind Memory: Visual Representations of Slavery in England and America, 1780–1865*. New York: Routledge, 2000.

Wu, Duncan. *Wordsworth's Reading, 1770–1799*. Cambridge: Cambridge University Press, 1995.

Young, Percy M. *A History of British Music*. London: Ernest Benn, 1967,

Ziegler, Philip. *The Black Death*. New York: Harper, 1969.

Zonana, Joyce. "'They Will Prove the Truth of My Tale': Safie's Letters as the Feminist Core of Mary Shelley's *Frankenstein*." *Journal of Narrative Technique* 21 (1991): 170–84.

Index

Acknowledgments

This work has been shaped by discussions with many people, including Anne Mellor, Candi France, Joan Dayan, Chuck Rzepka, Michael Macovski, Robert Ryan, Beth Lau, Dave Baulch, Gary Handwerk, Mona Modiano, Anya Taylor, Alex Dick, Angela Esterhammer, Nick Halmi, Michael Eberle-Sinatra, Anthony Harding, Greg Kucich, Jim McKusick, Nick Roe, Jack Stillinger, Christine Sutphin, Patsy Callaghan, Ed Stover, Robyn Fiebelkorn, Doug Mackie, Sheri Paddock, Sheila Kineke, Laurie MacDiarmid, and Duane Reed, who also designed the cover art. My colleagues at Washington State University, especially Michael Hanly, Al von Frank, Alex Hammond, Nick Keisling, Virginia Hyde, and Barbara Monroe, have generously supported my work, as well. I also am grateful to the students in my senior seminars on "Travel Literature of the Romantic Period" and "The Pleasures of Imagination," and to the students in my graduate seminar "Slavery and Romanticism," particularly Patsy Glatt.

I wish to thank the editors of the eight-volume series *Slavery, Abolition, and Emancipation*, from whom I have learned so much: Alan Richardson, Srinivas Aravamuden, David Dabydeen, Sukdev Sandhu, Jeff Cox, Alan Bewell; the advisory editors Anne Mellor and James Walvin; and my co-general editor, Peter J. Kitson.

For granting me permission to reproduce photographs, I thank Cambridge University Library, The British Library, The James Ford Bell Libaray at the University of Minnesota, The Bridgeman Art Gallery, The Wilberforce House, The National Museums and Galleries on Merseyside, The Walker Art Gallery, the Gemäldegalerie Berlin, the Bildarchiv Preußischer Kulturbesitz, Berlin, Pomona College, and the Houghton Library at Harvard University. For permission to reproduce her poem, I thank Nicole Jones. For timely advice about Stedman's watercolors, I thank Richard and Sally Price. For generous use of archival material and early printed books, I thank Wilberforce House Museum, National Maritime Museum, National Gallaries and Museums on Merseyside, Public Records Office Liverpool, Public Records Office London, Natural History Museum, The Rhodes House, Cambridge University Library, The British Library.

I owe a great debt to friends and colleagues who have read and re-read drafts of this book: Jerry Hogle, who advised and directed this project at its inception; John Willinsky, who encouraged my work in its earliest incarnations; Peter J. Kitson, Morton D. Paley, Bruce Graver, Alan Richardson, and Alan Bewell, who read and commented on specific chapters; Elizabeth Jones, who read the entire manuscript and checked it for clarity; my creative writing group, Dodie Forrest, Gail Pearlman, Jill Widner, and Shannon Hopkins; my collaborator, Tim Fulford, who provided everything from ideas and inspiration to footnotes and facts, and who read three different versions and listened to me talk through at least that many more; the two anonymous reveiwers of this manuscript for University of Pennsylvania Press, who provided excellent and detailed advice for revision; and my two editors at Penn Press, Jerry Singerman and Alison Anderson.

Thanks especially to Stephanie Lee and Myron Lee.